ROSARIO + VAMPIRE
Season II

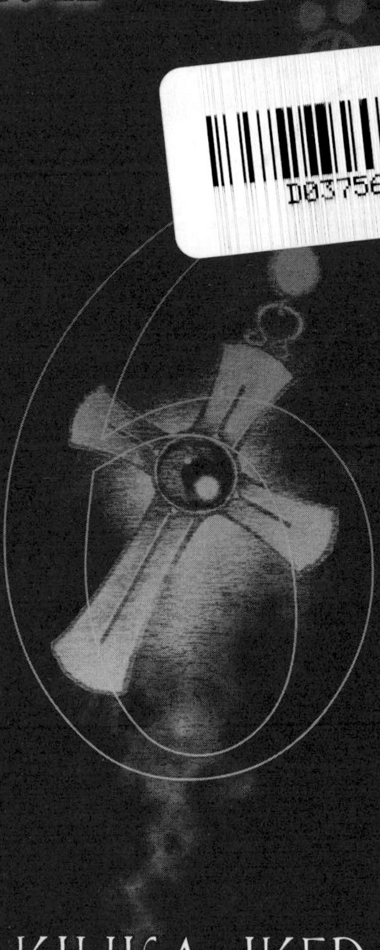

6

AKIHISA IKEDA

Horror Story Thus Far

Tsukune Aono accidentally enrolls in Yokai Academy, a high school for monsters! After befriending the school's cutest girl, Moka Akashiya, he decides to stay...even though Yokai has a zero-tolerance policy toward humans. (A *fatal* policy.) Tsukune has to hide his true identity while fending off attacks by monster gangs. He survives with the help of his News Club friends—Moka, Kurumu, Yukari and Mizore.

Now Tsukune and his friends are sophomores (although they nearly destroyed the school along the way), and have come back from summer vacation at a seaside resort. They battled an organization called "Fairy Tale" that was trying to capture the powers of a young Siren named San. As they learn about San's struggles to make it in the human world, our heroes begin to think about their futures...

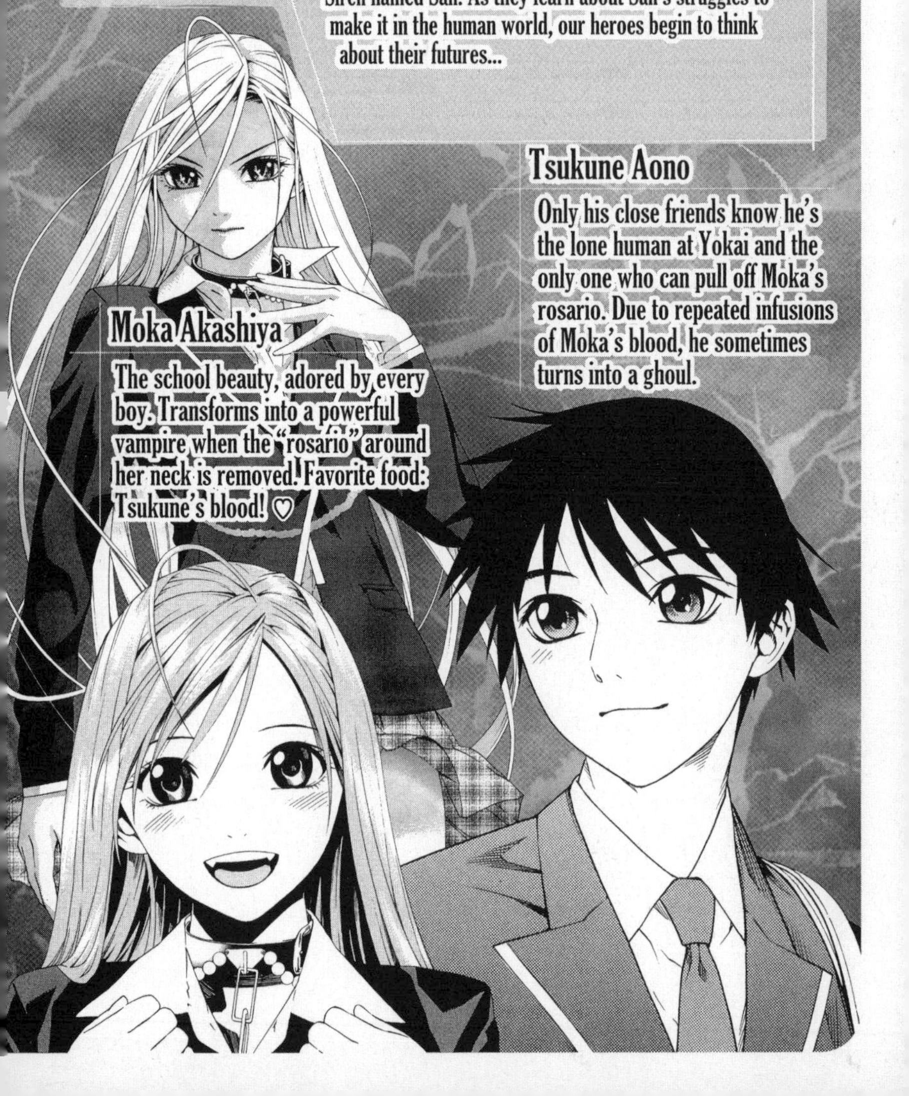
Tsukune Aono
Only his close friends know he's the lone human at Yokai and the only one who can pull off Moka's rosario. Due to repeated infusions of Moka's blood, he sometimes turns into a ghoul.
Moka Akashiya
The school beauty, adored by every boy. Transforms into a powerful vampire when the "rosario" around her neck is removed. Favorite food: Tsukune's blood! ♡

Kurumu Kurono

A succubus. Also adored by all the boys—for two obvious reasons. Fights with Moka over Tsukune.

Yukari Sendo

A mischievous witch. Much younger than the others. A genius who skipped several grades. Has quite a sharp tongue for such a cute little thing.

Mizore Shirayuki

A snow fairy who manipulates ice. She fell in love with Tsukune after reading his newspaper articles.

Ruby Tojo

A witch who only learned to trust humans after meeting Tsukune. Now employed as Yokai's head-master's assistant.

Koko Shuzen

Moka's stubborn little sister. Koko worships Moka's inner vampiric self but hates her sweet exterior. Koko's pet bat transforms into a weapon.

Ginnei Morioka

President of the News Club. Although his true form is a werewolf, he's more notorious as a wolf of a different kind—one who chases every girl in sight.

Tenmei Mikogami

The mysterious headmaster of Yokai Academy. Saved Tsukune when he transformed into a ghoul by sealing the monster inside him with a Spirit Lock.

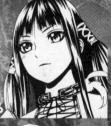

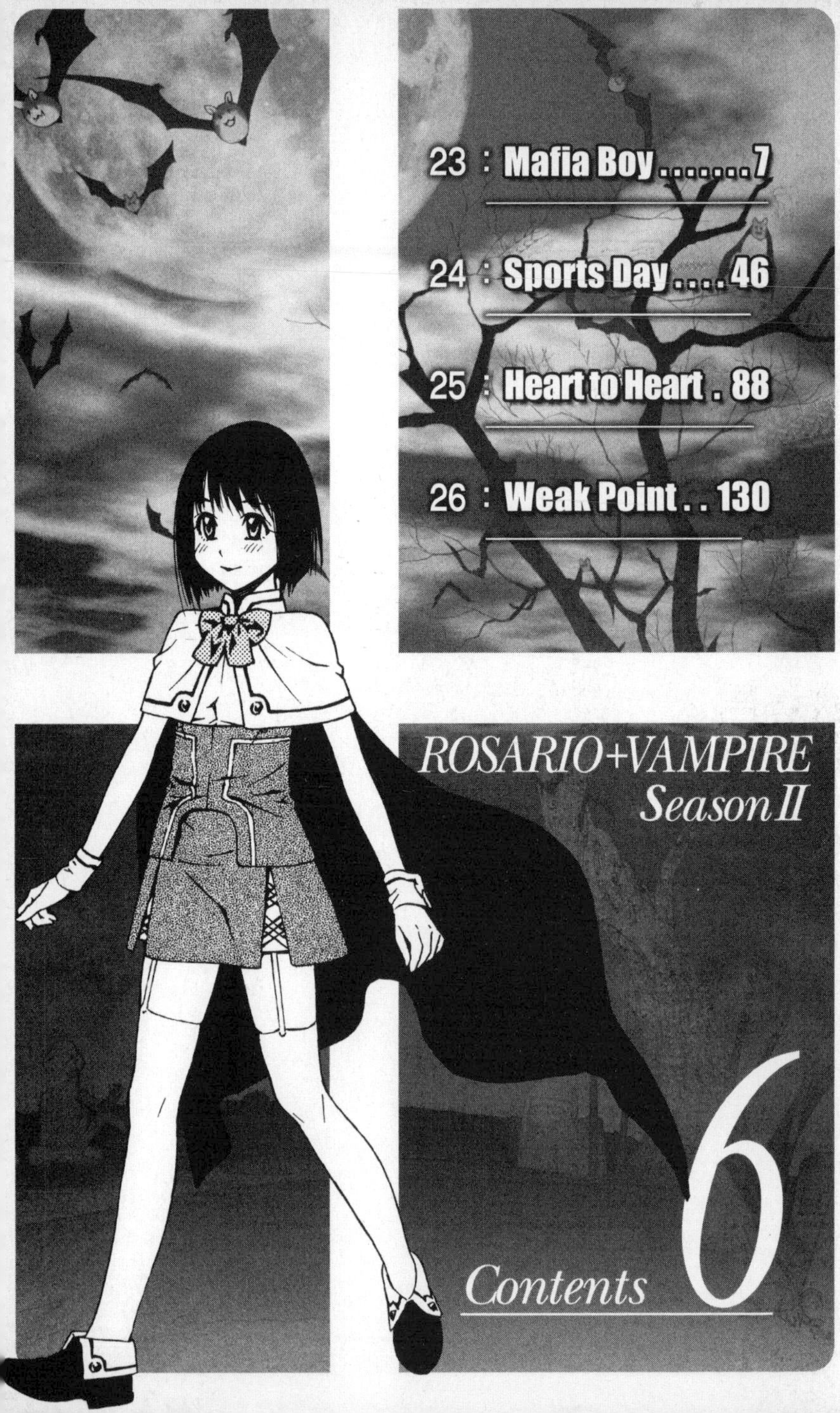

ROSARIO+VAMPIRE
Season II

Contents 6

23: Mafia Boy

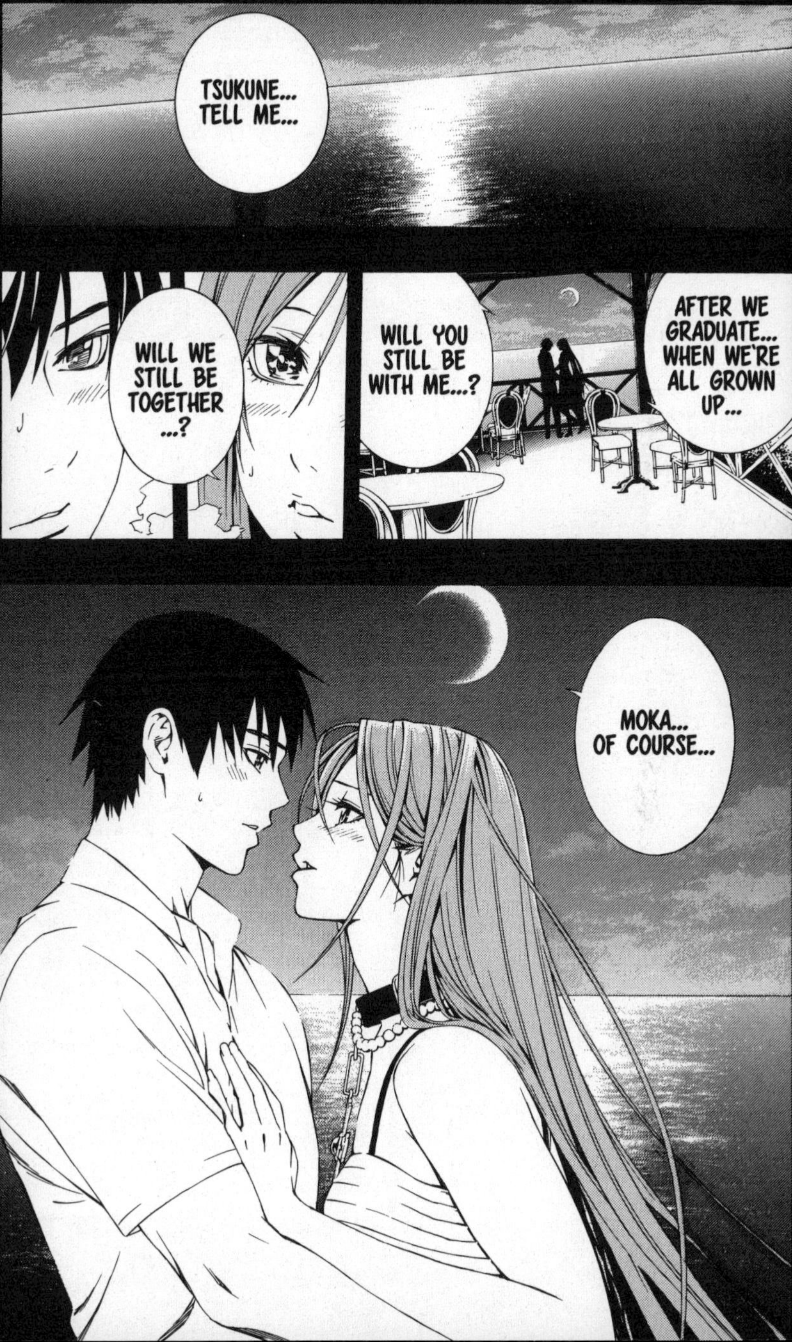
TSUKUNE... TELL ME...
AFTER WE GRADUATE... WHEN WE'RE ALL GROWN UP...
WILL YOU STILL BE WITH ME...?
WILL WE STILL BE TOGETHER ...?
MOKA... OF COURSE...

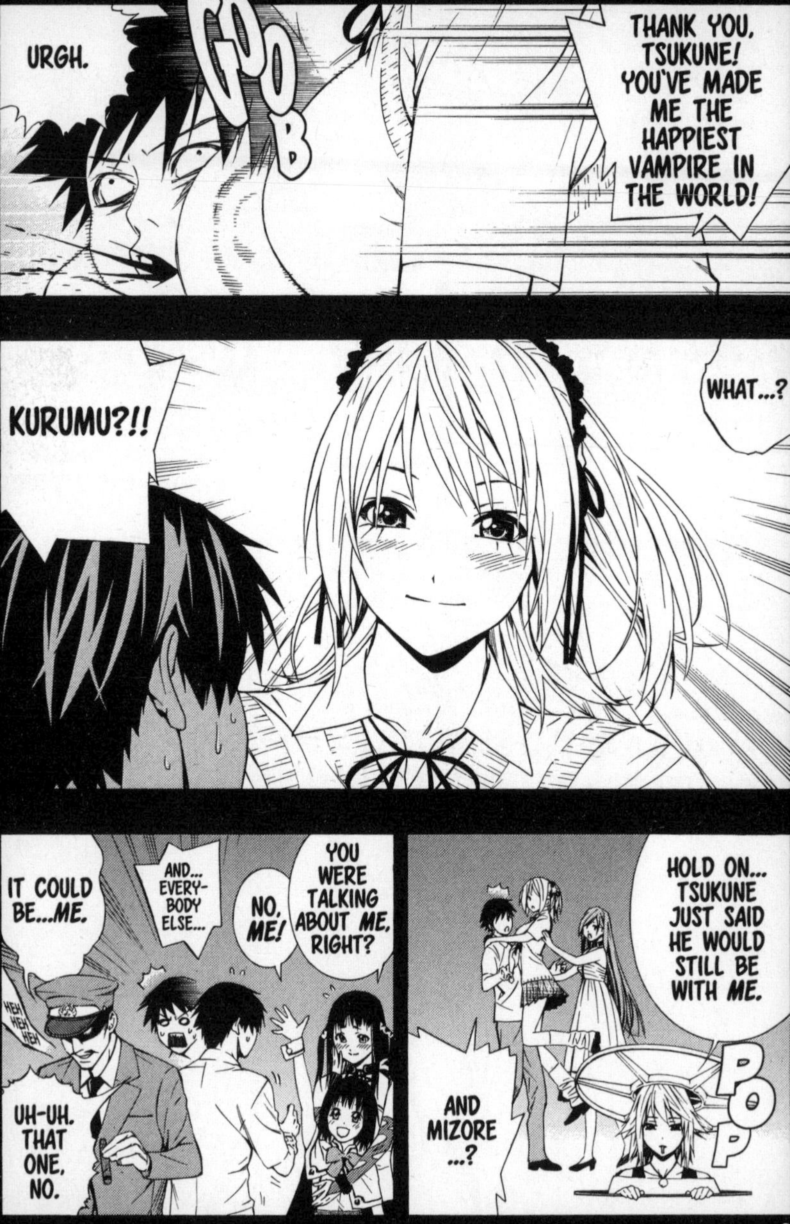
THANK YOU, TSUKUNE! YOU'VE MADE ME THE HAPPIEST VAMPIRE IN THE WORLD!
GOOB
URGH.
WHAT...?
KURUMU?!!
HOLD ON... TSUKUNE JUST SAID HE WOULD STILL BE WITH ME.
POP
AND MIZORE ...?
YOU WERE TALKING ABOUT ME, RIGHT?
NO, ME!
AND... EVERY-BODY ELSE...
IT COULD BE...ME.
HEH HEH HEH
UH-UH. THAT ONE, NO.

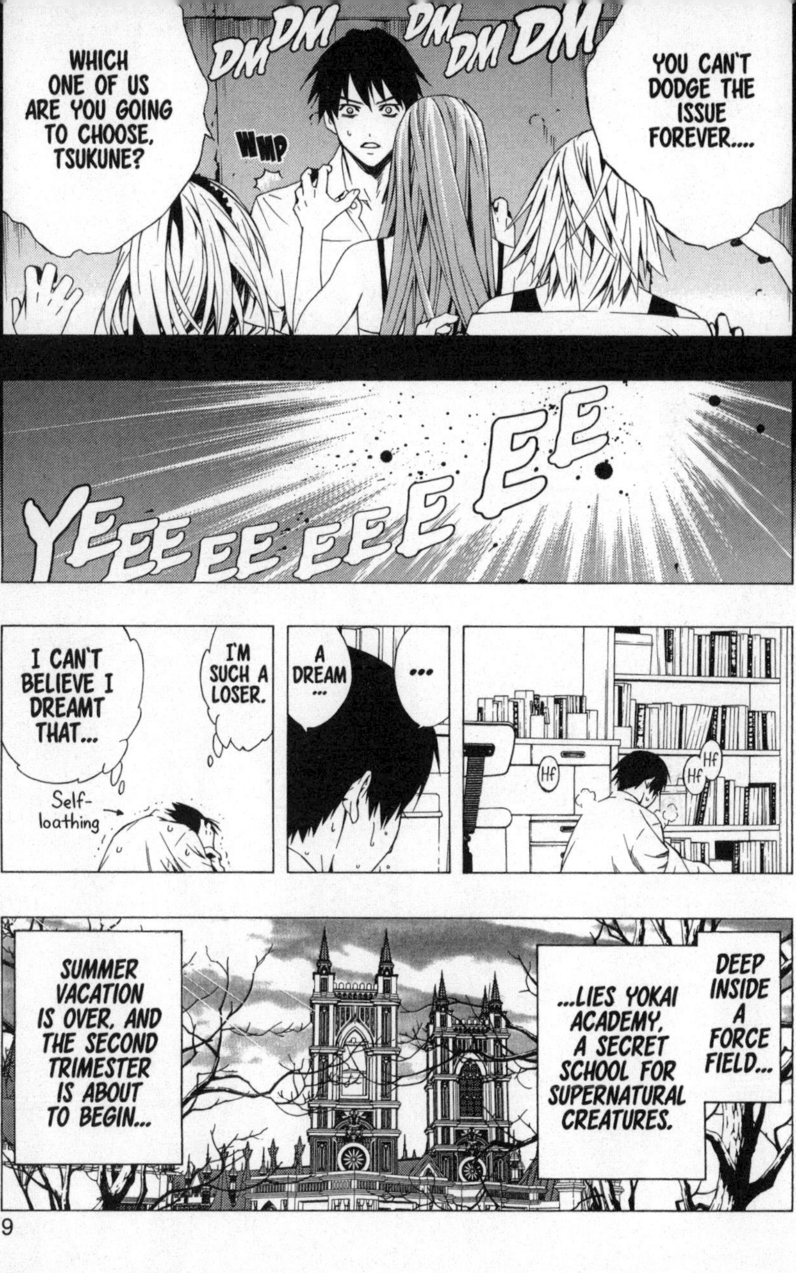
YOU CAN'T DODGE THE ISSUE FOREVER....
DM DM DM DM DM DM
WHICH ONE OF US ARE YOU GOING TO CHOOSE, TSUKUNE?
WMP
YEEEEEEEEEEE
Hf Hf Hf
...
A DREAM ...
I'M SUCH A LOSER.
I CAN'T BELIEVE I DREAMT THAT...
Self-loathing
DEEP INSIDE A FORCE FIELD...
...LIES YOKAI ACADEMY, A SECRET SCHOOL FOR SUPERNATURAL CREATURES.
SUMMER VACATION IS OVER, AND THE SECOND TRIMESTER IS ABOUT TO BEGIN...

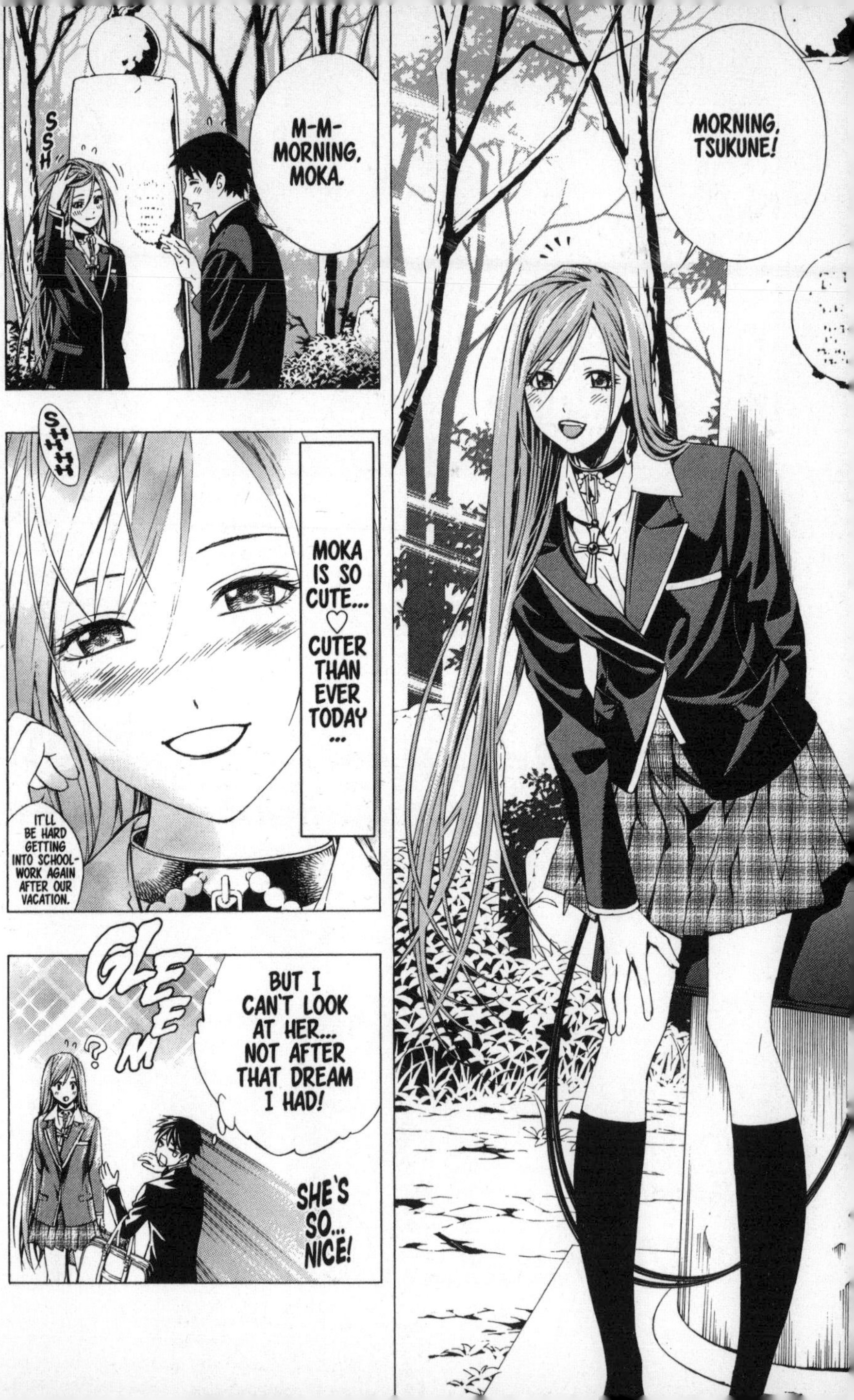
MORNING, TSUKUNE!
SSH
M-M-MORNING, MOKA.
SHHHH
MOKA IS SO CUTE... ♡ CUTER THAN EVER TODAY...
IT'LL BE HARD GETTING INTO SCHOOL-WORK AGAIN AFTER OUR VACATION.
GLEEM
BUT I CAN'T LOOK AT HER... NOT AFTER THAT DREAM I HAD!
SHE'S SO... NICE!

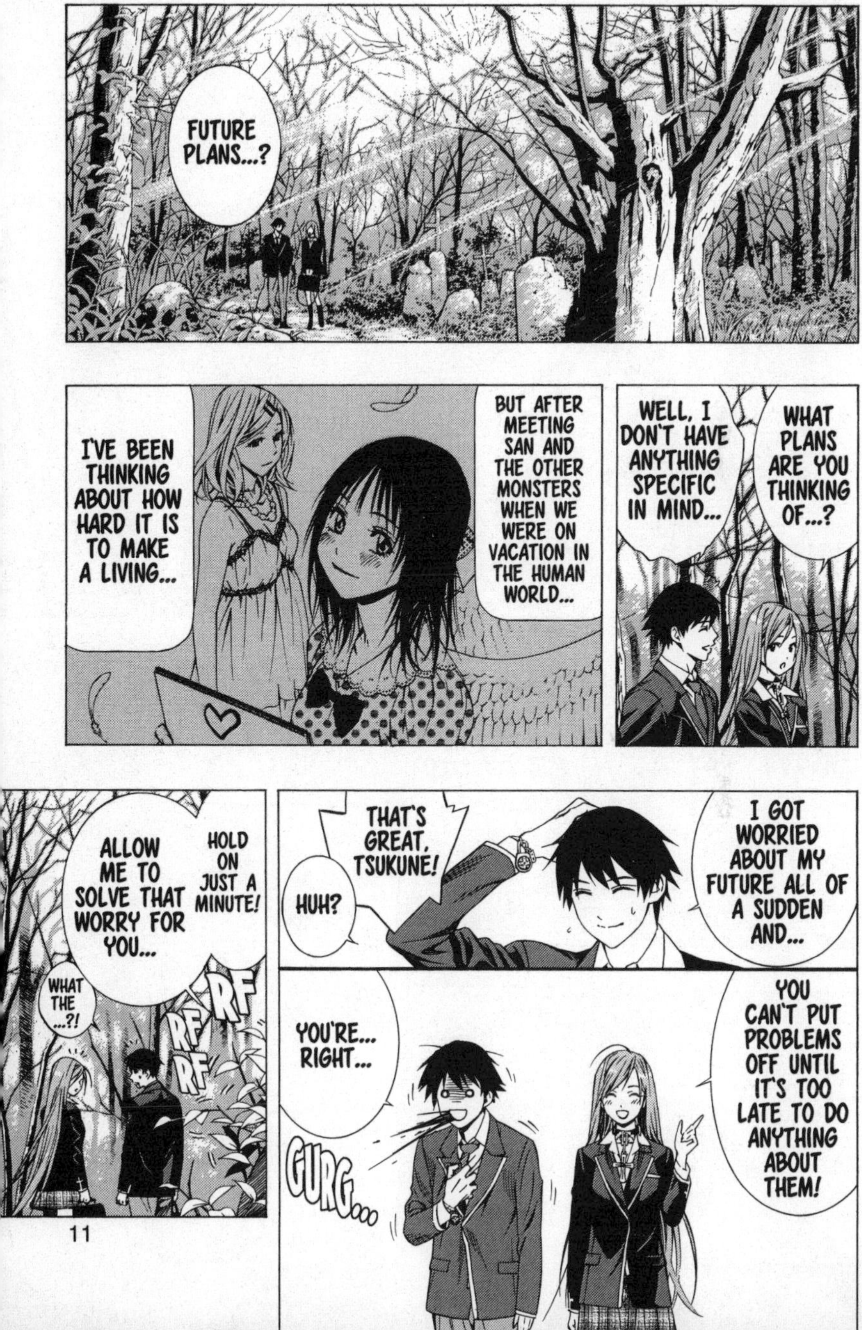
FUTURE PLANS...?
WHAT PLANS ARE YOU THINKING OF...?
WELL, I DON'T HAVE ANYTHING SPECIFIC IN MIND...
BUT AFTER MEETING SAN AND THE OTHER MONSTERS WHEN WE WERE ON VACATION IN THE HUMAN WORLD...
I'VE BEEN THINKING ABOUT HOW HARD IT IS TO MAKE A LIVING...
I GOT WORRIED ABOUT MY FUTURE ALL OF A SUDDEN AND...
THAT'S GREAT, TSUKUNE!
HUH?
YOU CAN'T PUT PROBLEMS OFF UNTIL IT'S TOO LATE TO DO ANYTHING ABOUT THEM!
YOU'RE... RIGHT...
GURG...
HOLD ON JUST A MINUTE!
ALLOW ME TO SOLVE THAT WORRY FOR YOU...
RF
RF
RF
WHAT THE ...?!

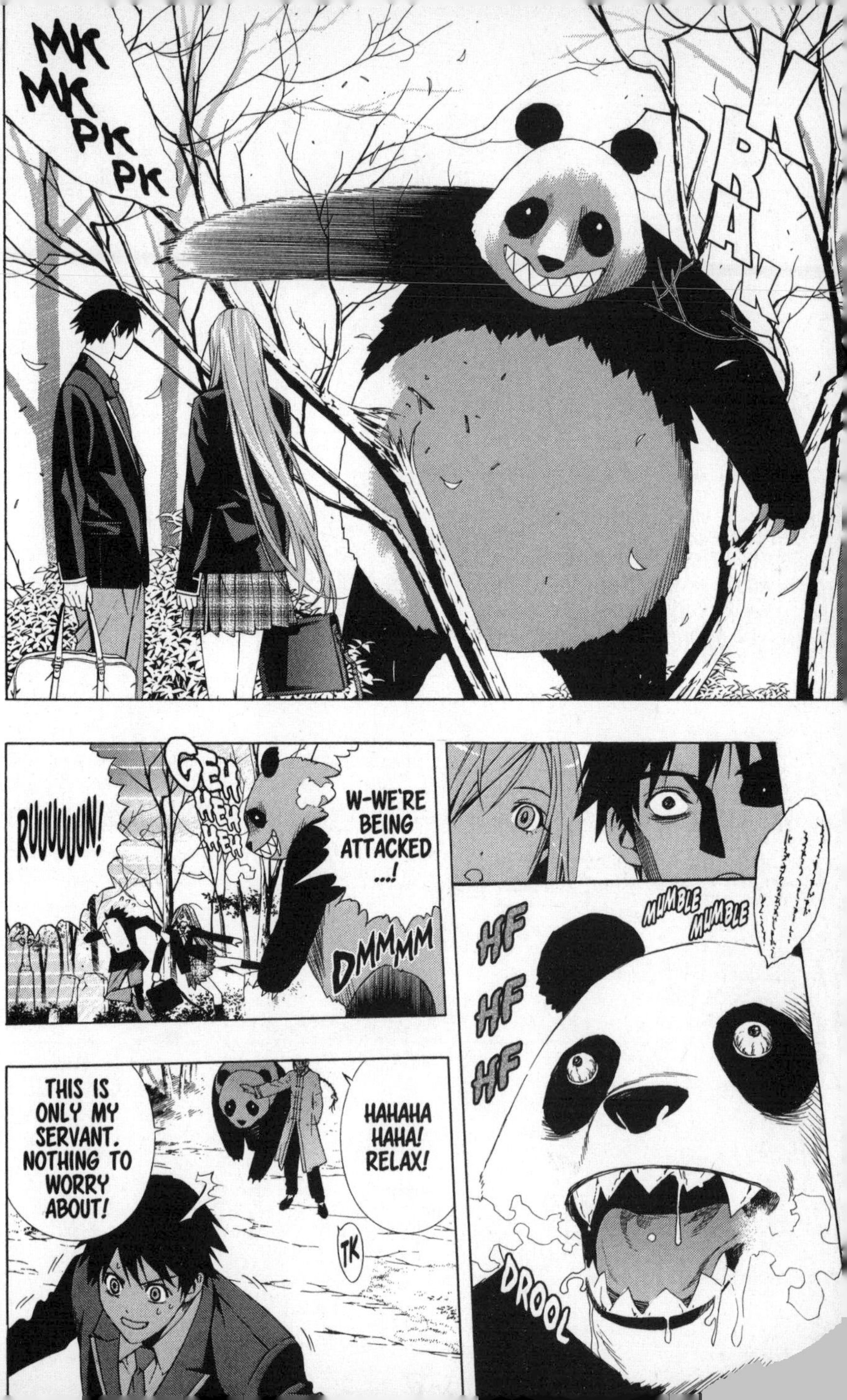
KRAK
MK MK PK PK
GEH HEH HEH
W-WE'RE BEING ATTACKED ...!
RUUUUUN!
DMMMM
MUMBLE MUMBLE
HF HF HF
DROOL
HAHAHA HAHA! RELAX!
THIS IS ONLY MY SERVANT. NOTHING TO WORRY ABOUT!
TK

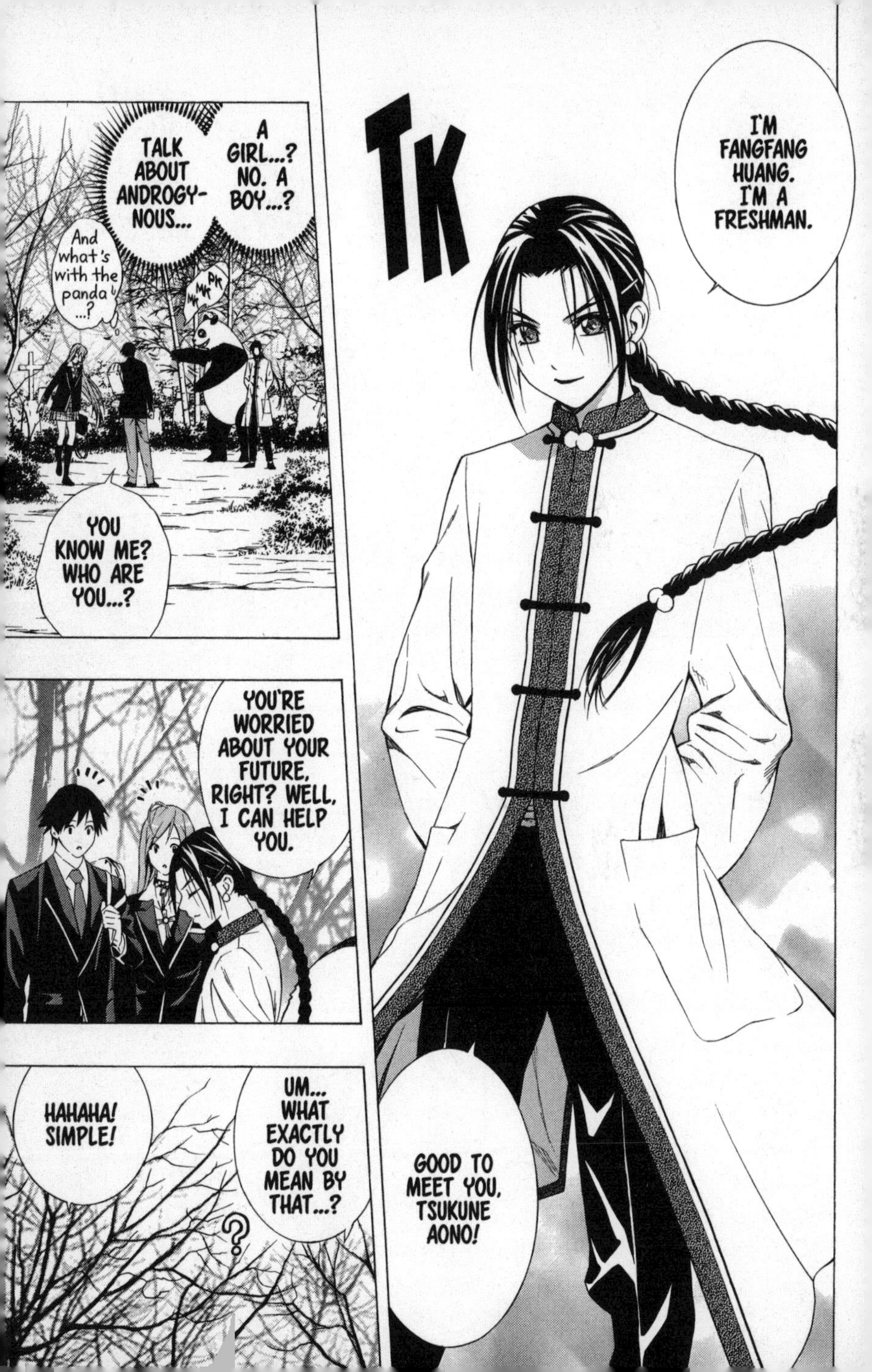
I'M FANGFANG HUANG. I'M A FRESHMAN.
TK
GOOD TO MEET YOU, TSUKUNE AONO!
A GIRL...? NO. A BOY...?
TALK ABOUT ANDROGY-NOUS...
And what's with the panda...?
PK MK MK
YOU KNOW ME? WHO ARE YOU...?
YOU'RE WORRIED ABOUT YOUR FUTURE, RIGHT? WELL, I CAN HELP YOU.
UM... WHAT EXACTLY DO YOU MEAN BY THAT...?
HAHAHA! SIMPLE!
?

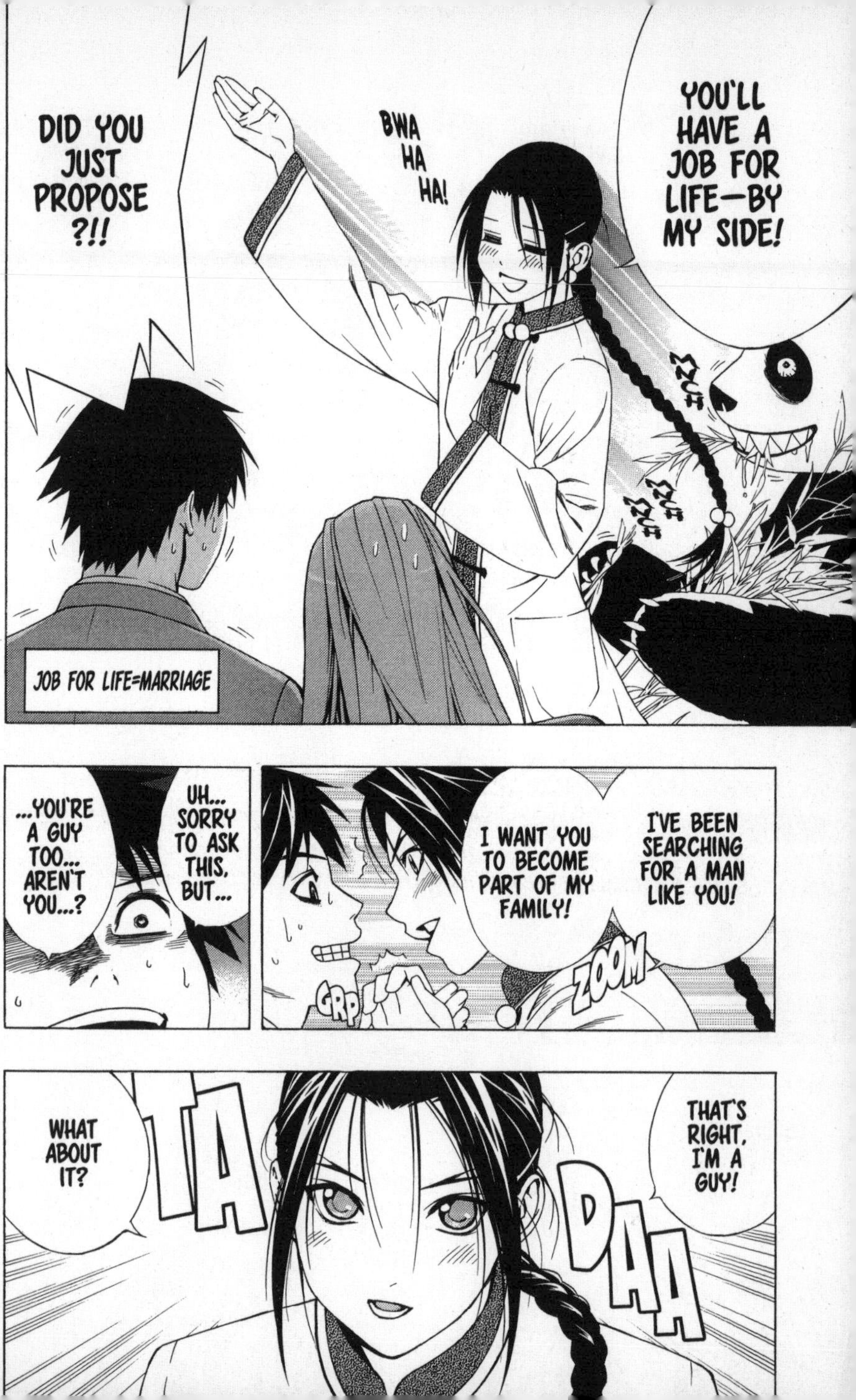
YOU'LL HAVE A JOB FOR LIFE—BY MY SIDE!
BWA HA HA!
MNCH
MNCH MNCH
DID YOU JUST PROPOSE ?!!
JOB FOR LIFE=MARRIAGE
I'VE BEEN SEARCHING FOR A MAN LIKE YOU!
I WANT YOU TO BECOME PART OF MY FAMILY!
ZOOM
GRP
UH... SORRY TO ASK THIS, BUT...
...YOU'RE A GUY TOO... AREN'T YOU...?
THAT'S RIGHT, I'M A GUY!
TA DAA
WHAT ABOUT IT?

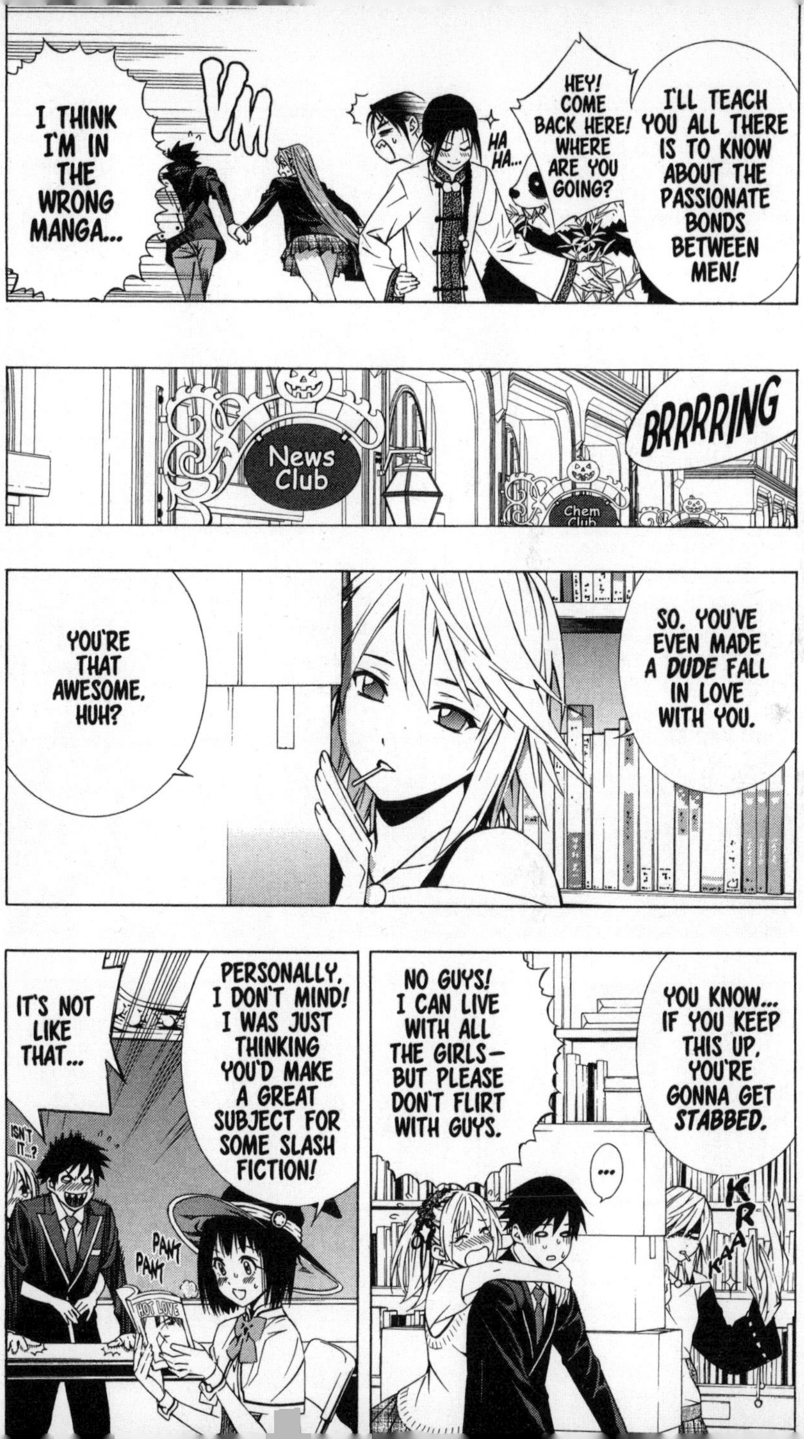
I'LL TEACH YOU ALL THERE IS TO KNOW ABOUT THE PASSIONATE BONDS BETWEEN MEN!
HEY! COME BACK HERE! WHERE ARE YOU GOING?
HA HA...
VM
I THINK I'M IN THE WRONG MANGA...
BRRRRING
News Club
Chem Club
SO. YOU'VE EVEN MADE A DUDE FALL IN LOVE WITH YOU.
YOU'RE THAT AWESOME, HUH?
YOU KNOW... IF YOU KEEP THIS UP, YOU'RE GONNA GET STABBED.
KRA
KAA
...
NO GUYS! I CAN LIVE WITH ALL THE GIRLS— BUT PLEASE DON'T FLIRT WITH GUYS.
PERSONALLY, I DON'T MIND! I WAS JUST THINKING YOU'D MAKE A GREAT SUBJECT FOR SOME SLASH FICTION!
IT'S NOT LIKE THAT...
ISN'T IT...?
PANT PANT
HOT LOVE

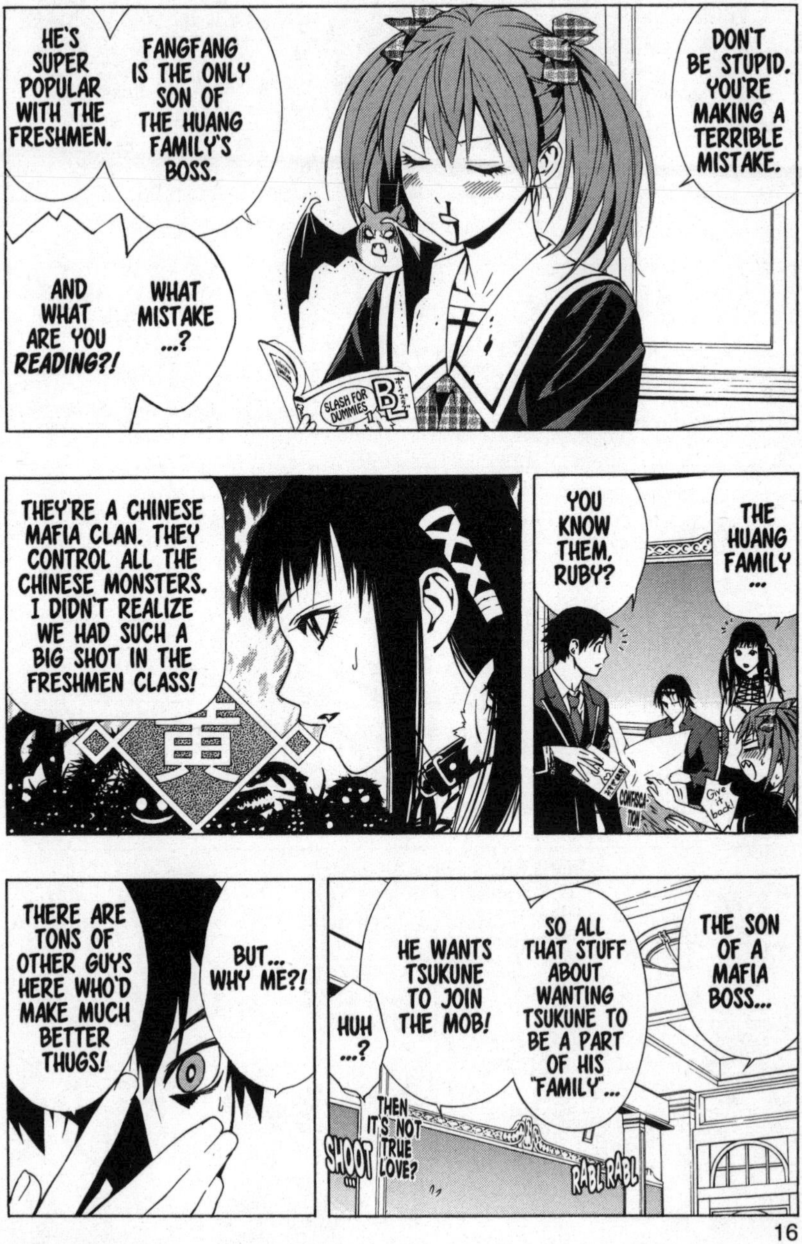
DON'T BE STUPID. YOU'RE MAKING A TERRIBLE MISTAKE.
FANGFANG IS THE ONLY SON OF THE HUANG FAMILY'S BOSS.
HE'S SUPER POPULAR WITH THE FRESHMEN.
WHAT MISTAKE ...?
AND WHAT ARE YOU *READING?!*
SLASH FOR DUMMIES
BL
THE HUANG FAMILY ...
YOU KNOW THEM, RUBY?
CONFISCATION
Give it back!
THEY'RE A CHINESE MAFIA CLAN. THEY CONTROL ALL THE CHINESE MONSTERS. I DIDN'T REALIZE WE HAD SUCH A BIG SHOT IN THE FRESHMEN CLASS!
THE SON OF A MAFIA BOSS...
SO ALL THAT STUFF ABOUT WANTING TSUKUNE TO BE A PART OF HIS "FAMILY"...
HE WANTS TSUKUNE TO JOIN THE MOB!
HUH ...?
THEN IT'S NOT TRUE LOVE?
SHOOT ...
RABL RABL
BUT... WHY ME?!
THERE ARE TONS OF OTHER GUYS HERE WHO'D MAKE MUCH BETTER THUGS!

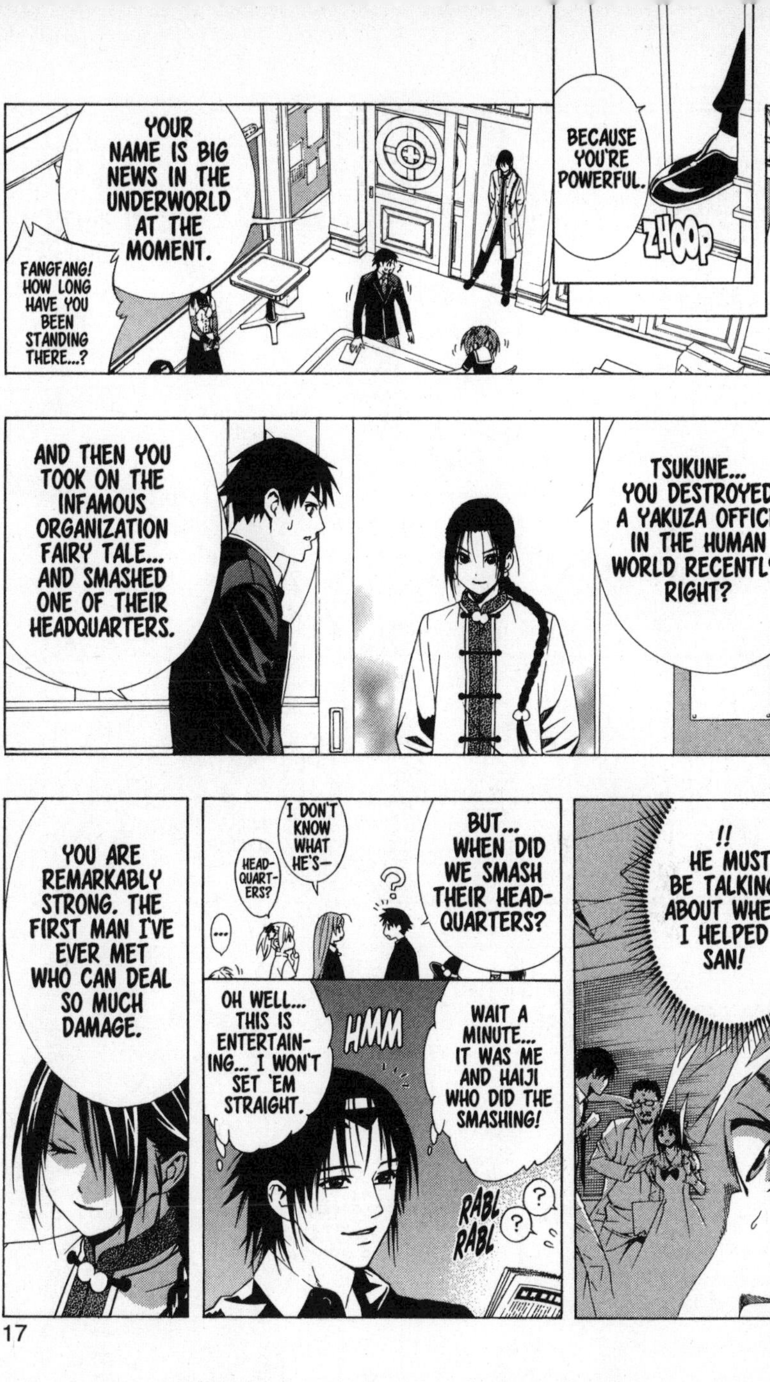
BECAUSE YOU'RE POWERFUL.
ZHOOP
YOUR NAME IS BIG NEWS IN THE UNDERWORLD AT THE MOMENT.
FANGFANG! HOW LONG HAVE YOU BEEN STANDING THERE...?
TSUKUNE... YOU DESTROYED A YAKUZA OFFICE IN THE HUMAN WORLD RECENTLY, RIGHT?
AND THEN YOU TOOK ON THE INFAMOUS ORGANIZATION FAIRY TALE... AND SMASHED ONE OF THEIR HEADQUARTERS.
!! HE MUST BE TALKING ABOUT WHEN I HELPED SAN!
BUT... WHEN DID WE SMASH THEIR HEAD-QUARTERS?
I DON'T KNOW WHAT HE'S—
HEAD-QUART-ERS?
...
WAIT A MINUTE... IT WAS ME AND HAIJI WHO DID THE SMASHING!
HMM
OH WELL... THIS IS ENTERTAIN-ING... I WON'T SET 'EM STRAIGHT.
RABL RABL
?
?
YOU ARE REMARKABLY STRONG. THE FIRST MAN I'VE EVER MET WHO CAN DEAL SO MUCH DAMAGE.

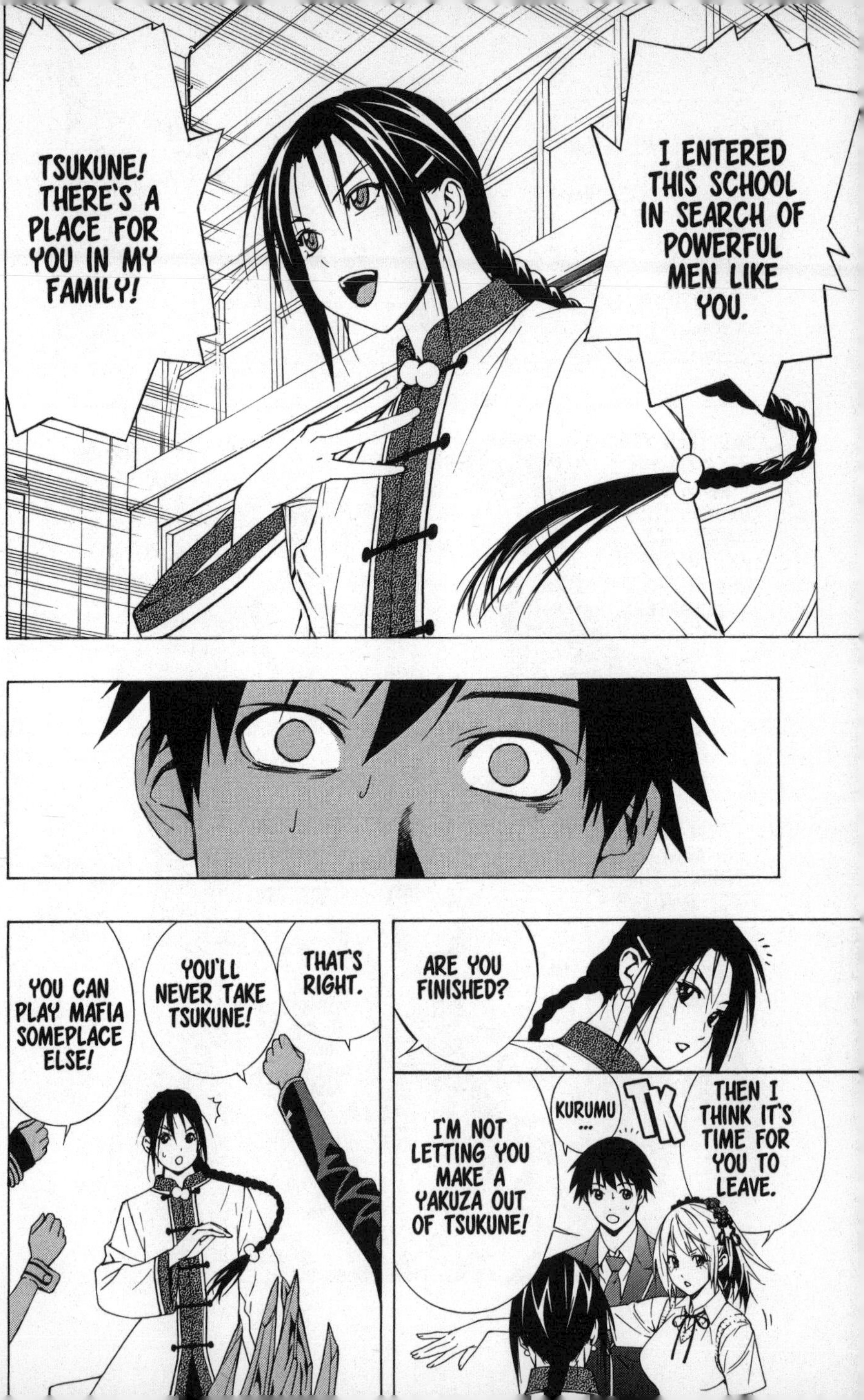
I ENTERED THIS SCHOOL IN SEARCH OF POWERFUL MEN LIKE YOU.
TSUKUNE! THERE'S A PLACE FOR YOU IN MY FAMILY!
ARE YOU FINISHED?
THEN I THINK IT'S TIME FOR YOU TO LEAVE.
TK
KURUMU...
I'M NOT LETTING YOU MAKE A YAKUZA OUT OF TSUKUNE!
THAT'S RIGHT.
YOU'LL NEVER TAKE TSUKUNE!
YOU CAN PLAY MAFIA SOMEPLACE ELSE!

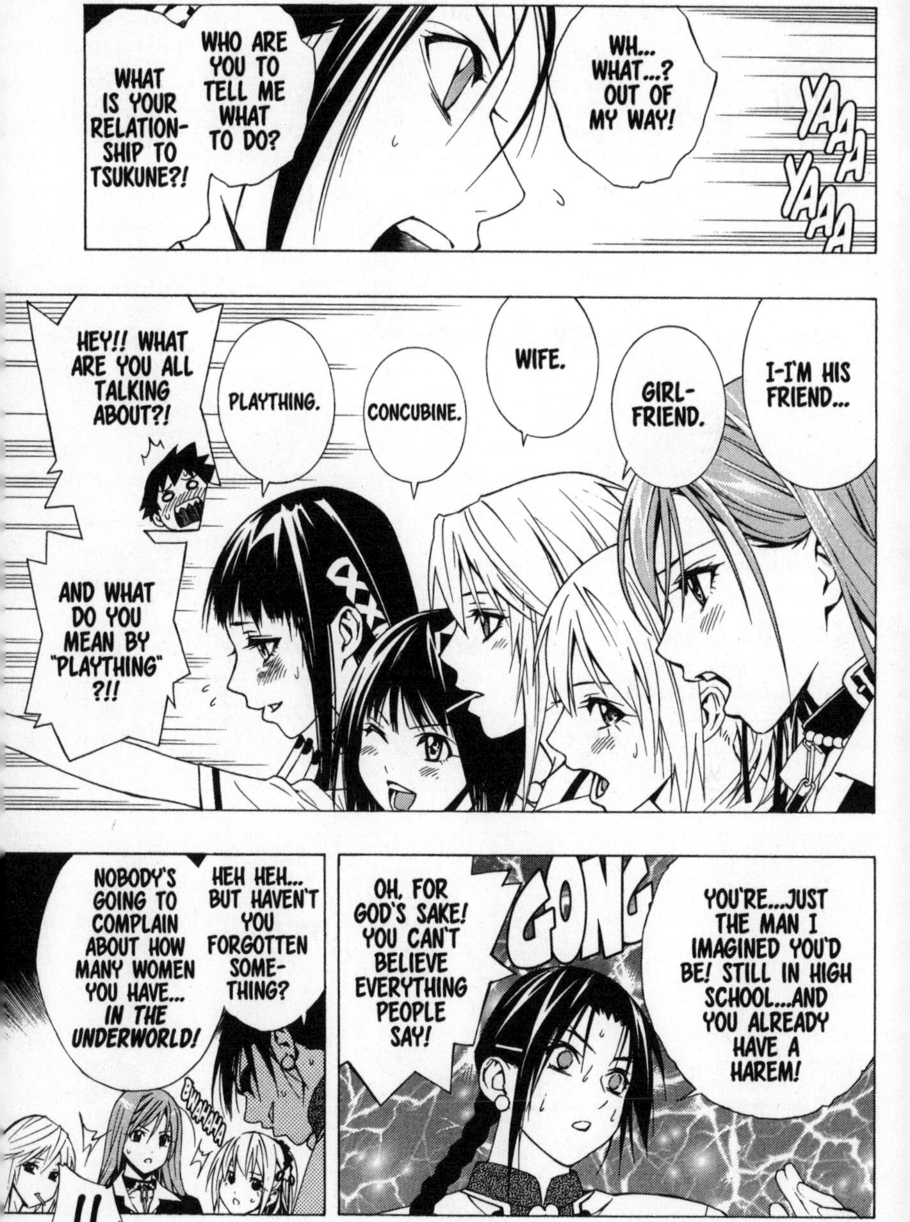
YAAA YAAA
WH... WHAT...? OUT OF MY WAY!
WHO ARE YOU TO TELL ME WHAT TO DO?
WHAT IS YOUR RELATION-SHIP TO TSUKUNE?!
I-I'M HIS FRIEND...
GIRL-FRIEND.
WIFE.
CONCUBINE.
PLAYTHING.
HEY!! WHAT ARE YOU ALL TALKING ABOUT?!
AND WHAT DO YOU MEAN BY "PLAYTHING"?!!
YOU'RE...JUST THE MAN I IMAGINED YOU'D BE! STILL IN HIGH SCHOOL...AND YOU ALREADY HAVE A HAREM!
GONG
OH, FOR GOD'S SAKE! YOU CAN'T BELIEVE EVERYTHING PEOPLE SAY!
HEH HEH... BUT HAVEN'T YOU FORGOTTEN SOME-THING?
NOBODY'S GOING TO COMPLAIN ABOUT HOW MANY WOMEN YOU HAVE... IN THE UNDERWORLD!
BWAHAHA
!!

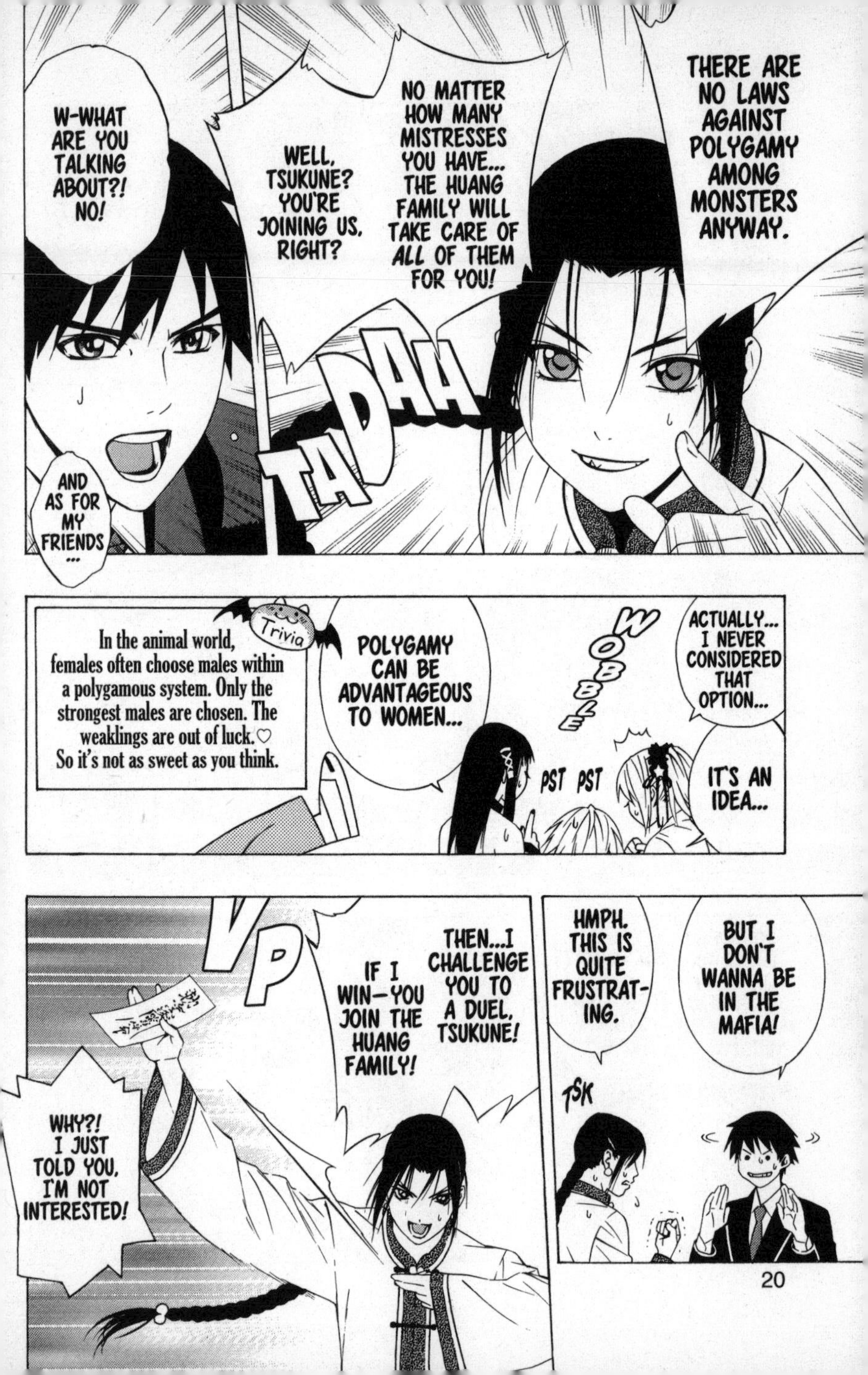
THERE ARE NO LAWS AGAINST POLYGAMY AMONG MONSTERS ANYWAY.
NO MATTER HOW MANY MISTRESSES YOU HAVE... THE HUANG FAMILY WILL TAKE CARE OF ALL OF THEM FOR YOU!
WELL, TSUKUNE? YOU'RE JOINING US, RIGHT?
TADAH
W-WHAT ARE YOU TALKING ABOUT?! NO!
AND AS FOR MY FRIENDS...
ACTUALLY... I NEVER CONSIDERED THAT OPTION...
IT'S AN IDEA...
WOBBLE
PST PST
POLYGAMY CAN BE ADVANTAGEOUS TO WOMEN...
Trivia
In the animal world, females often choose males within a polygamous system. Only the strongest males are chosen. The weaklings are out of luck.♡ So it's not as sweet as you think.
BUT I DON'T WANNA BE IN THE MAFIA!
HMPH. THIS IS QUITE FRUSTRAT-ING.
TSK
THEN...I CHALLENGE YOU TO A DUEL, TSUKUNE!
IF I WIN—YOU JOIN THE HUANG FAMILY!
VP
WHY?! I JUST TOLD YOU, I'M NOT INTERESTED!

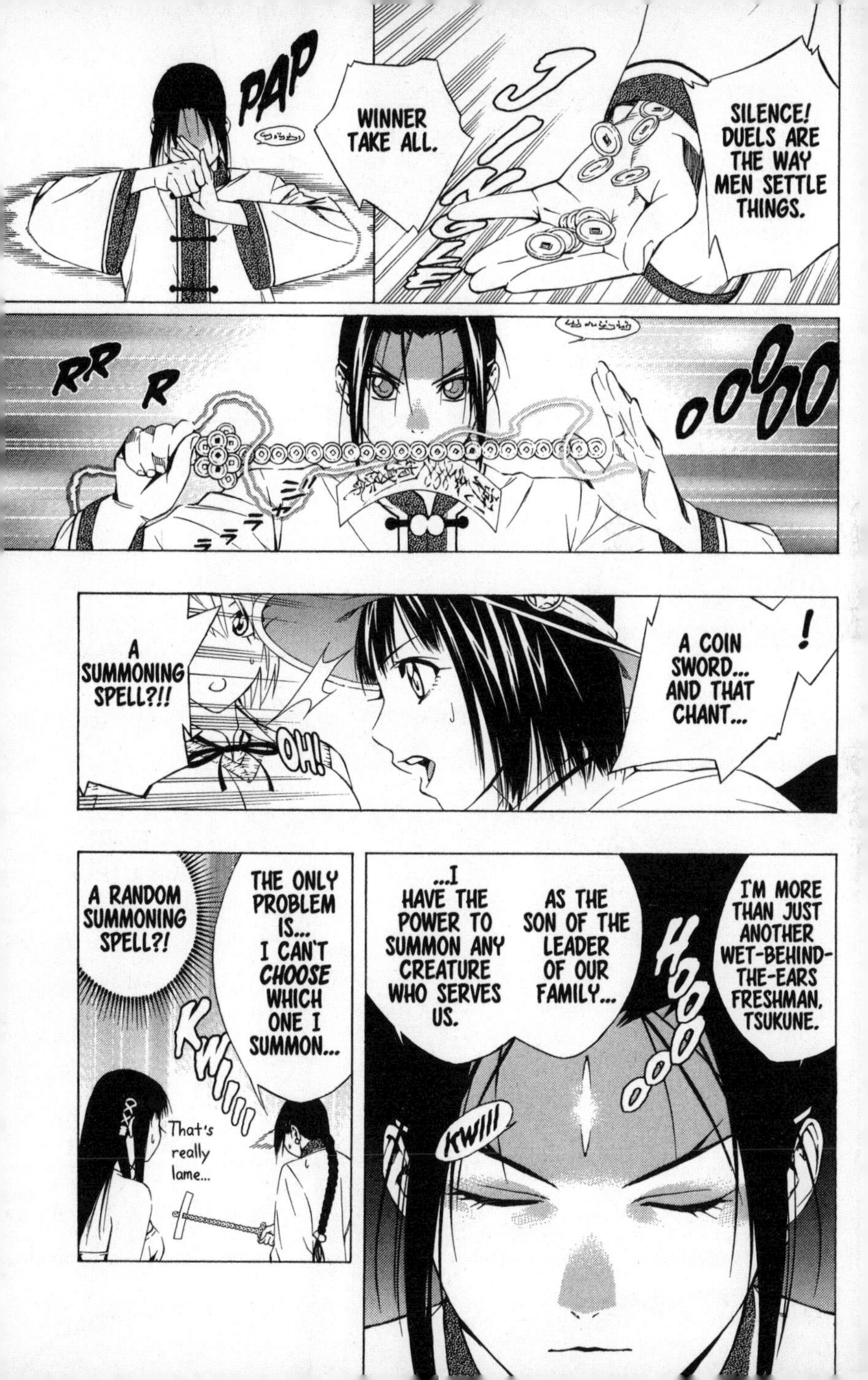
SILENCE! DUELS ARE THE WAY MEN SETTLE THINGS.
WINNER TAKE ALL.
PAP
RRR
OOOOO
!
A COIN SWORD... AND THAT CHANT...
A SUMMONING SPELL?!!
OH!
I'M MORE THAN JUST ANOTHER WET-BEHIND-THE-EARS FRESHMAN, TSUKUNE.
AS THE SON OF THE LEADER OF OUR FAMILY...
...I HAVE THE POWER TO SUMMON ANY CREATURE WHO SERVES US.
HOOOOO
KWIII
THE ONLY PROBLEM IS... I CAN'T *CHOOSE* WHICH ONE I SUMMON...
A RANDOM SUMMONING SPELL?!
KWIIII
That's really lame...

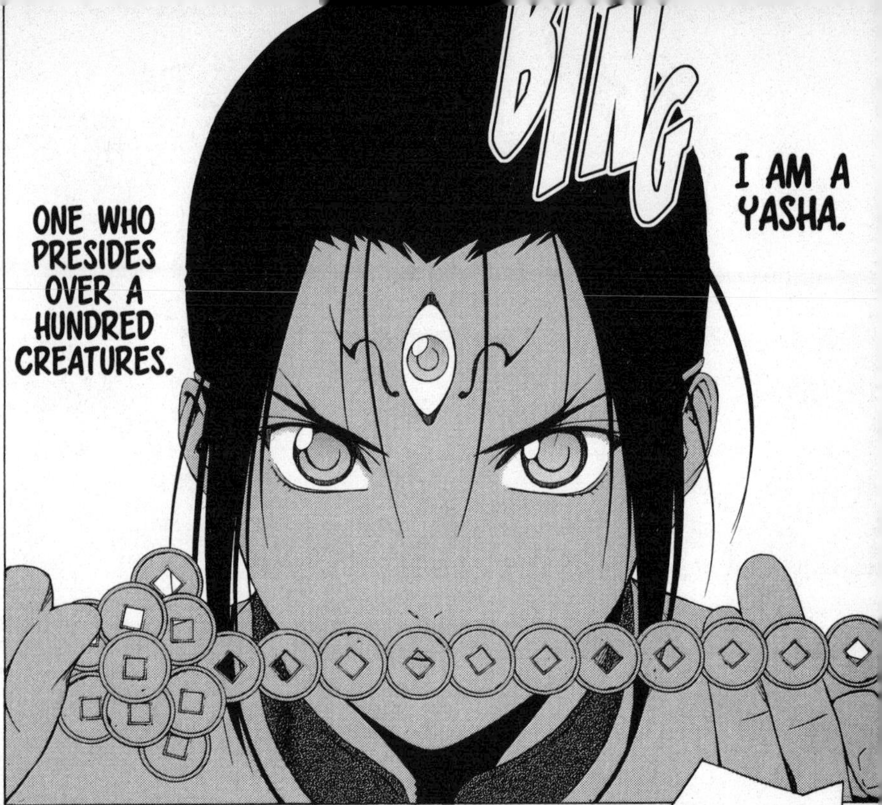
BING
I AM A YASHA.
ONE WHO PRESIDES OVER A HUNDRED CREATURES.

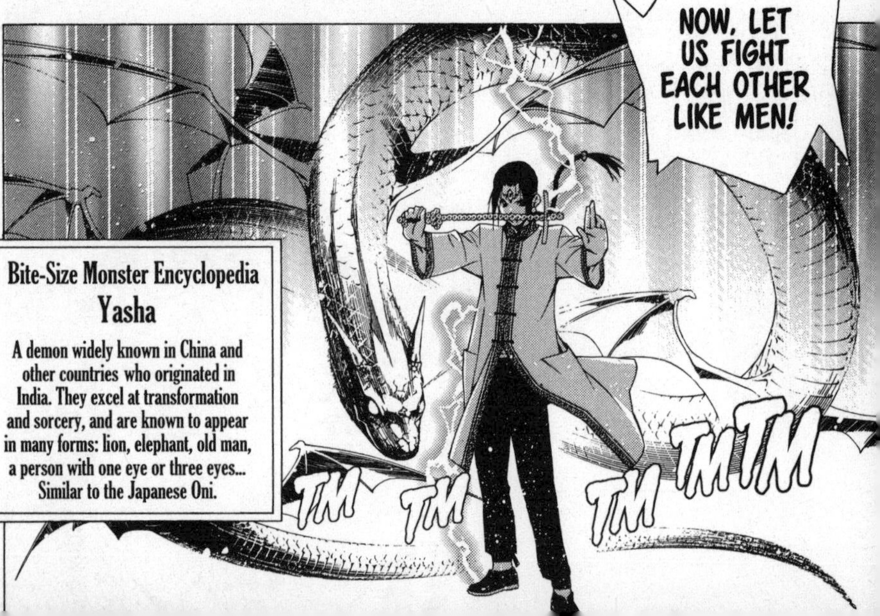
NOW, LET US FIGHT EACH OTHER LIKE MEN!
TMTM
TM
TM
TM

Bite-Size Monster Encyclopedia
Yasha

A demon widely known in China and other countries who originated in India. They excel at transformation and sorcery, and are known to appear in many forms: lion, elephant, old man, a person with one eye or three eyes... Similar to the Japanese Oni.

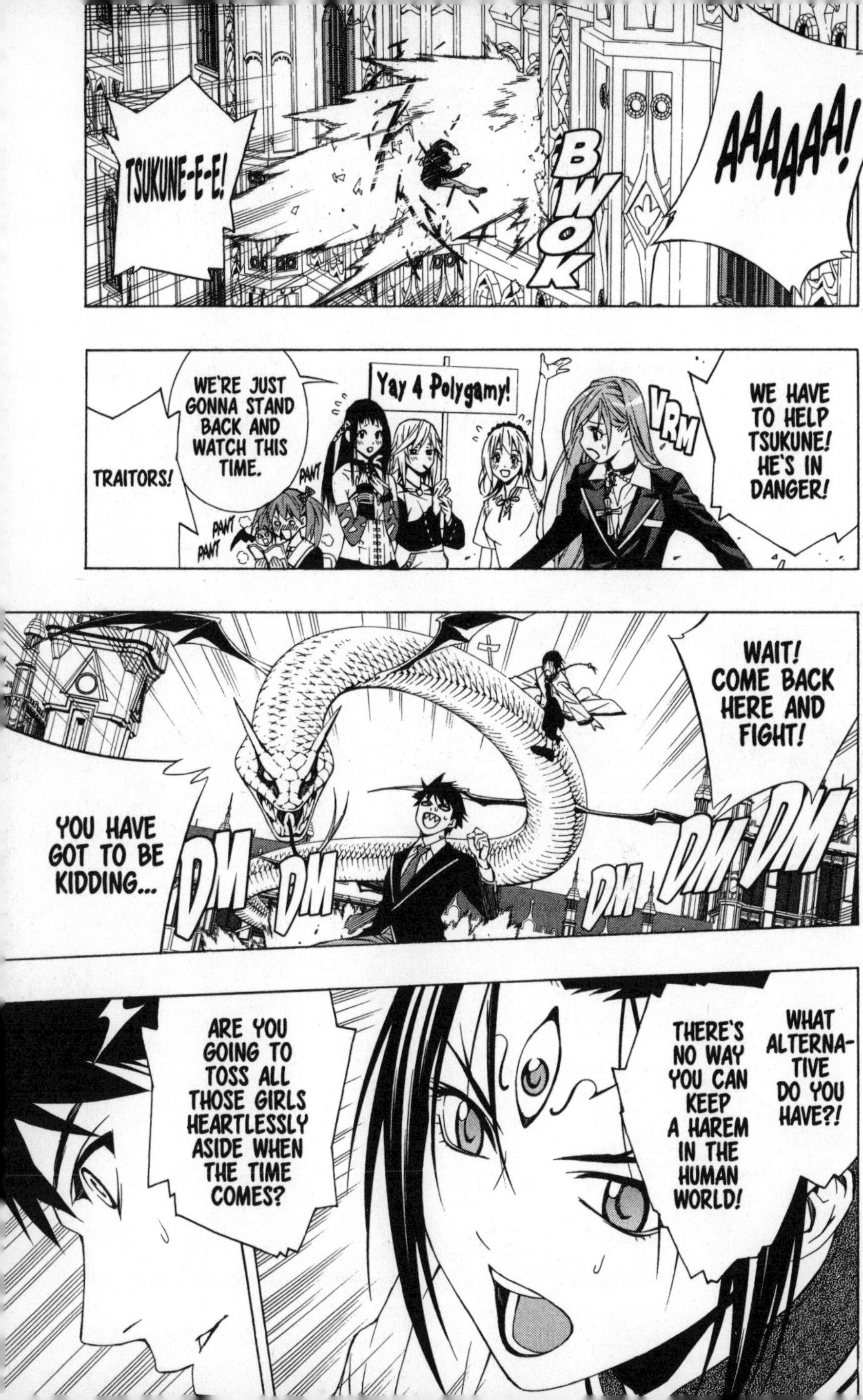
AAAAAA!
BWOK
TSUKUNE-E-E!
WE HAVE TO HELP TSUKUNE! HE'S IN DANGER!
VRM
Yay 4 Polygamy!
WE'RE JUST GONNA STAND BACK AND WATCH THIS TIME.
PANT
TRAITORS!
PANT PANT
WAIT! COME BACK HERE AND FIGHT!
DM DM DM DM
DM DM
YOU HAVE GOT TO BE KIDDING...
WHAT ALTERNA-TIVE DO YOU HAVE?!
THERE'S NO WAY YOU CAN KEEP A HAREM IN THE HUMAN WORLD!
ARE YOU GOING TO TOSS ALL THOSE GIRLS HEARTLESSLY ASIDE WHEN THE TIME COMES?

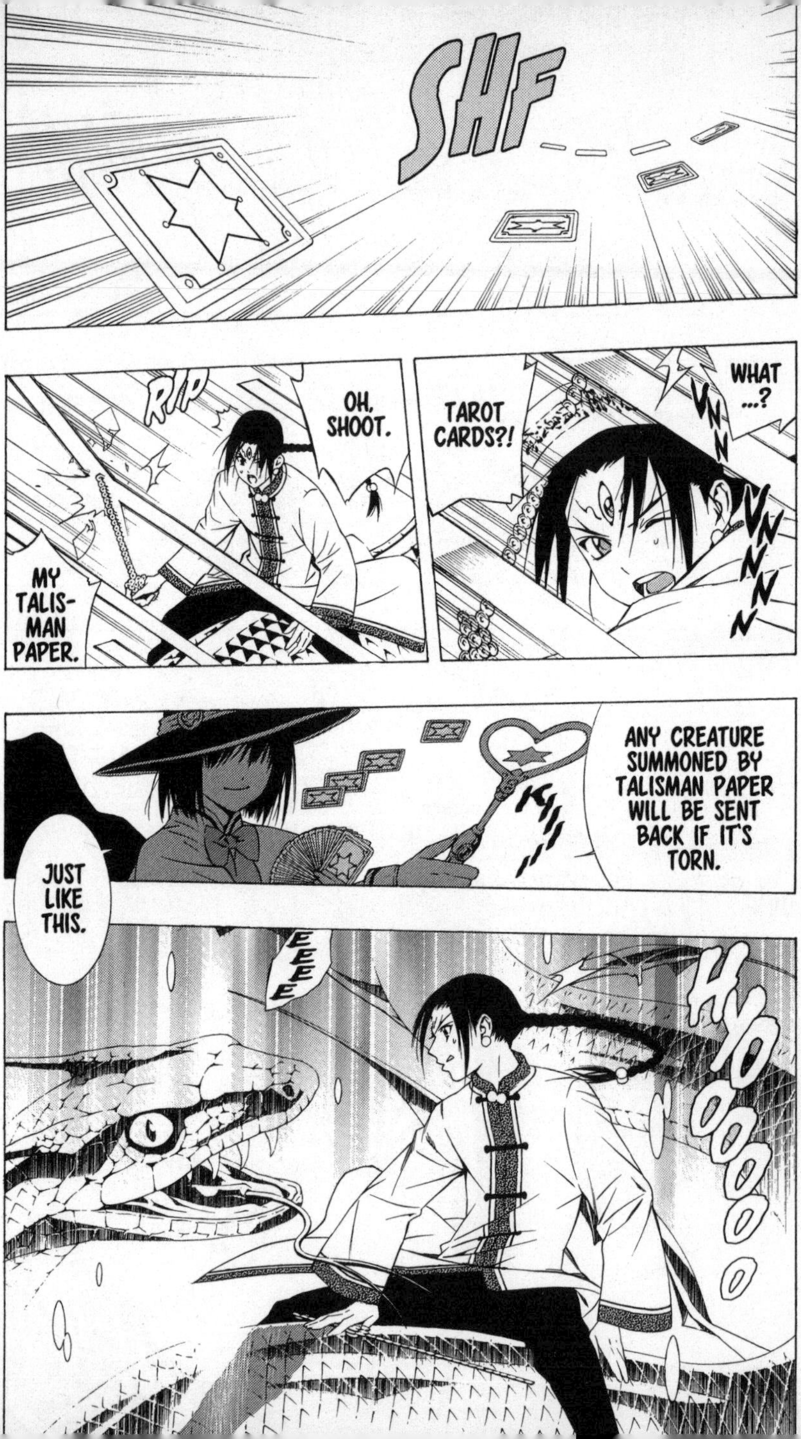
SHF
WHAT ...?
VNNNNNNN
TAROT CARDS?!
OH, SHOOT.
RIP
MY TALISMAN PAPER.
ANY CREATURE SUMMONED BY TALISMAN PAPER WILL BE SENT BACK IF IT'S TORN.
KII
JUST LIKE THIS.
HYOOOOOOO
EEEE

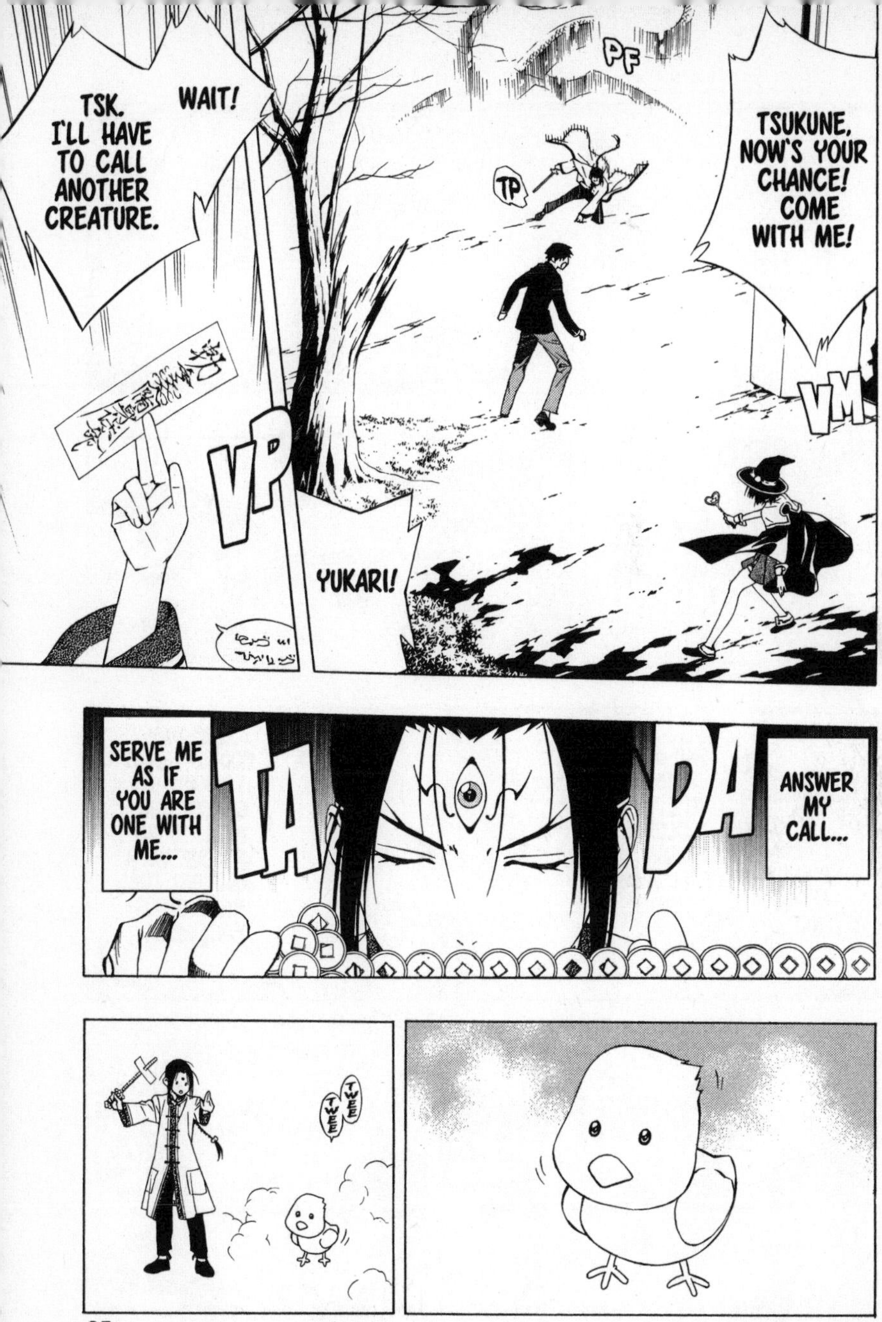
PF
TSUKUNE, NOW'S YOUR CHANCE! COME WITH ME!
TP
WAIT!
TSK. I'LL HAVE TO CALL ANOTHER CREATURE.
VM
VP
YUKARI!
ANSWER MY CALL...
DA
TA
SERVE ME AS IF YOU ARE ONE WITH ME...
TWEE
TWEE

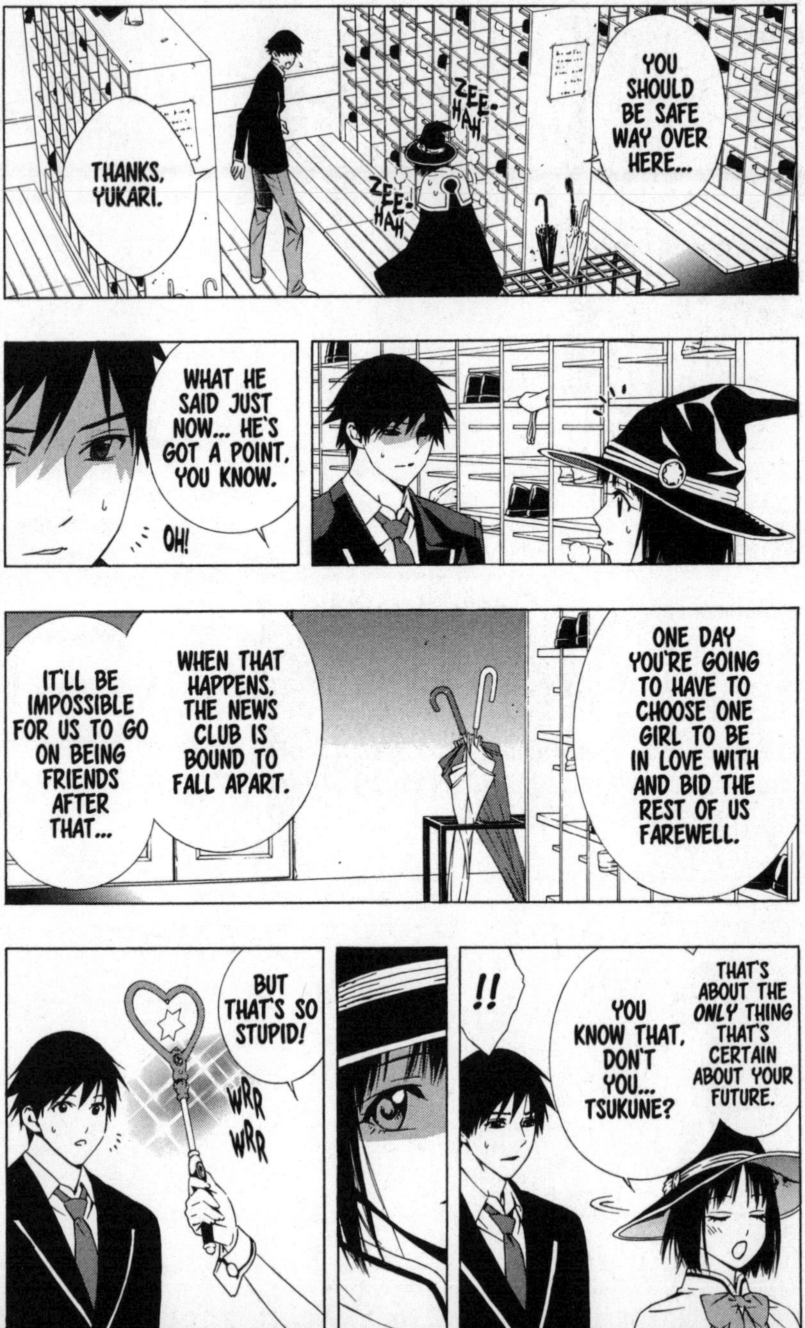
YOU SHOULD BE SAFE WAY OVER HERE...
ZEE-HAH
ZEE-HAH
THANKS, YUKARI.
WHAT HE SAID JUST NOW... HE'S GOT A POINT, YOU KNOW.
OH!
ONE DAY YOU'RE GOING TO HAVE TO CHOOSE ONE GIRL TO BE IN LOVE WITH AND BID THE REST OF US FAREWELL.
WHEN THAT HAPPENS, THE NEWS CLUB IS BOUND TO FALL APART.
IT'LL BE IMPOSSIBLE FOR US TO GO ON BEING FRIENDS AFTER THAT...
THAT'S ABOUT THE *ONLY* THING THAT'S CERTAIN ABOUT YOUR FUTURE.
YOU KNOW THAT, DON'T YOU... TSUKUNE?
!!
BUT THAT'S SO STUPID!
WRR WRR

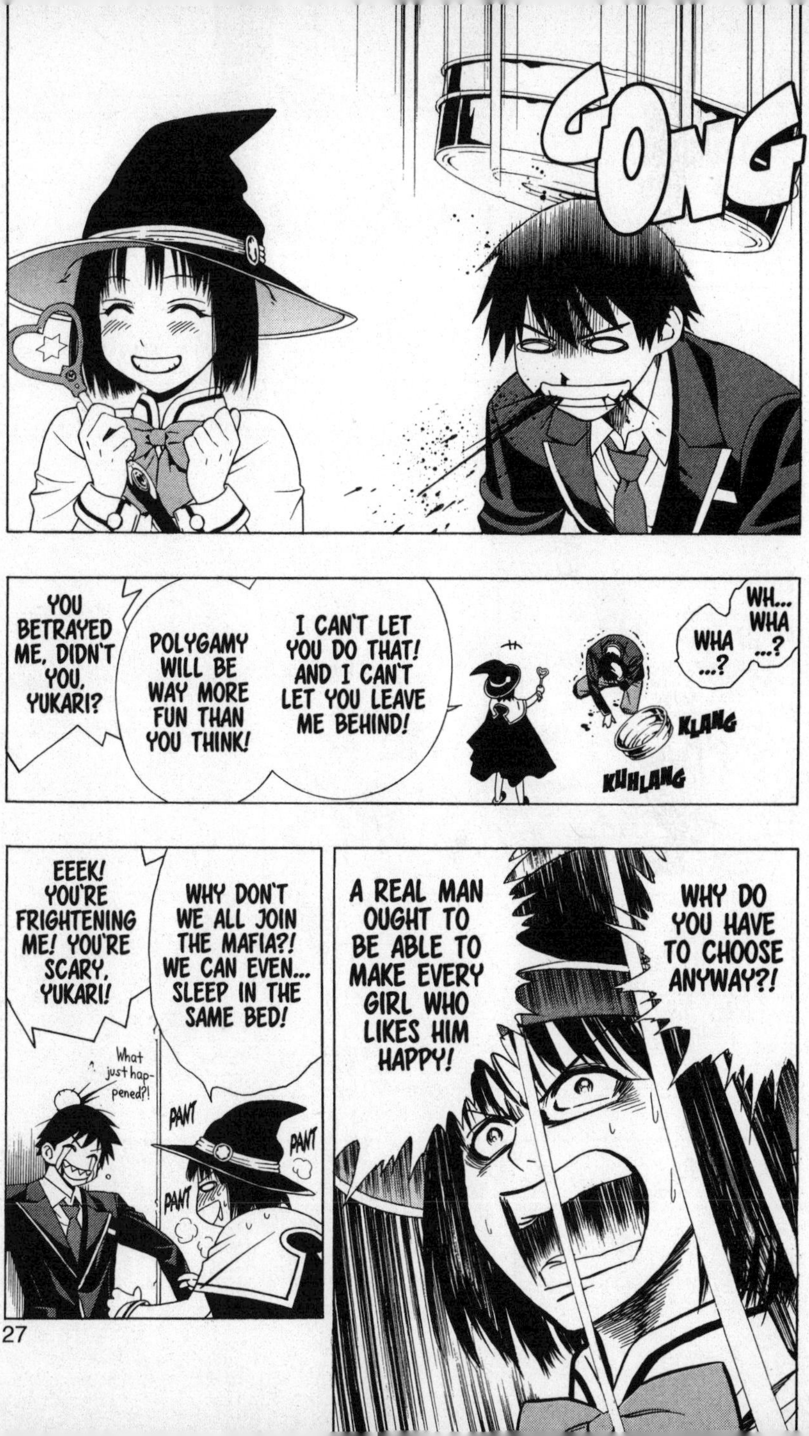
GONG
WH... WHA ...?
WHA ...?
KLANG
KUHLANG
I CAN'T LET YOU DO THAT! AND I CAN'T LET YOU LEAVE ME BEHIND!
POLYGAMY WILL BE WAY MORE FUN THAN YOU THINK!
YOU BETRAYED ME, DIDN'T YOU, YUKARI?
WHY DO YOU HAVE TO CHOOSE ANYWAY?!
A REAL MAN OUGHT TO BE ABLE TO MAKE EVERY GIRL WHO LIKES HIM HAPPY!
WHY DON'T WE ALL JOIN THE MAFIA?! WE CAN EVEN... SLEEP IN THE SAME BED!
EEEK! YOU'RE FRIGHTENING ME! YOU'RE SCARY, YUKARI!
What just happened?!
PANT
PANT
PANT

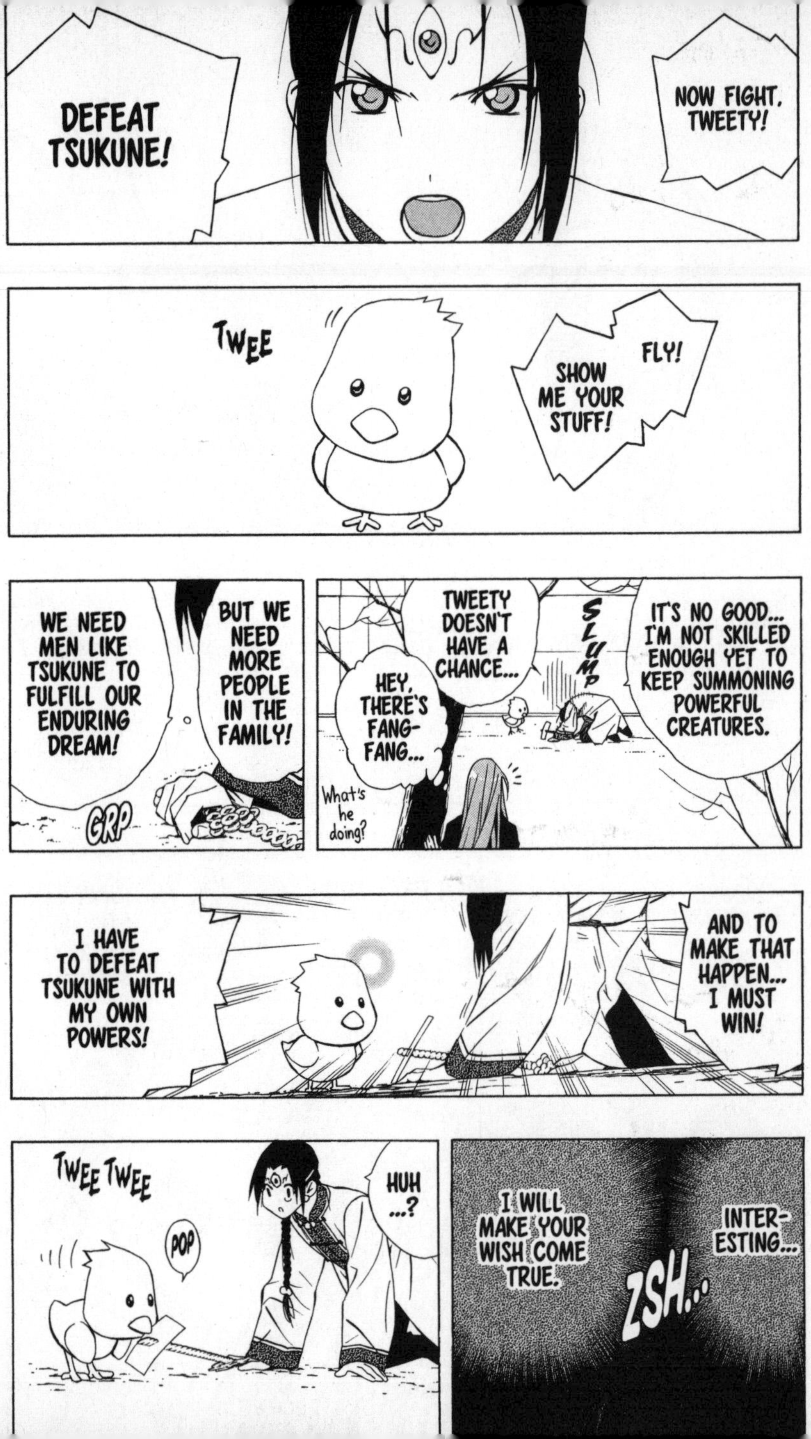
NOW FIGHT, TWEETY!
DEFEAT TSUKUNE!
FLY!
SHOW ME YOUR STUFF!
TWEE
IT'S NO GOOD... I'M NOT SKILLED ENOUGH YET TO KEEP SUMMONING POWERFUL CREATURES.
SLUMP
TWEETY DOESN'T HAVE A CHANCE...
HEY, THERE'S FANG-FANG...
What's he doing?
BUT WE NEED MORE PEOPLE IN THE FAMILY!
WE NEED MEN LIKE TSUKUNE TO FULFILL OUR ENDURING DREAM!
GRP
AND TO MAKE THAT HAPPEN... I MUST WIN!
I HAVE TO DEFEAT TSUKUNE WITH MY OWN POWERS!
INTER-ESTING...
I WILL MAKE YOUR WISH COME TRUE.
ZSH...
HUH ...?
TWEE TWEE
POP

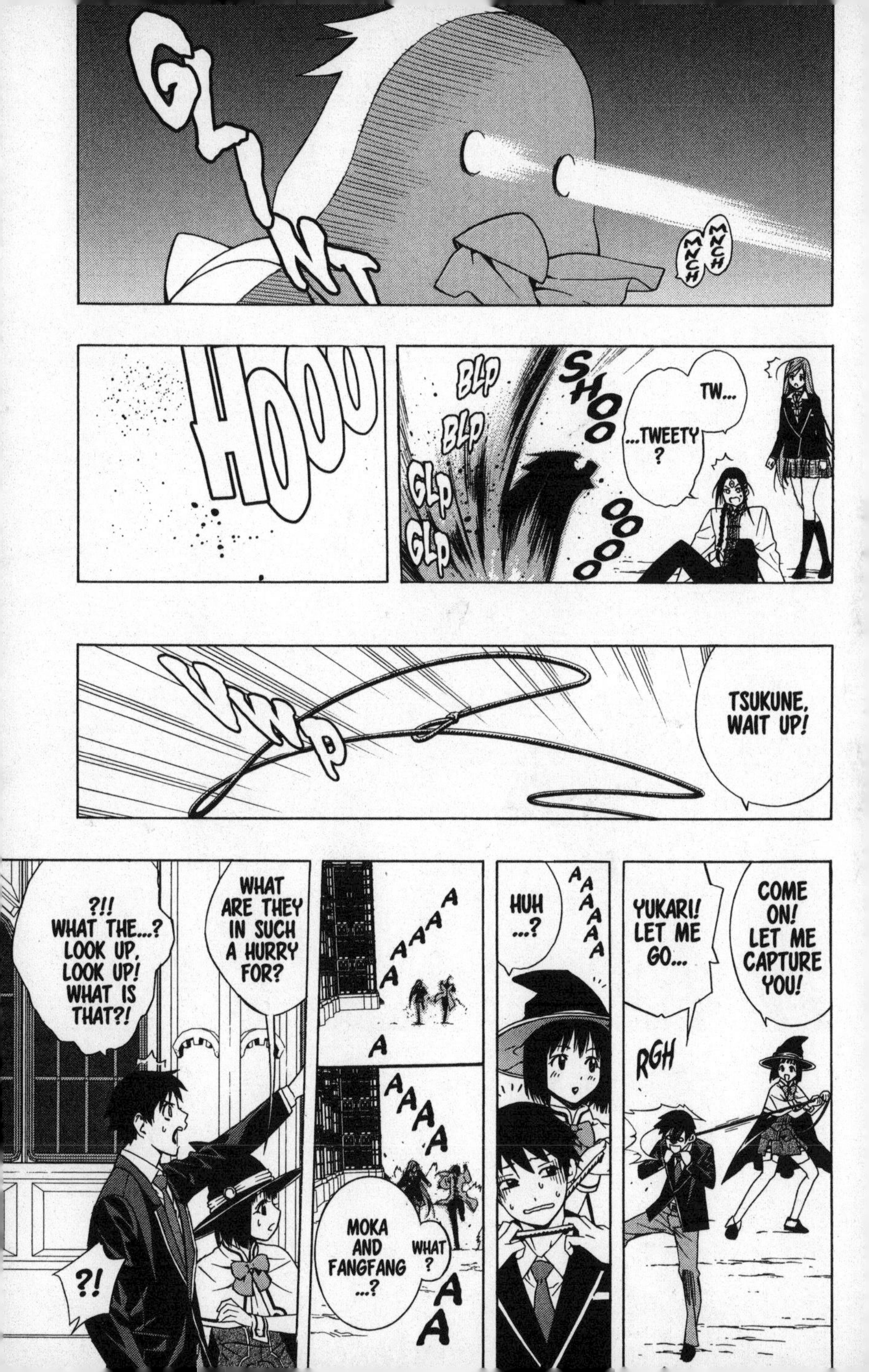
MNCH MNCH
GLNT
TW... ...TWEETY?
SHOO
BLP BLP GLP GLP
OOOO
HOOOO
TSUKUNE, WAIT UP!
VWNP
COME ON! LET ME CAPTURE YOU!
YUKARI! LET ME GO...
RGH
AAAAAA
HUH ...?
AAAAA A
AAAAA
WHAT?
MOKA AND FANGFANG ...?
AA
WHAT ARE THEY IN SUCH A HURRY FOR?
?!! WHAT THE...? LOOK UP, LOOK UP! WHAT IS THAT?!
?!

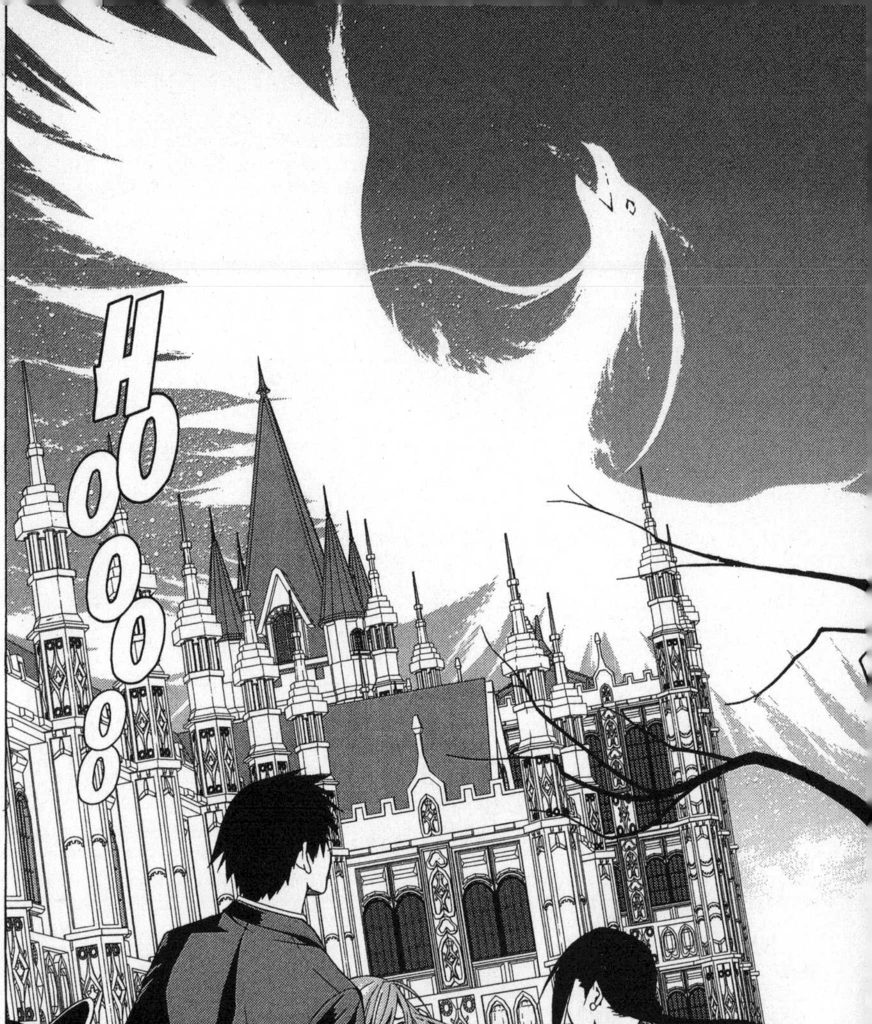
HOOOOOO

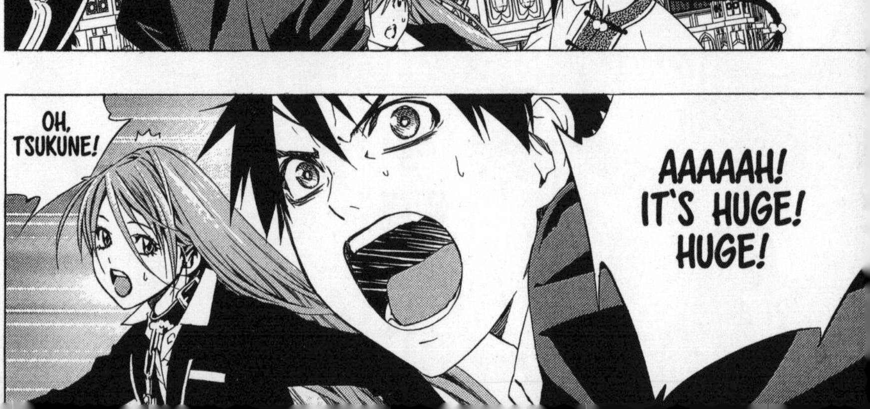
AAAAAH! IT'S HUGE! HUGE!
OH, TSUKUNE!

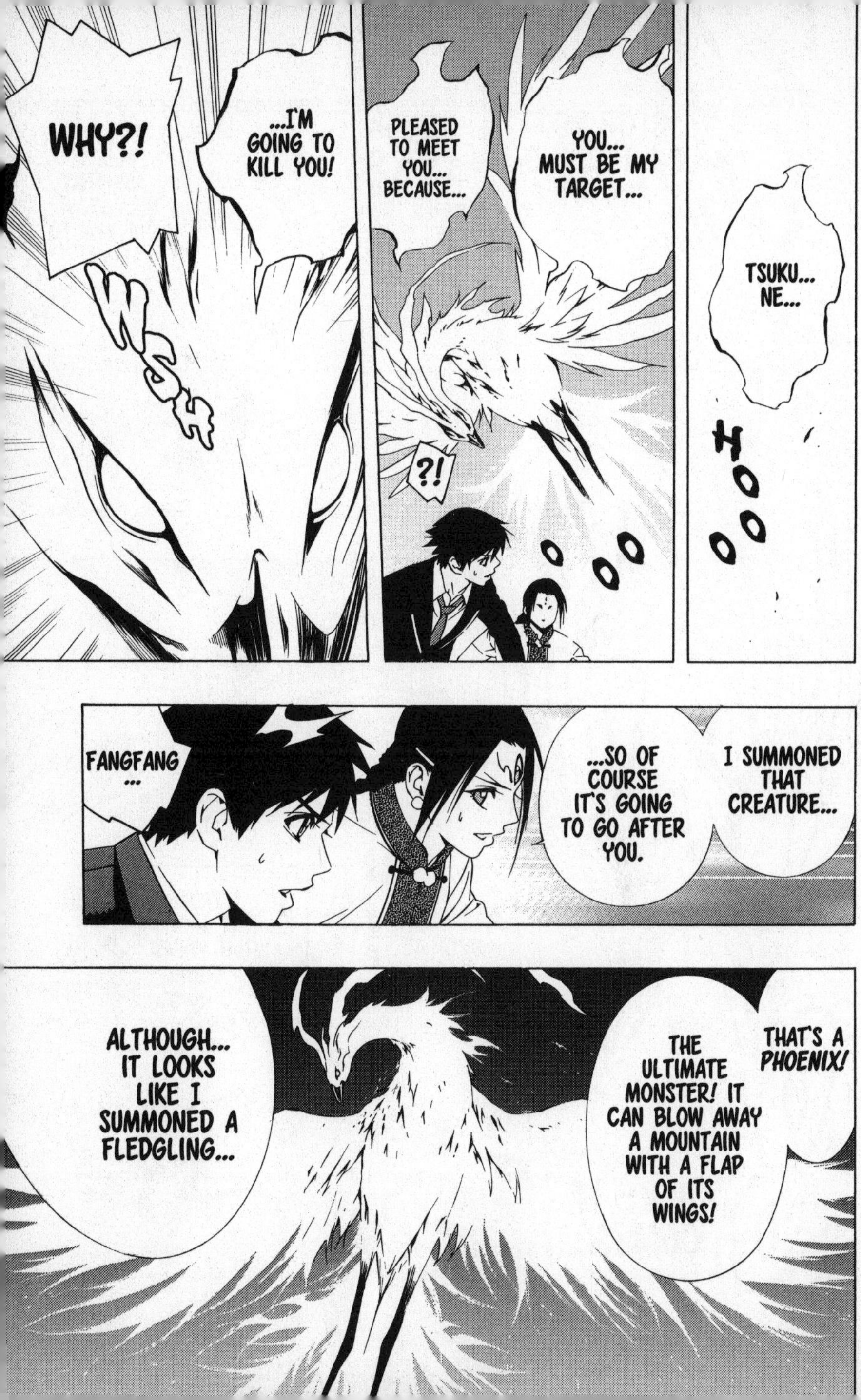
TSUKU... NE...
HOOOO
YOU... MUST BE MY TARGET...
PLEASED TO MEET YOU... BECAUSE...
OOO
?!
...I'M GOING TO KILL YOU!
WHY?!
WSH
I SUMMONED THAT CREATURE...
...SO OF COURSE IT'S GOING TO GO AFTER YOU.
FANGFANG...
THAT'S A PHOENIX!
THE ULTIMATE MONSTER! IT CAN BLOW AWAY A MOUNTAIN WITH A FLAP OF ITS WINGS!
ALTHOUGH... IT LOOKS LIKE I SUMMONED A FLEDGLING...

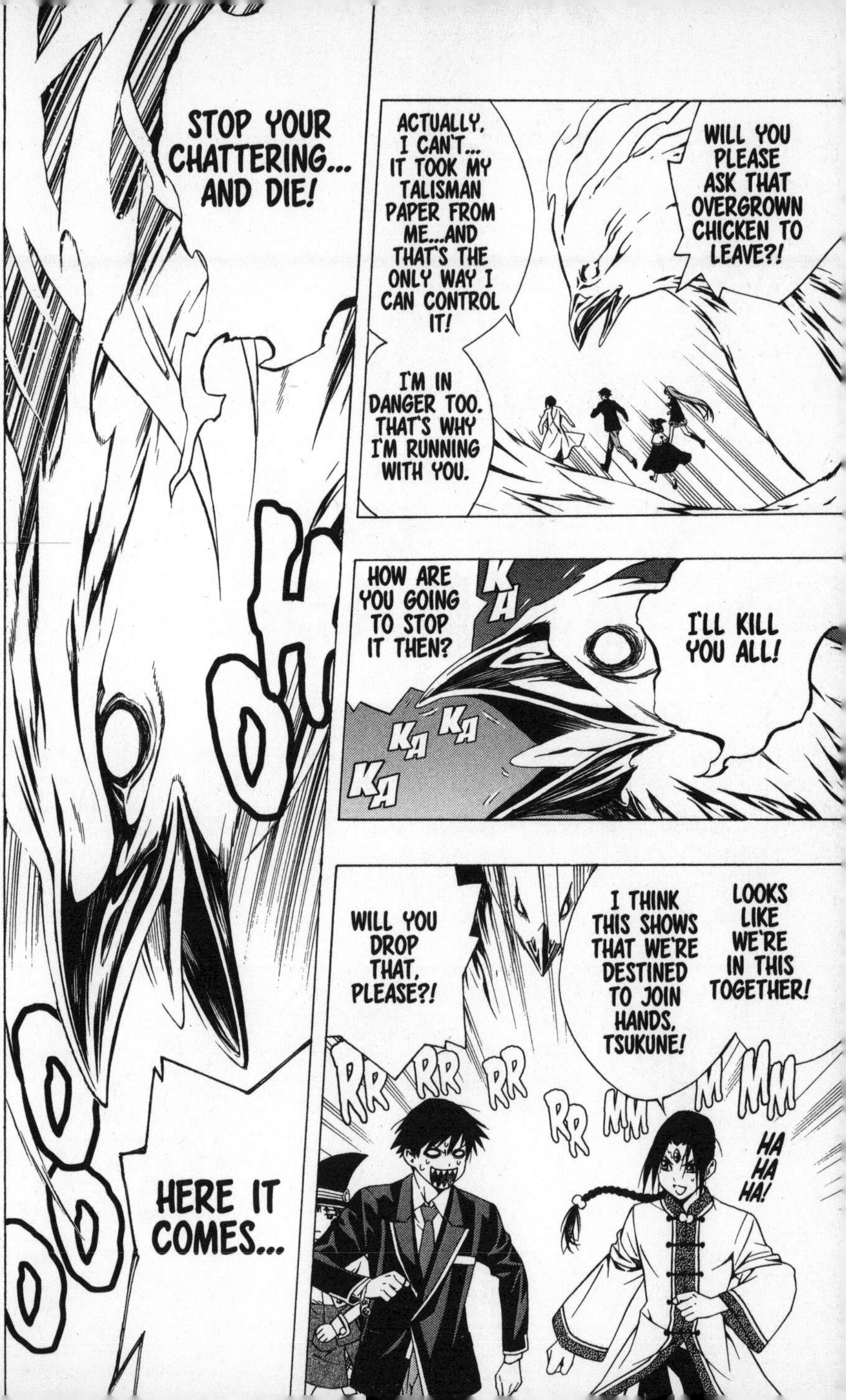
WILL YOU PLEASE ASK THAT OVERGROWN CHICKEN TO LEAVE?!
ACTUALLY, I CAN'T... IT TOOK MY TALISMAN PAPER FROM ME...AND THAT'S THE ONLY WAY I CAN CONTROL IT!
I'M IN DANGER TOO. THAT'S WHY I'M RUNNING WITH YOU.
KA
I'LL KILL YOU ALL!
HOW ARE YOU GOING TO STOP IT THEN?
KA KA KA
LOOKS LIKE WE'RE IN THIS TOGETHER!
I THINK THIS SHOWS THAT WE'RE DESTINED TO JOIN HANDS, TSUKUNE!
WILL YOU DROP THAT, PLEASE?!
RR RR RR RR
MM M MM
HA HA HA!
STOP YOUR CHATTERING... AND DIE!
HERE IT COMES...

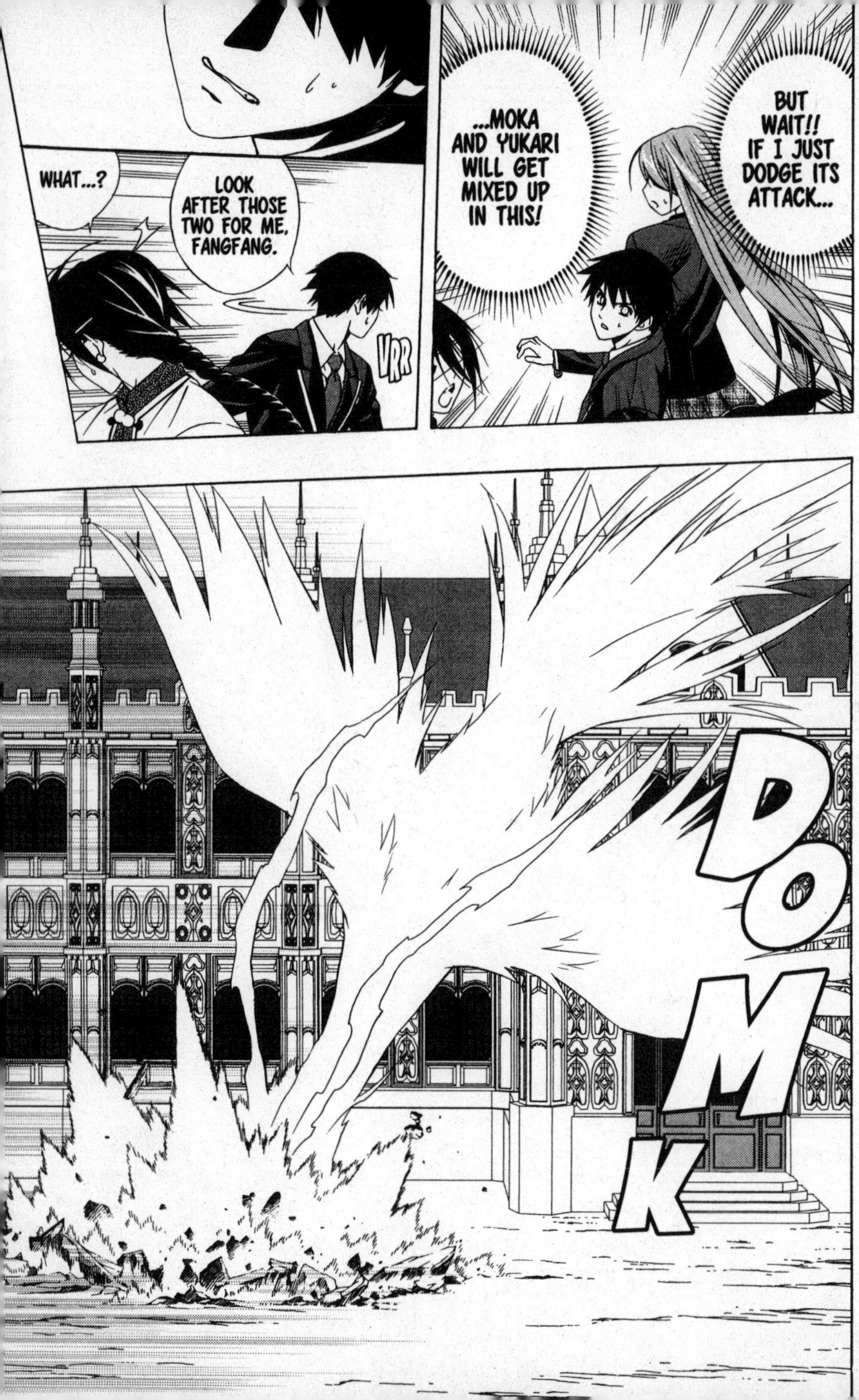
BUT WAIT!! IF I JUST DODGE ITS ATTACK...
...MOKA AND YUKARI WILL GET MIXED UP IN THIS!
VRR
LOOK AFTER THOSE TWO FOR ME, FANGFANG.
WHAT...?
DOMK

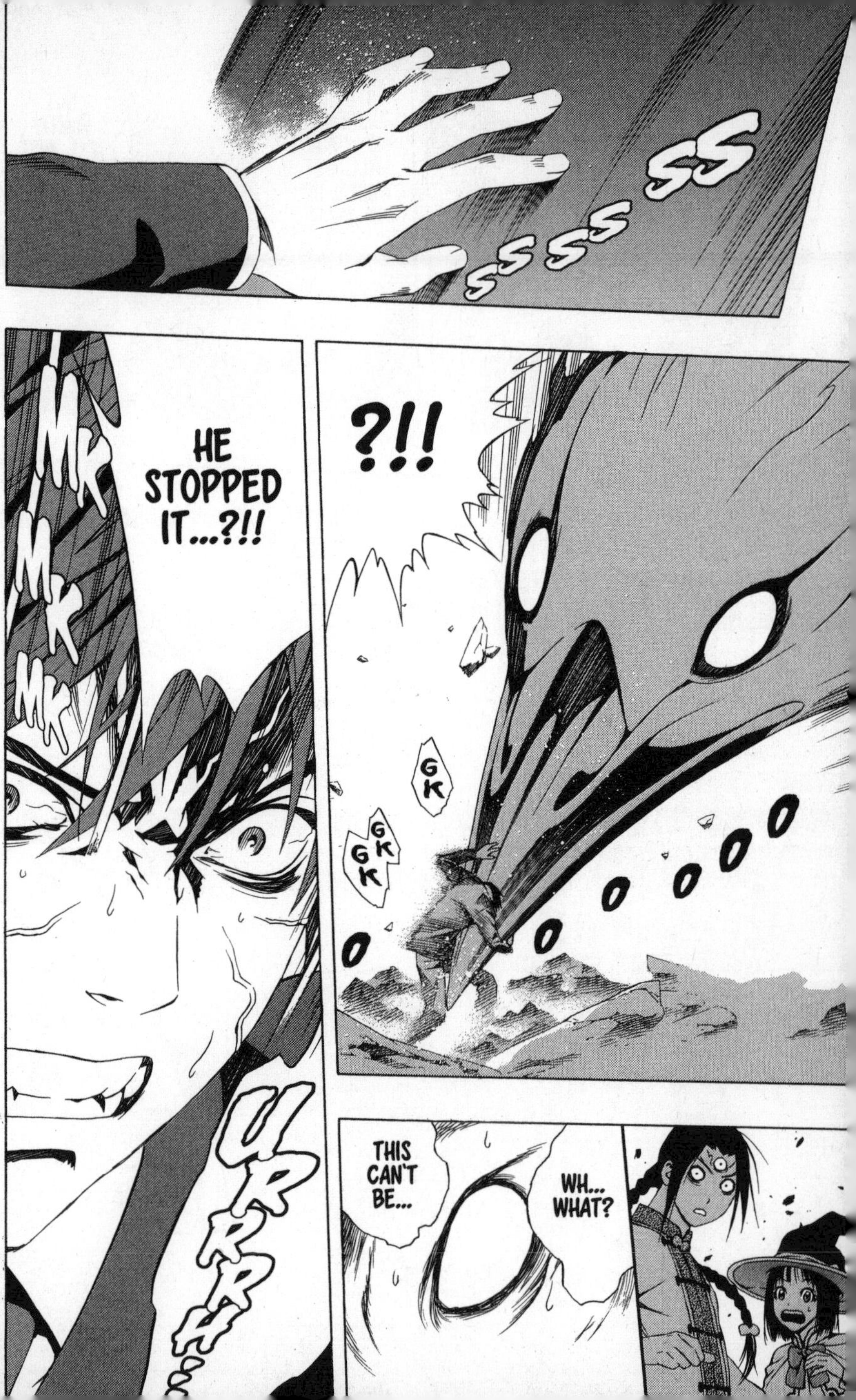
SSSSSSS
?!!
GK
GK GK
OOOOOOOOOO
WH... WHAT?
THIS CAN'T BE...
MK MK MK
HE STOPPED IT...?!!
URRRR

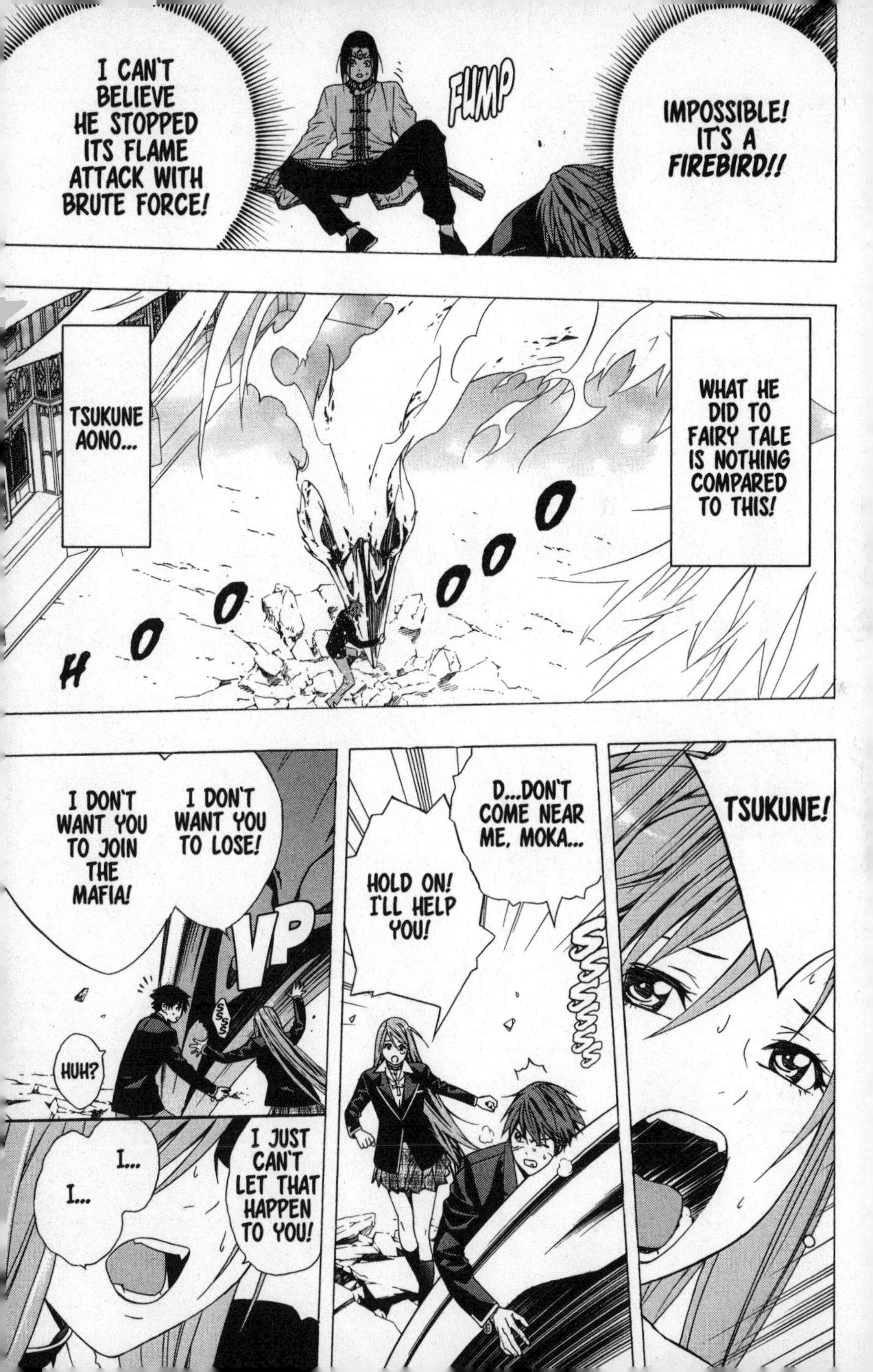
IMPOSSIBLE! IT'S A FIREBIRD!!
FUMP
I CAN'T BELIEVE HE STOPPED ITS FLAME ATTACK WITH BRUTE FORCE!
WHAT HE DID TO FAIRY TALE IS NOTHING COMPARED TO THIS!
TSUKUNE AONO...
HOOOOO
TSUKUNE!
D...DON'T COME NEAR ME, MOKA...
HOLD ON! I'LL HELP YOU!
I DON'T WANT YOU TO LOSE!
I DON'T WANT YOU TO JOIN THE MAFIA!
VP
HUH?
I JUST CAN'T LET THAT HAPPEN TO YOU!
I...
I...

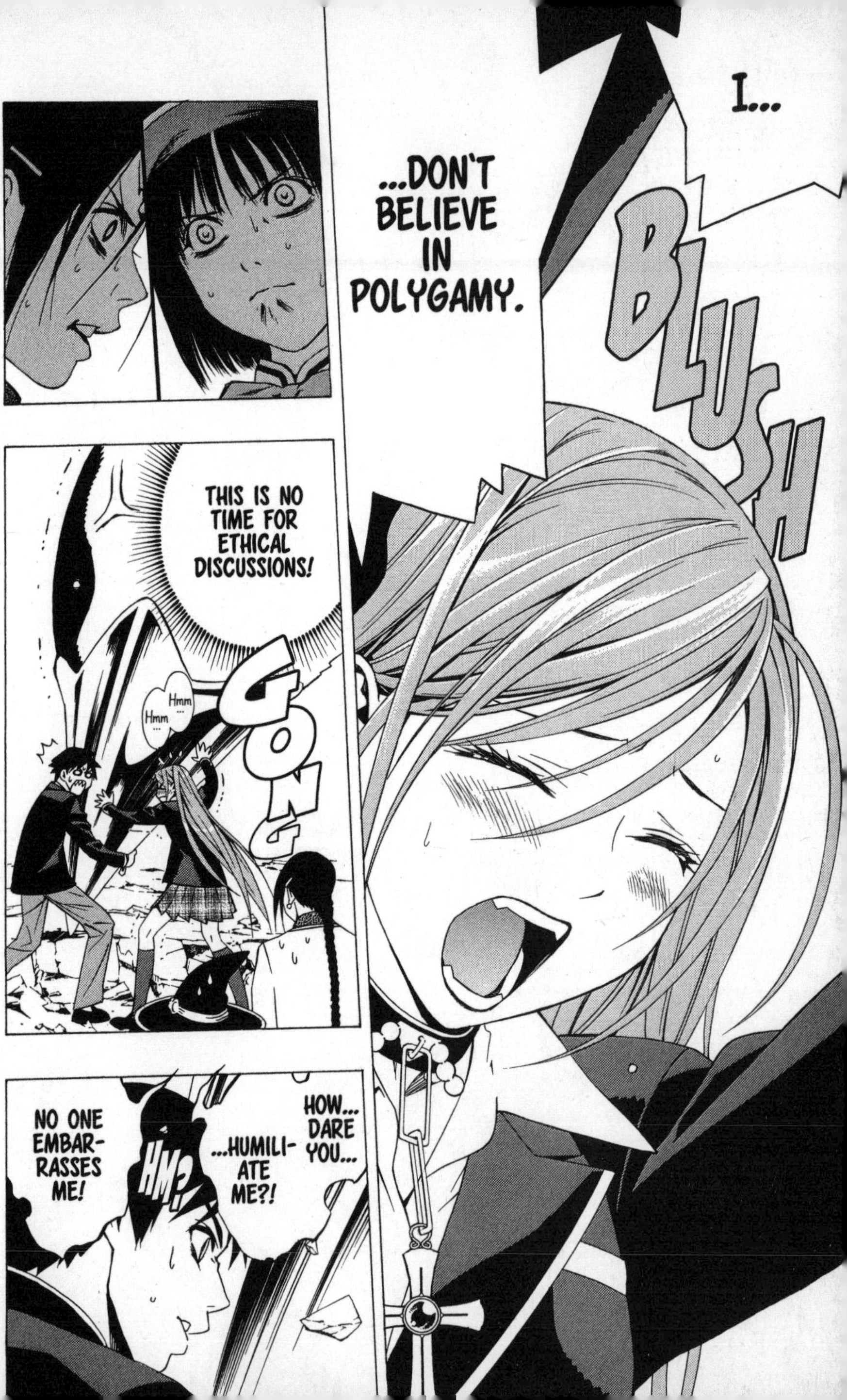
I...
...DON'T BELIEVE IN POLYGAMY.
BLUSH
THIS IS NO TIME FOR ETHICAL DISCUSSIONS!
Hmm...
Hmm...
GONG
HOW... DARE YOU...
...HUMILI-ATE ME?!
HM?
NO ONE EMBAR-RASSES ME!

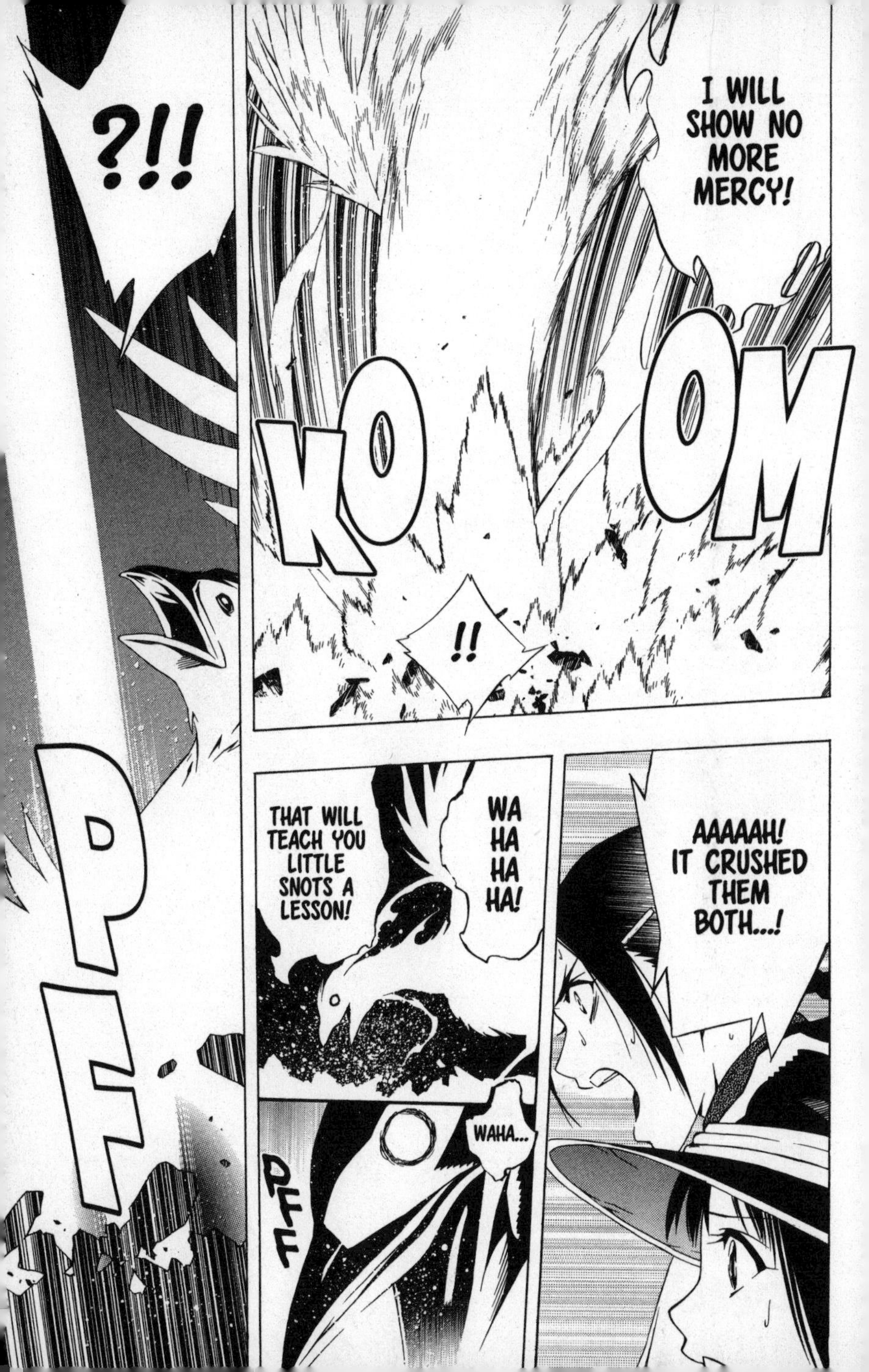
I WILL SHOW NO MORE MERCY!
KOOM
!!
AAAAAH! IT CRUSHED THEM BOTH...!
WA HA HA HA!
THAT WILL TEACH YOU LITTLE SNOTS A LESSON!
WAHA...
PFF
?!!
PFF

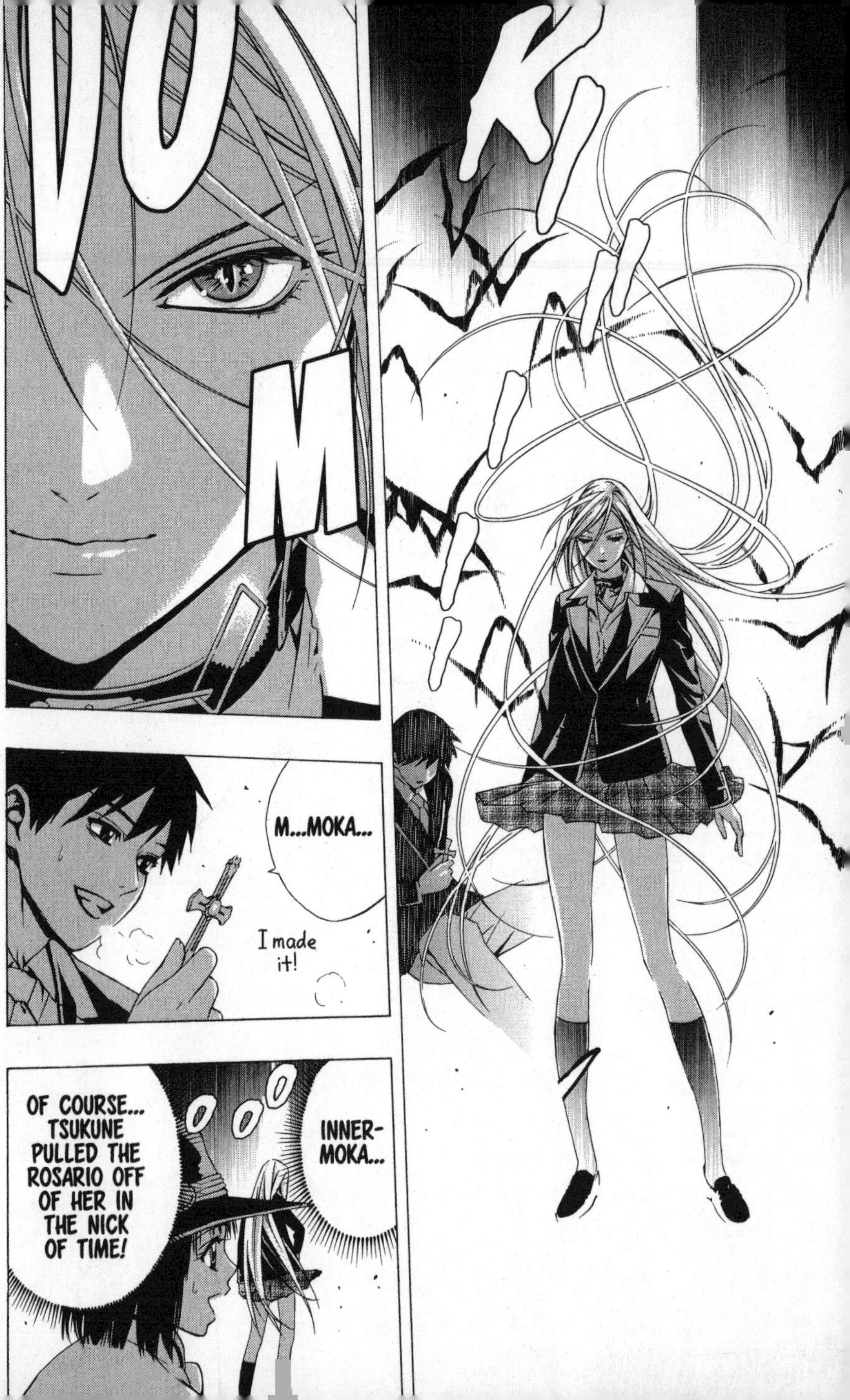
M...MOKA...
I made it!
INNER-MOKA...
OF COURSE... TSUKUNE PULLED THE ROSARIO OFF OF HER IN THE NICK OF TIME!

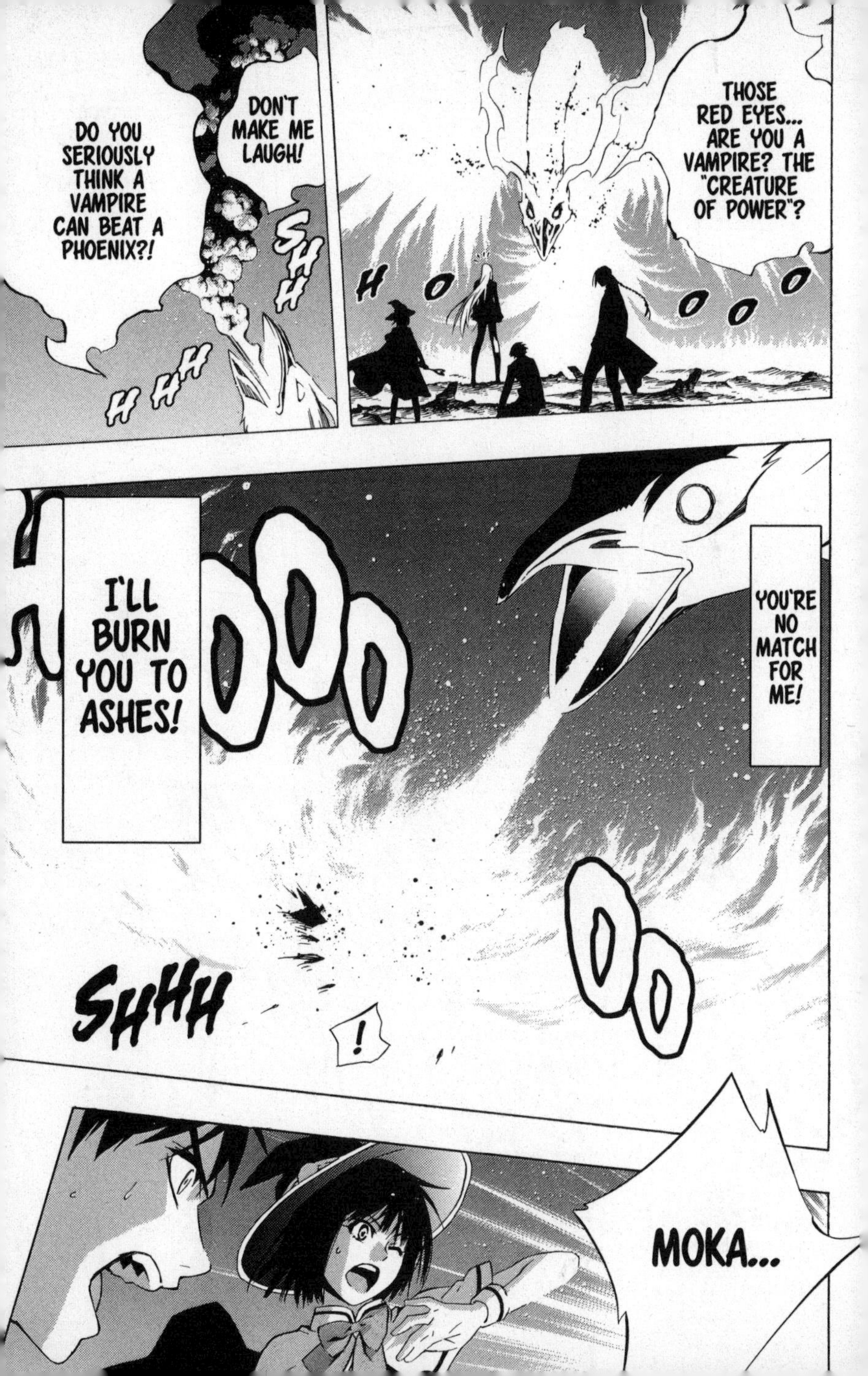
THOSE RED EYES... ARE YOU A VAMPIRE? THE "CREATURE OF POWER"?
HOOOOO
DON'T MAKE ME LAUGH!
DO YOU SERIOUSLY THINK A VAMPIRE CAN BEAT A PHOENIX?!
SHHHHH
YOU'RE NO MATCH FOR ME!
I'LL BURN YOU TO ASHES!
OOOO
OO
SHHH
!
MOKA...

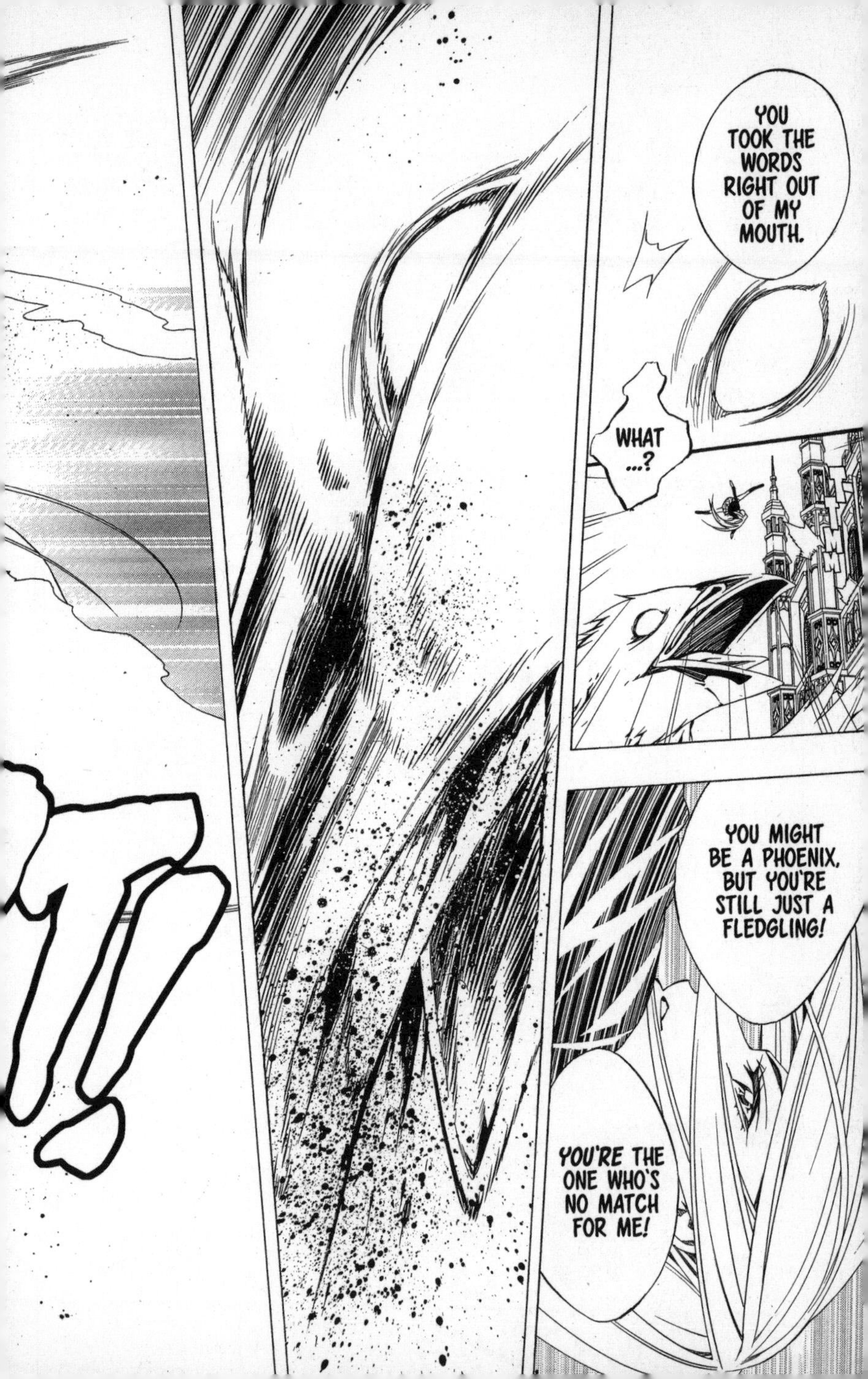
YOU TOOK THE WORDS RIGHT OUT OF MY MOUTH.
WHAT ...?
YOU MIGHT BE A PHOENIX, BUT YOU'RE STILL JUST A FLEDGLING!
YOU'RE THE ONE WHO'S NO MATCH FOR ME!
!!

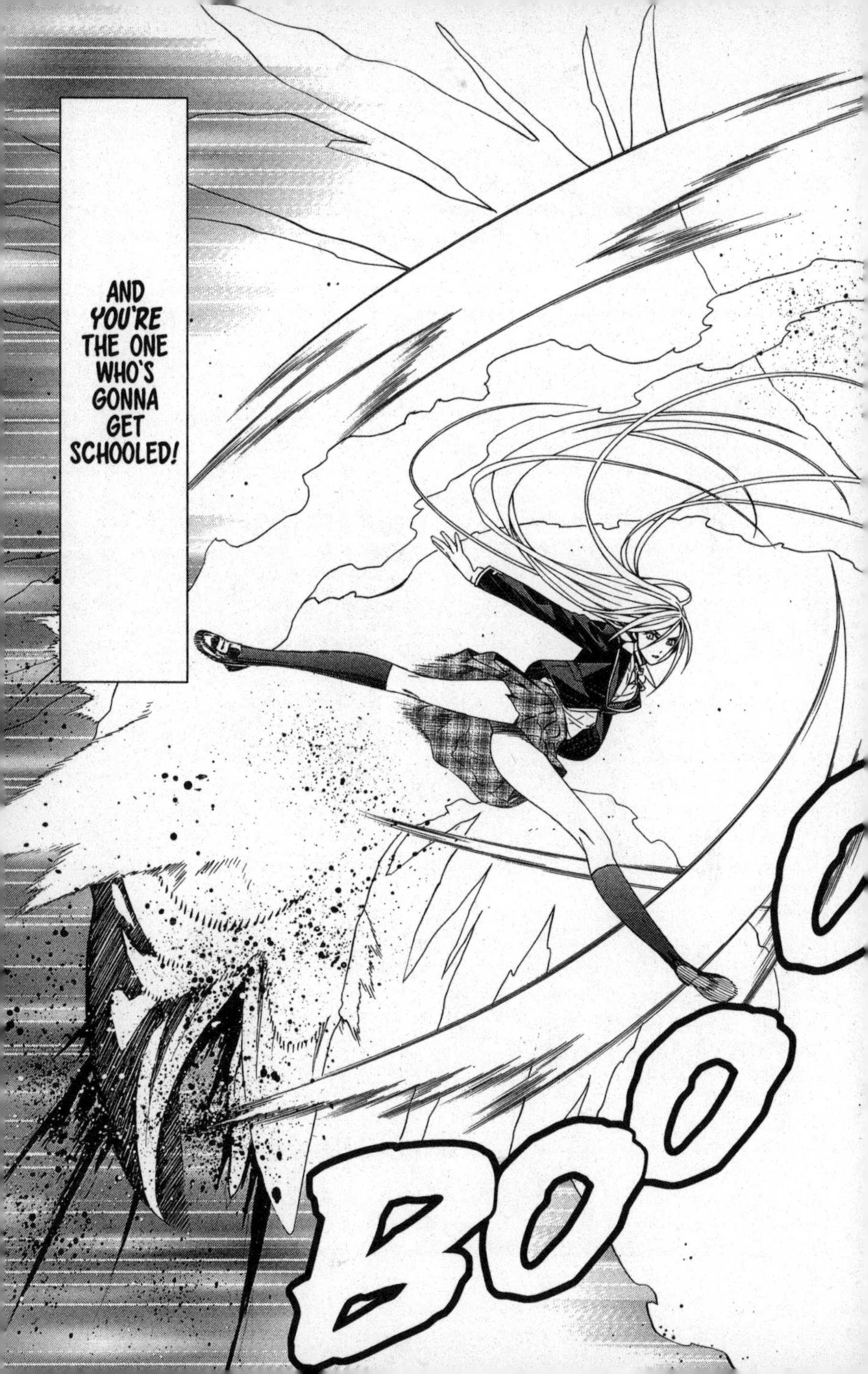
AND YOU'RE THE ONE WHO'S GONNA GET SCHOOLED!
BOOO

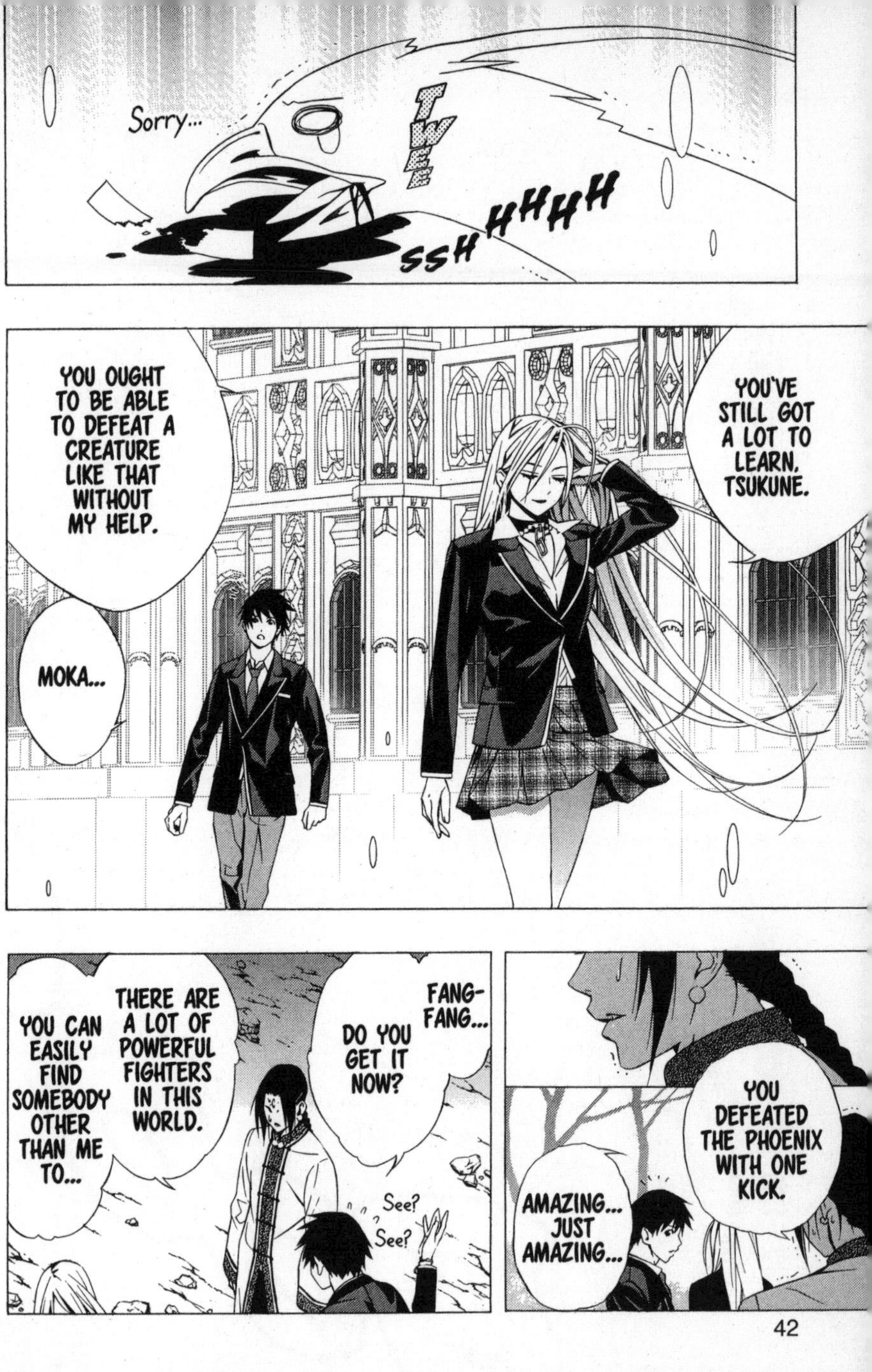

Sorry...
TWEE
SSHHHHHH
YOU'VE STILL GOT A LOT TO LEARN, TSUKUNE.
YOU OUGHT TO BE ABLE TO DEFEAT A CREATURE LIKE THAT WITHOUT MY HELP.
MOKA...
YOU DEFEATED THE PHOENIX WITH ONE KICK.
AMAZING... JUST AMAZING...
FANG-FANG...
DO YOU GET IT NOW?
See?
See?
THERE ARE A LOT OF POWERFUL FIGHTERS IN THIS WORLD.
YOU CAN EASILY FIND SOMEBODY OTHER THAN ME TO...

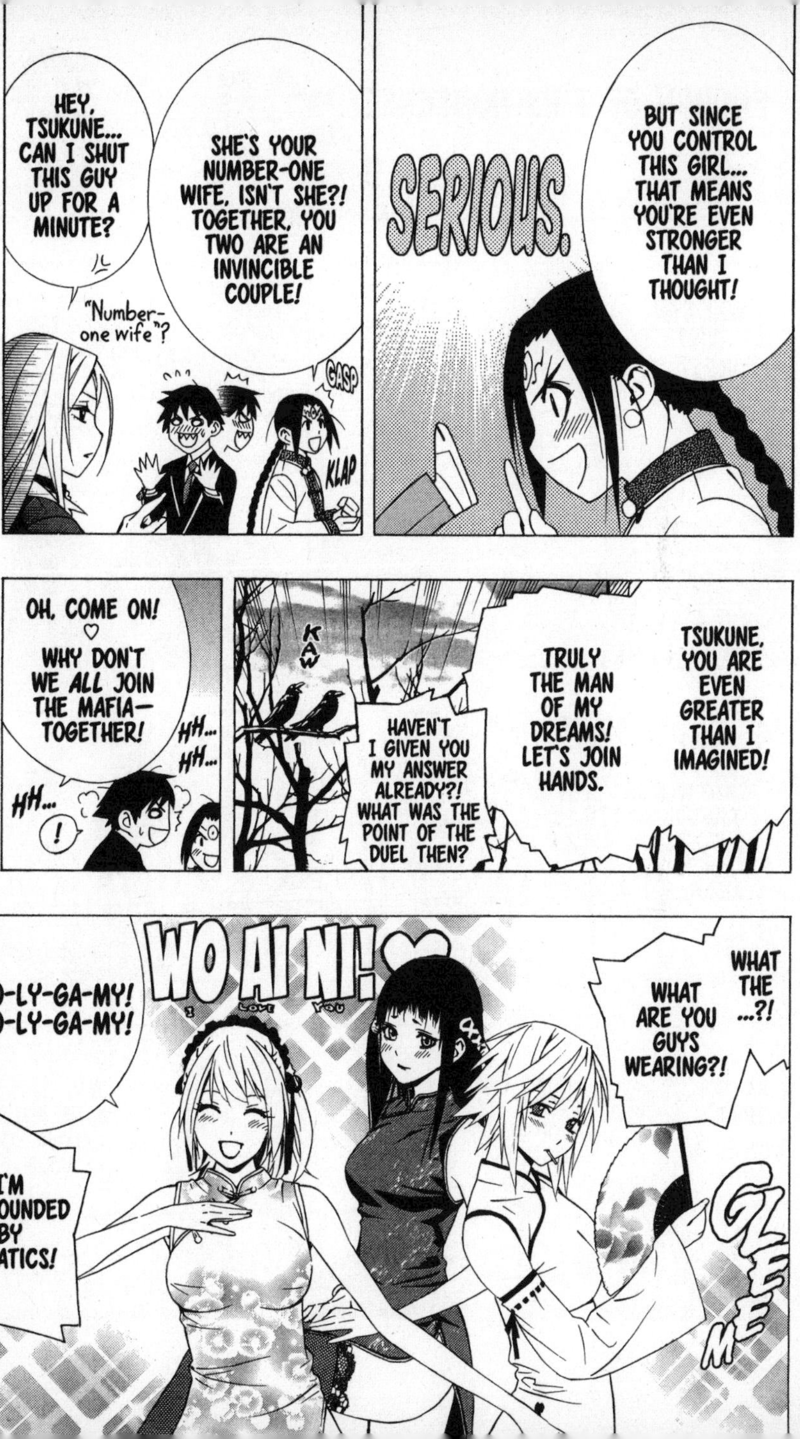
SERIOUS.
BUT SINCE YOU CONTROL THIS GIRL... THAT MEANS YOU'RE EVEN STRONGER THAN I THOUGHT!
SHE'S YOUR NUMBER-ONE WIFE, ISN'T SHE?! TOGETHER, YOU TWO ARE AN INVINCIBLE COUPLE!
GASP
KLAP
HEY, TSUKUNE... CAN I SHUT THIS GUY UP FOR A MINUTE?
"Number-one wife"?
TSUKUNE, YOU ARE EVEN GREATER THAN I IMAGINED!
TRULY THE MAN OF MY DREAMS! LET'S JOIN HANDS.
KAW
HAVEN'T I GIVEN YOU MY ANSWER ALREADY?! WHAT WAS THE POINT OF THE DUEL THEN?
OH, COME ON! ♡ WHY DON'T WE *ALL* JOIN THE MAFIA—TOGETHER!
HH... HH...
HH...
!
WHAT THE ...?!
WHAT ARE YOU GUYS WEARING?!
WO AI NI! ♡
I LOVE YOU
PO-LY-GA-MY! PO-LY-GA-MY!
GLEEM
I'M SURROUNDED BY LUNATICS!

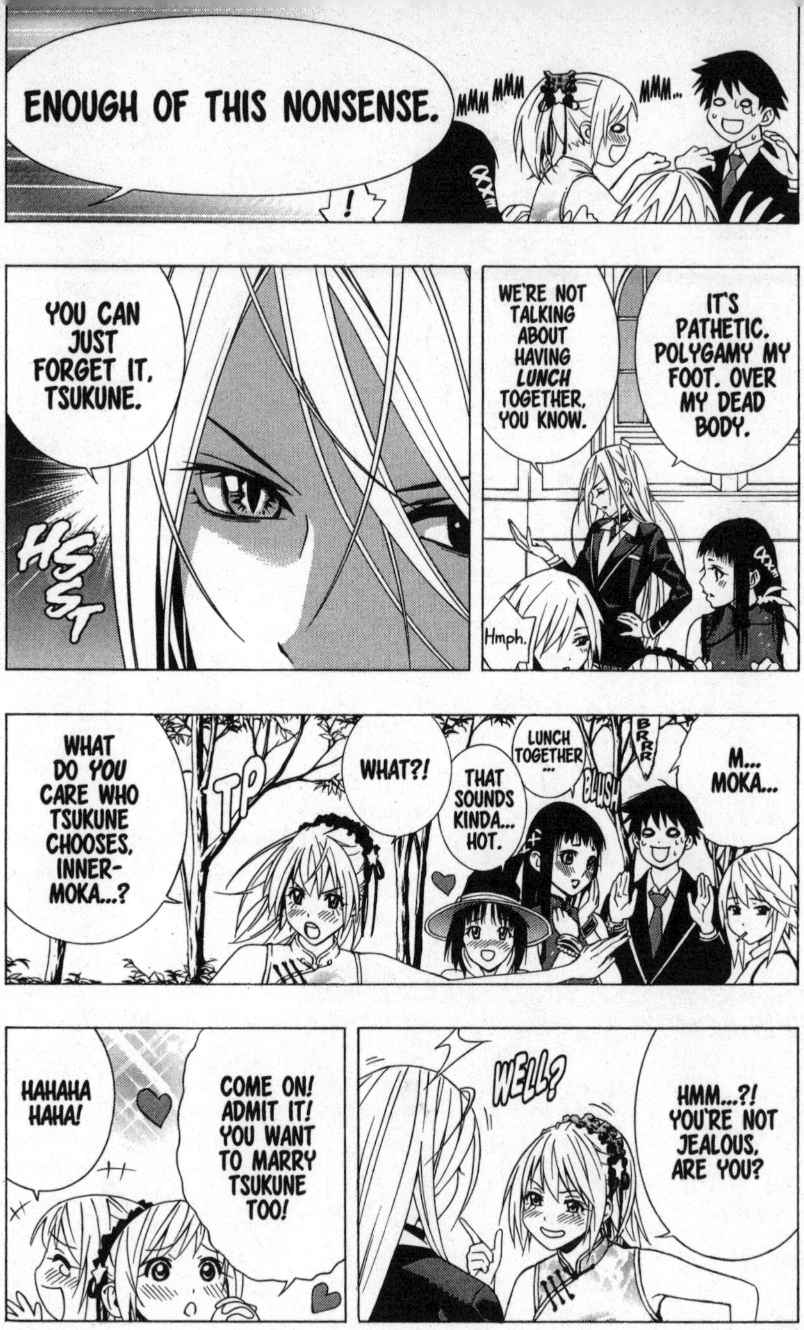
MMM...
MMM MMM
ENOUGH OF THIS NONSENSE.
!
IT'S PATHETIC. POLYGAMY MY FOOT. OVER MY DEAD BODY.
WE'RE NOT TALKING ABOUT HAVING LUNCH TOGETHER, YOU KNOW.
Hmph.
YOU CAN JUST FORGET IT, TSUKUNE.
HSST
M... MOKA...
BRRR
LUNCH TOGETHER...
BLUSH
THAT SOUNDS KINDA... HOT.
WHAT?!
TP
WHAT DO YOU CARE WHO TSUKUNE CHOOSES, INNER-MOKA...?
HMM...?! YOU'RE NOT JEALOUS, ARE YOU?
WELL?
COME ON! ADMIT IT! YOU WANT TO MARRY TSUKUNE TOO!
HAHAHA HAHA!

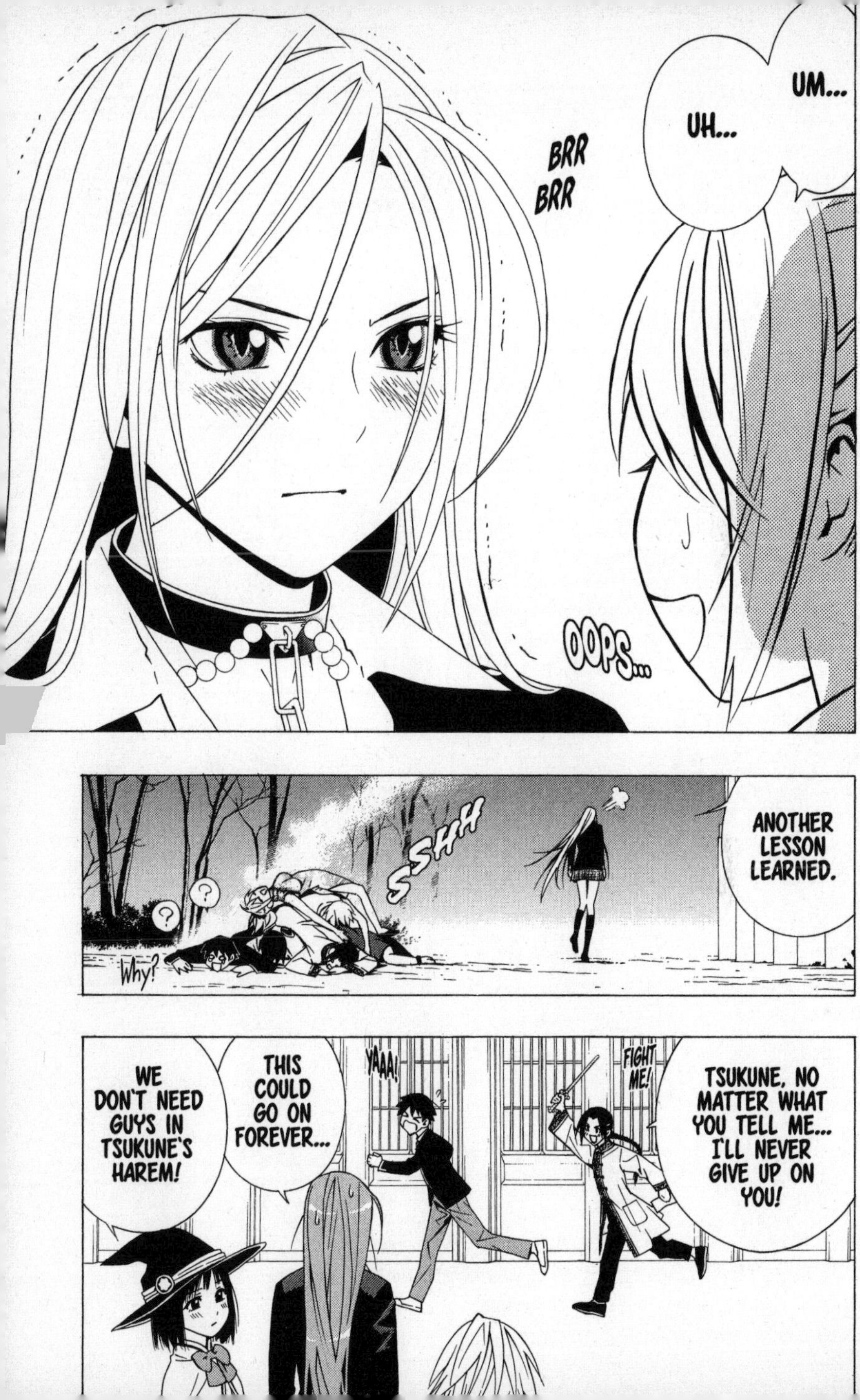
UM...
UH...
BRR
BRR
OOPS...
ANOTHER LESSON LEARNED.
SSHH
?
?
Why?
TSUKUNE, NO MATTER WHAT YOU TELL ME... I'LL NEVER GIVE UP ON YOU!
FIGHT ME!
YAAA!
THIS COULD GO ON FOREVER...
WE DON'T NEED GUYS IN TSUKUNE'S HAREM!

24: Sports Day

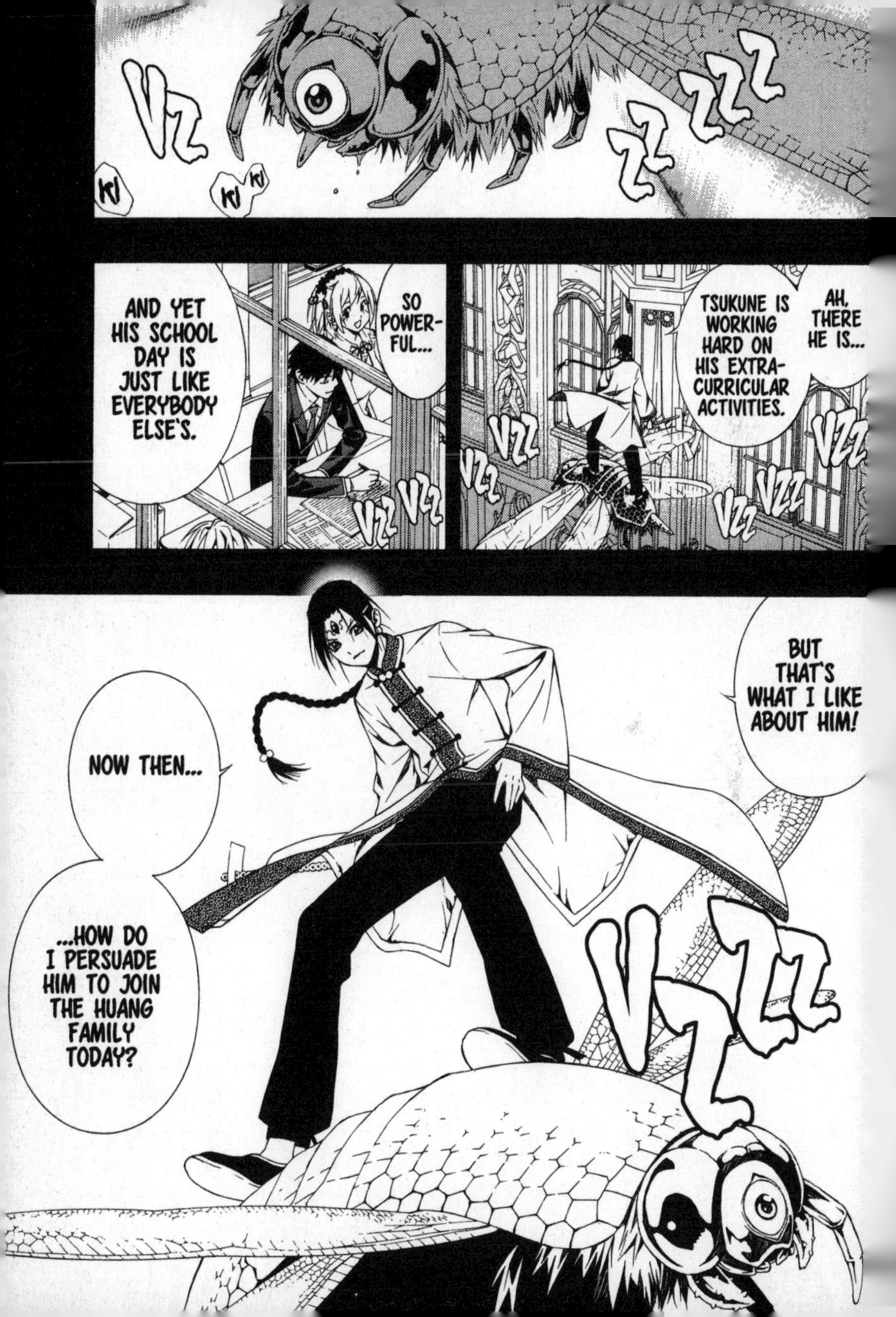
VZZZZZZ
KI
KI KI
AH, THERE HE IS...
TSUKUNE IS WORKING HARD ON HIS EXTRA-CURRICULAR ACTIVITIES.
VZZ
VZZ
VZZ
VZZ
VZZ
SO POWER-FUL...
AND YET HIS SCHOOL DAY IS JUST LIKE EVERYBODY ELSE'S.
VZZ
VZZ
BUT THAT'S WHAT I LIKE ABOUT HIM!
NOW THEN...
...HOW DO I PERSUADE HIM TO JOIN THE HUANG FAMILY TODAY?
VZZZ

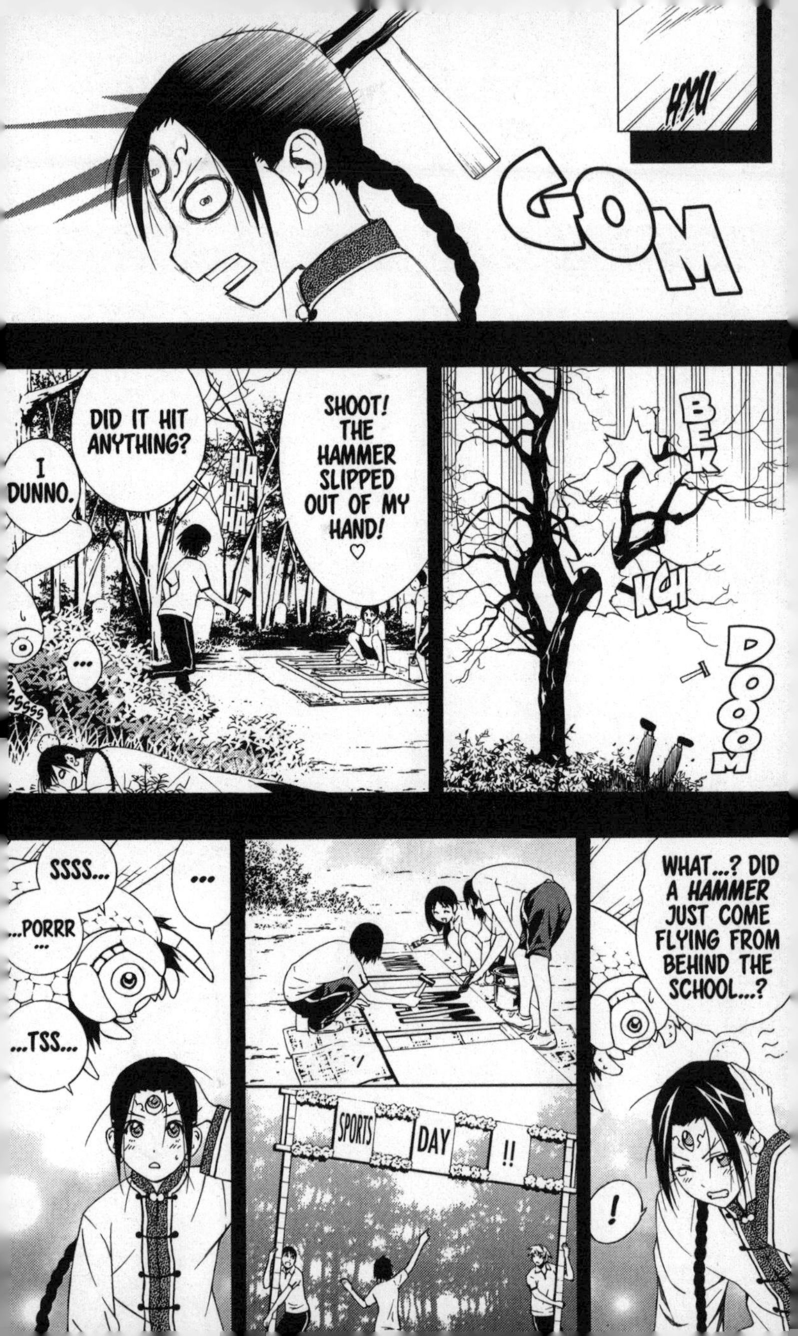
HYU
GOM
BEK
KCH
DOOOOM
SHOOT! THE HAMMER SLIPPED OUT OF MY HAND! ♡
HA HA HA
DID IT HIT ANYTHING?
I DUNNO.
...
SSSSS
WHAT...? DID A HAMMER JUST COME FLYING FROM BEHIND THE SCHOOL...?
!
SPORTS DAY !!
...
SSSS...
...PORRR ...
...TSS...

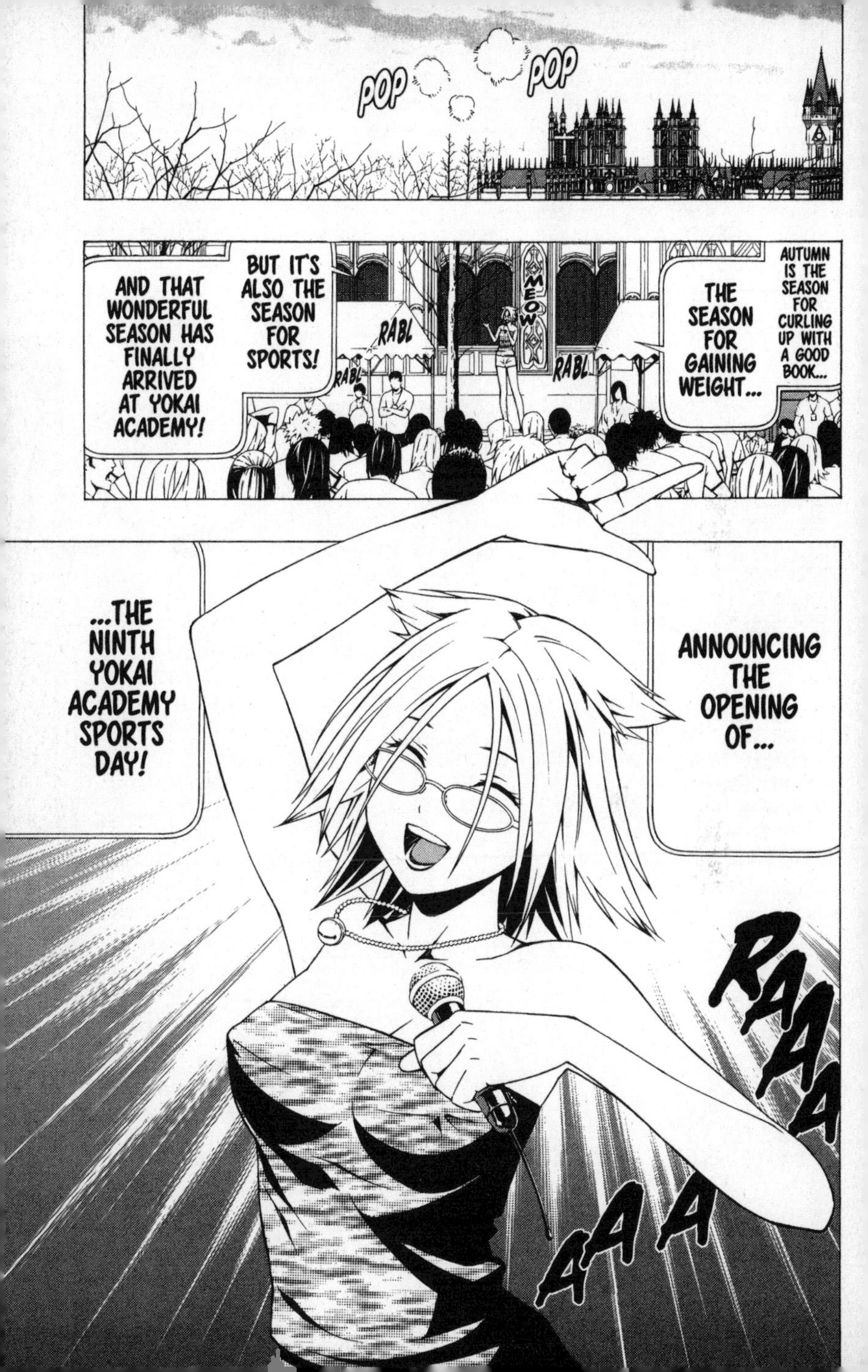
POP
POP
AUTUMN IS THE SEASON FOR CURLING UP WITH A GOOD BOOK...
THE SEASON FOR GAINING WEIGHT...
MEOW
RABL
RABL
RABL
BUT IT'S ALSO THE SEASON FOR SPORTS!
AND THAT WONDERFUL SEASON HAS FINALLY ARRIVED AT YOKAI ACADEMY!
ANNOUNCING THE OPENING OF...
...THE NINTH YOKAI ACADEMY SPORTS DAY!
RAAAAAAA

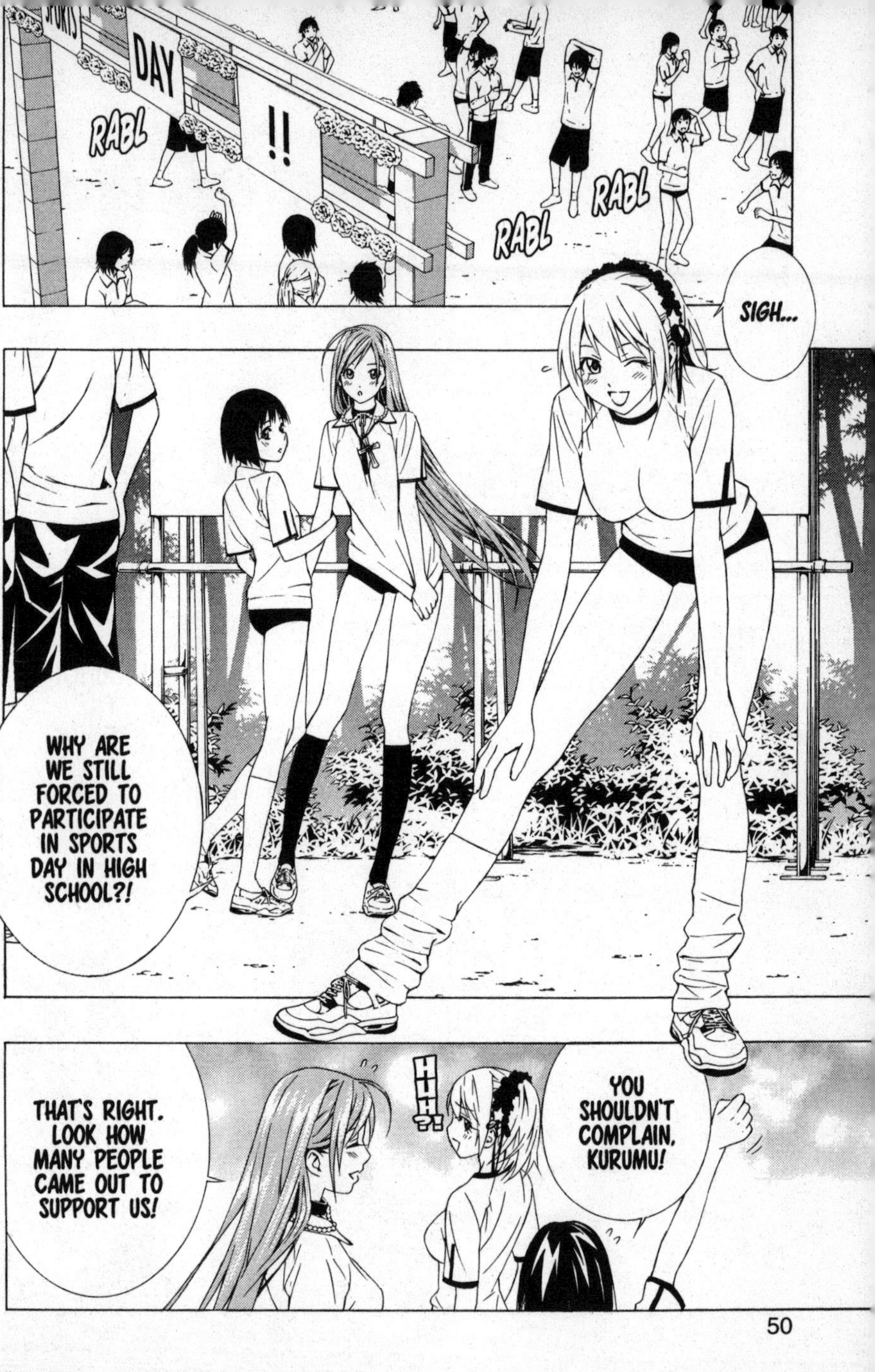
SPORTS DAY !!
RABL
RABL
RABL
SIGH...
WHY ARE WE STILL FORCED TO PARTICIPATE IN SPORTS DAY IN HIGH SCHOOL?!
YOU SHOULDN'T COMPLAIN, KURUMU!
HUH?!
THAT'S RIGHT. LOOK HOW MANY PEOPLE CAME OUT TO SUPPORT US!

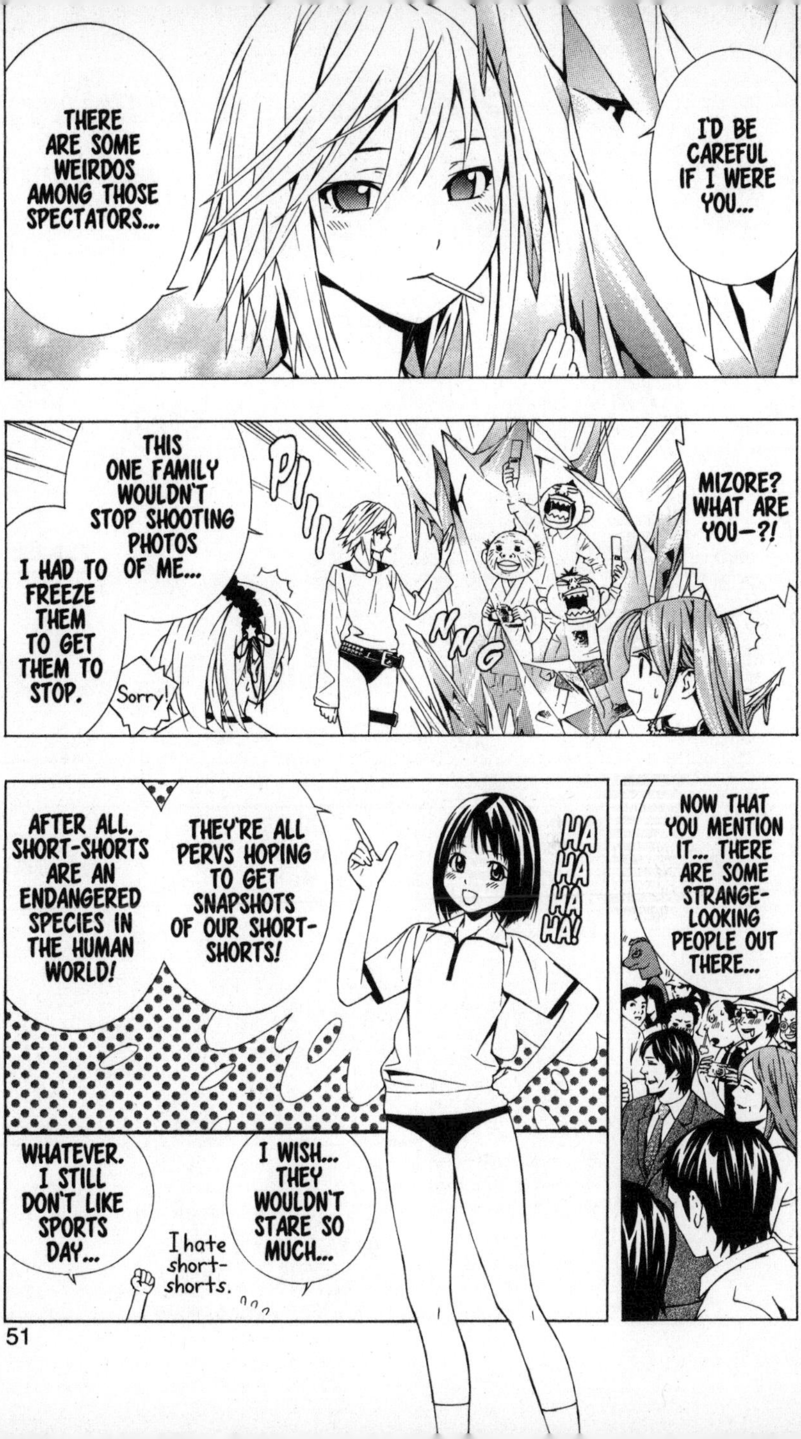
I'D BE CAREFUL IF I WERE YOU...
THERE ARE SOME WEIRDOS AMONG THOSE SPECTATORS...
MIZORE? WHAT ARE YOU—?!
PIIII
NNG
THIS ONE FAMILY WOULDN'T STOP SHOOTING PHOTOS OF ME...
I HAD TO FREEZE THEM TO GET THEM TO STOP.
Sorry!
NOW THAT YOU MENTION IT... THERE ARE SOME STRANGE-LOOKING PEOPLE OUT THERE...
HA HA HA HA!
THEY'RE ALL PERVS HOPING TO GET SNAPSHOTS OF OUR SHORT-SHORTS!
AFTER ALL, SHORT-SHORTS ARE AN ENDANGERED SPECIES IN THE HUMAN WORLD!
I WISH... THEY WOULDN'T STARE SO MUCH...
I hate short-shorts.
WHATEVER. I STILL DON'T LIKE SPORTS DAY...

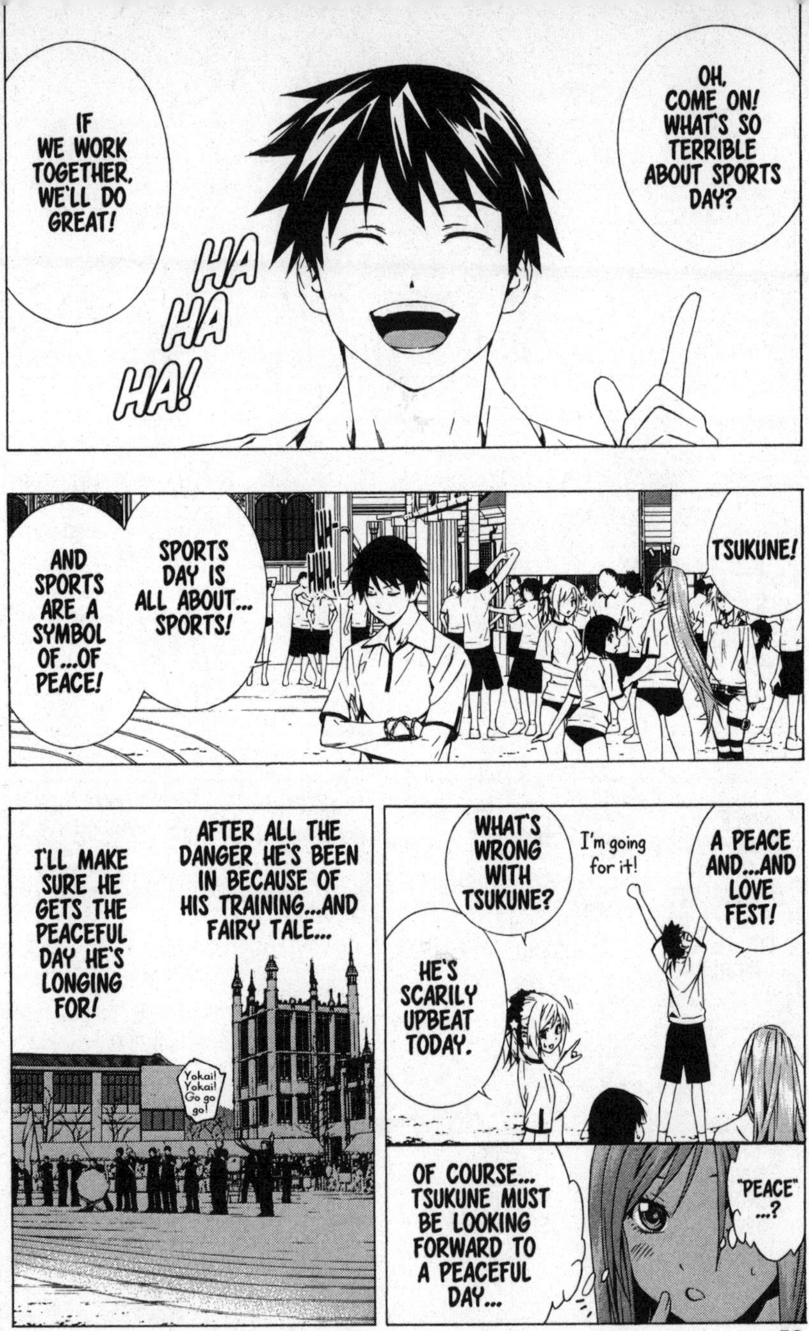
OH, COME ON! WHAT'S SO TERRIBLE ABOUT SPORTS DAY?
HA HA HA!
IF WE WORK TOGETHER, WE'LL DO GREAT!
TSUKUNE!
SPORTS DAY IS ALL ABOUT... SPORTS!
AND SPORTS ARE A SYMBOL OF...OF PEACE!
A PEACE AND...AND LOVE FEST!
I'm going for it!
WHAT'S WRONG WITH TSUKUNE?
HE'S SCARILY UPBEAT TODAY.
"PEACE" ...?
OF COURSE... TSUKUNE MUST BE LOOKING FORWARD TO A PEACEFUL DAY...
AFTER ALL THE DANGER HE'S BEEN IN BECAUSE OF HIS TRAINING...AND FAIRY TALE...
I'LL MAKE SURE HE GETS THE PEACEFUL DAY HE'S LONGING FOR!
Yokai! Yokai! Go go go!

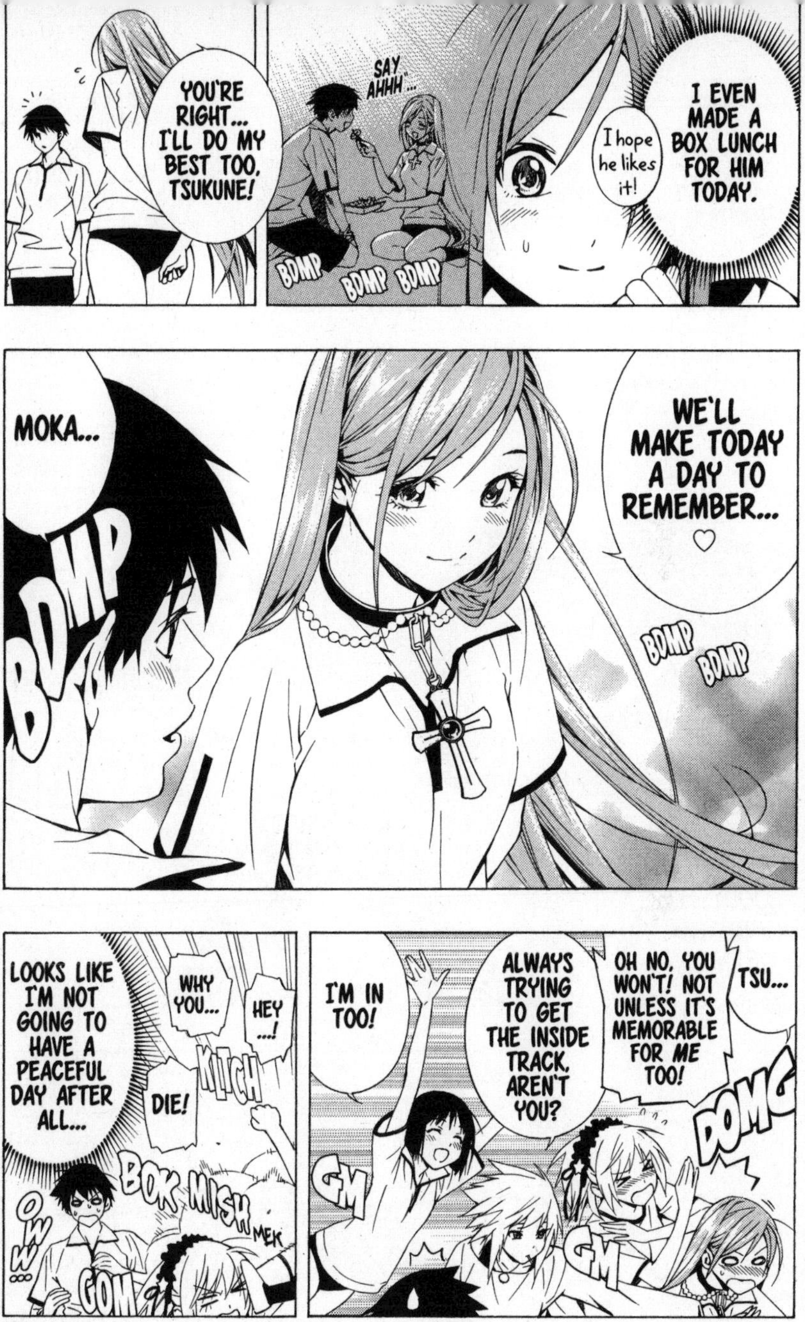
I EVEN MADE A BOX LUNCH FOR HIM TODAY.
I hope he likes it!
SAY AHHH...
BDMP BDMP BDMP
YOU'RE RIGHT... I'LL DO MY BEST TOO, TSUKUNE!
WE'LL MAKE TODAY A DAY TO REMEMBER... ♡
BDMP BDMP
MOKA...
BDMP
TSU...
OH NO, YOU WON'T! NOT UNLESS IT'S MEMORABLE FOR *ME* TOO!
ALWAYS TRYING TO GET THE INSIDE TRACK, AREN'T YOU?
I'M IN TOO!
DOMG
GM
GM
HEY ...!
WHY YOU...
KITCH
DIE!
LOOKS LIKE I'M NOT GOING TO HAVE A PEACEFUL DAY AFTER ALL...
BOK MISH
MEK
OWW...
GOM

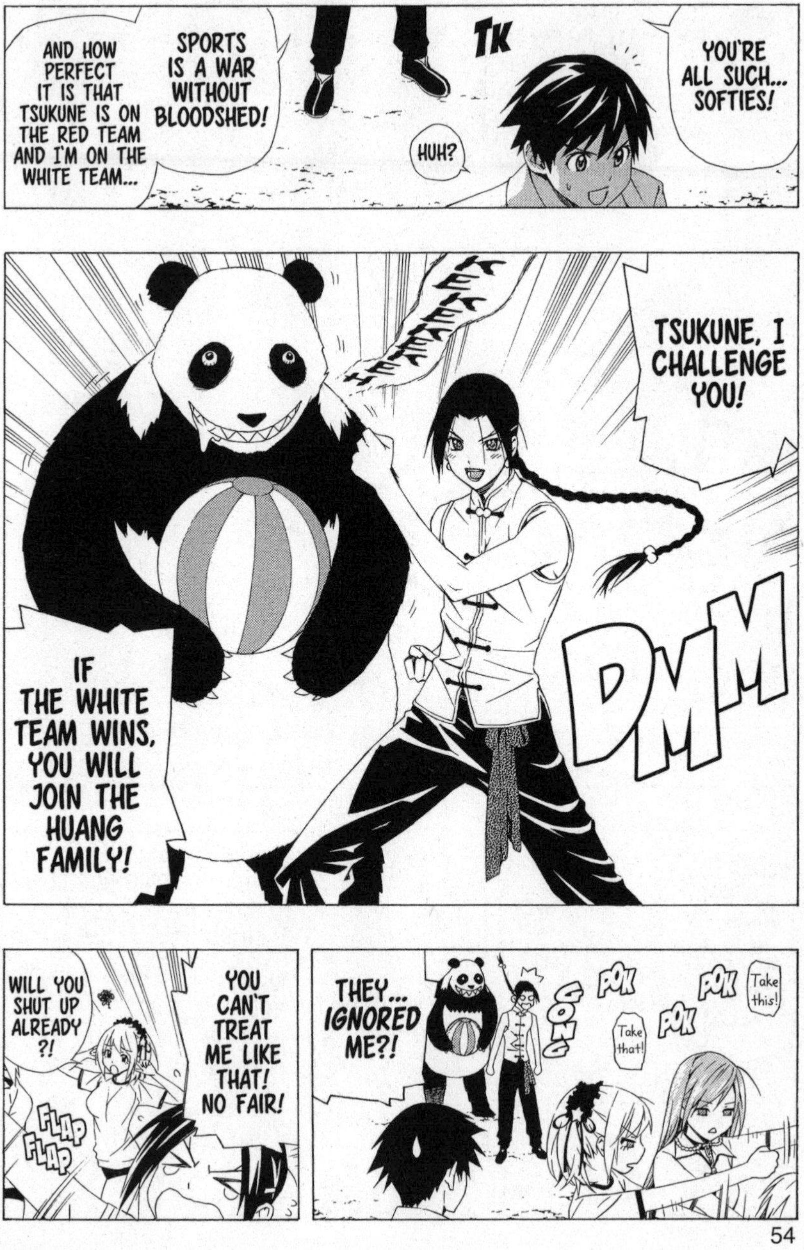
YOU'RE ALL SUCH... SOFTIES!
HUH?
TK
SPORTS IS A WAR WITHOUT BLOODSHED!
AND HOW PERFECT IT IS THAT TSUKUNE IS ON THE RED TEAM AND I'M ON THE WHITE TEAM...
TSUKUNE, I CHALLENGE YOU!
KEKEKEKEH
DMM
IF THE WHITE TEAM WINS, YOU WILL JOIN THE HUANG FAMILY!
Take this!
POK
POK
Take that!
POK
GONG
THEY... IGNORED ME?!
YOU CAN'T TREAT ME LIKE THAT! NO FAIR!
WILL YOU SHUT UP ALREADY?!
FLAP FLAP

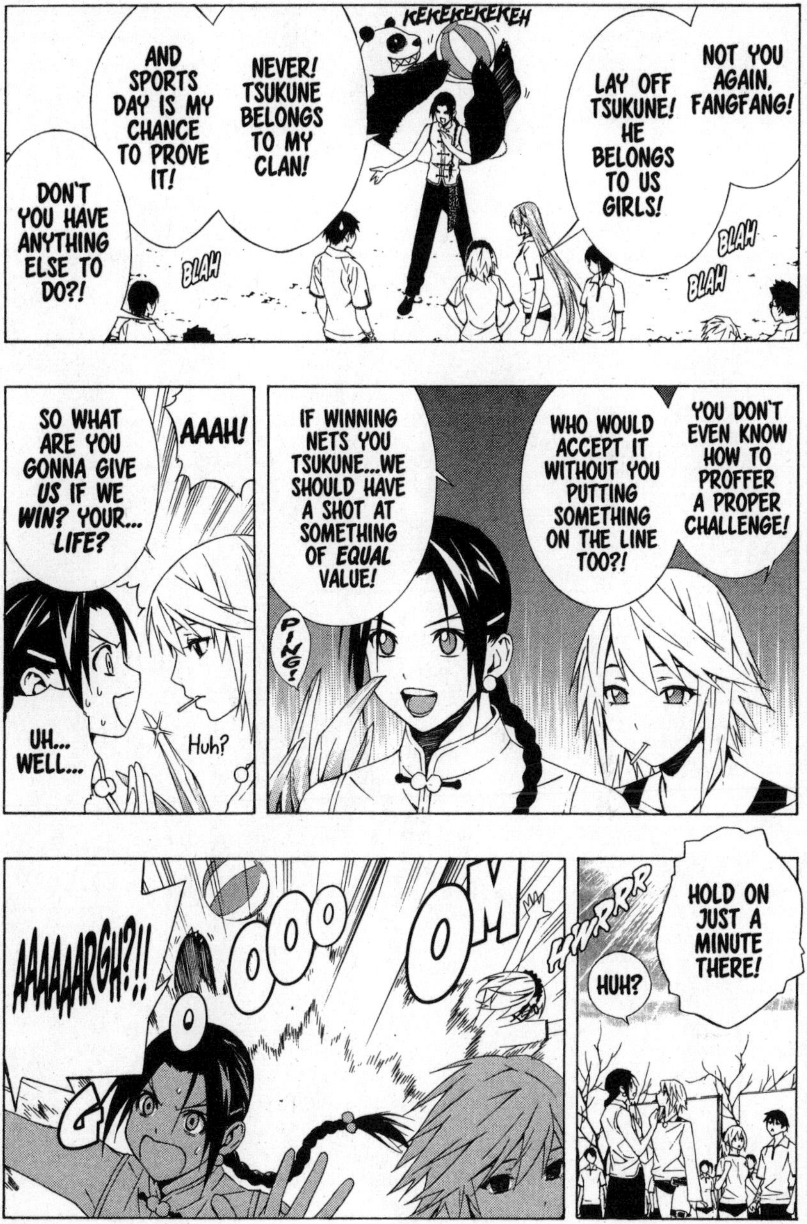
NOT YOU AGAIN, FANGFANG!
LAY OFF TSUKUNE! HE BELONGS TO US GIRLS!
BLAH
BLAH
KEKEREKEREKEH
NEVER! TSUKUNE BELONGS TO MY CLAN!
AND SPORTS DAY IS MY CHANCE TO PROVE IT!
BLAH
DON'T YOU HAVE ANYTHING ELSE TO DO?!
YOU DON'T EVEN KNOW HOW TO PROFFER A PROPER CHALLENGE!
WHO WOULD ACCEPT IT WITHOUT YOU PUTTING SOMETHING ON THE LINE TOO?!
IF WINNING NETS YOU TSUKUNE...WE SHOULD HAVE A SHOT AT SOMETHING OF *EQUAL* VALUE!
PING!
AAAH!
SO WHAT ARE YOU GONNA GIVE US IF WE *WIN*? YOUR... *LIFE*?
Huh?
UH... WELL...
HOLD ON JUST A MINUTE THERE!
HWRRR
HUH?
GOOOOOM
AAAAAARGH?!!

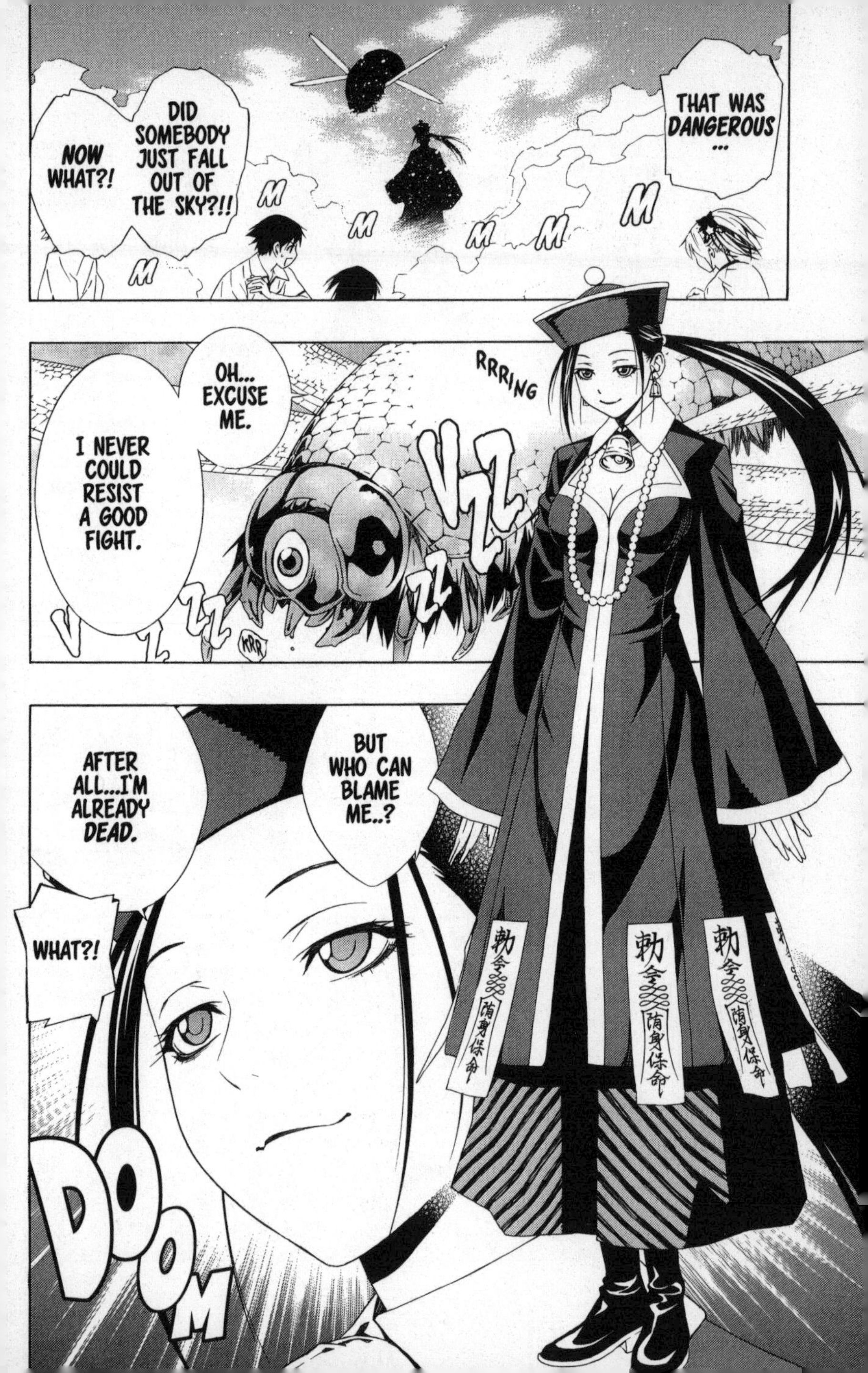
THAT WAS DANGEROUS ...
DID SOMEBODY JUST FALL OUT OF THE SKY?!!
NOW WHAT?!
M M M M M M M
RRRING
OH... EXCUSE ME.
I NEVER COULD RESIST A GOOD FIGHT.
VZZ
VZZ
KRR
BUT WHO CAN BLAME ME..?
AFTER ALL...I'M ALREADY DEAD.
WHAT?!
DOOM

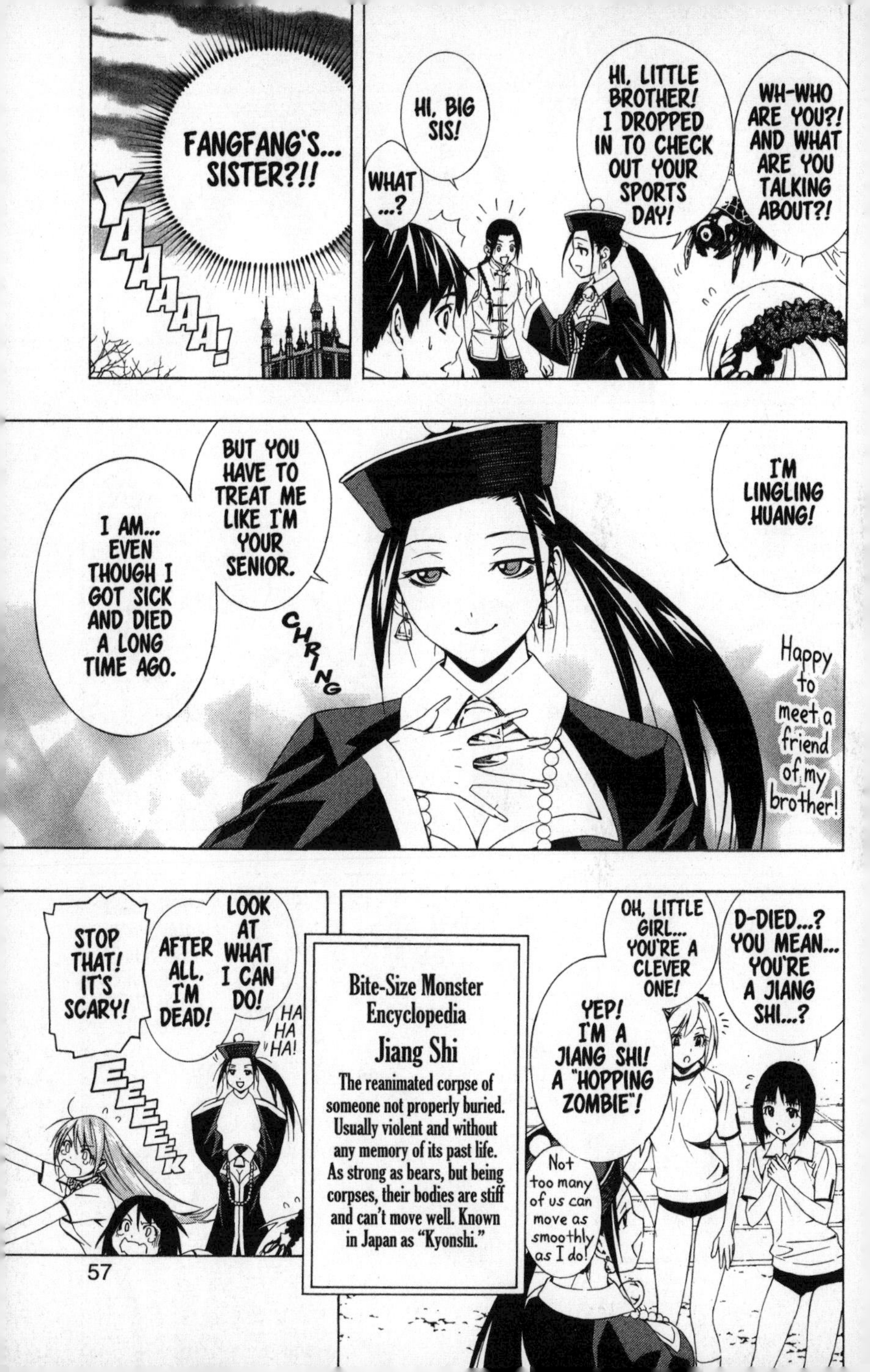
WH-WHO ARE YOU?! AND WHAT ARE YOU TALKING ABOUT?!
HI, LITTLE BROTHER! I DROPPED IN TO CHECK OUT YOUR SPORTS DAY!
HI, BIG SIS!
WHAT ...?
FANGFANG'S... SISTER?!!
YAAAAAA!
I'M LINGLING HUANG!
Happy to meet a friend of my brother!
BUT YOU HAVE TO TREAT ME LIKE I'M YOUR SENIOR.
CHRING
I AM... EVEN THOUGH I GOT SICK AND DIED A LONG TIME AGO.
D-DIED...? YOU MEAN... YOU'RE A JIANG SHI...?
OH, LITTLE GIRL... YOU'RE A CLEVER ONE!
YEP! I'M A JIANG SHI! A "HOPPING ZOMBIE"!
Not too many of us can move as smoothly as I do!
Bite-Size Monster Encyclopedia
Jiang Shi
The reanimated corpse of someone not properly buried. Usually violent and without any memory of its past life. As strong as bears, but being corpses, their bodies are stiff and can't move well. Known in Japan as "Kyonshi."
LOOK AT WHAT I CAN DO!
AFTER ALL, I'M DEAD!
HA HA HA!
STOP THAT! IT'S SCARY!
EEEEEEK

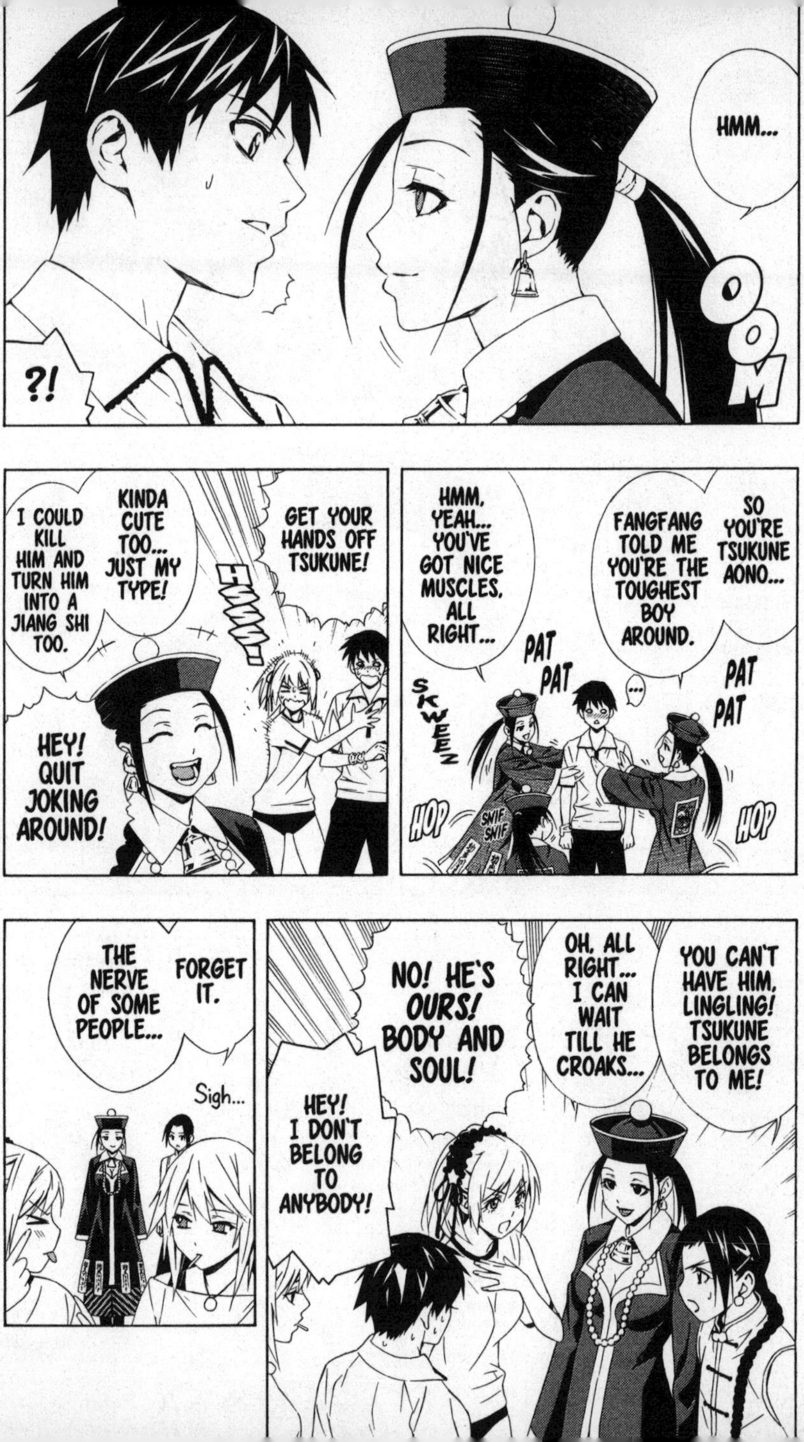
HMM...
OOOM
?!
SO YOU'RE TSUKUNE AONO...
FANGFANG TOLD ME YOU'RE THE TOUGHEST BOY AROUND.
HMM, YEAH... YOU'VE GOT NICE MUSCLES, ALL RIGHT...
PAT PAT
...
PAT PAT
SKWEEZ
HOP
SNIF SNIF
HOP
GET YOUR HANDS OFF TSUKUNE!
KINDA CUTE TOO... JUST MY TYPE!
I COULD KILL HIM AND TURN HIM INTO A JIANG SHI TOO.
HEY! QUIT JOKING AROUND!
YOU CAN'T HAVE HIM, LINGLING! TSUKUNE BELONGS TO ME!
OH, ALL RIGHT... I CAN WAIT TILL HE CROAKS...
NO! HE'S OURS! BODY AND SOUL!
HEY! I DON'T BELONG TO ANYBODY!
FORGET IT.
THE NERVE OF SOME PEOPLE...
Sigh...

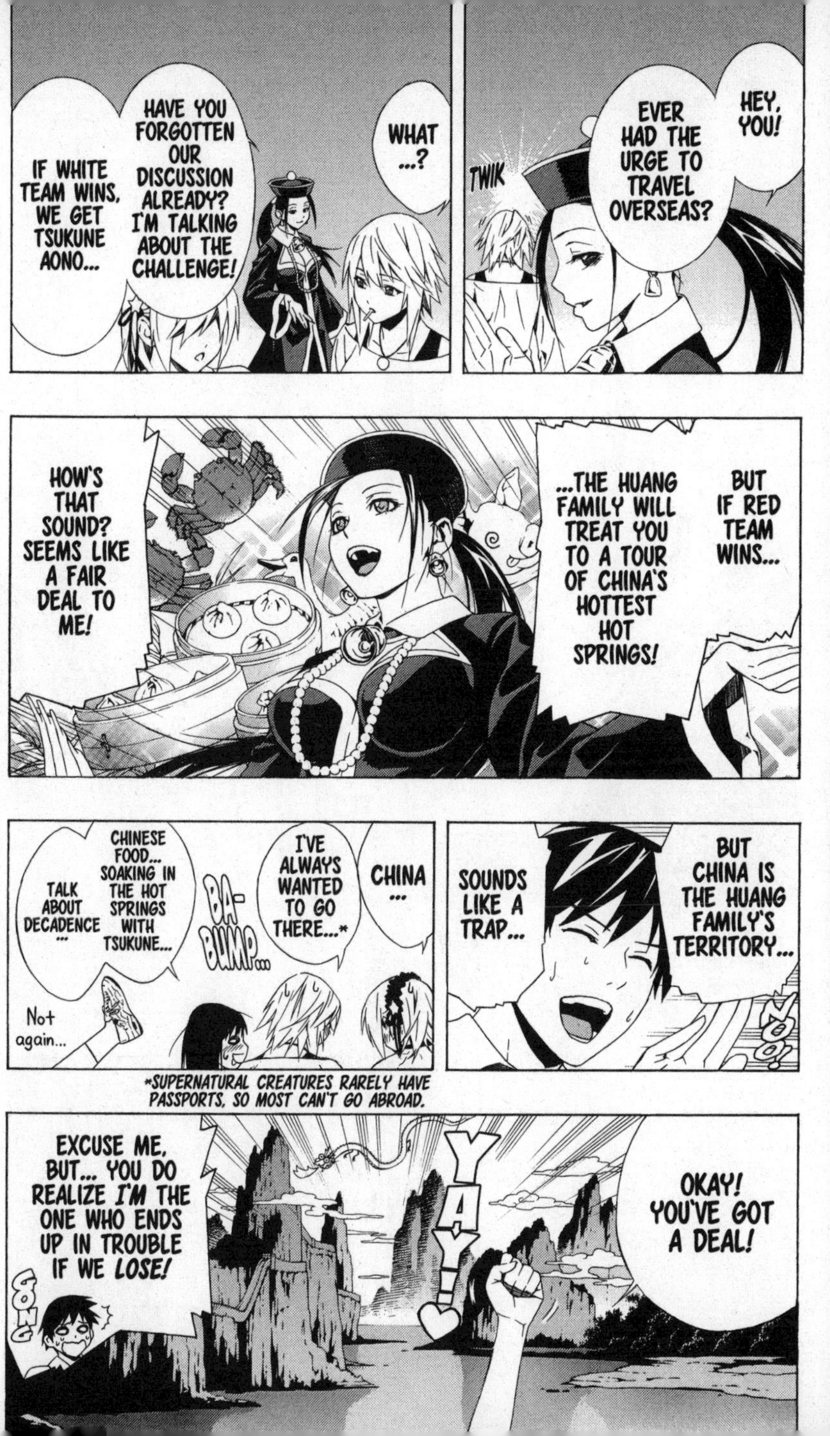
HEY, YOU!
EVER HAD THE URGE TO TRAVEL OVERSEAS?
TWIK
WHAT ...?
HAVE YOU FORGOTTEN OUR DISCUSSION ALREADY? I'M TALKING ABOUT THE CHALLENGE!
IF WHITE TEAM WINS, WE GET TSUKUNE AONO...
BUT IF RED TEAM WINS...
...THE HUANG FAMILY WILL TREAT YOU TO A TOUR OF CHINA'S HOTTEST HOT SPRINGS!
HOW'S THAT SOUND? SEEMS LIKE A FAIR DEAL TO ME!
BUT CHINA IS THE HUANG FAMILY'S TERRITORY...
SOUNDS LIKE A TRAP...
MOO!
CHINA ...
I'VE ALWAYS WANTED TO GO THERE...*
BA-BUMP...
CHINESE FOOD... SOAKING IN THE HOT SPRINGS WITH TSUKUNE...
TALK ABOUT DECADENCE ...
Not again...
*SUPERNATURAL CREATURES RARELY HAVE PASSPORTS, SO MOST CAN'T GO ABROAD.
OKAY! YOU'VE GOT A DEAL!
YAY!
EXCUSE ME, BUT... YOU DO REALIZE *I'M* THE ONE WHO ENDS UP IN TROUBLE IF WE *LOSE*!
GONG

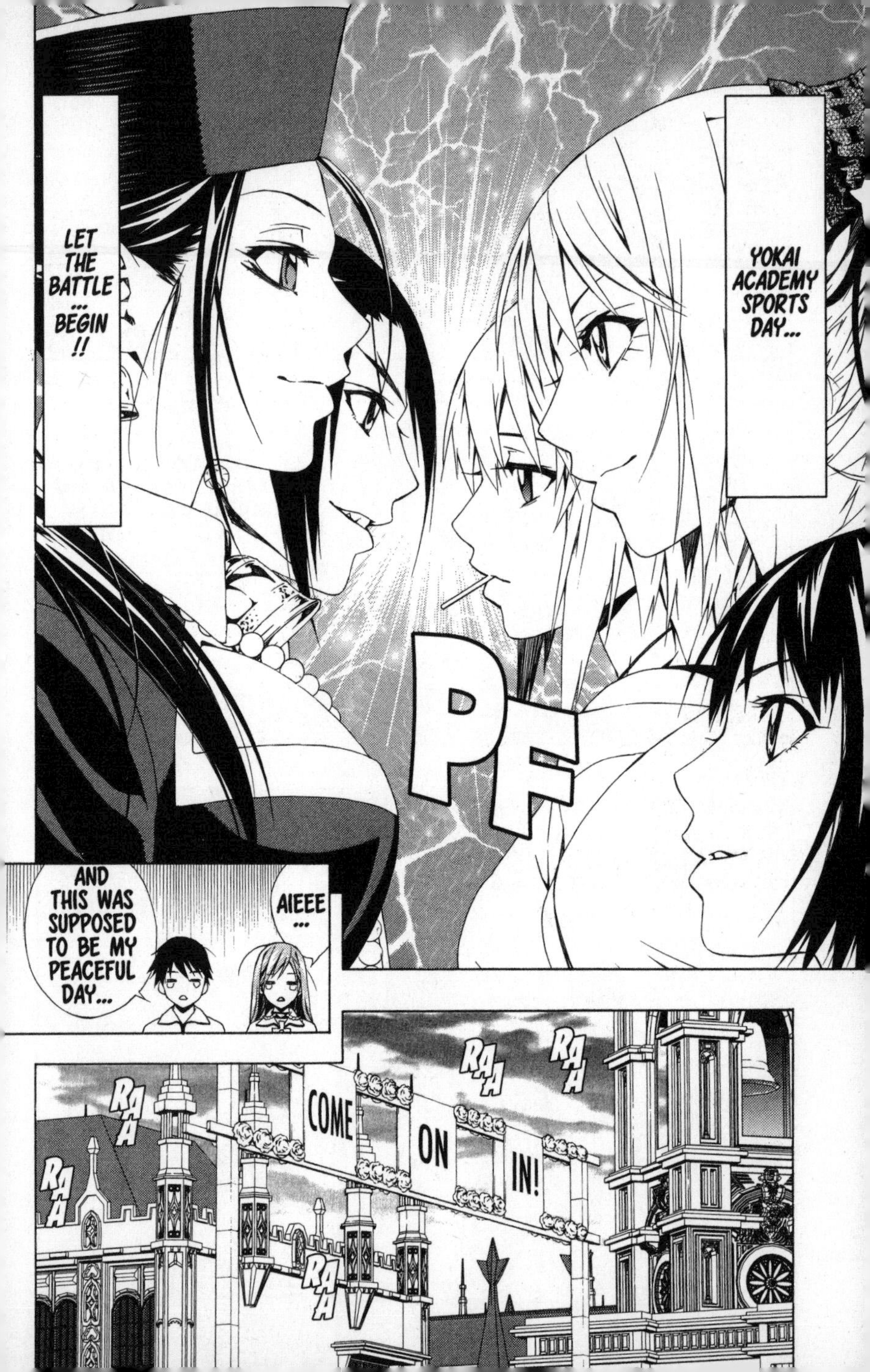
YOKAI ACADEMY SPORTS DAY...
LET THE BATTLE ... BEGIN!!
PF
AIEEE ...
AND THIS WAS SUPPOSED TO BE MY PEACEFUL DAY...
RAA
RAA
COME ON IN!
RAA
RAA
RAA

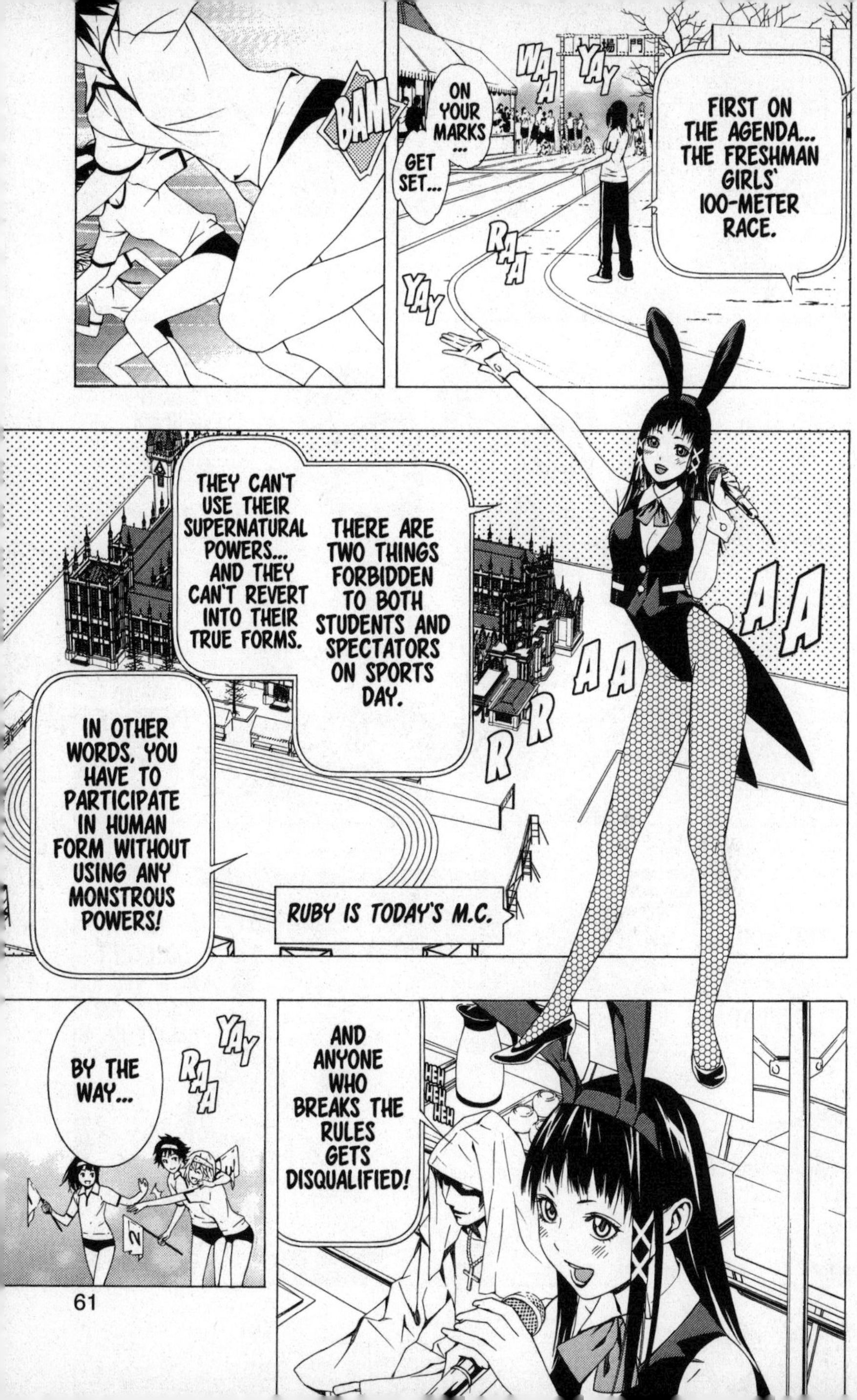
FIRST ON THE AGENDA... THE FRESHMAN GIRLS' 100-METER RACE.
WAA
YAY
ON YOUR MARKS ...
GET SET...
RAA
YAY
BAM
THERE ARE TWO THINGS FORBIDDEN TO BOTH STUDENTS AND SPECTATORS ON SPORTS DAY.
THEY CAN'T USE THEIR SUPERNATURAL POWERS... AND THEY CAN'T REVERT INTO THEIR TRUE FORMS.
AA
AA
RR
IN OTHER WORDS, YOU HAVE TO PARTICIPATE IN HUMAN FORM WITHOUT USING ANY MONSTROUS POWERS!
RUBY IS TODAY'S M.C.
AND ANYONE WHO BREAKS THE RULES GETS DISQUALIFIED!
HEH HEH HEH
YAY
RAA
BY THE WAY...

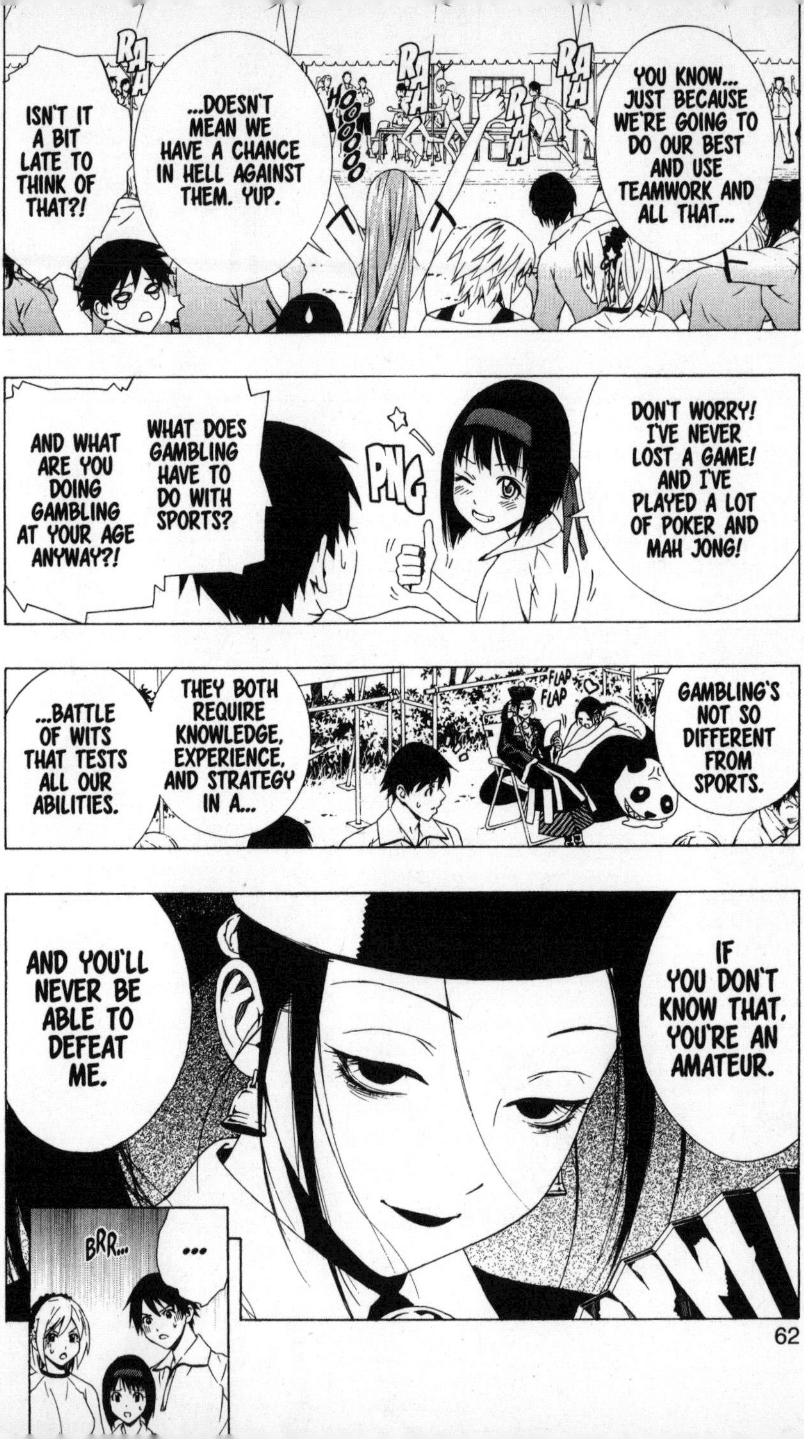
RAA
RAA
RAA
RAA
HOOOOOOO
YOU KNOW... JUST BECAUSE WE'RE GOING TO DO OUR BEST AND USE TEAMWORK AND ALL THAT...
...DOESN'T MEAN WE HAVE A CHANCE IN HELL AGAINST THEM. YUP.
ISN'T IT A BIT LATE TO THINK OF THAT?!
DON'T WORRY! I'VE NEVER LOST A GAME! AND I'VE PLAYED A LOT OF POKER AND MAH JONG!
PNG
WHAT DOES GAMBLING HAVE TO DO WITH SPORTS?
AND WHAT ARE YOU DOING GAMBLING AT YOUR AGE ANYWAY?!
GAMBLING'S NOT SO DIFFERENT FROM SPORTS.
FLAP FLAP
THEY BOTH REQUIRE KNOWLEDGE, EXPERIENCE, AND STRATEGY IN A...
...BATTLE OF WITS THAT TESTS ALL OUR ABILITIES.
IF YOU DON'T KNOW THAT, YOU'RE AN AMATEUR.
AND YOU'LL NEVER BE ABLE TO DEFEAT ME.
...
BRR...

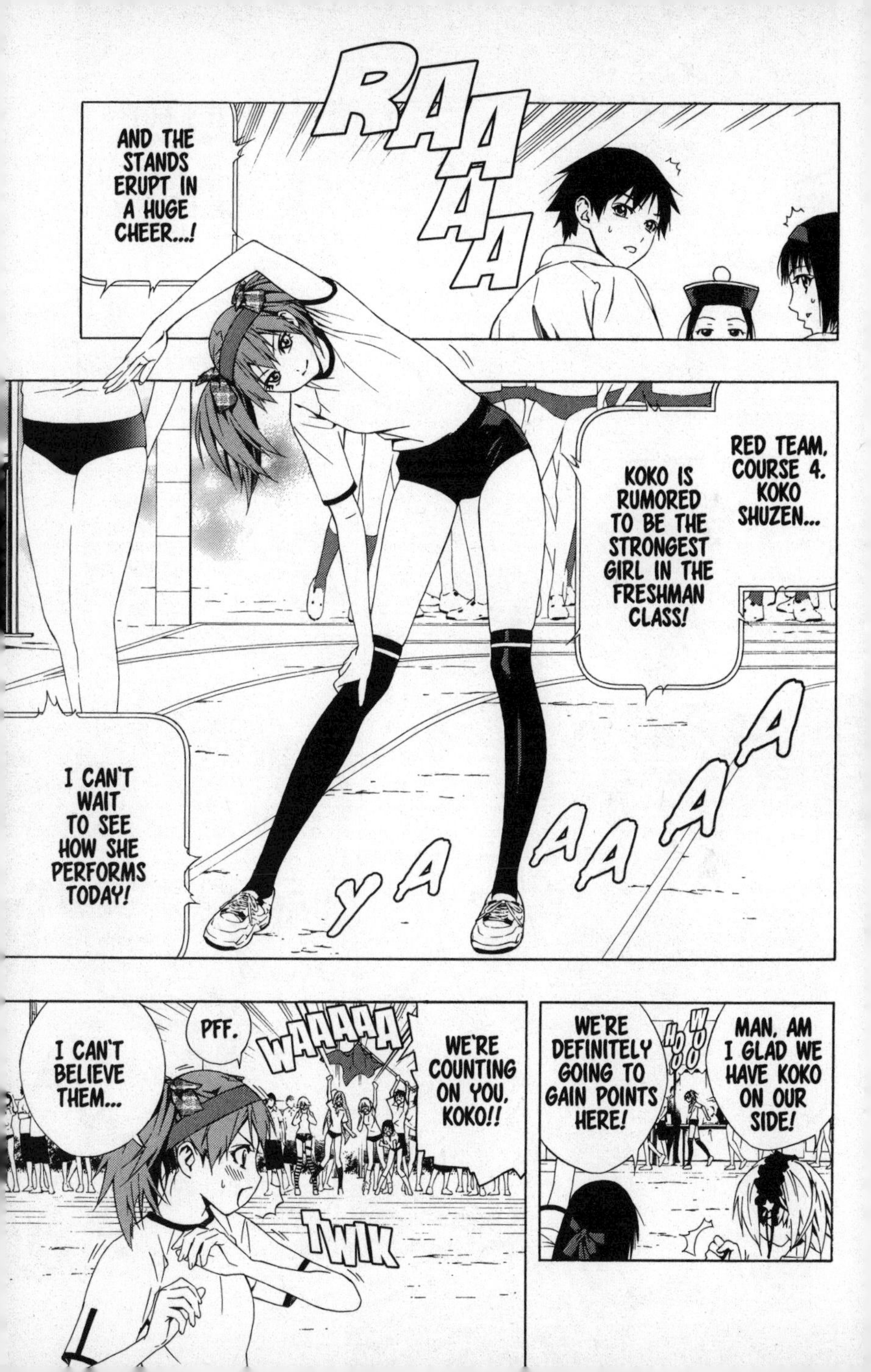

RAAAAA
AND THE STANDS ERUPT IN A HUGE CHEER...!
RED TEAM, COURSE 4. KOKO SHUZEN...
KOKO IS RUMORED TO BE THE STRONGEST GIRL IN THE FRESHMAN CLASS!
YAAAAAA
I CAN'T WAIT TO SEE HOW SHE PERFORMS TODAY!
MAN, AM I GLAD WE HAVE KOKO ON OUR SIDE!
WOO HOO
WE'RE DEFINITELY GOING TO GAIN POINTS HERE!
WE'RE COUNTING ON YOU, KOKO!!
WAAAAA
PFF.
I CAN'T BELIEVE THEM...
TWIK

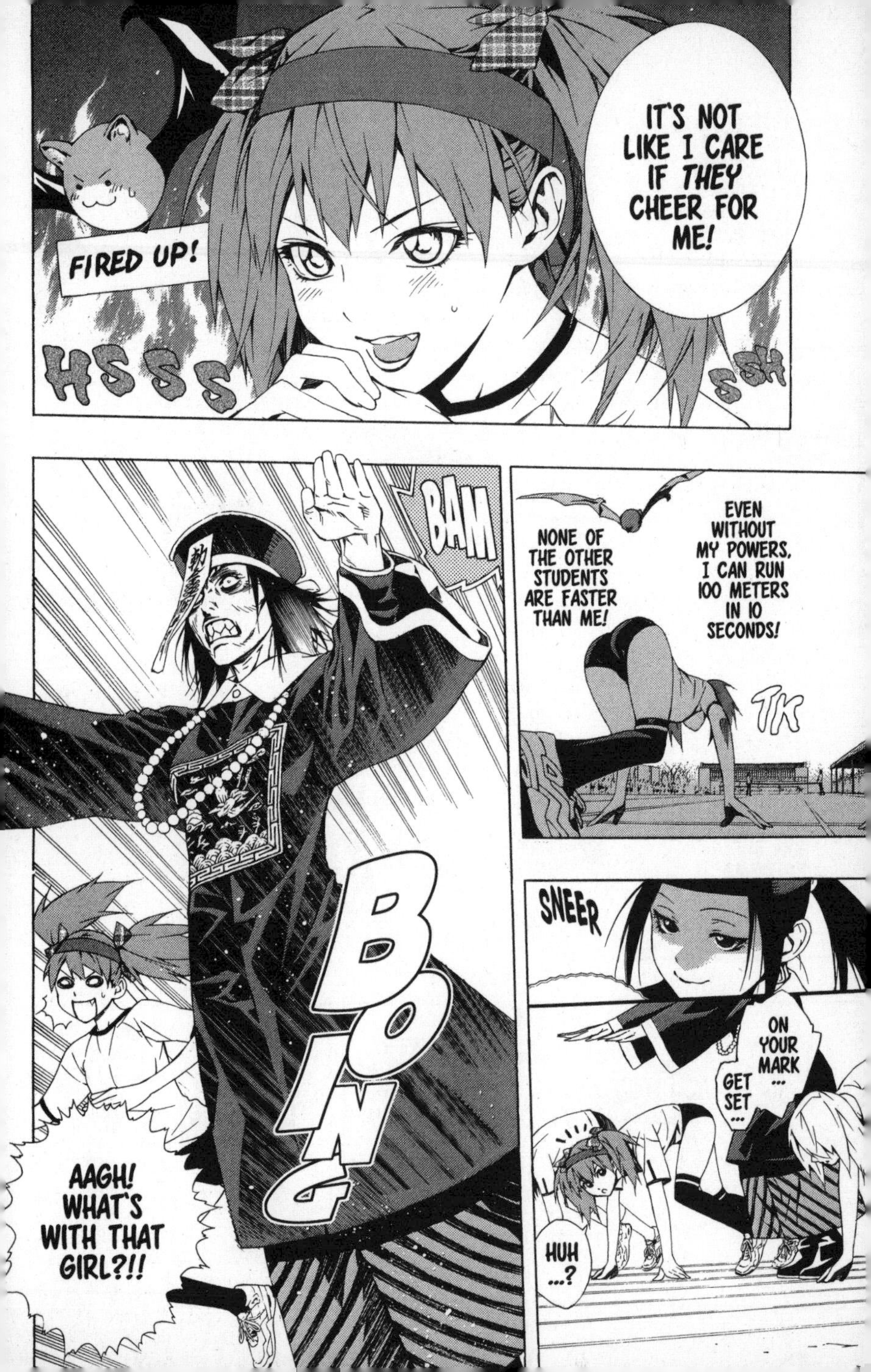
IT'S NOT LIKE I CARE IF THEY CHEER FOR ME!
FIRED UP!
SSH
HSSS
EVEN WITHOUT MY POWERS, I CAN RUN 100 METERS IN 10 SECONDS!
NONE OF THE OTHER STUDENTS ARE FASTER THAN ME!
TK
SNEER
ON YOUR MARK...
GET SET...
HUH...?
BAM
BOING
AAGH! WHAT'S WITH THAT GIRL?!!

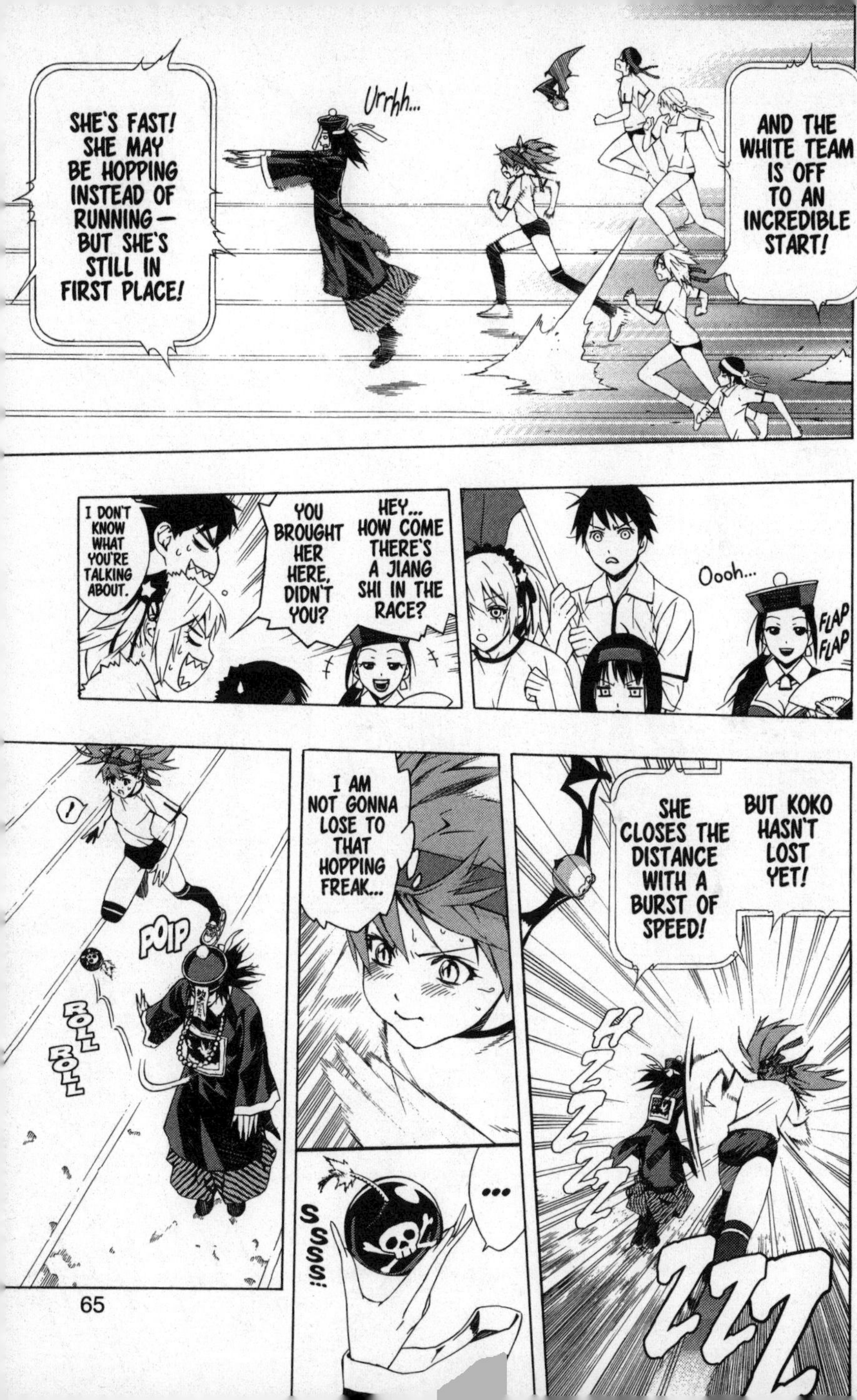
AND THE WHITE TEAM IS OFF TO AN INCREDIBLE START!
Urrhh...
SHE'S FAST! SHE MAY BE HOPPING INSTEAD OF RUNNING—BUT SHE'S STILL IN FIRST PLACE!
Oooh...
FLAP FLAP
HEY... HOW COME THERE'S A JIANG SHI IN THE RACE?
YOU BROUGHT HER HERE, DIDN'T YOU?
I DON'T KNOW WHAT YOU'RE TALKING ABOUT.
BUT KOKO HASN'T LOST YET!
SHE CLOSES THE DISTANCE WITH A BURST OF SPEED!
HZZZZZ
ZZZ
I AM NOT GONNA LOSE TO THAT HOPPING FREAK...
...
SSSS!!
!
POIP
ROLL ROLL

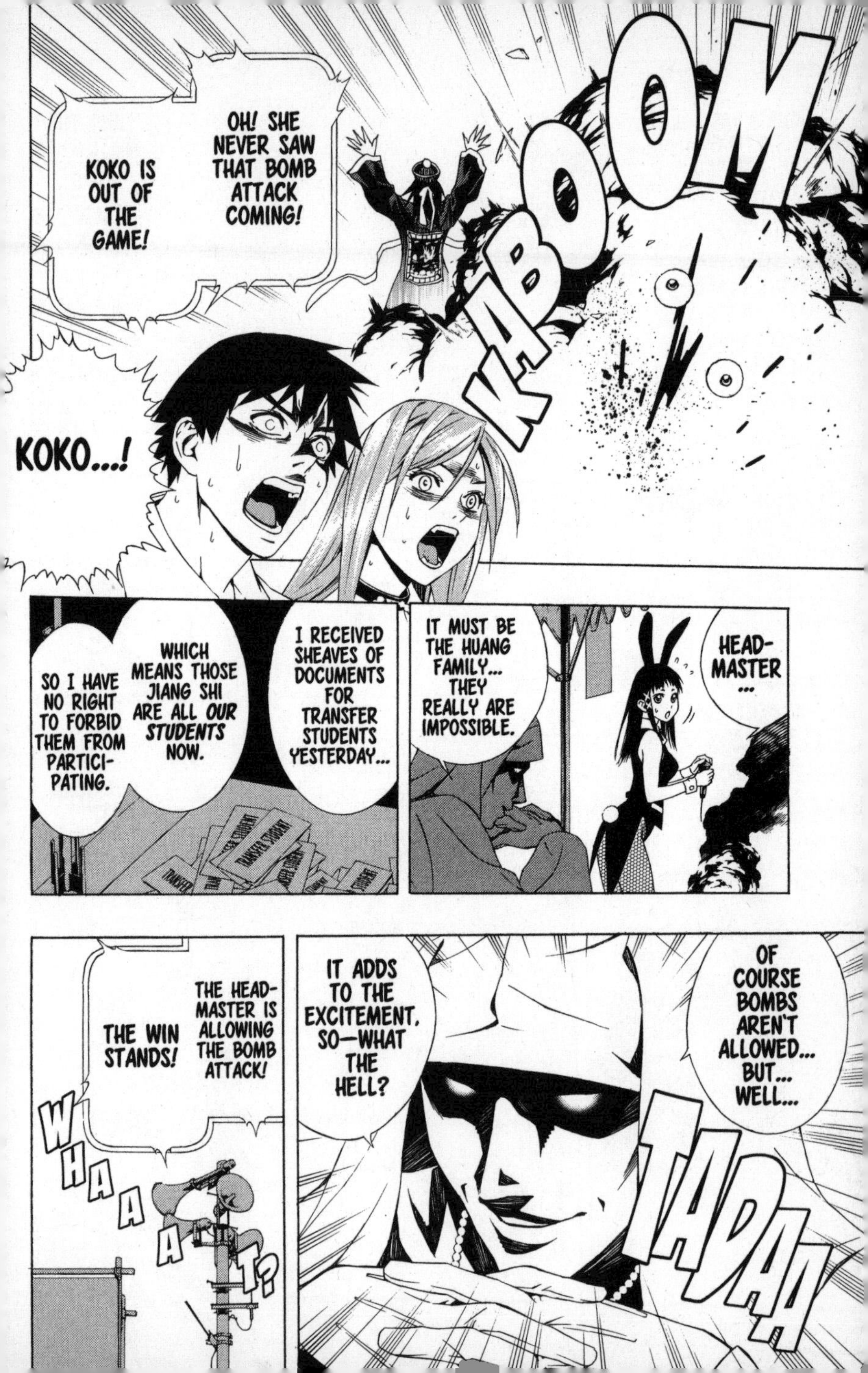
KABOOM
OH! SHE NEVER SAW THAT BOMB ATTACK COMING!
KOKO IS OUT OF THE GAME!
KOKO...!
HEAD-MASTER...
IT MUST BE THE HUANG FAMILY... THEY REALLY ARE IMPOSSIBLE.
I RECEIVED SHEAVES OF DOCUMENTS FOR TRANSFER STUDENTS YESTERDAY...
WHICH MEANS THOSE JIANG SHI ARE ALL *OUR STUDENTS* NOW.
SO I HAVE NO RIGHT TO FORBID THEM FROM PARTICI-PATING.
TRANSFER STUDENT
OF COURSE BOMBS AREN'T ALLOWED... BUT... WELL...
TADAA
IT ADDS TO THE EXCITEMENT, SO—WHAT THE HELL?
THE HEAD-MASTER IS ALLOWING THE BOMB ATTACK!
THE WIN STANDS!
WHAAAAT?

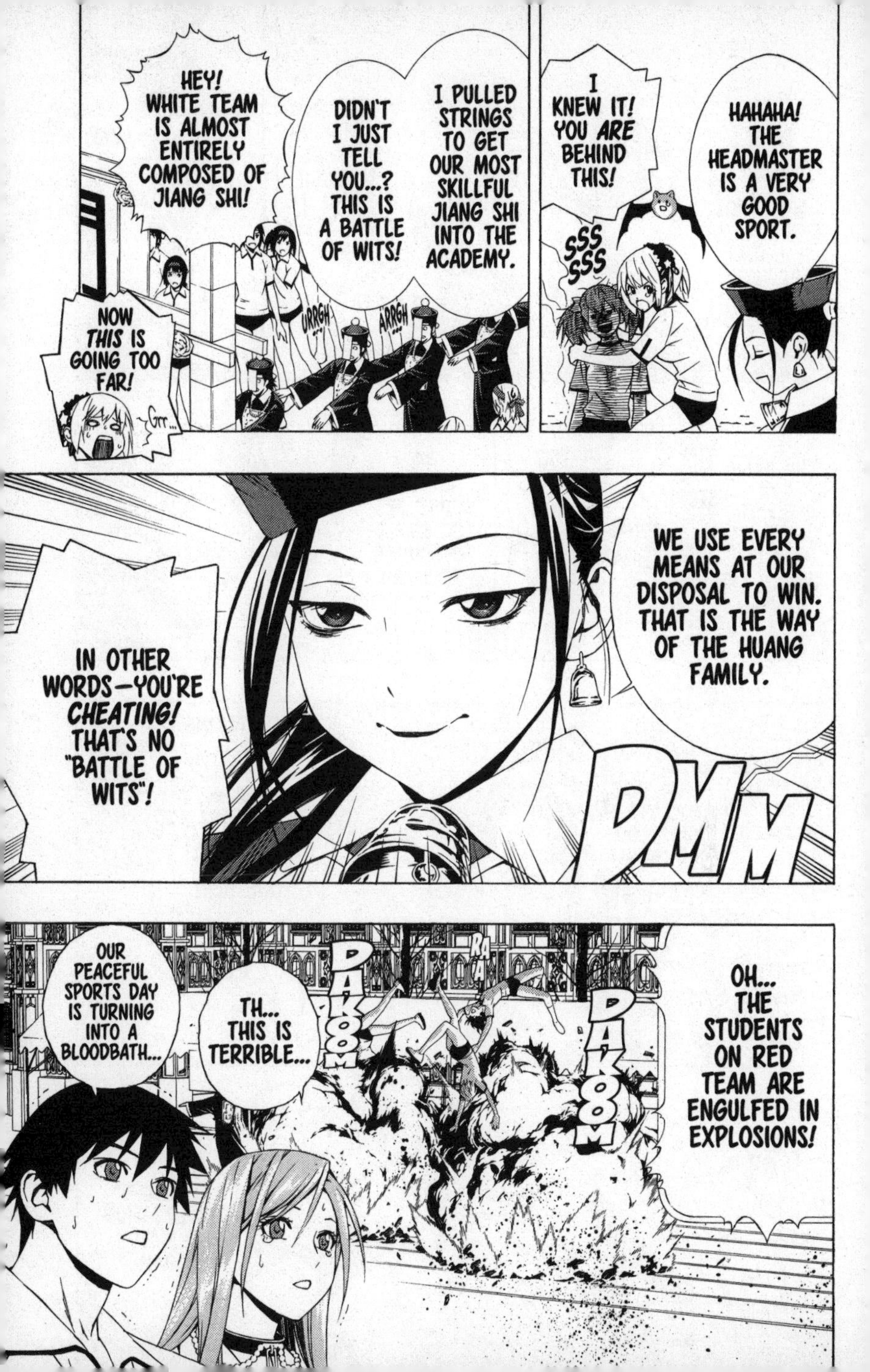
HAHAHA! THE HEADMASTER IS A VERY GOOD SPORT.
I KNEW IT! YOU ARE BEHIND THIS!
SSS SSS
HEY! WHITE TEAM IS ALMOST ENTIRELY COMPOSED OF JIANG SHI!
DIDN'T I JUST TELL YOU...? THIS IS A BATTLE OF WITS!
I PULLED STRINGS TO GET OUR MOST SKILLFUL JIANG SHI INTO THE ACADEMY.
ARRGH
URRGH
NOW THIS IS GOING TOO FAR!
Grr...
WE USE EVERY MEANS AT OUR DISPOSAL TO WIN. THAT IS THE WAY OF THE HUANG FAMILY.
IN OTHER WORDS—YOU'RE CHEATING! THAT'S NO "BATTLE OF WITS"!
DMM
OH... THE STUDENTS ON RED TEAM ARE ENGULFED IN EXPLOSIONS!
DAKOOM
RA
DAKOOM
TH... THIS IS TERRIBLE...
OUR PEACEFUL SPORTS DAY IS TURNING INTO A BLOODBATH...

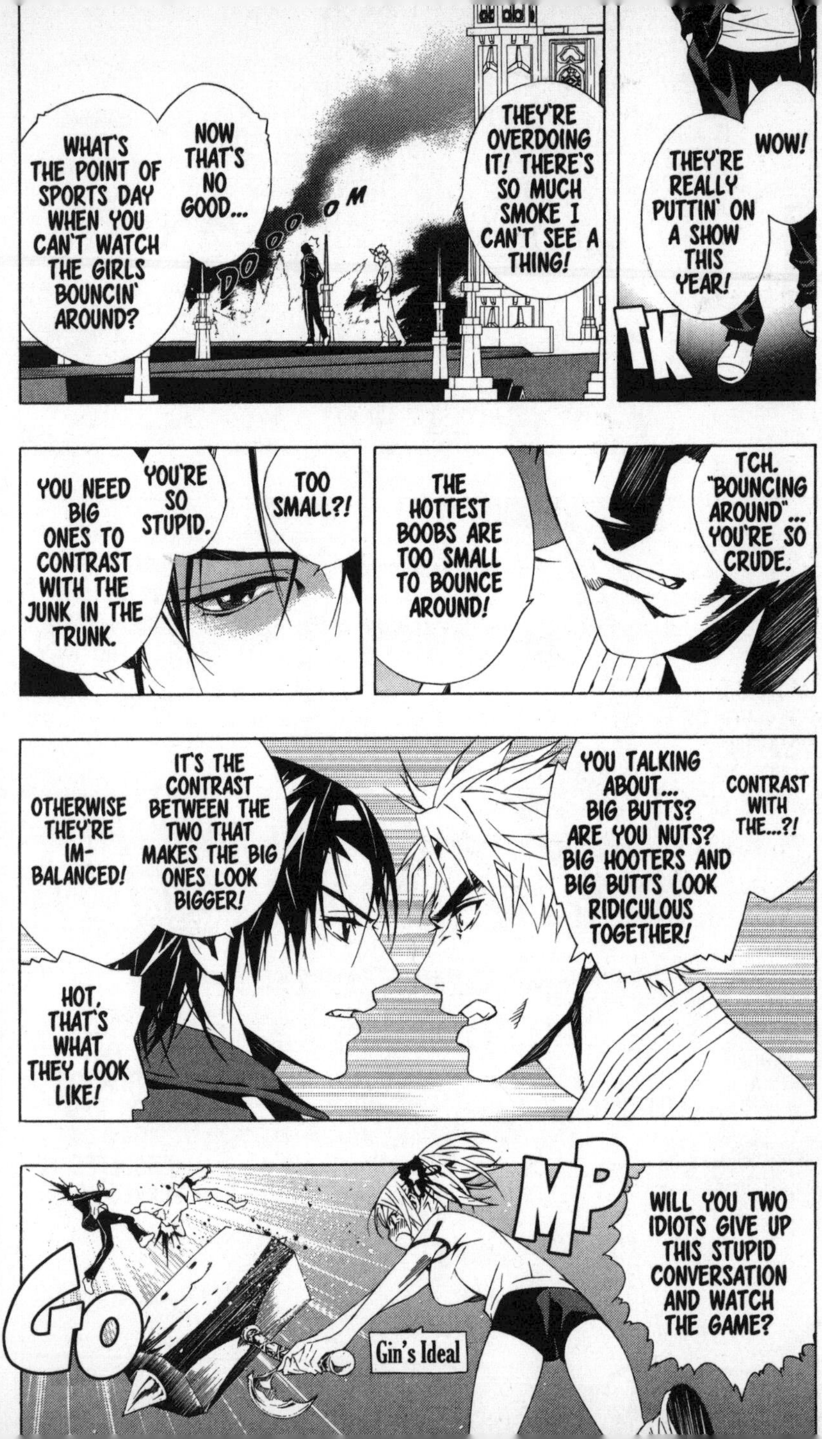
WOW!
THEY'RE REALLY PUTTIN' ON A SHOW THIS YEAR!
TK
THEY'RE OVERDOING IT! THERE'S SO MUCH SMOKE I CAN'T SEE A THING!
DOOOOOM
NOW THAT'S NO GOOD...
WHAT'S THE POINT OF SPORTS DAY WHEN YOU CAN'T WATCH THE GIRLS BOUNCIN' AROUND?
TCH. "BOUNCING AROUND"... YOU'RE SO CRUDE.
THE HOTTEST BOOBS ARE TOO SMALL TO BOUNCE AROUND!
TOO SMALL?!
YOU'RE SO STUPID.
YOU NEED BIG ONES TO CONTRAST WITH THE JUNK IN THE TRUNK.
CONTRAST WITH THE...?!
YOU TALKING ABOUT... BIG BUTTS? ARE YOU NUTS? BIG HOOTERS AND BIG BUTTS LOOK RIDICULOUS TOGETHER!
IT'S THE CONTRAST BETWEEN THE TWO THAT MAKES THE BIG ONES LOOK BIGGER!
OTHERWISE THEY'RE IM-BALANCED!
HOT, THAT'S WHAT THEY LOOK LIKE!
WILL YOU TWO IDIOTS GIVE UP THIS STUPID CONVERSATION AND WATCH THE GAME?
GO
MP
Gin's Ideal

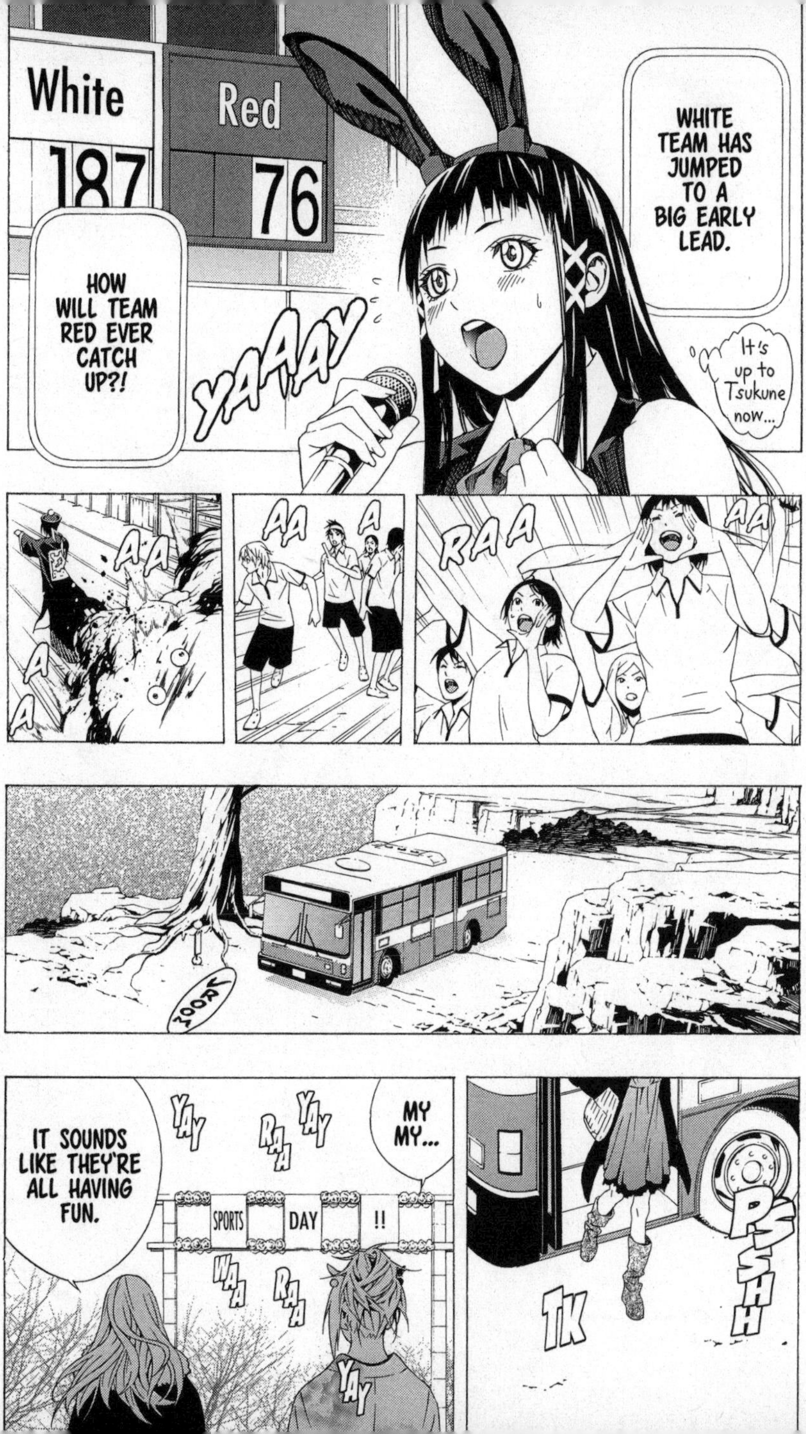
WHITE TEAM HAS JUMPED TO A BIG EARLY LEAD.
White
Red
187
76
It's up to Tsukune now...
HOW WILL TEAM RED EVER CATCH UP?!
YAAAY
RAA
AA
AA
A
AA
A
A
VROOOM
PSSHH
TK
MY MY...
YAY
RAA
YAY
SPORTS
DAY
!!
WAA
RAA
YAY
IT SOUNDS LIKE THEY'RE ALL HAVING FUN.

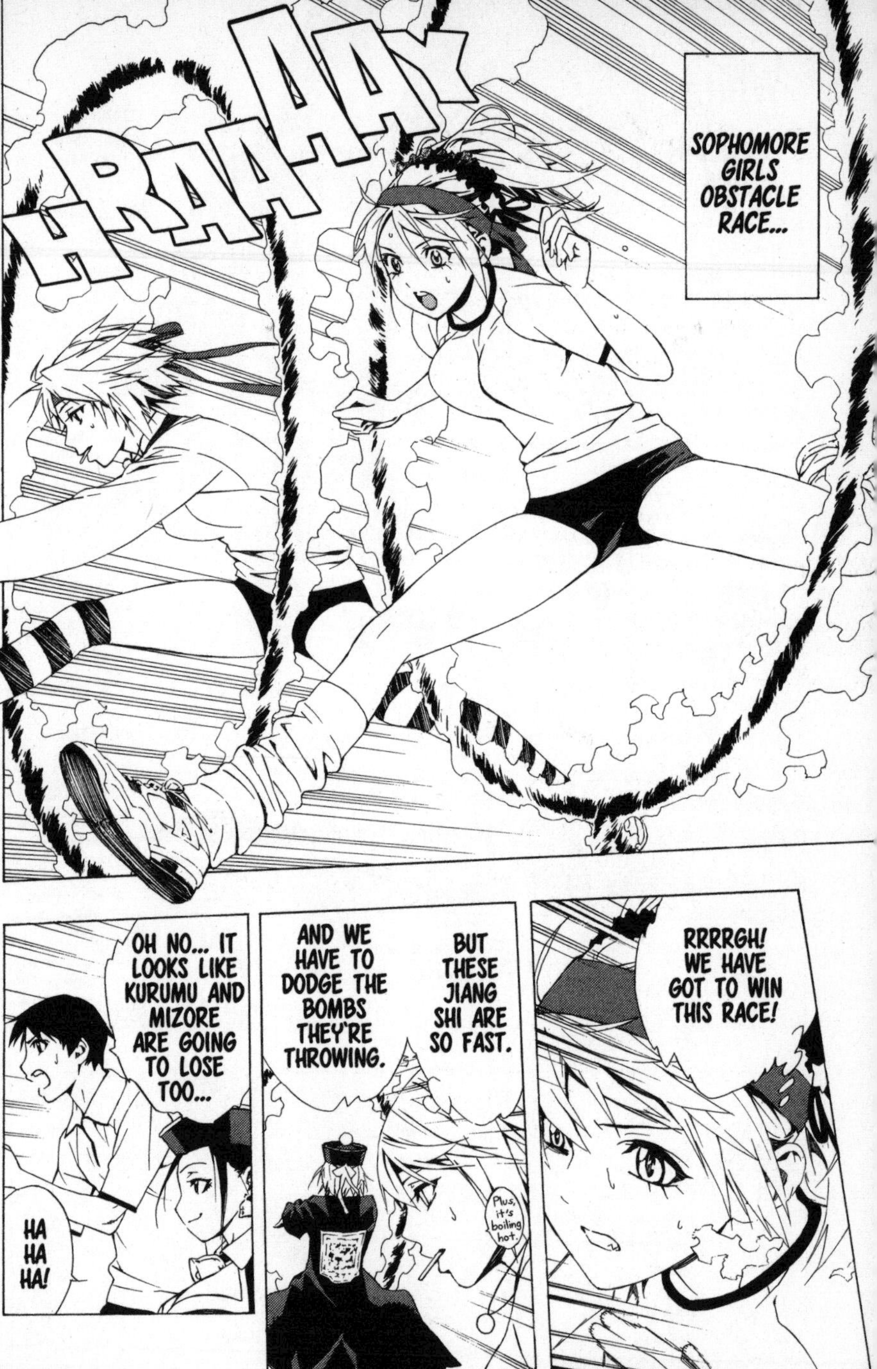
SOPHOMORE GIRLS OBSTACLE RACE...
HRAAAAAY
RRRRGH! WE HAVE GOT TO WIN THIS RACE!
BUT THESE JIANG SHI ARE SO FAST.
AND WE HAVE TO DODGE THE BOMBS THEY'RE THROWING.
Plus, it's boiling hot.
OH NO... IT LOOKS LIKE KURUMU AND MIZORE ARE GOING TO LOSE TOO...
HA HA HA!

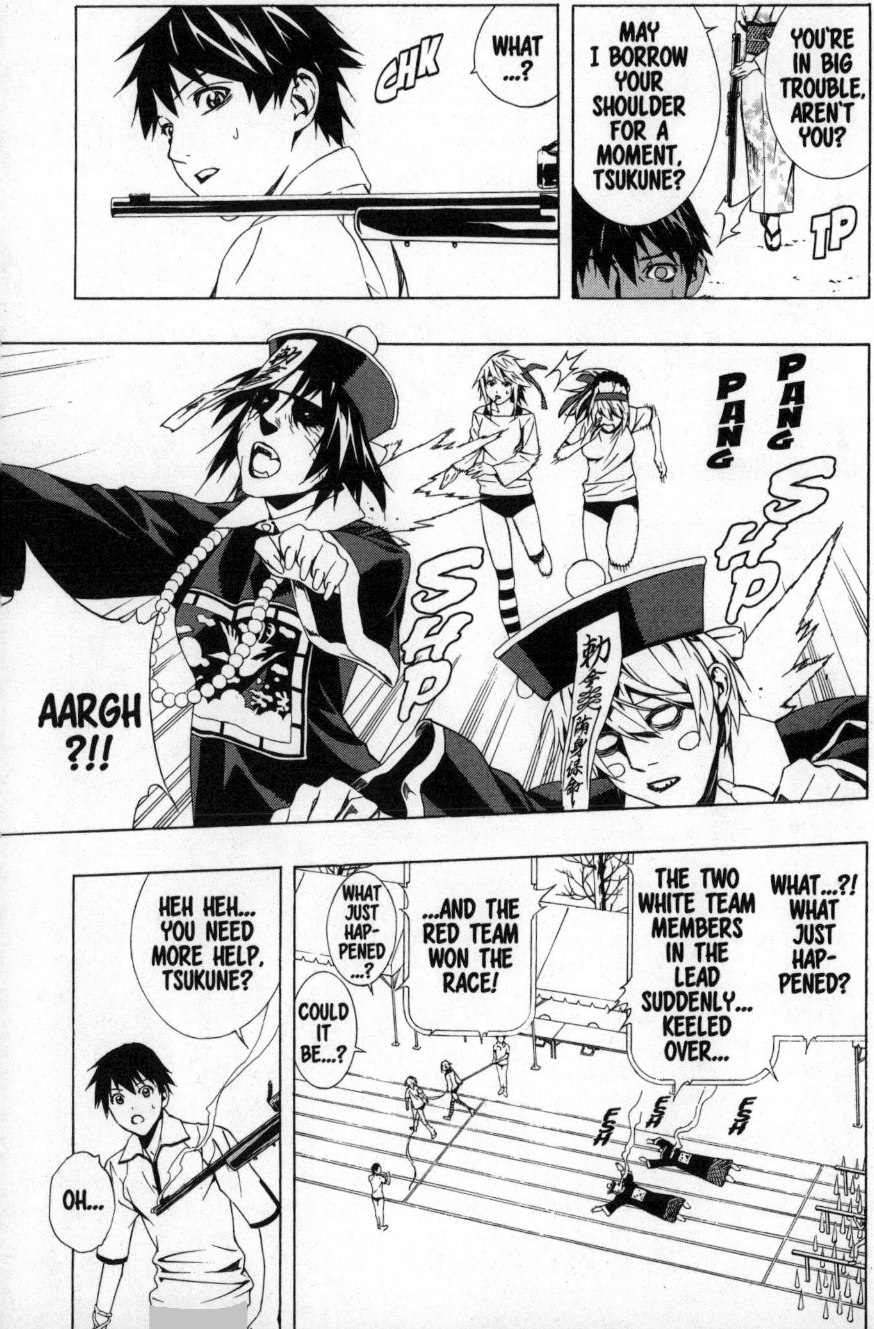

YOU'RE IN BIG TROUBLE, AREN'T YOU?
TP
MAY I BORROW YOUR SHOULDER FOR A MOMENT, TSUKUNE?
WHAT ...?
CHK
PANG
PANG
SHP
SHP
AARGH ?!!
WHAT...?! WHAT JUST HAP-PENED?
THE TWO WHITE TEAM MEMBERS IN THE LEAD SUDDENLY... KEELED OVER...
...AND THE RED TEAM WON THE RACE!
WHAT JUST HAP-PENED ...?
COULD IT BE...?
ESH
ESH
ESH
HEH HEH... YOU NEED MORE HELP, TSUKUNE?
OH...

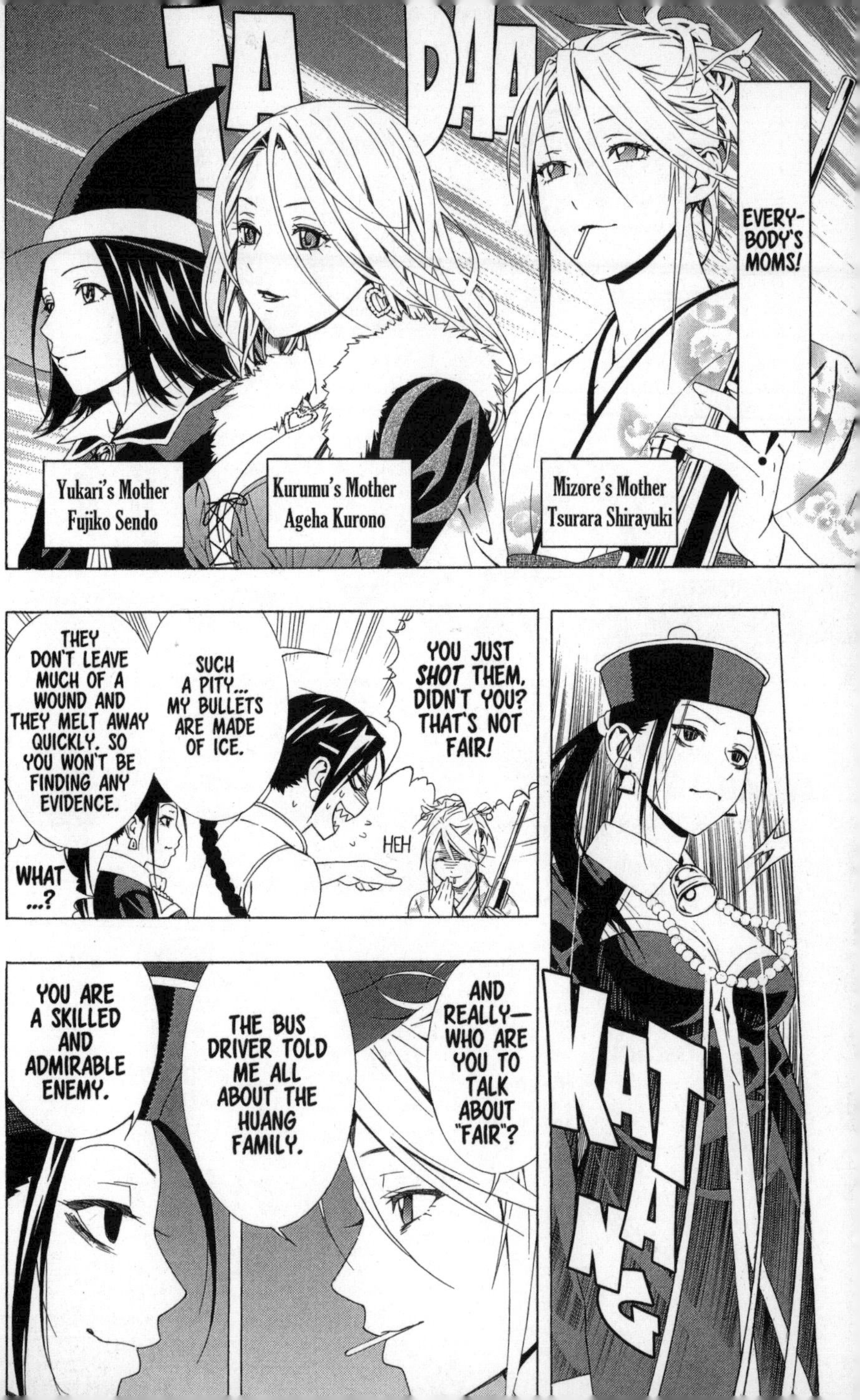
TA DAA
EVERY-BODY'S MOMS!
Mizore's Mother Tsurara Shirayuki
Kurumu's Mother Ageha Kurono
Yukari's Mother Fujiko Sendo
KATNANG
YOU JUST SHOT THEM, DIDN'T YOU? THAT'S NOT FAIR!
HEH
SUCH A PITY... MY BULLETS ARE MADE OF ICE.
THEY DON'T LEAVE MUCH OF A WOUND AND THEY MELT AWAY QUICKLY. SO YOU WON'T BE FINDING ANY EVIDENCE.
WHAT ...?
AND REALLY— WHO ARE YOU TO TALK ABOUT "FAIR"?
THE BUS DRIVER TOLD ME ALL ABOUT THE HUANG FAMILY.
YOU ARE A SKILLED AND ADMIRABLE ENEMY.

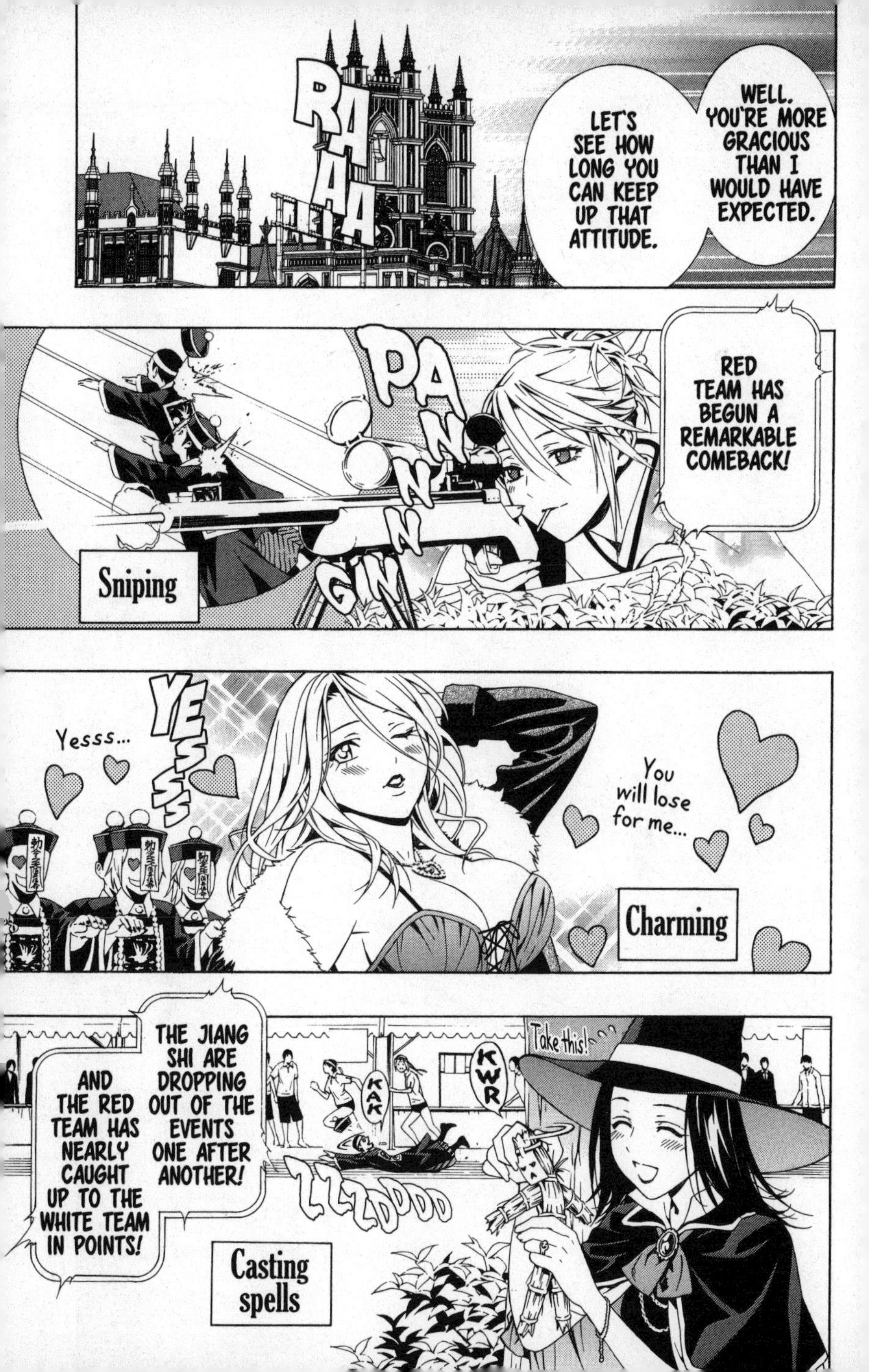

WELL. YOU'RE MORE GRACIOUS THAN I WOULD HAVE EXPECTED.
LET'S SEE HOW LONG YOU CAN KEEP UP THAT ATTITUDE.
RAAA
RED TEAM HAS BEGUN A REMARKABLE COMEBACK!
PANNNGIN
Sniping
You will lose for me...
YESSS
Yesss...
Charming
Take this!
KWR
KAK
THE JIANG SHI ARE DROPPING OUT OF THE EVENTS ONE AFTER ANOTHER!
AND THE RED TEAM HAS NEARLY CAUGHT UP TO THE WHITE TEAM IN POINTS!
Casting spells

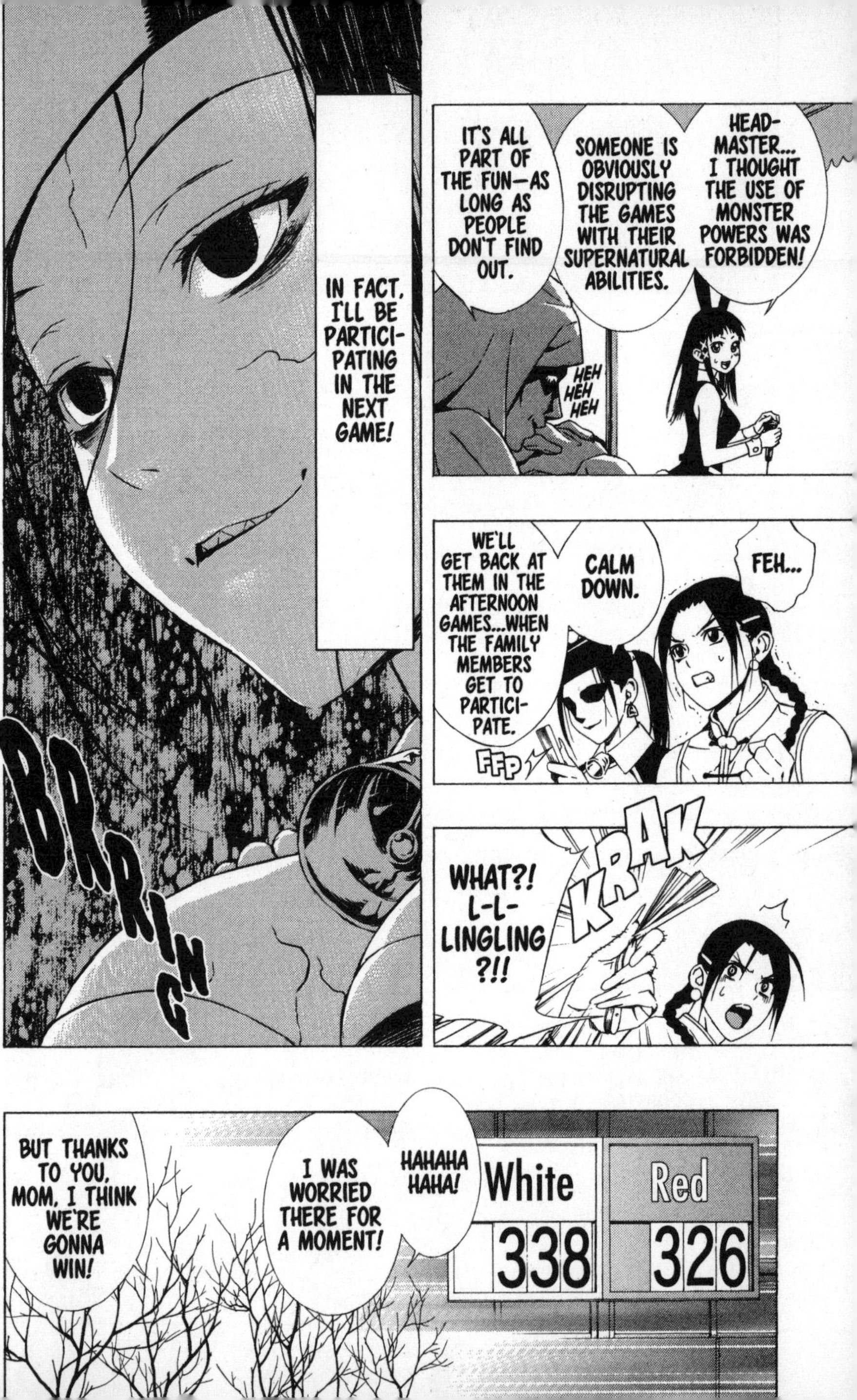
HEAD-MASTER... I THOUGHT THE USE OF MONSTER POWERS WAS FORBIDDEN!
SOMEONE IS OBVIOUSLY DISRUPTING THE GAMES WITH THEIR SUPERNATURAL ABILITIES.
IT'S ALL PART OF THE FUN—AS LONG AS PEOPLE DON'T FIND OUT.
HEH HEH HEH
FEH...
CALM DOWN.
WE'LL GET BACK AT THEM IN THE AFTERNOON GAMES...WHEN THE FAMILY MEMBERS GET TO PARTICI-PATE.
FFP
KRAK
WHAT?! L-L-LINGLING ?!!
IN FACT, I'LL BE PARTICI-PATING IN THE NEXT GAME!
BRRRING
White
Red
338
326
HAHAHA HAHA!
I WAS WORRIED THERE FOR A MOMENT!
BUT THANKS TO YOU, MOM, I THINK WE'RE GONNA WIN!

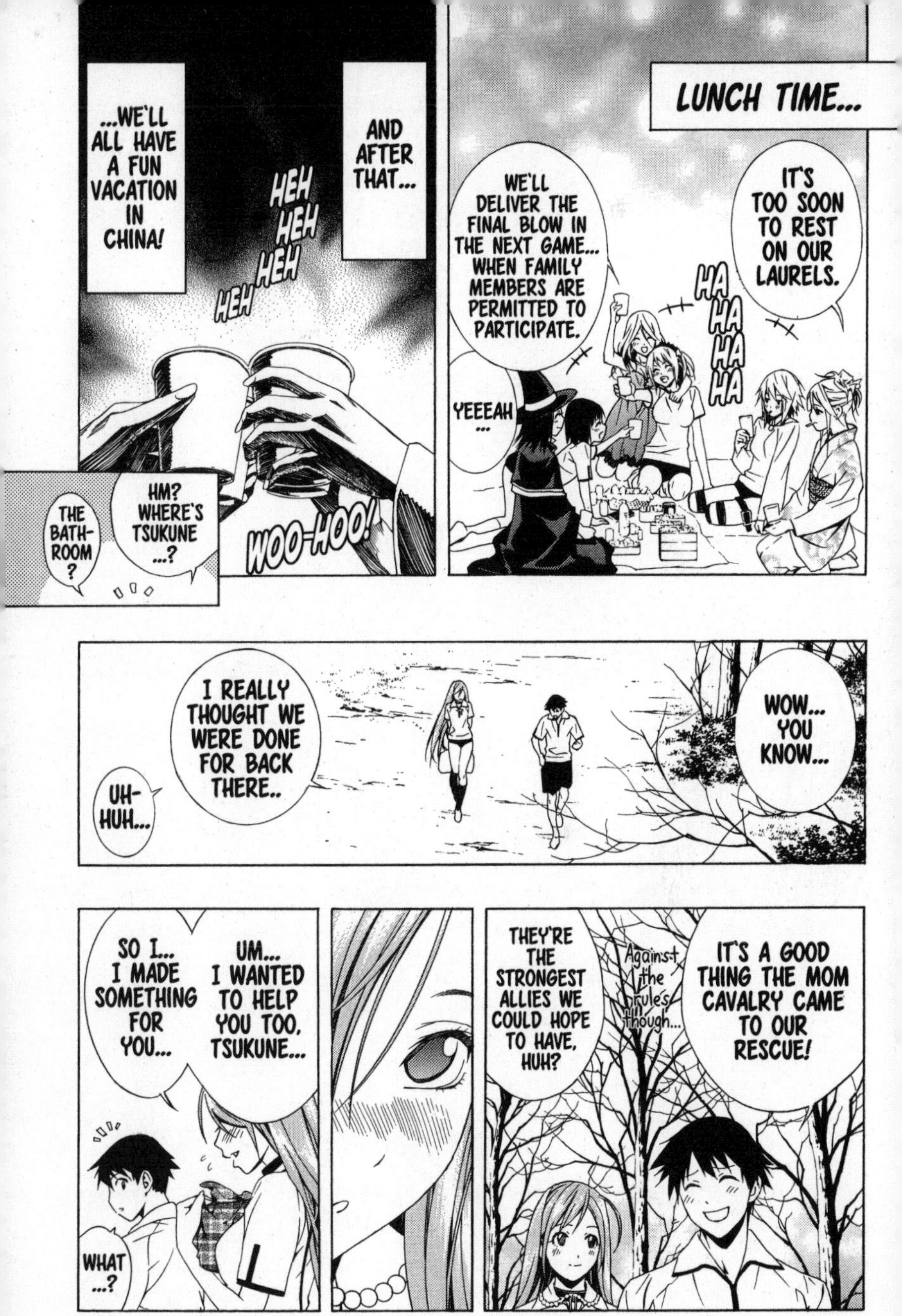
LUNCH TIME...
IT'S TOO SOON TO REST ON OUR LAURELS.
HA HA HA HA
WE'LL DELIVER THE FINAL BLOW IN THE NEXT GAME... WHEN FAMILY MEMBERS ARE PERMITTED TO PARTICIPATE.
YEEEAH...
AND AFTER THAT...
...WE'LL ALL HAVE A FUN VACATION IN CHINA!
HEH HEH HEH HEH
WOO-HOO!
HM? WHERE'S TSUKUNE...?
THE BATH-ROOM?
WOW... YOU KNOW...
I REALLY THOUGHT WE WERE DONE FOR BACK THERE..
UH-HUH...
IT'S A GOOD THING THE MOM CAVALRY CAME TO OUR RESCUE!
Against the rules though...
THEY'RE THE STRONGEST ALLIES WE COULD HOPE TO HAVE, HUH?
UM... I WANTED TO HELP YOU TOO, TSUKUNE...
SO I... I MADE SOMETHING FOR YOU...
WHAT...?

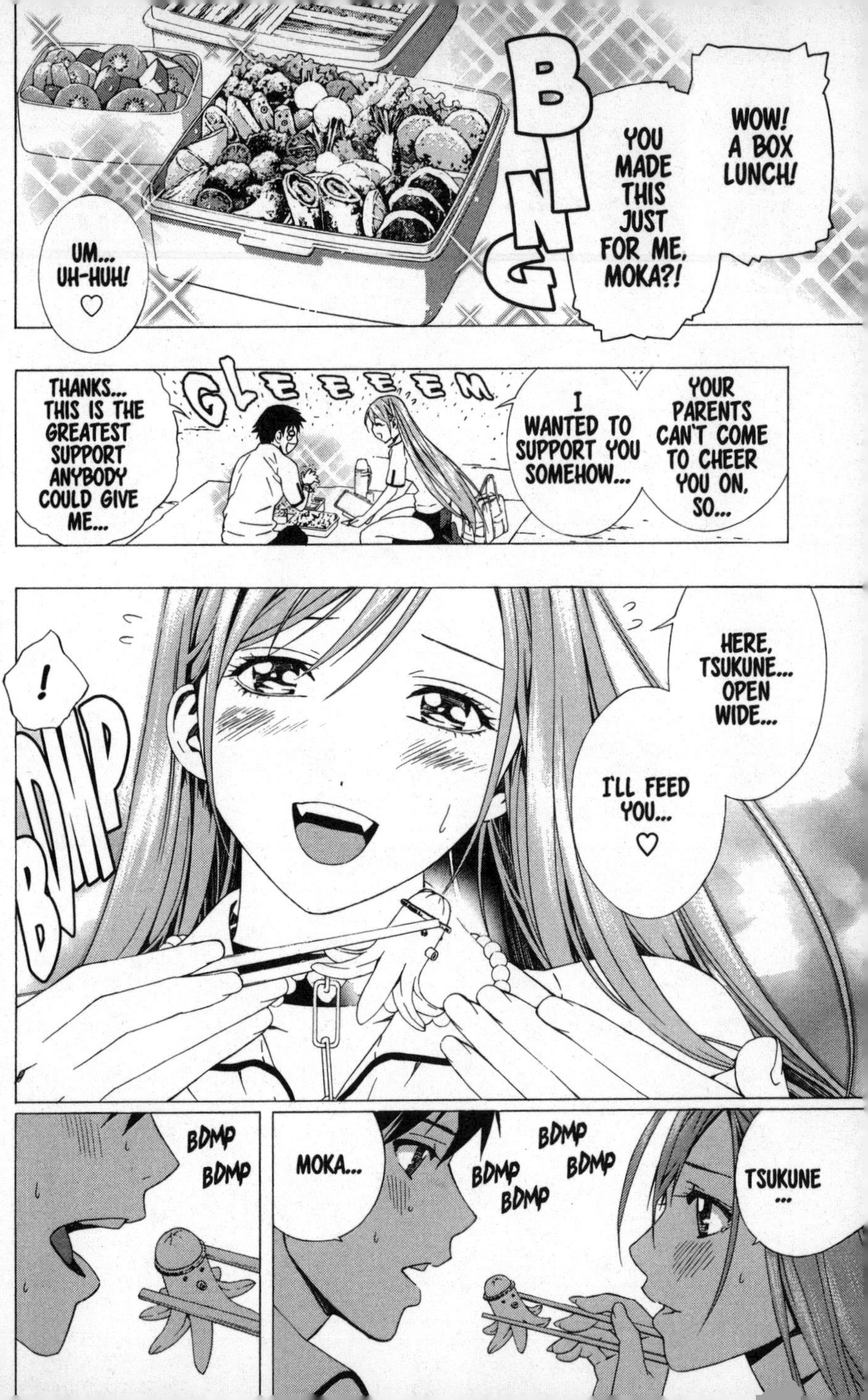
WOW! A BOX LUNCH!
YOU MADE THIS JUST FOR ME, MOKA?!
BING
UM... UH-HUH! ♡
YOUR PARENTS CAN'T COME TO CHEER YOU ON, SO...
I WANTED TO SUPPORT YOU SOMEHOW...
GLEEEEEM
THANKS... THIS IS THE GREATEST SUPPORT ANYBODY COULD GIVE ME...
HERE, TSUKUNE... OPEN WIDE...
I'LL FEED YOU... ♡
!
BDMP
TSUKUNE ...
BDMP
BDMP
BDMP
BDMP
MOKA...
BDMP
BDMP

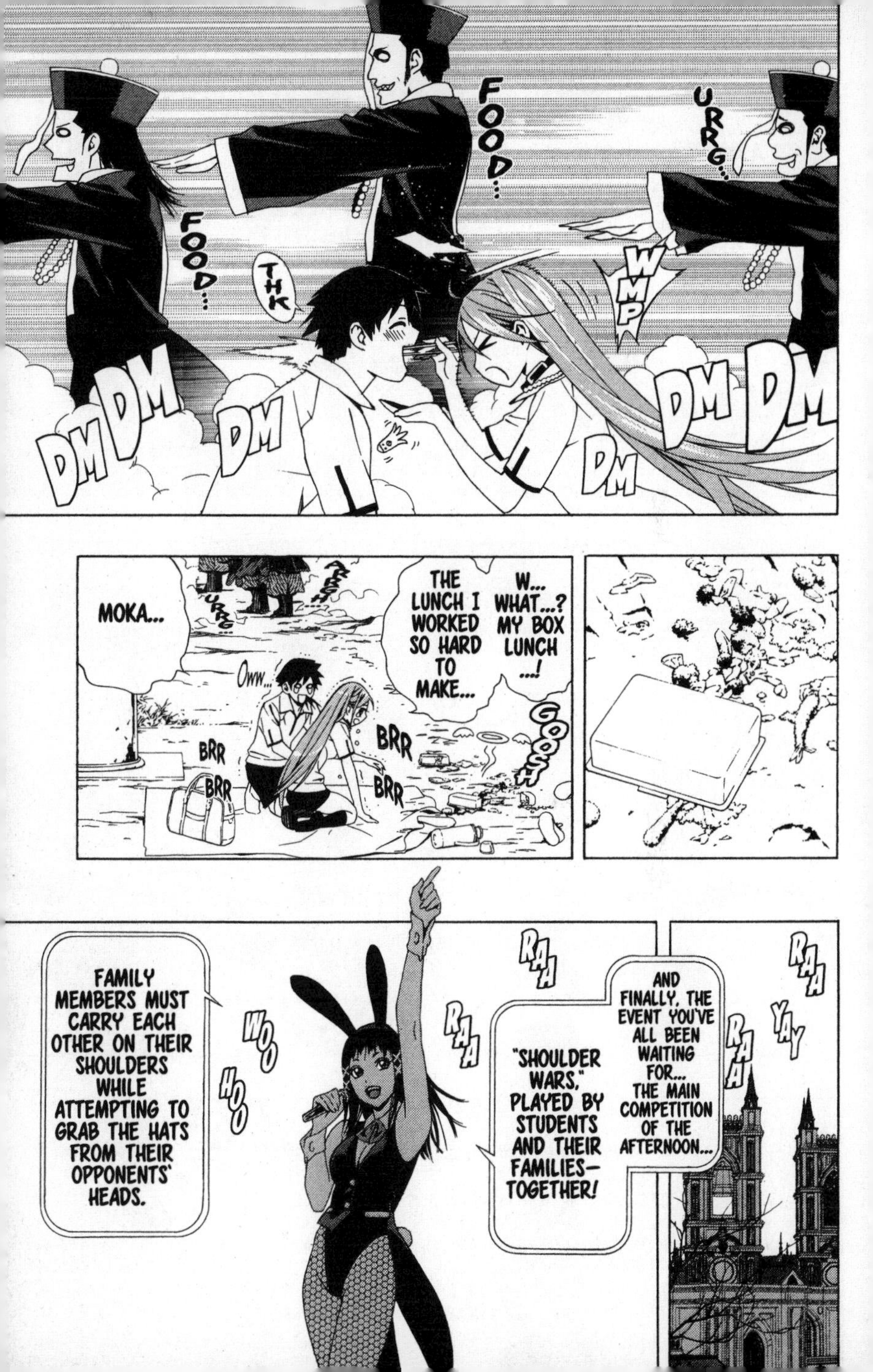
URRG...
FOOD...
WMP
THK
FOOD...
DM DM
DM
DM
DM DM
W... WHAT...? MY BOX LUNCH ...!
THE LUNCH I WORKED SO HARD TO MAKE...
URRG...
MOKA...
GOOSH
OWW...
BRR
BRR
BRR
BRR
RAA
YAY
RAA
AND FINALLY, THE EVENT YOU'VE ALL BEEN WAITING FOR... THE MAIN COMPETITION OF THE AFTERNOON...
RAA
"SHOULDER WARS," PLAYED BY STUDENTS AND THEIR FAMILIES—TOGETHER!
RAA
WOO HOO
FAMILY MEMBERS MUST CARRY EACH OTHER ON THEIR SHOULDERS WHILE ATTEMPTING TO GRAB THE HATS FROM THEIR OPPONENTS' HEADS.

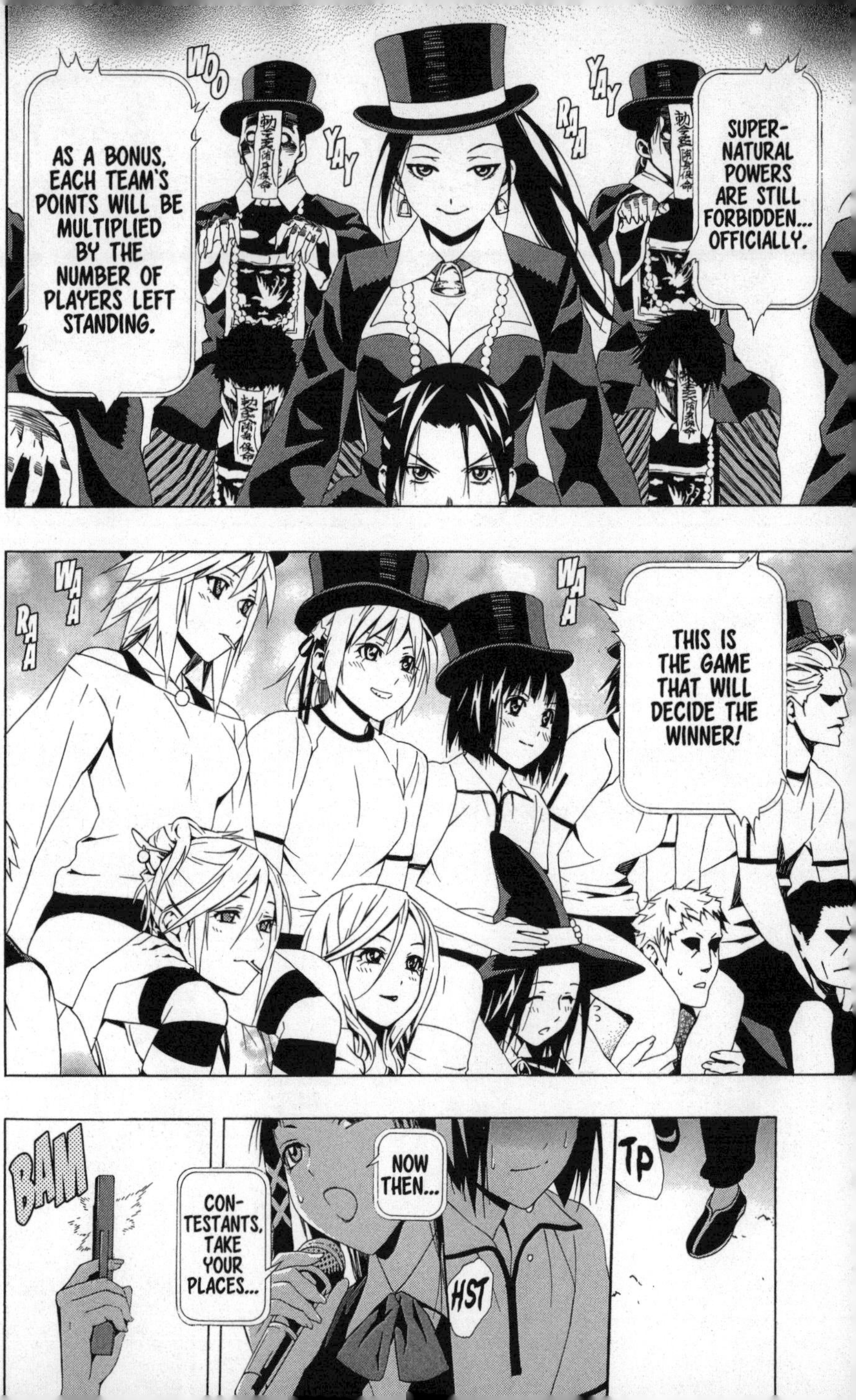
SUPER-NATURAL POWERS ARE STILL FORBIDDEN... OFFICIALLY.
YAY
RAA
YAY
WOO
AS A BONUS, EACH TEAM'S POINTS WILL BE MULTIPLIED BY THE NUMBER OF PLAYERS LEFT STANDING.
WAA
THIS IS THE GAME THAT WILL DECIDE THE WINNER!
WAA
RAA
TP
HST
NOW THEN...
CON-TESTANTS, TAKE YOUR PLACES...
BAM

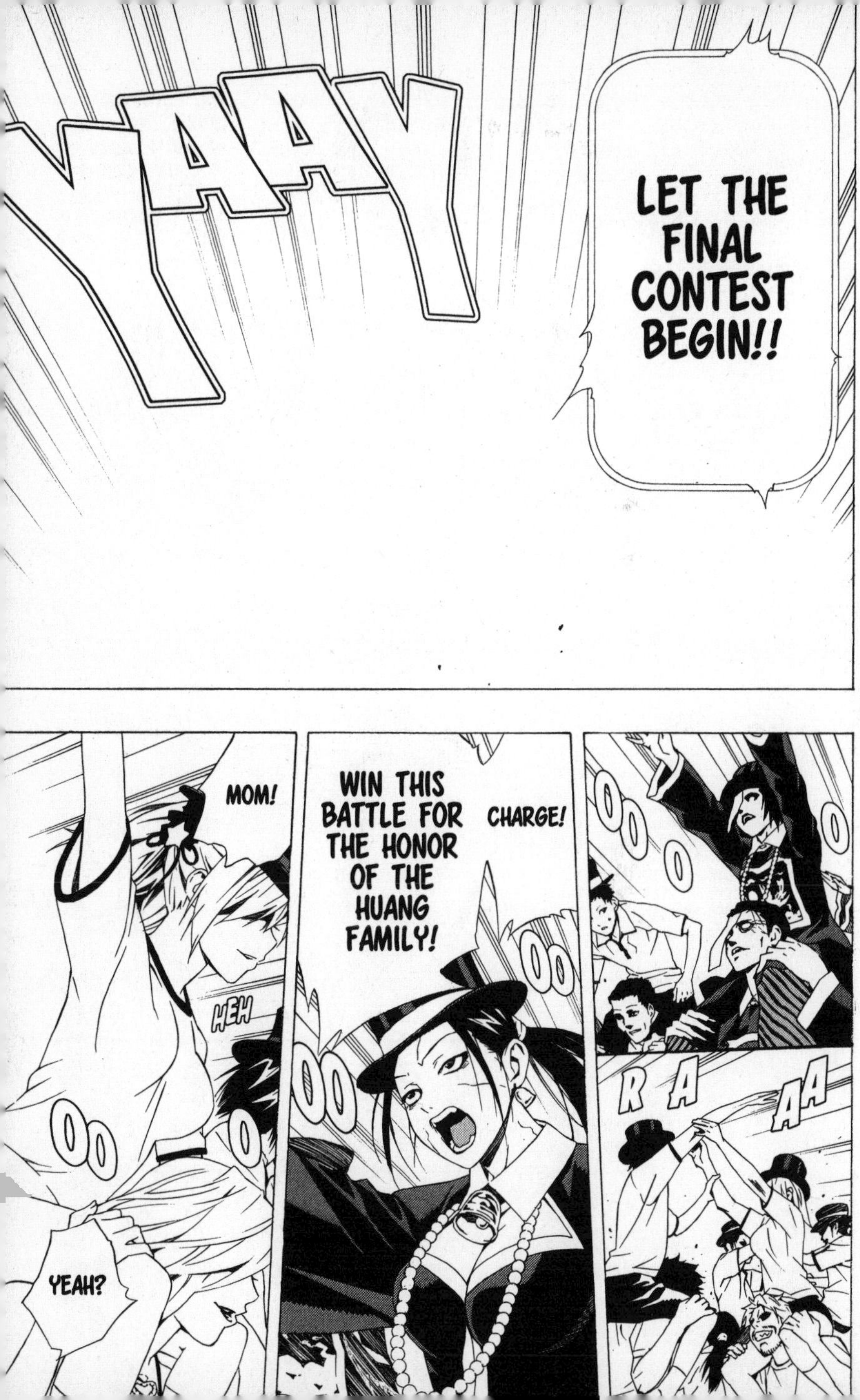
LET THE FINAL CONTEST BEGIN!!
YAAY
OOOO
RAAA
CHARGE!
WIN THIS BATTLE FOR THE HONOR OF THE HUANG FAMILY!
OO
OO
MOM!
HEH
OO
O
YEAH?

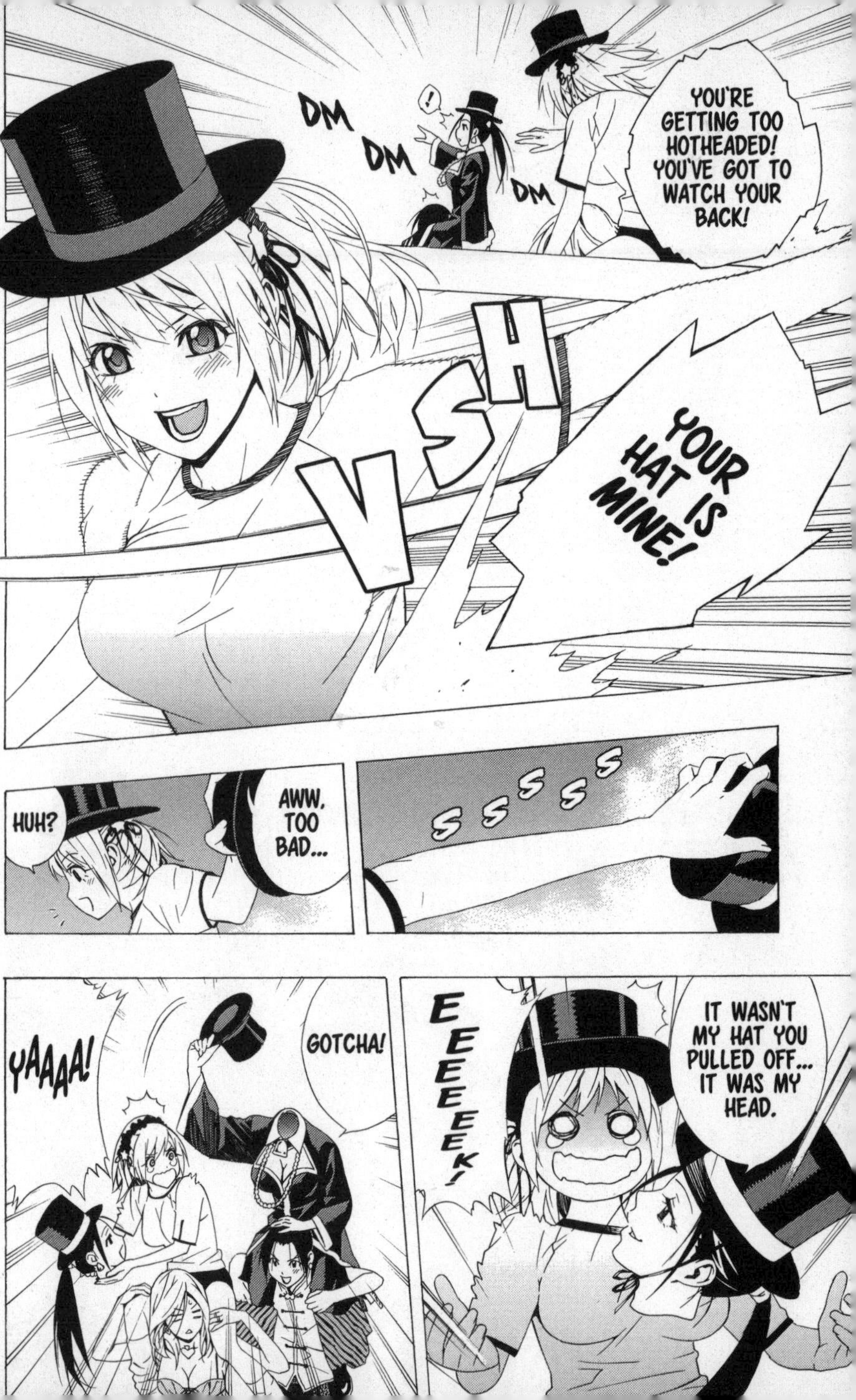
YOU'RE GETTING TOO HOTHEADED! YOU'VE GOT TO WATCH YOUR BACK!
!
DM
DM
DM
VSH
YOUR HAT IS MINE!
SSSSS
AWW, TOO BAD...
HUH?
IT WASN'T MY HAT YOU PULLED OFF... IT WAS MY HEAD.
EEEEEEEK!
GOTCHA!
YAAAA!

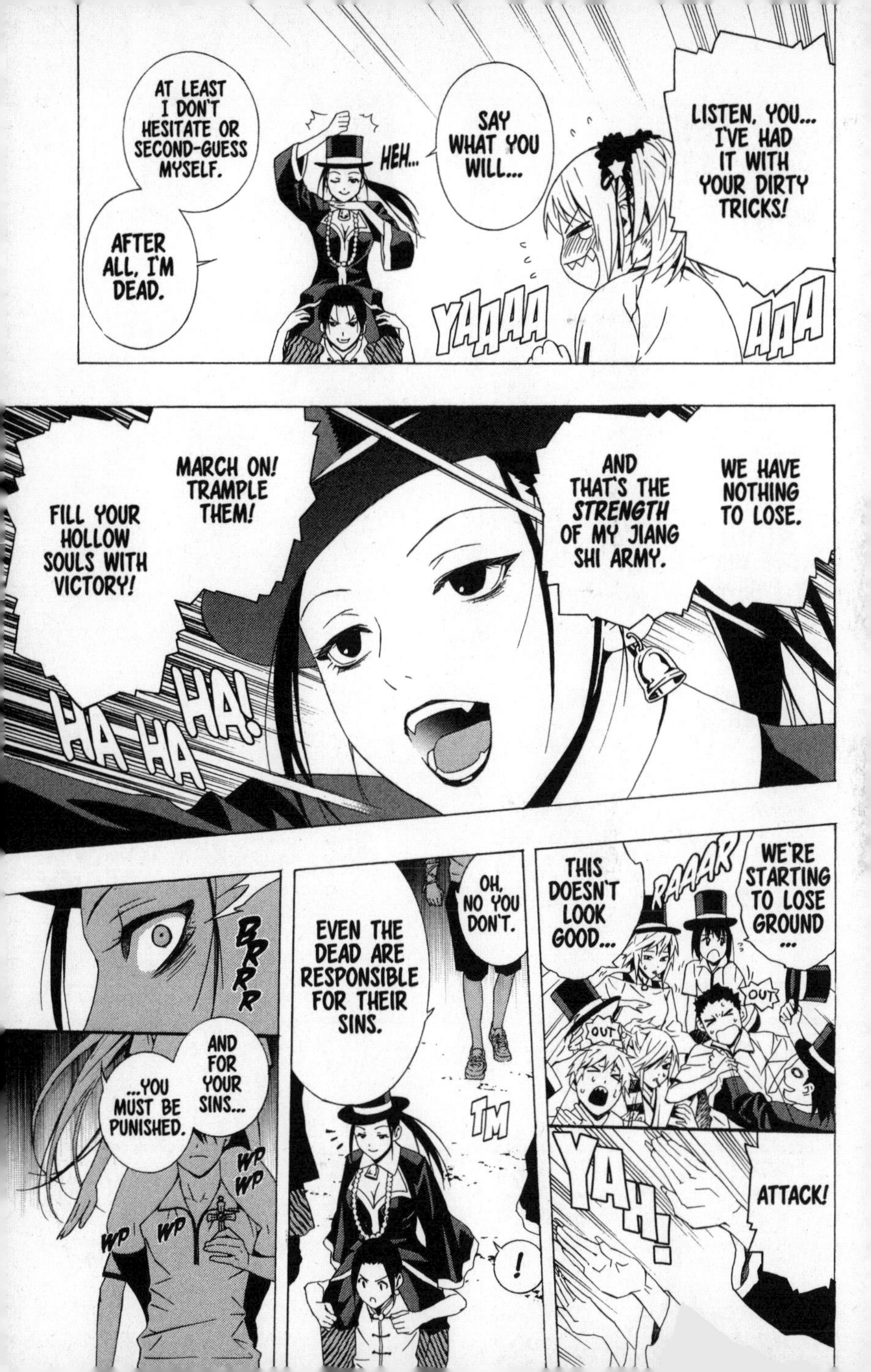
LISTEN, YOU... I'VE HAD IT WITH YOUR DIRTY TRICKS!
YAAAAAAA
SAY WHAT YOU WILL...
HEH...
AT LEAST I DON'T HESITATE OR SECOND-GUESS MYSELF.
AFTER ALL, I'M DEAD.
WE HAVE NOTHING TO LOSE.
AND THAT'S THE *STRENGTH* OF MY JIANG SHI ARMY.
MARCH ON! TRAMPLE THEM!
FILL YOUR HOLLOW SOULS WITH VICTORY!
HA HA HA!
WE'RE STARTING TO LOSE GROUND...
RAAAR
THIS DOESN'T LOOK GOOD...
OUT
OUT
ATTACK!
YAH!
OH, NO YOU DON'T.
EVEN THE DEAD ARE RESPONSIBLE FOR THEIR SINS.
TM
!
BRRR
AND FOR YOUR SINS...
...YOU MUST BE PUNISHED.
WP
WP
WP
WP

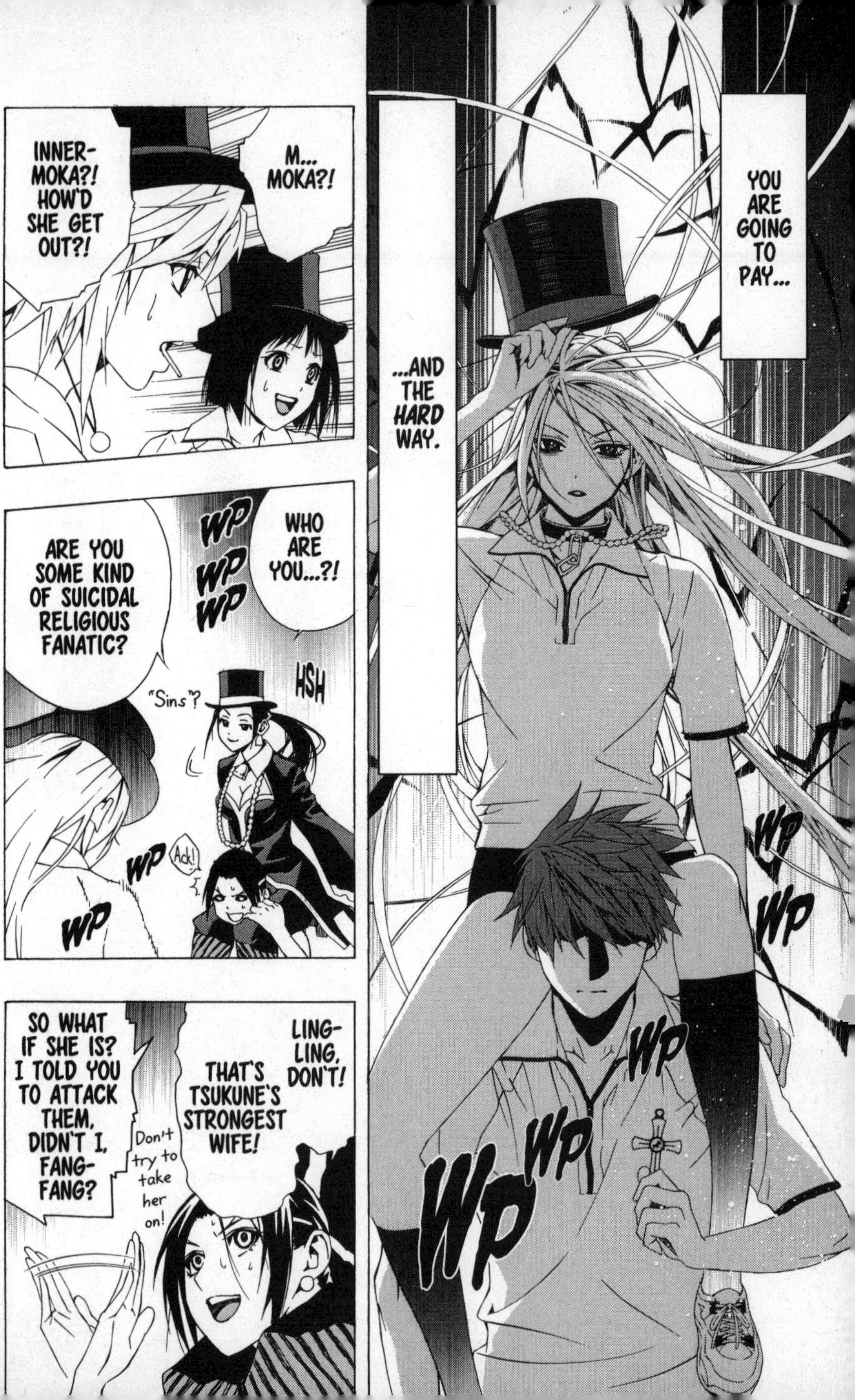
YOU ARE GOING TO PAY...
...AND THE HARD WAY.
WP
WP
WP
WP
WP
M... MOKA?!
INNER-MOKA?! HOW'D SHE GET OUT?!
WHO ARE YOU...?!
WP WP WP
ARE YOU SOME KIND OF SUICIDAL RELIGIOUS FANATIC?
HSH
"Sins"?
Ack!
WP
WP
LING-LING, DON'T!
THAT'S TSUKUNE'S STRONGEST WIFE!
Don't try to take her on!
SO WHAT IF SHE IS? I TOLD YOU TO ATTACK THEM, DIDN'T I, FANG-FANG?

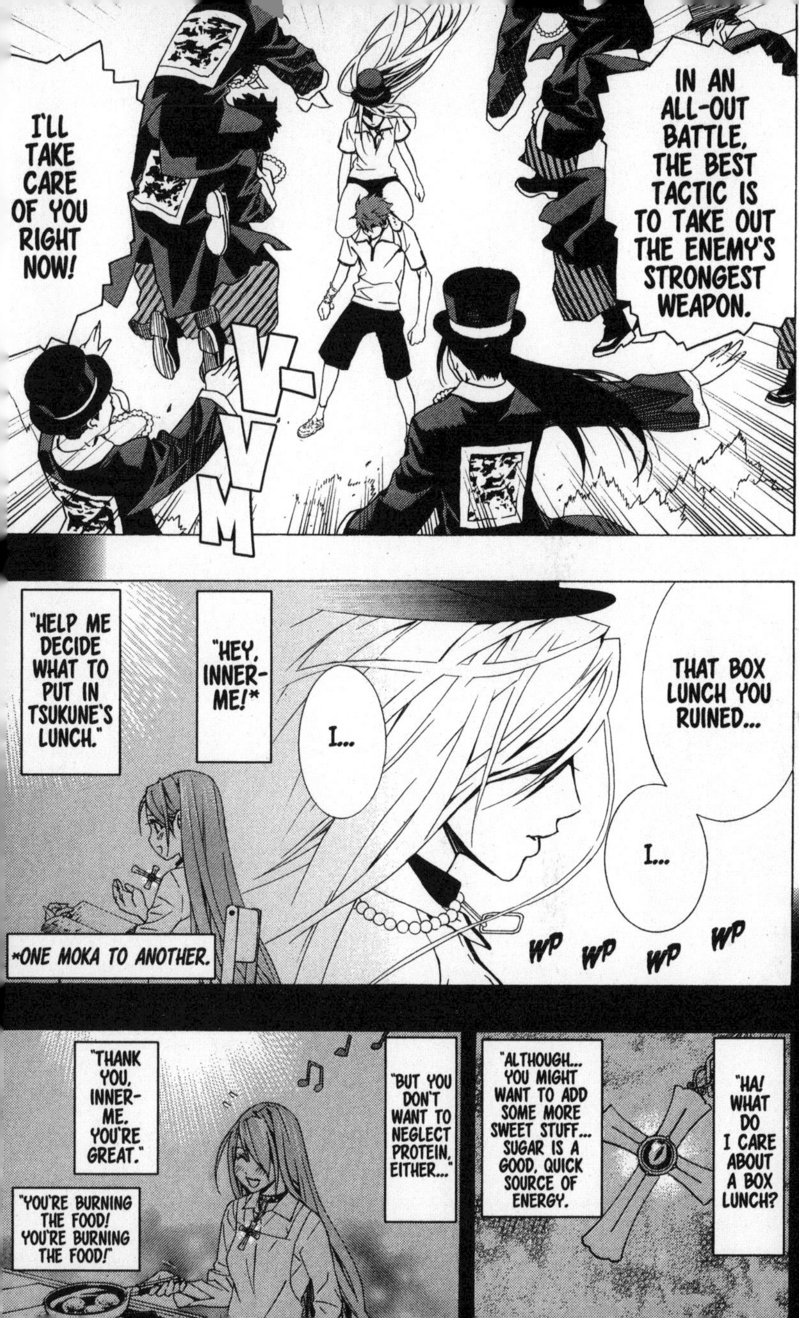
IN AN ALL-OUT BATTLE, THE BEST TACTIC IS TO TAKE OUT THE ENEMY'S STRONGEST WEAPON.
I'LL TAKE CARE OF YOU RIGHT NOW!
V-VVM
THAT BOX LUNCH YOU RUINED...
I...
I...
"HEY, INNER-ME!*
"HELP ME DECIDE WHAT TO PUT IN TSUKUNE'S LUNCH."
WP WP WP WP
*ONE MOKA TO ANOTHER.
"HA! WHAT DO I CARE ABOUT A BOX LUNCH?
"ALTHOUGH... YOU MIGHT WANT TO ADD SOME MORE SWEET STUFF... SUGAR IS A GOOD, QUICK SOURCE OF ENERGY.
"BUT YOU DON'T WANT TO NEGLECT PROTEIN, EITHER..."
"THANK YOU, INNER-ME. YOU'RE GREAT."
"YOU'RE BURNING THE FOOD! YOU'RE BURNING THE FOOD!"

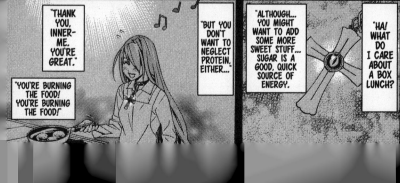

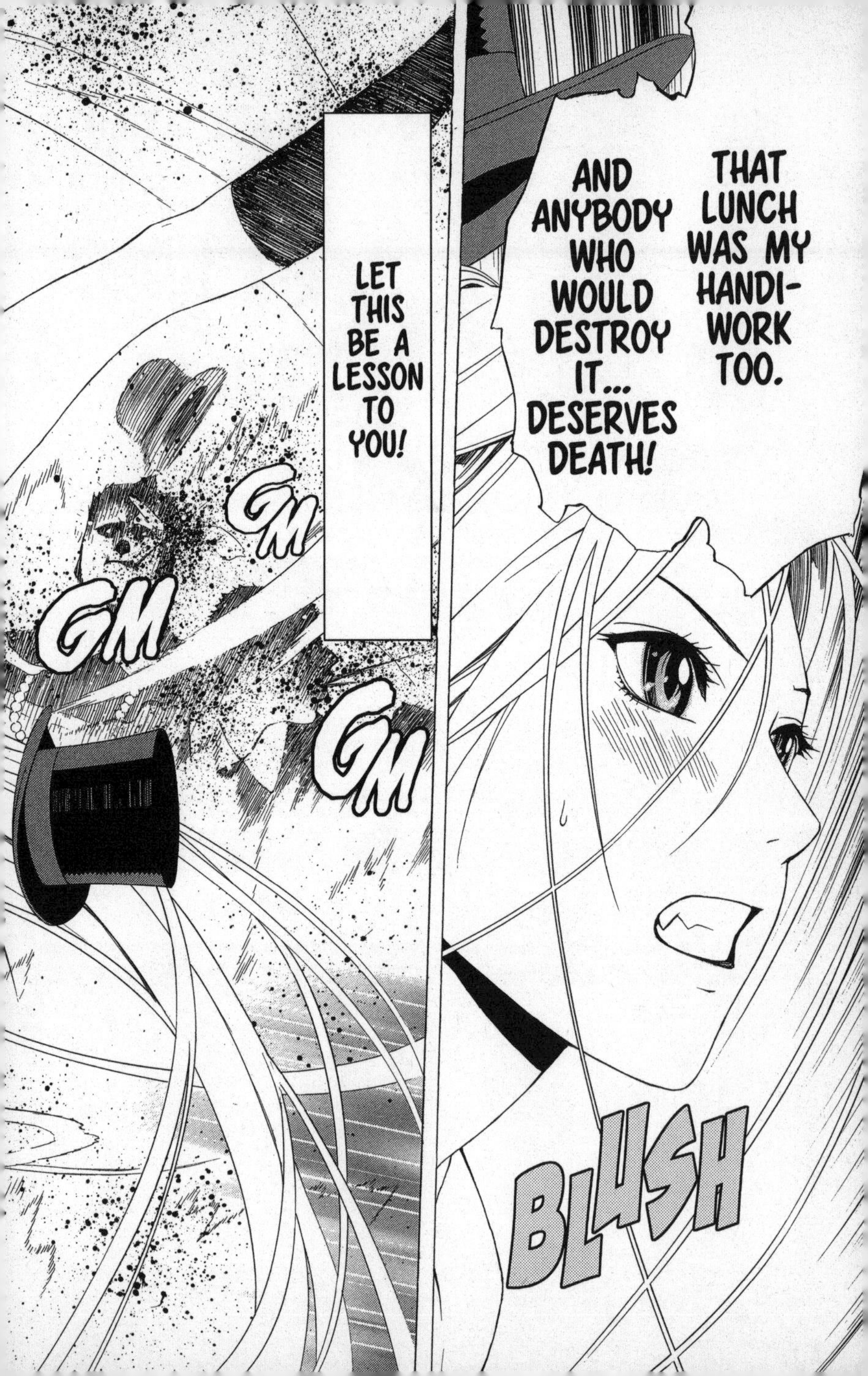
THAT LUNCH WAS MY HANDIWORK TOO.
AND ANYBODY WHO WOULD DESTROY IT... DESERVES DEATH!
BLUSH
LET THIS BE A LESSON TO YOU!
GM
GM
GM

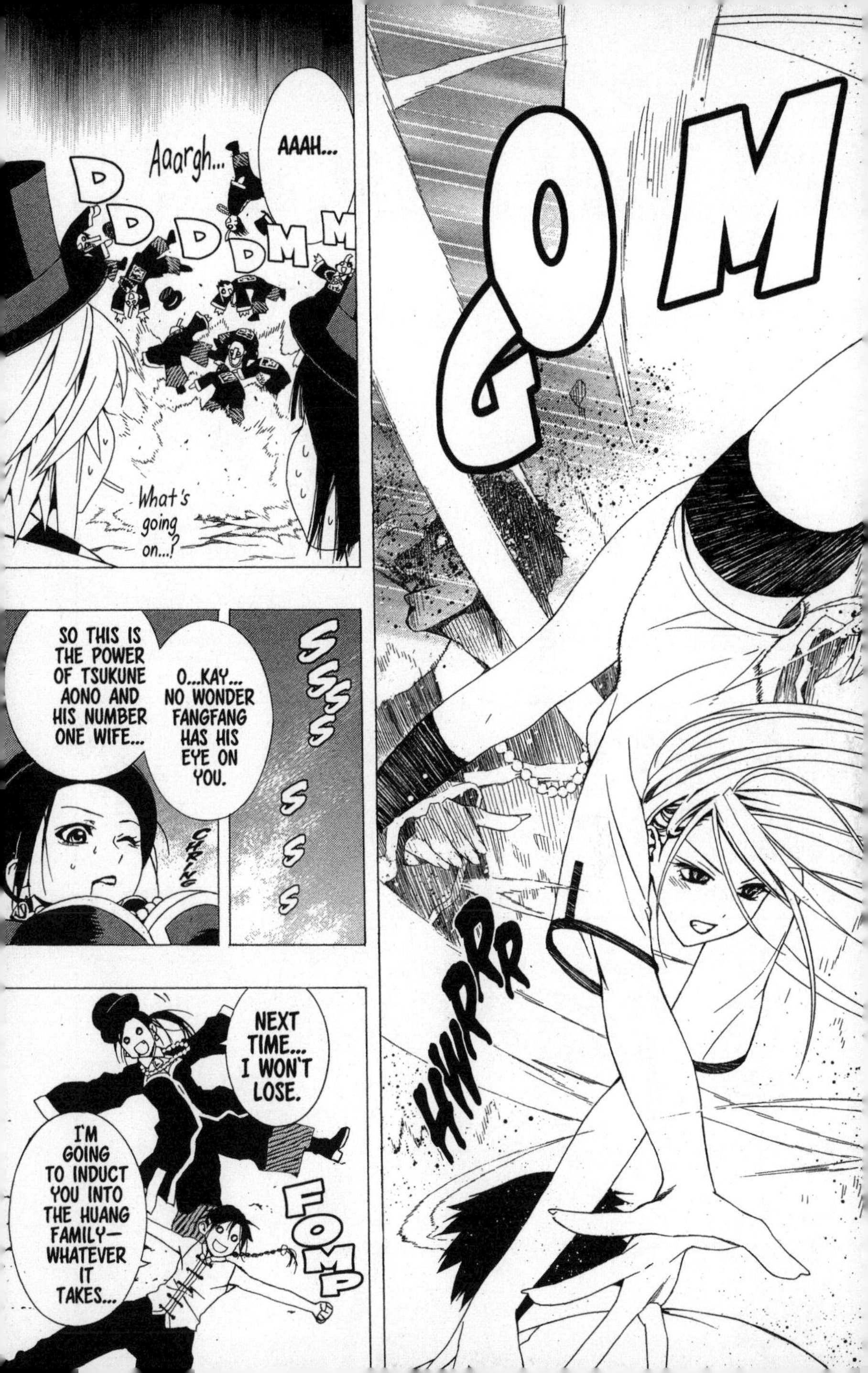
GOM
HWRRR
AAAH...
Aaargh...
DDDDDMMM
What's going on...?
SSSS SSS
CHRING
SO THIS IS THE POWER OF TSUKUNE AONO AND HIS NUMBER ONE WIFE...
O...KAY... NO WONDER FANGFANG HAS HIS EYE ON YOU.
NEXT TIME... I WON'T LOSE.
I'M GOING TO INDUCT YOU INTO THE HUANG FAMILY—WHATEVER IT TAKES...
FOMP

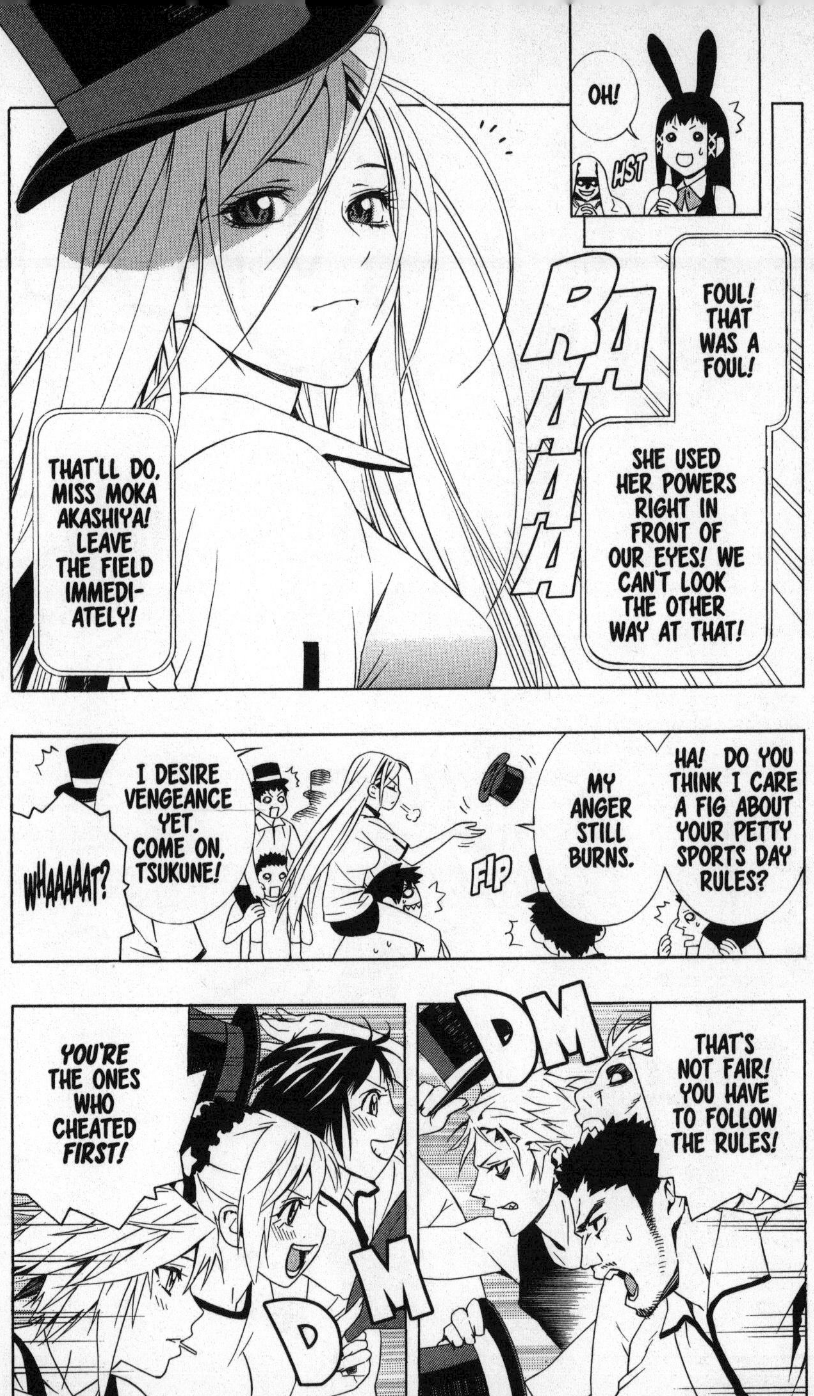
OH!
HST
FOUL! THAT WAS A FOUL!
SHE USED HER POWERS RIGHT IN FRONT OF OUR EYES! WE CAN'T LOOK THE OTHER WAY AT THAT!
RAAAAA
THAT'LL DO, MISS MOKA AKASHIYA! LEAVE THE FIELD IMMEDI-ATELY!
HA! DO YOU THINK I CARE A FIG ABOUT YOUR PETTY SPORTS DAY RULES?
MY ANGER STILL BURNS.
FLIP
I DESIRE VENGEANCE YET. COME ON, TSUKUNE!
WHAAAAAT?
THAT'S NOT FAIR! YOU HAVE TO FOLLOW THE RULES!
DM
YOU'RE THE ONES WHO CHEATED FIRST!
DM

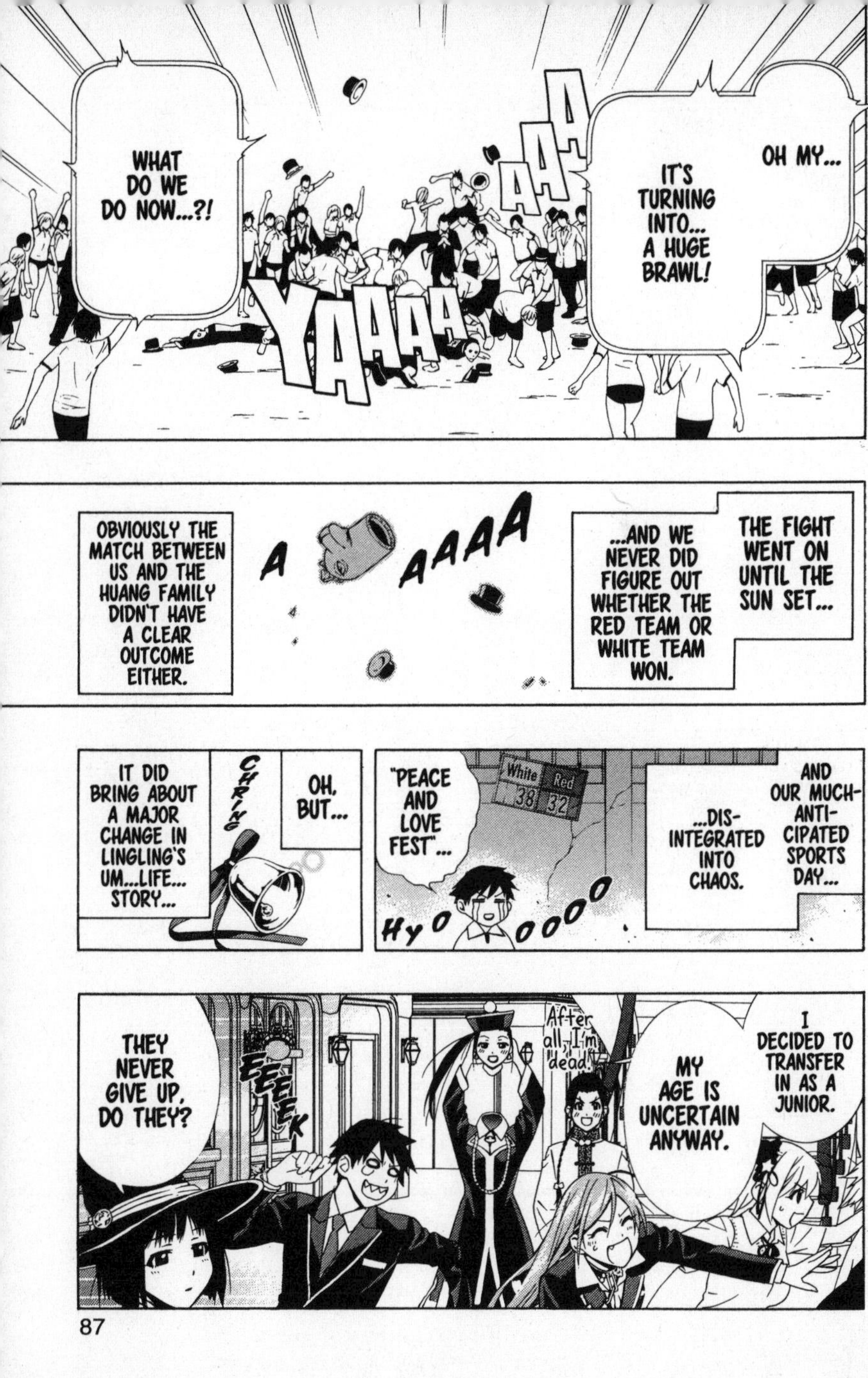
OH MY...
IT'S TURNING INTO... A HUGE BRAWL!
AAAA
YAAAA
WHAT DO WE DO NOW...?!
THE FIGHT WENT ON UNTIL THE SUN SET...
...AND WE NEVER DID FIGURE OUT WHETHER THE RED TEAM OR WHITE TEAM WON.
A AAAA
OBVIOUSLY THE MATCH BETWEEN US AND THE HUANG FAMILY DIDN'T HAVE A CLEAR OUTCOME EITHER.
AND OUR MUCH-ANTICIPATED SPORTS DAY...
...DIS-INTEGRATED INTO CHAOS.
White 38
Red 32
"PEACE AND LOVE FEST"...
HyOOOOO
OH, BUT...
CHRING
IT DID BRING ABOUT A MAJOR CHANGE IN LINGLING'S UM...LIFE... STORY...
I DECIDED TO TRANSFER IN AS A JUNIOR.
MY AGE IS UNCERTAIN ANYWAY.
After all, I'm dead.
EEEEEK
THEY NEVER GIVE UP, DO THEY?

25: Heart to Heart

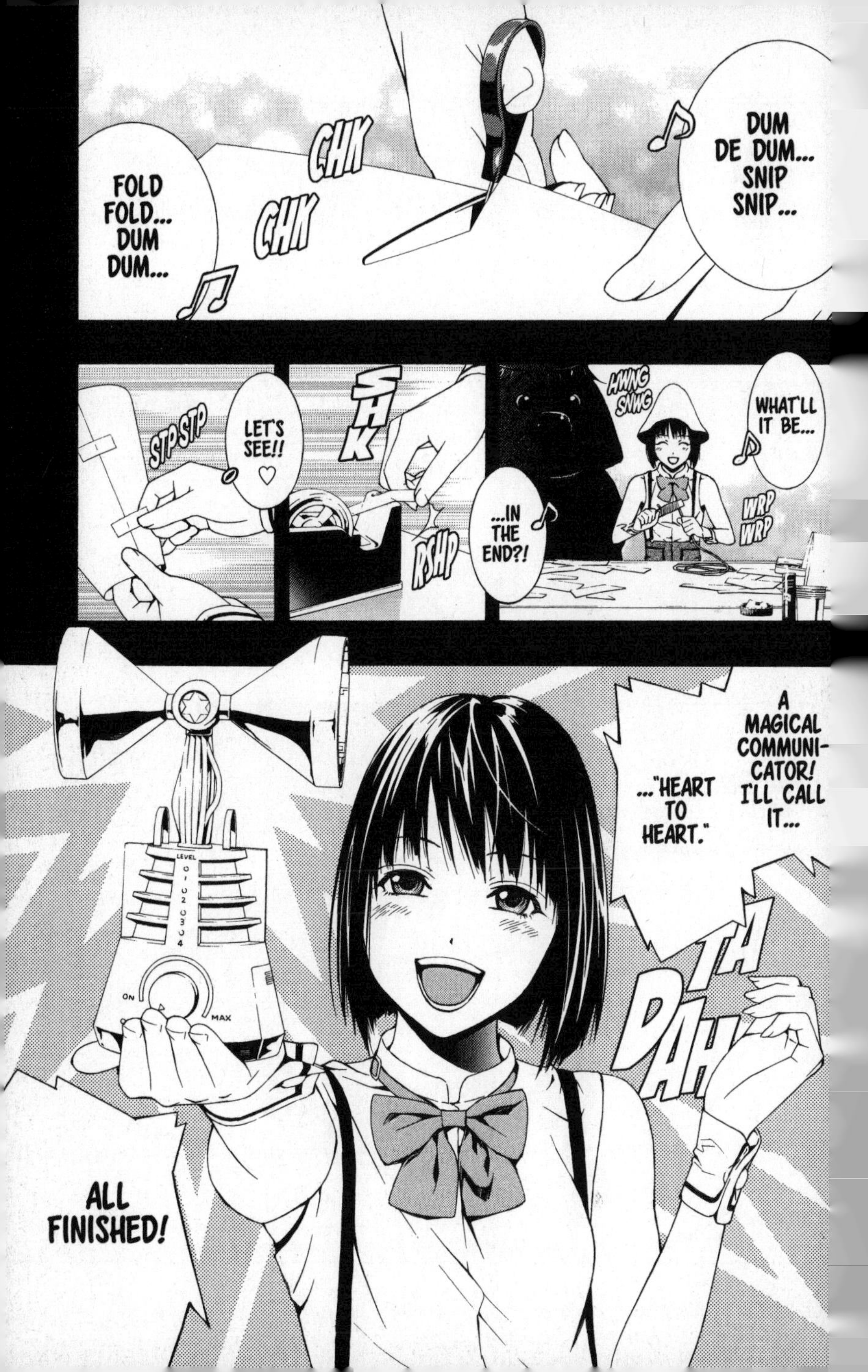
DUM DE DUM... SNIP SNIP...
CHK
CHK
FOLD FOLD... DUM DUM...
WHAT'LL IT BE...
...IN THE END?!
HWNG SNWG
WRP WRP
SHK
RSHP
LET'S SEE!! ♡
STP STP
A MAGICAL COMMUNI-CATOR! I'LL CALL IT...
..."HEART TO HEART."
TA DAH
ALL FINISHED!
LEVEL
0 1 2 3 4
ON
MAX

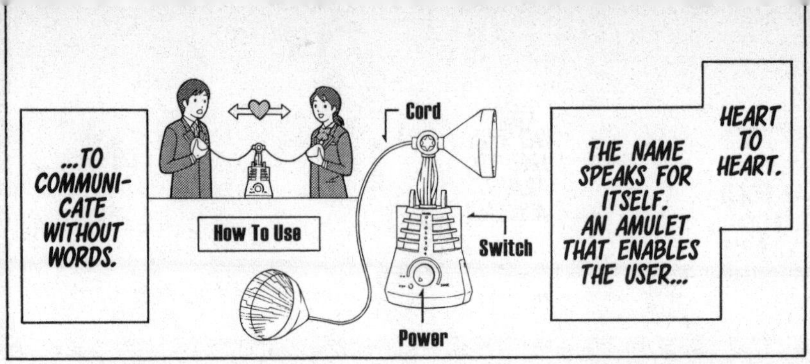
HEART TO HEART.
THE NAME SPEAKS FOR ITSELF. AN AMULET THAT ENABLES THE USER...
Cord
Switch
Power
How To Use
...TO COMMUNI-CATE WITHOUT WORDS.

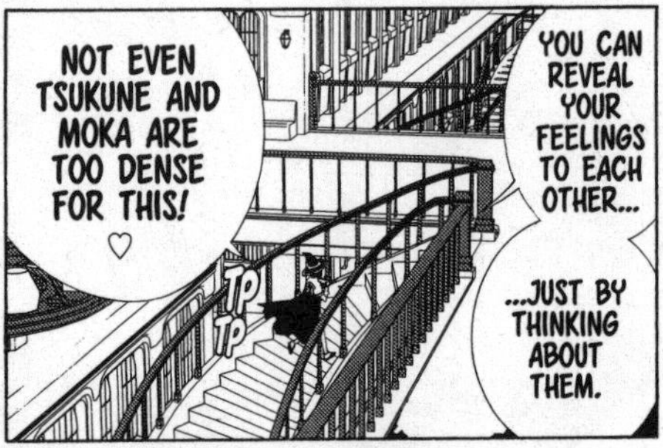
YOU CAN REVEAL YOUR FEELINGS TO EACH OTHER...
...JUST BY THINKING ABOUT THEM.
NOT EVEN TSUKUNE AND MOKA ARE TOO DENSE FOR THIS! ♡
TP TP

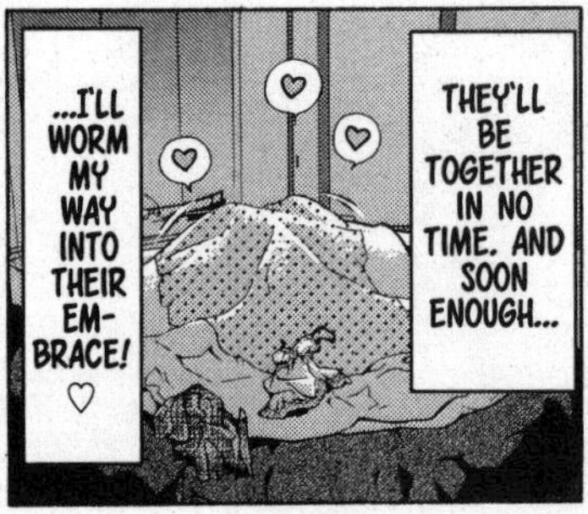
THEY'LL BE TOGETHER IN NO TIME. AND SOON ENOUGH...
...I'LL WORM MY WAY INTO THEIR EM-BRACE! ♡

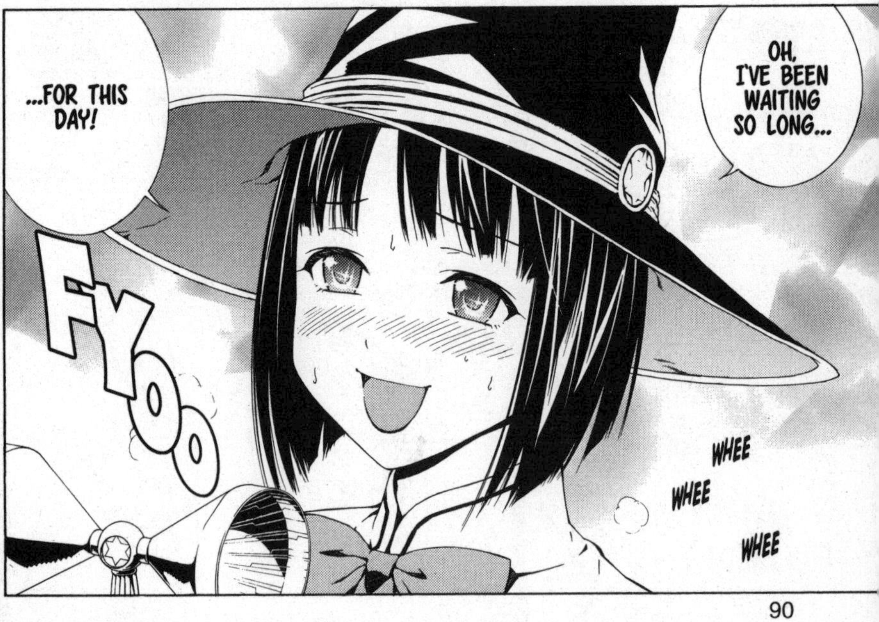
OH, I'VE BEEN WAITING SO LONG...
...FOR THIS DAY!
FYOOO
WHEE
WHEE
WHEE

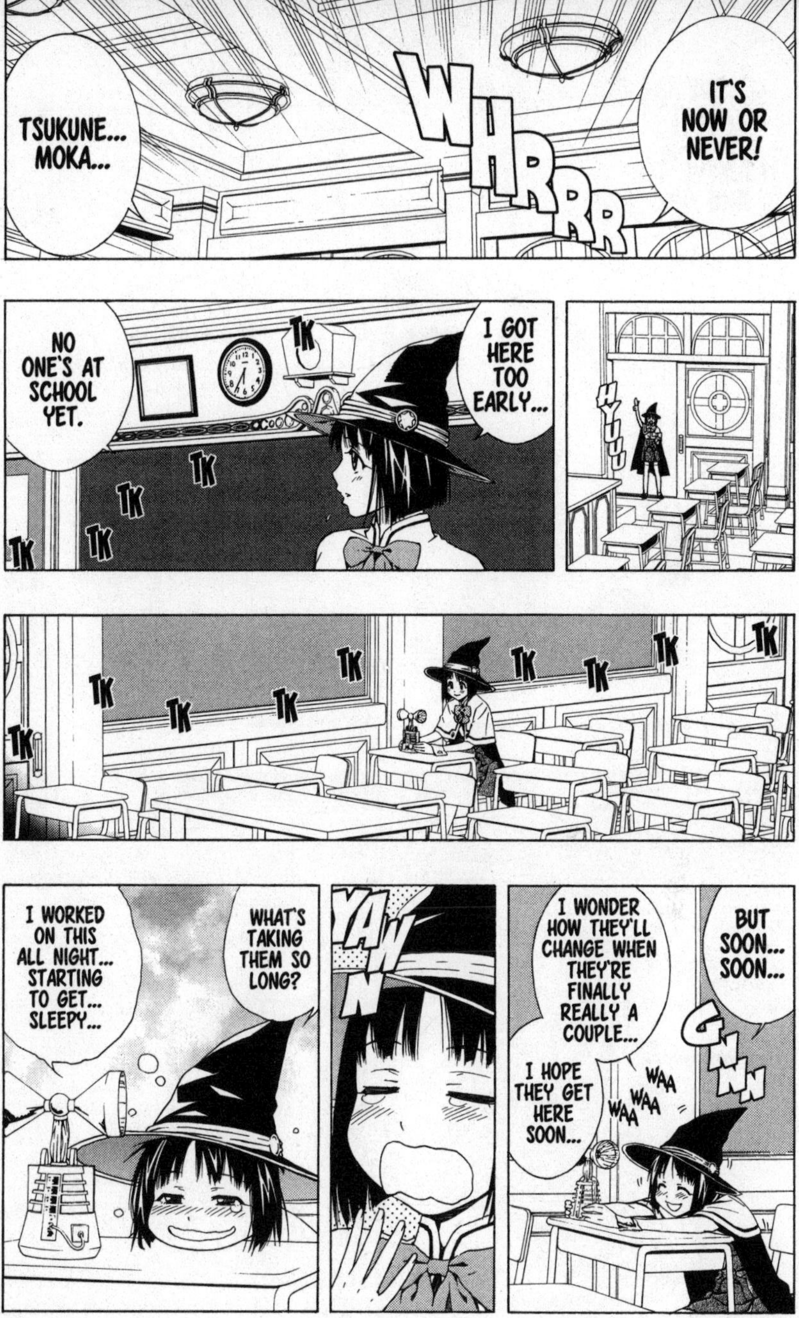
IT'S NOW OR NEVER!
WHRRRR
TSUKUNE... MOKA...
HYUUU
I GOT HERE TOO EARLY...
NO ONE'S AT SCHOOL YET.
TK TK TK TK TK
TK TK TK TK TK TK TK TK TK
BUT SOON... SOON...
GNNN
I WONDER HOW THEY'LL CHANGE WHEN THEY'RE FINALLY REALLY A COUPLE...
I HOPE THEY GET HERE SOON...
WAA WAA WAA
YAWN
WHAT'S TAKING THEM SO LONG?
I WORKED ON THIS ALL NIGHT... STARTING TO GET... SLEEPY...

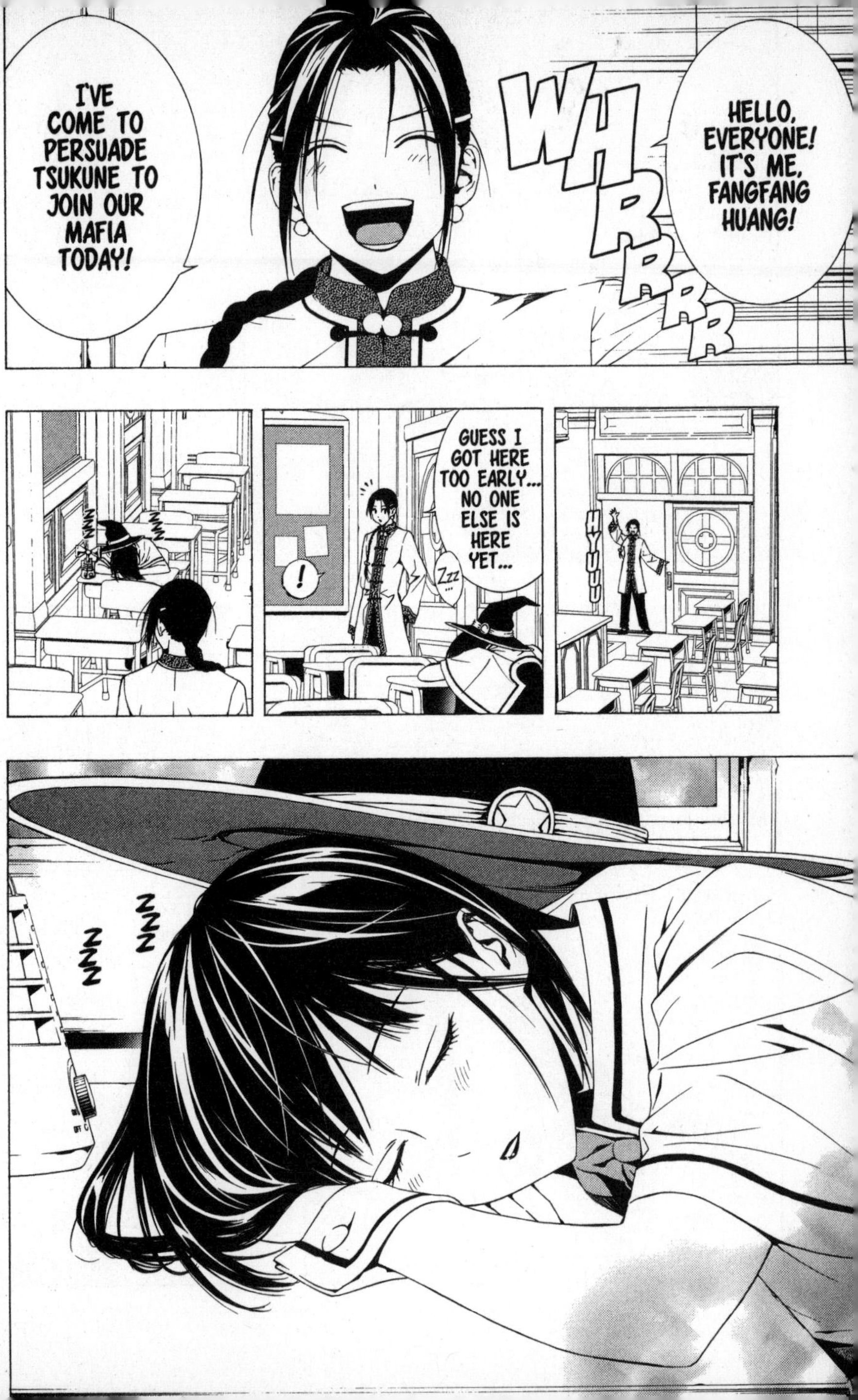
HELLO, EVERYONE! IT'S ME, FANGFANG HUANG!
WHRRRR
I'VE COME TO PERSUADE TSUKUNE TO JOIN OUR MAFIA TODAY!
HYUUU
GUESS I GOT HERE TOO EARLY... NO ONE ELSE IS HERE YET...
!
Zzz...
ZZZ
ZZZ
ZZZ
ZZZ

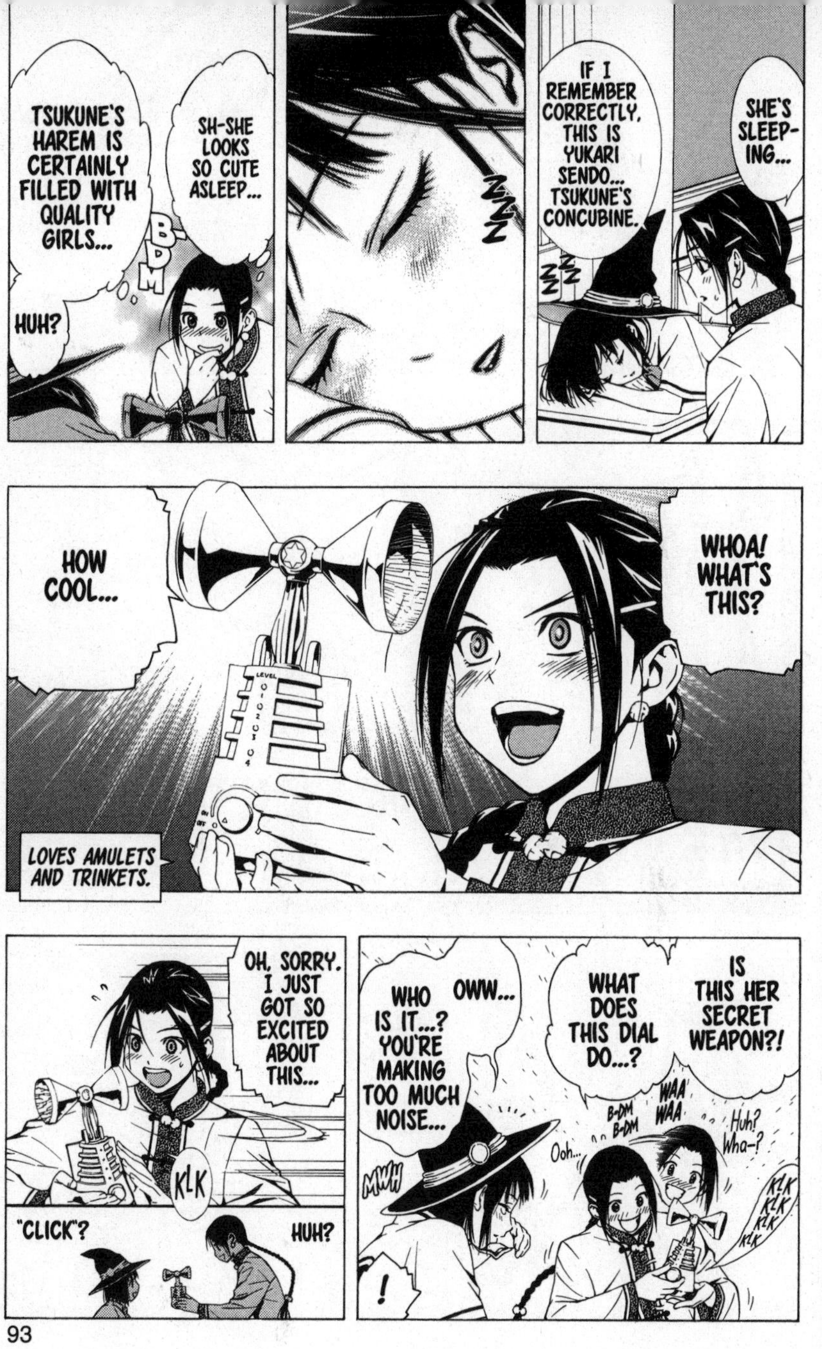
SHE'S SLEEPING...
IF I REMEMBER CORRECTLY, THIS IS YUKARI SENDO... TSUKUNE'S CONCUBINE.
ZZZ
ZZZ
SH-SHE LOOKS SO CUTE ASLEEP...
TSUKUNE'S HAREM IS CERTAINLY FILLED WITH QUALITY GIRLS...
BDM
HUH?
WHOA! WHAT'S THIS?
HOW COOL...
LOVES AMULETS AND TRINKETS.
IS THIS HER SECRET WEAPON?!
WHAT DOES THIS DIAL DO...?
OWW...
WHO IS IT...? YOU'RE MAKING TOO MUCH NOISE...
WAA WAA
B-DM B-DM
Huh? Wha-?
Ooh...
KLK KLK KLK KLK
MWH
!
OH, SORRY. I JUST GOT SO EXCITED ABOUT THIS...
KLK
HUH?
"CLICK"?

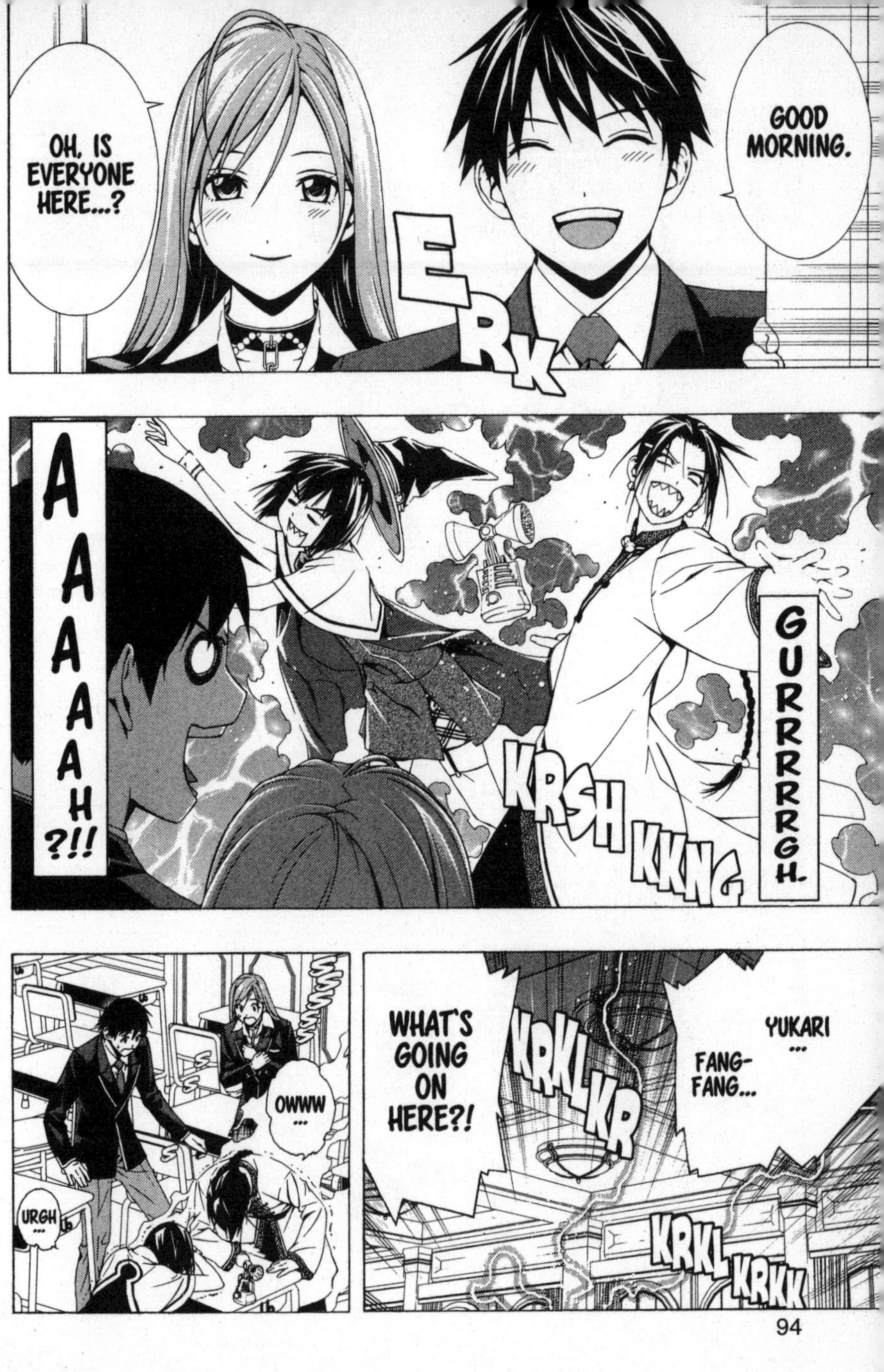
GOOD MORNING.
OH, IS EVERYONE HERE...?
ERK
GURRRRRGH.
KKNG
KRSH
AAAAAH?!!
YUKARI...
FANG-FANG...
KRKLKR
WHAT'S GOING ON HERE?!
KRKL KRKK
OWWW...
URGH...

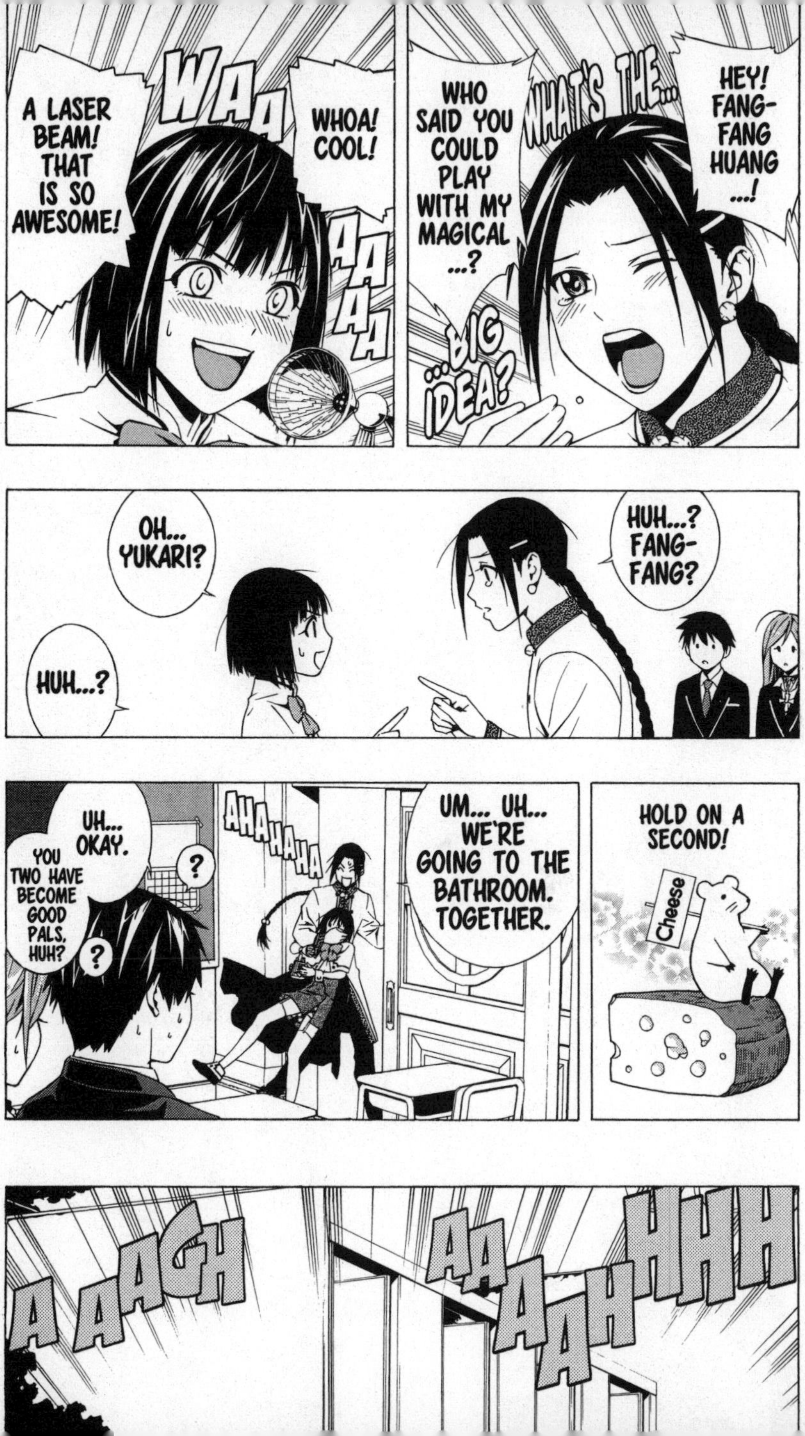
HEY! FANG-FANG HUANG ...!
WHAT'S THE...
WHO SAID YOU COULD PLAY WITH MY MAGICAL ...?
...BIG IDEA?
WHOA! COOL!
WAA AAAA
A LASER BEAM! THAT IS SO AWESOME!
HUH...? FANG-FANG?
OH... YUKARI?
HUH...?
HOLD ON A SECOND!
Cheese
UM... UH... WE'RE GOING TO THE BATHROOM. TOGETHER.
AHAHAHAHA
?
UH... OKAY.
YOU TWO HAVE BECOME GOOD PALS, HUH?
?
AAAAAHHHHH
A AAAGH

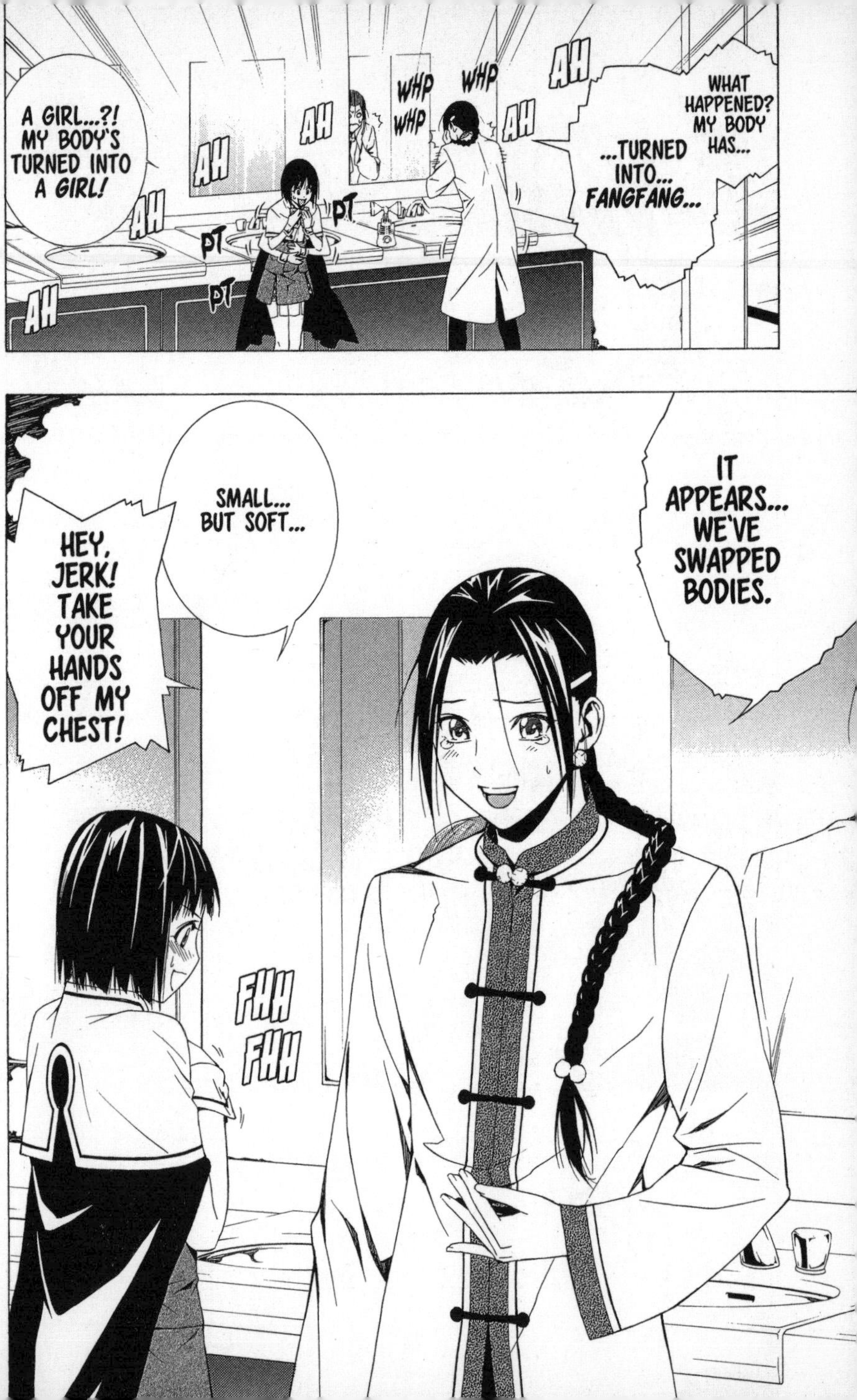
AH
WHAT HAPPENED? MY BODY HAS...
...TURNED INTO... FANGFANG...
AH
WHP WHP
WHP
AH
AH
A GIRL...?! MY BODY'S TURNED INTO A GIRL!
AH
PT
PT
PT
AH
IT APPEARS... WE'VE SWAPPED BODIES.
SMALL... BUT SOFT...
HEY, JERK! TAKE YOUR HANDS OFF MY CHEST!
FHH FHH

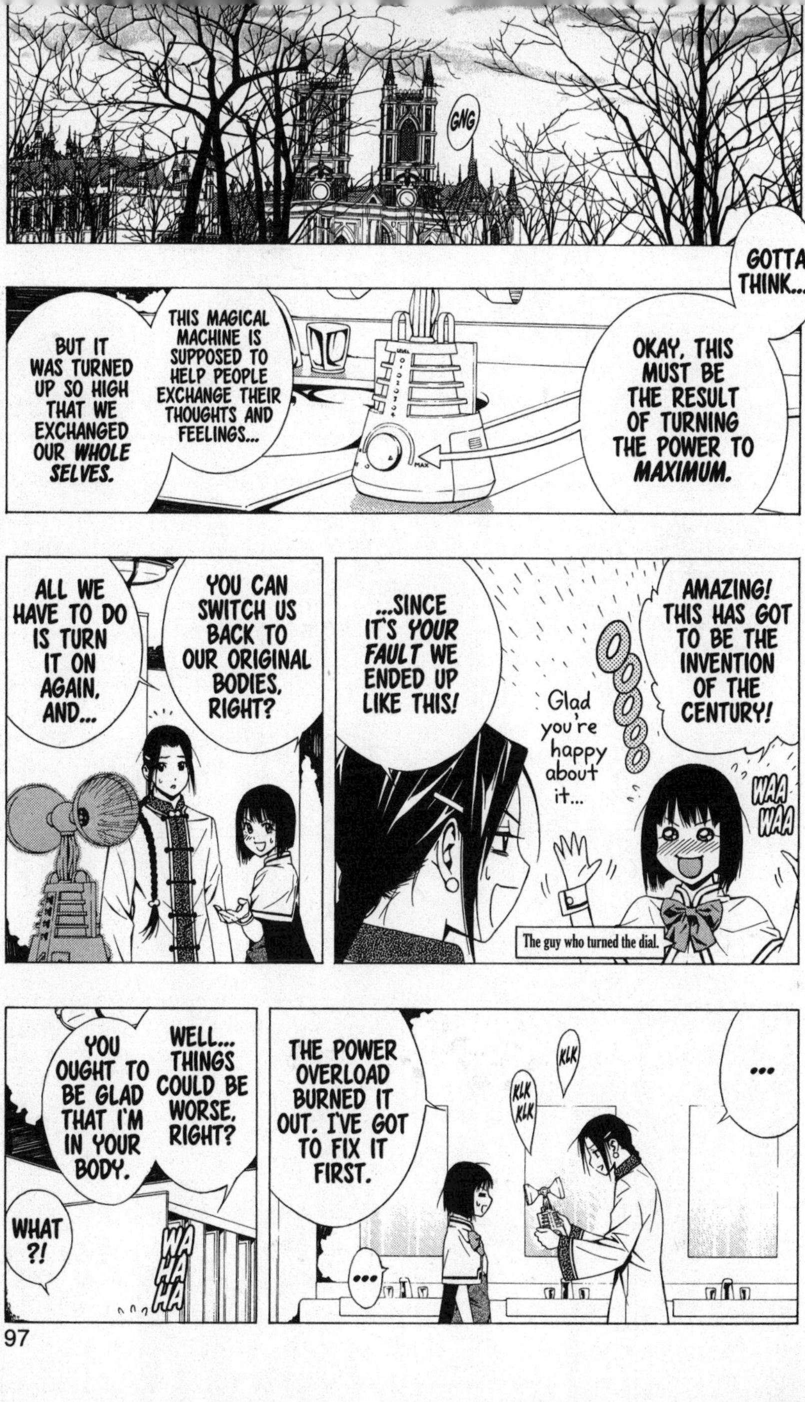
GNG
GOTTA THINK...
OKAY, THIS MUST BE THE RESULT OF TURNING THE POWER TO *MAXIMUM.*
THIS MAGICAL MACHINE IS SUPPOSED TO HELP PEOPLE EXCHANGE THEIR THOUGHTS AND FEELINGS...
BUT IT WAS TURNED UP SO HIGH THAT WE EXCHANGED OUR *WHOLE SELVES.*
AMAZING! THIS HAS GOT TO BE THE INVENTION OF THE CENTURY!
WAA WAA
Glad you're happy about it...
...SINCE IT'S *YOUR FAULT* WE ENDED UP LIKE THIS!
The guy who turned the dial.
YOU CAN SWITCH US BACK TO OUR ORIGINAL BODIES, RIGHT?
ALL WE HAVE TO DO IS TURN IT ON AGAIN, AND...
...
KLK
KLK KLK
THE POWER OVERLOAD BURNED IT OUT. I'VE GOT TO FIX IT FIRST.
...
WELL... THINGS COULD BE WORSE, RIGHT?
YOU OUGHT TO BE GLAD THAT I'M IN YOUR BODY.
WHAT?!
WA HA HA HA

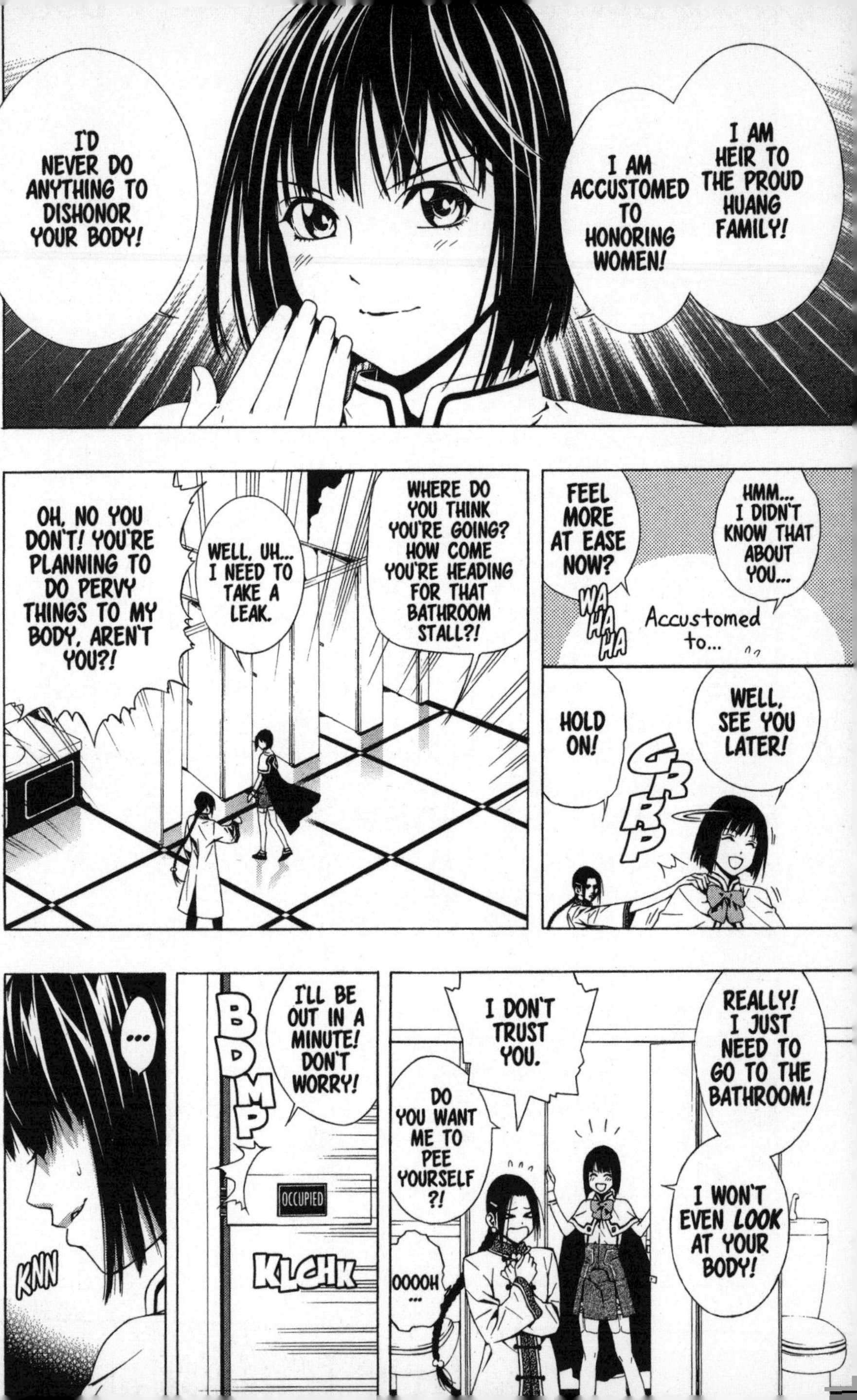
I AM HEIR TO THE PROUD HUANG FAMILY!
I AM ACCUSTOMED TO HONORING WOMEN!
I'D NEVER DO ANYTHING TO DISHONOR YOUR BODY!
HMM... I DIDN'T KNOW THAT ABOUT YOU...
Accustomed to...
FEEL MORE AT EASE NOW?
WA HA HA
WELL, SEE YOU LATER!
HOLD ON!
GRRP
WHERE DO YOU THINK YOU'RE GOING? HOW COME YOU'RE HEADING FOR THAT BATHROOM STALL?!
WELL, UH... I NEED TO TAKE A LEAK.
OH, NO YOU DON'T! YOU'RE PLANNING TO DO PERVY THINGS TO MY BODY, AREN'T YOU?!
REALLY! I JUST NEED TO GO TO THE BATHROOM!
I DON'T TRUST YOU.
I WON'T EVEN *LOOK* AT YOUR BODY!
DO YOU WANT ME TO PEE YOURSELF?!
OOOOH...
I'LL BE OUT IN A MINUTE! DON'T WORRY!
BDMP
OCCUPIED
KLCHK
...
KNN

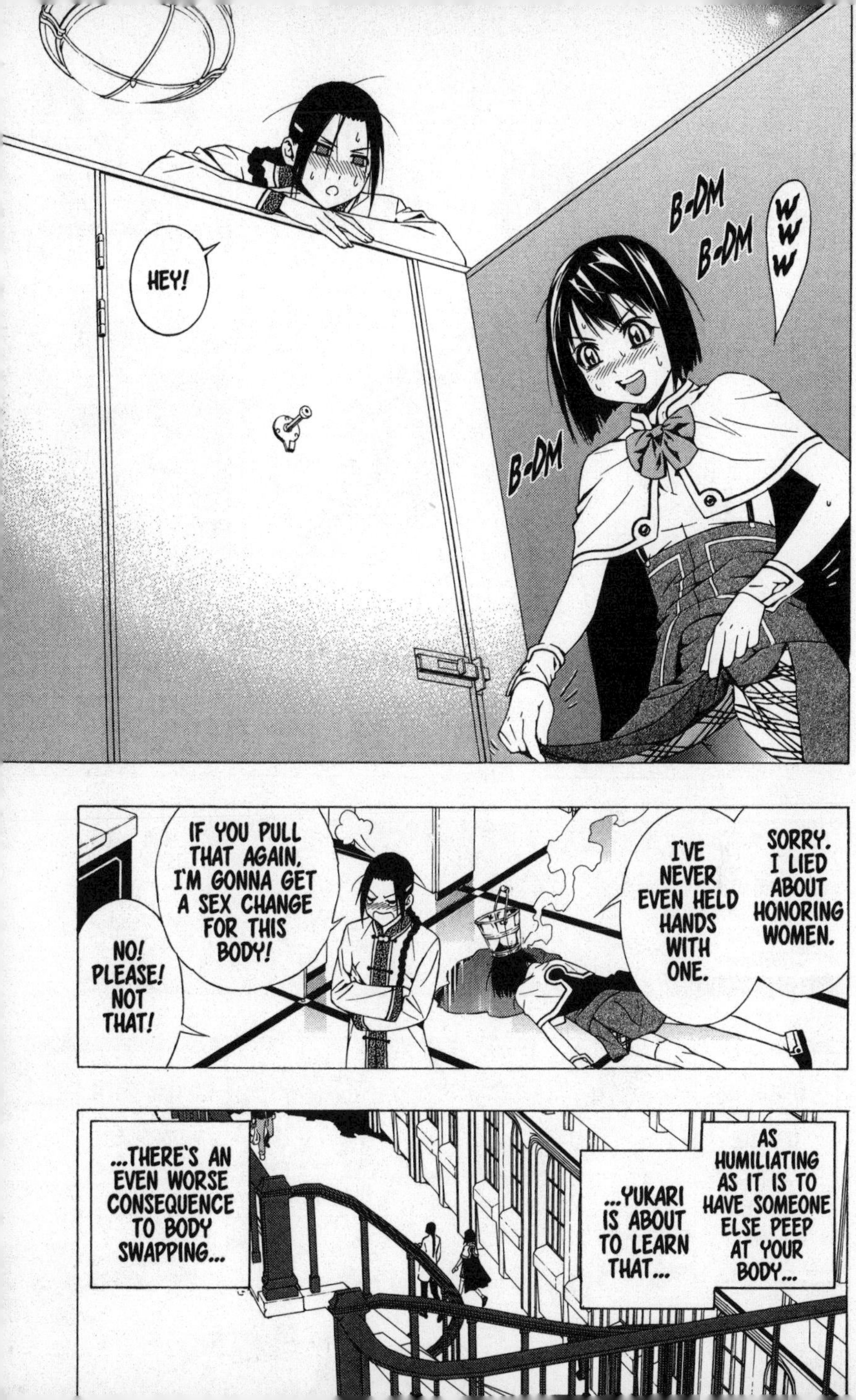
WWW
B-DM
B-DM
HEY!
B-DM
SORRY. I LIED ABOUT HONORING WOMEN.
I'VE NEVER EVEN HELD HANDS WITH ONE.
IF YOU PULL THAT AGAIN, I'M GONNA GET A SEX CHANGE FOR THIS BODY!
NO! PLEASE! NOT THAT!
AS HUMILIATING AS IT IS TO HAVE SOMEONE ELSE PEEP AT YOUR BODY...
...YUKARI IS ABOUT TO LEARN THAT...
...THERE'S AN EVEN WORSE CONSEQUENCE TO BODY SWAPPING...

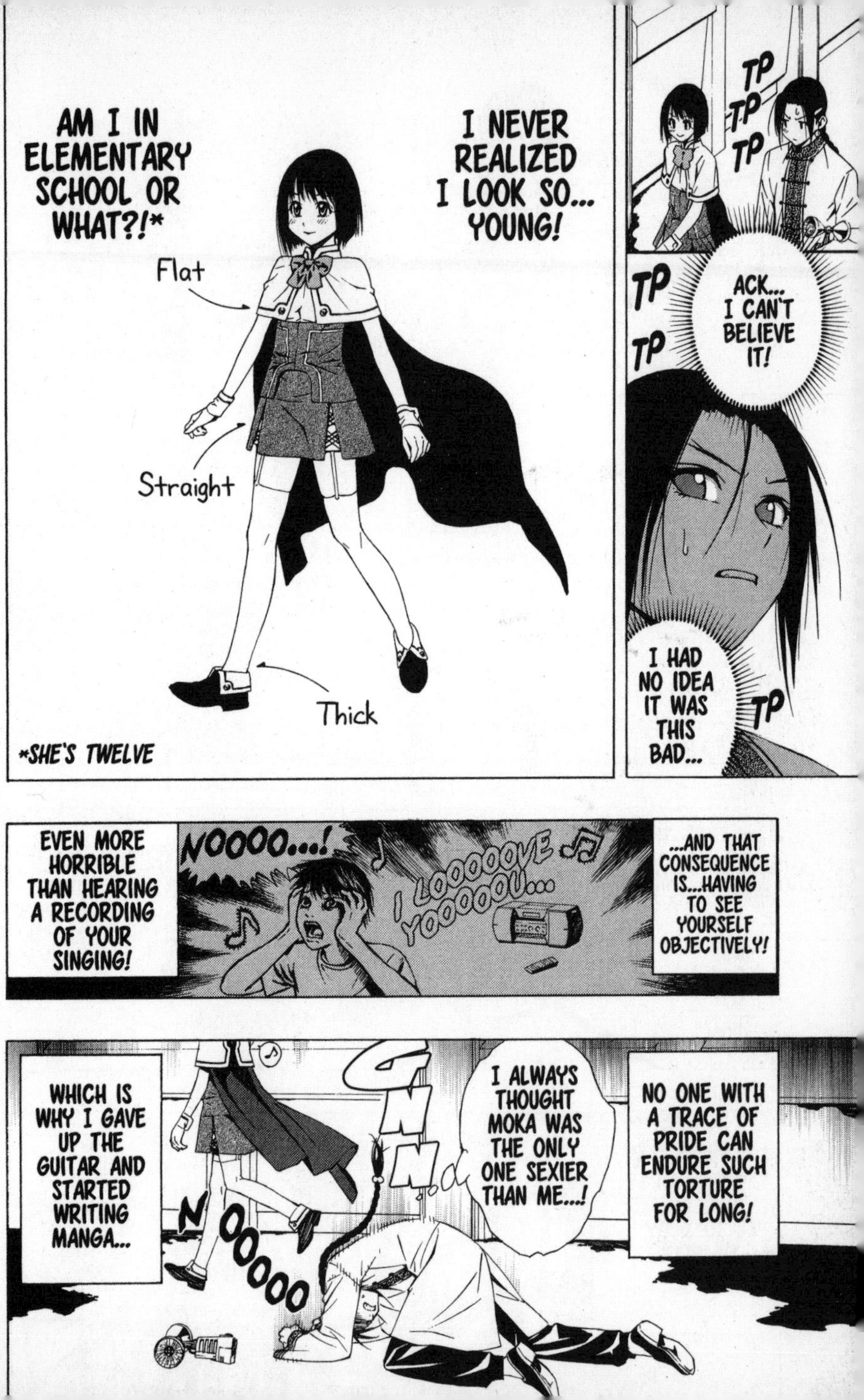
TP
TP
TP
TP
TP
ACK... I CAN'T BELIEVE IT!
I HAD NO IDEA IT WAS THIS BAD...
TP
I NEVER REALIZED I LOOK SO... YOUNG!
AM I IN ELEMENTARY SCHOOL OR WHAT?!*
Flat
Straight
Thick
*SHE'S TWELVE
...AND THAT CONSEQUENCE IS...HAVING TO SEE YOURSELF OBJECTIVELY!
I LOOOOOVE YOOOOOU...
NOOOO...!
EVEN MORE HORRIBLE THAN HEARING A RECORDING OF YOUR SINGING!
NO ONE WITH A TRACE OF PRIDE CAN ENDURE SUCH TORTURE FOR LONG!
I ALWAYS THOUGHT MOKA WAS THE ONLY ONE SEXIER THAN ME...!
NOOOOO
WHICH IS WHY I GAVE UP THE GUITAR AND STARTED WRITING MANGA...

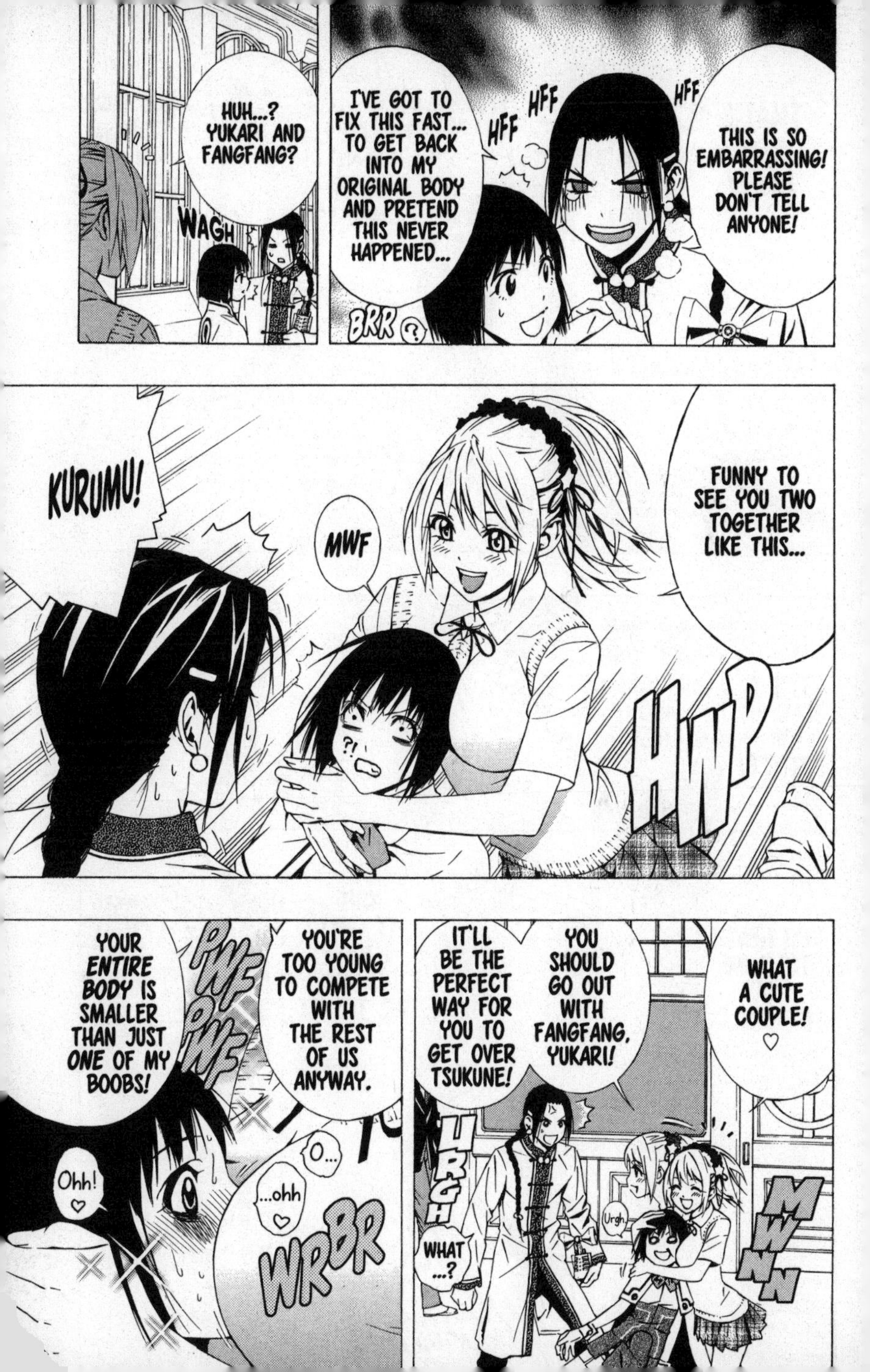
THIS IS SO EMBARRASSING! PLEASE DON'T TELL ANYONE!
HFF
HFF
HFF
I'VE GOT TO FIX THIS FAST... TO GET BACK INTO MY ORIGINAL BODY AND PRETEND THIS NEVER HAPPENED...
BRR
?
HUH...? YUKARI AND FANGFANG?
WAGH
FUNNY TO SEE YOU TWO TOGETHER LIKE THIS...
HNP
MWF
KURUMU!
?!
WHAT A CUTE COUPLE! ♡
YOU SHOULD GO OUT WITH FANGFANG, YUKARI!
IT'LL BE THE PERFECT WAY FOR YOU TO GET OVER TSUKUNE!
URGH
WHAT ...?
Urgh
MWNN
YOU'RE TOO YOUNG TO COMPETE WITH THE REST OF US ANYWAY.
YOUR ENTIRE BODY IS SMALLER THAN JUST ONE OF MY BOOBS!
PWF
PWF
O... ...ohh ♡
WRBR
Ohh! ♡

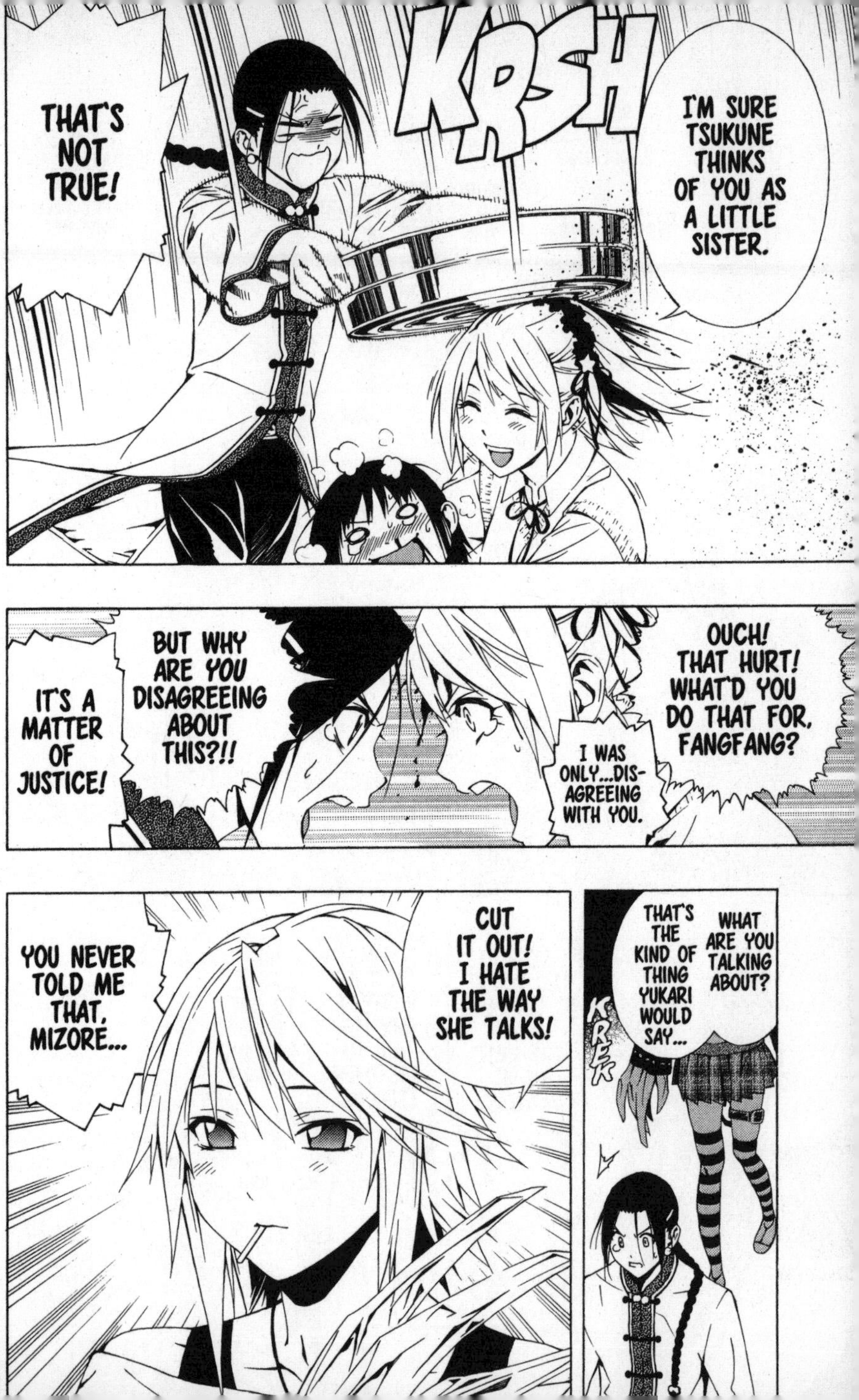
I'M SURE TSUKUNE THINKS OF YOU AS A LITTLE SISTER.
KRSH
THAT'S NOT TRUE!
OUCH! THAT HURT! WHAT'D YOU DO THAT FOR, FANGFANG?
I WAS ONLY...DIS-AGREEING WITH YOU.
BUT WHY ARE YOU DISAGREEING ABOUT THIS?!!
IT'S A MATTER OF JUSTICE!
WHAT ARE YOU TALKING ABOUT?
THAT'S THE KIND OF THING YUKARI WOULD SAY...
KREK
CUT IT OUT! I HATE THE WAY SHE TALKS!
YOU NEVER TOLD ME THAT, MIZORE...

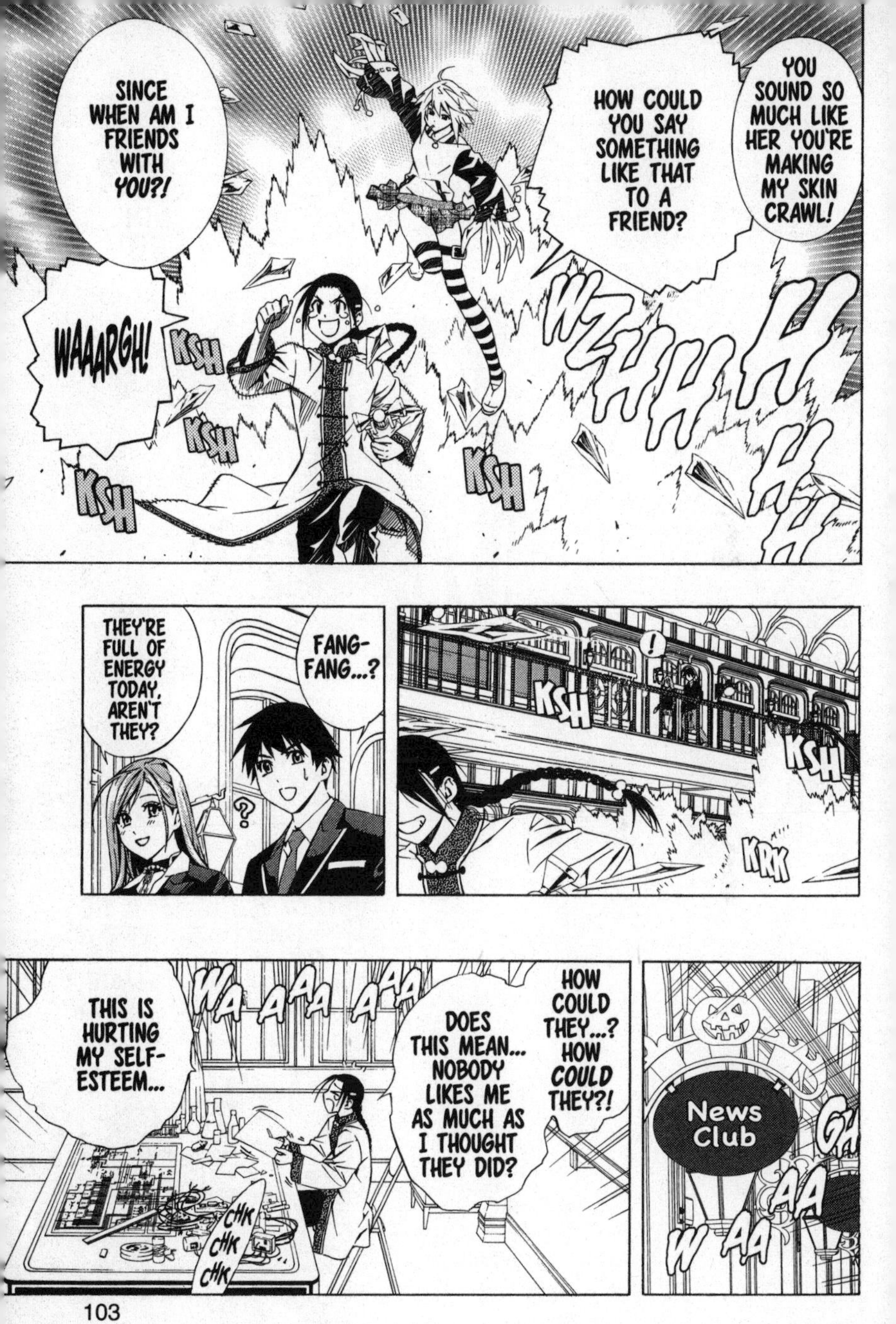
YOU SOUND SO MUCH LIKE HER YOU'RE MAKING MY SKIN CRAWL!
HOW COULD YOU SAY SOMETHING LIKE THAT TO A FRIEND?
SINCE WHEN AM I FRIENDS WITH YOU?!
WZHHHHH
WAAARGH!
KSH
KSH
KSH
KSH
!
KSH
KSH
KRK
FANG-FANG...?
THEY'RE FULL OF ENERGY TODAY, AREN'T THEY?
?
News Club
GA
AA
W AA
HOW COULD THEY...? HOW COULD THEY?!
DOES THIS MEAN... NOBODY LIKES ME AS MUCH AS I THOUGHT THEY DID?
WA A AA A AA
THIS IS HURTING MY SELF-ESTEEM...
CHK CHK CHK

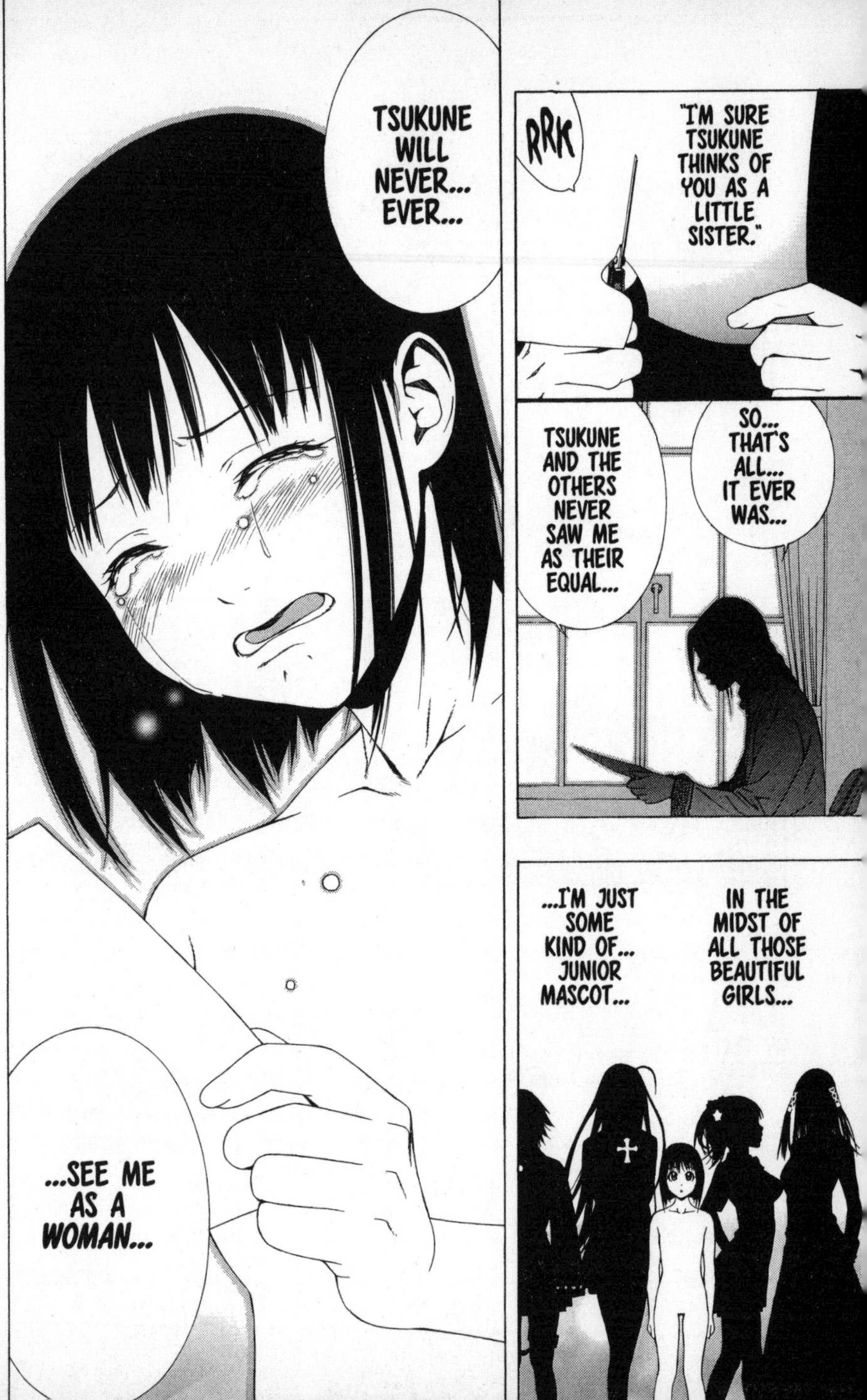
"I'M SURE TSUKUNE THINKS OF YOU AS A LITTLE SISTER."
RRK
SO... THAT'S ALL... IT EVER WAS...
TSUKUNE AND THE OTHERS NEVER SAW ME AS THEIR EQUAL...
IN THE MIDST OF ALL THOSE BEAUTIFUL GIRLS...
...I'M JUST SOME KIND OF... JUNIOR MASCOT...
TSUKUNE WILL NEVER... EVER...
...SEE ME AS A WOMAN...

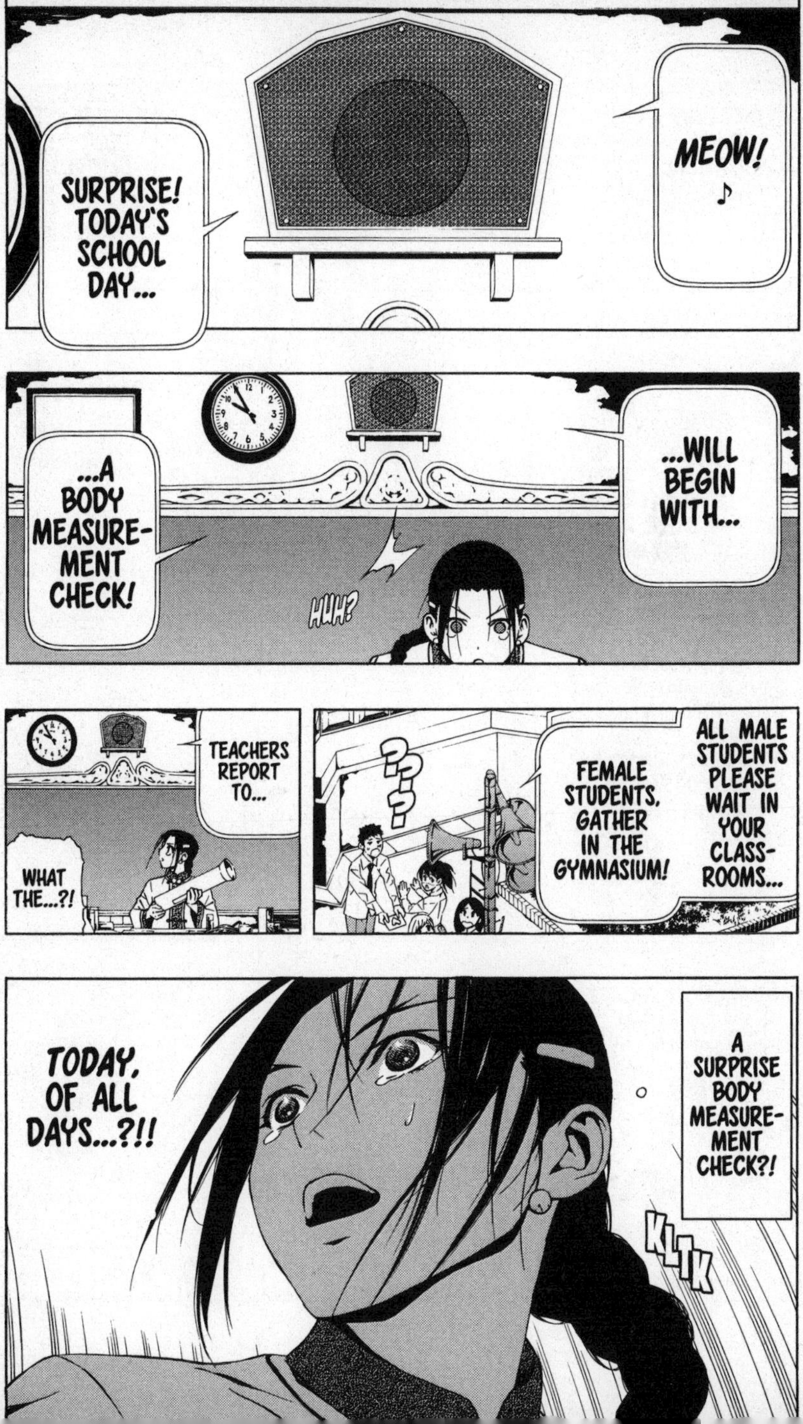
MEOW! ♪
SURPRISE! TODAY'S SCHOOL DAY...
...WILL BEGIN WITH...
...A BODY MEASUREMENT CHECK!
HUH?
ALL MALE STUDENTS PLEASE WAIT IN YOUR CLASSROOMS...
FEMALE STUDENTS, GATHER IN THE GYMNASIUM!
?!?!
TEACHERS REPORT TO...
WHAT THE...?!
A SURPRISE BODY MEASUREMENT CHECK?!
KLIK
TODAY, OF ALL DAYS...?!!

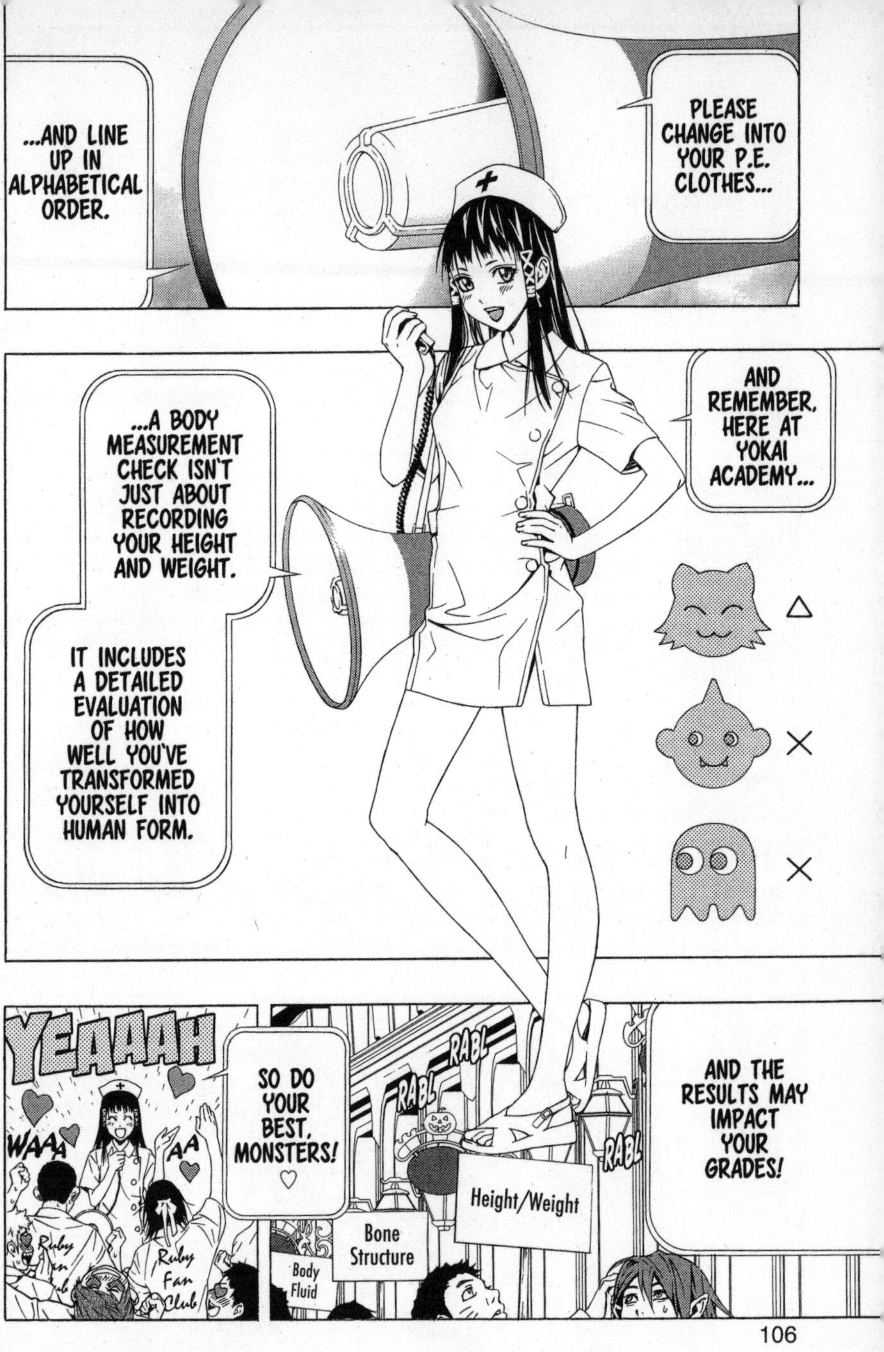
PLEASE CHANGE INTO YOUR P.E. CLOTHES...
...AND LINE UP IN ALPHABETICAL ORDER.
AND REMEMBER, HERE AT YOKAI ACADEMY...
...A BODY MEASUREMENT CHECK ISN'T JUST ABOUT RECORDING YOUR HEIGHT AND WEIGHT.
IT INCLUDES A DETAILED EVALUATION OF HOW WELL YOU'VE TRANSFORMED YOURSELF INTO HUMAN FORM.
AND THE RESULTS MAY IMPACT YOUR GRADES!
RABL
RABL
RABL
Height/Weight
Bone Structure
Body Fluid
SO DO YOUR BEST, MONSTERS! ♡
YEAAAH
WAAA
AA
Ruby Fan Club

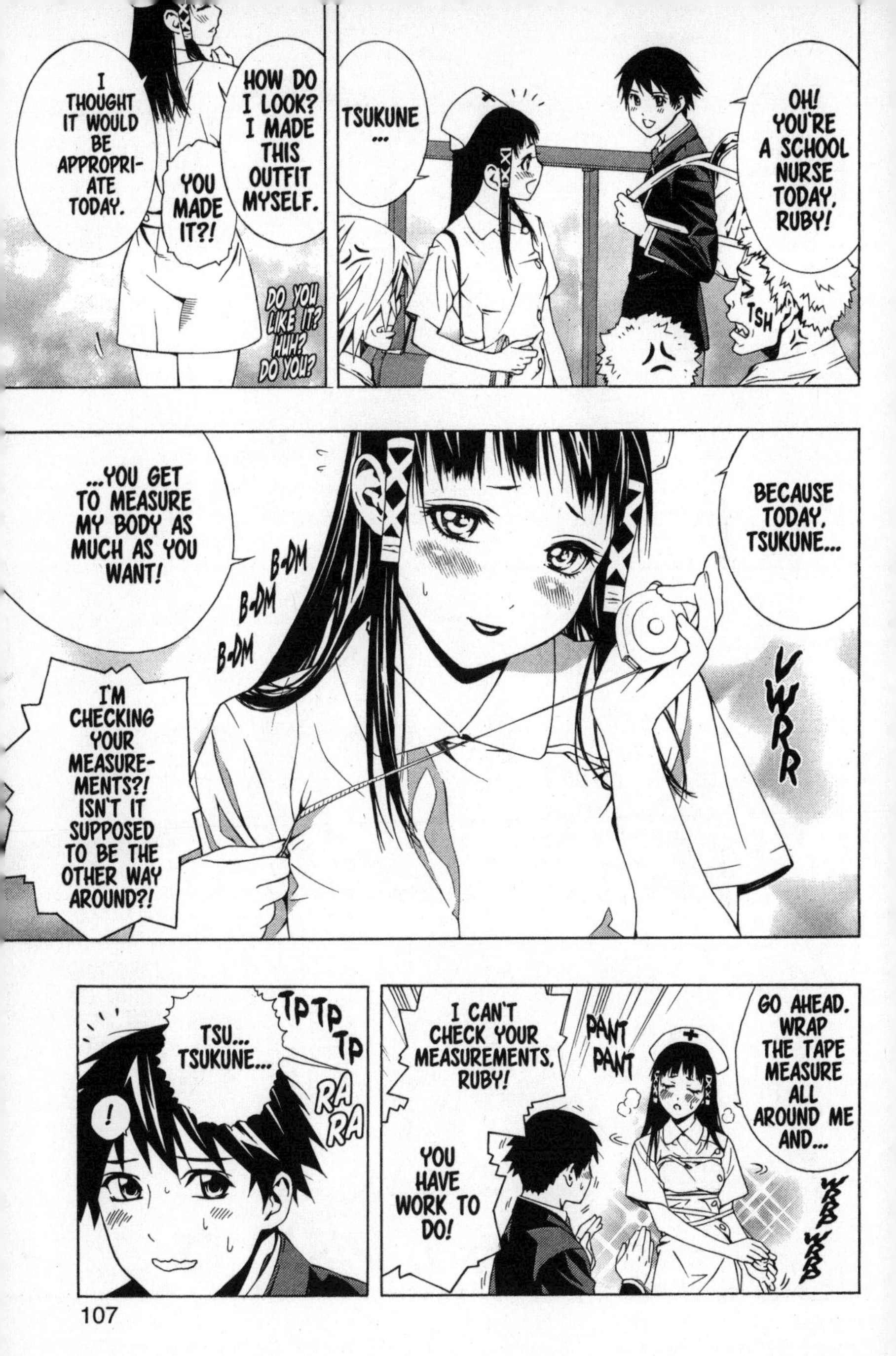
OH! YOU'RE A SCHOOL NURSE TODAY, RUBY!
TSH
TSUKUNE...
HOW DO I LOOK? I MADE THIS OUTFIT MYSELF.
YOU MADE IT?!
I THOUGHT IT WOULD BE APPROPRIATE TODAY.
DO YOU LIKE IT? HUH? DO YOU?
BECAUSE TODAY, TSUKUNE...
...YOU GET TO MEASURE MY BODY AS MUCH AS YOU WANT!
B-DM B-DM B-DM
VWRR
I'M CHECKING YOUR MEASUREMENTS?! ISN'T IT SUPPOSED TO BE THE OTHER WAY AROUND?!
GO AHEAD. WRAP THE TAPE MEASURE ALL AROUND ME AND...
WRRP WRRP
PANT PANT
I CAN'T CHECK YOUR MEASUREMENTS, RUBY!
YOU HAVE WORK TO DO!
TP TP TP TP
RA RA
TSU... TSUKUNE...
!

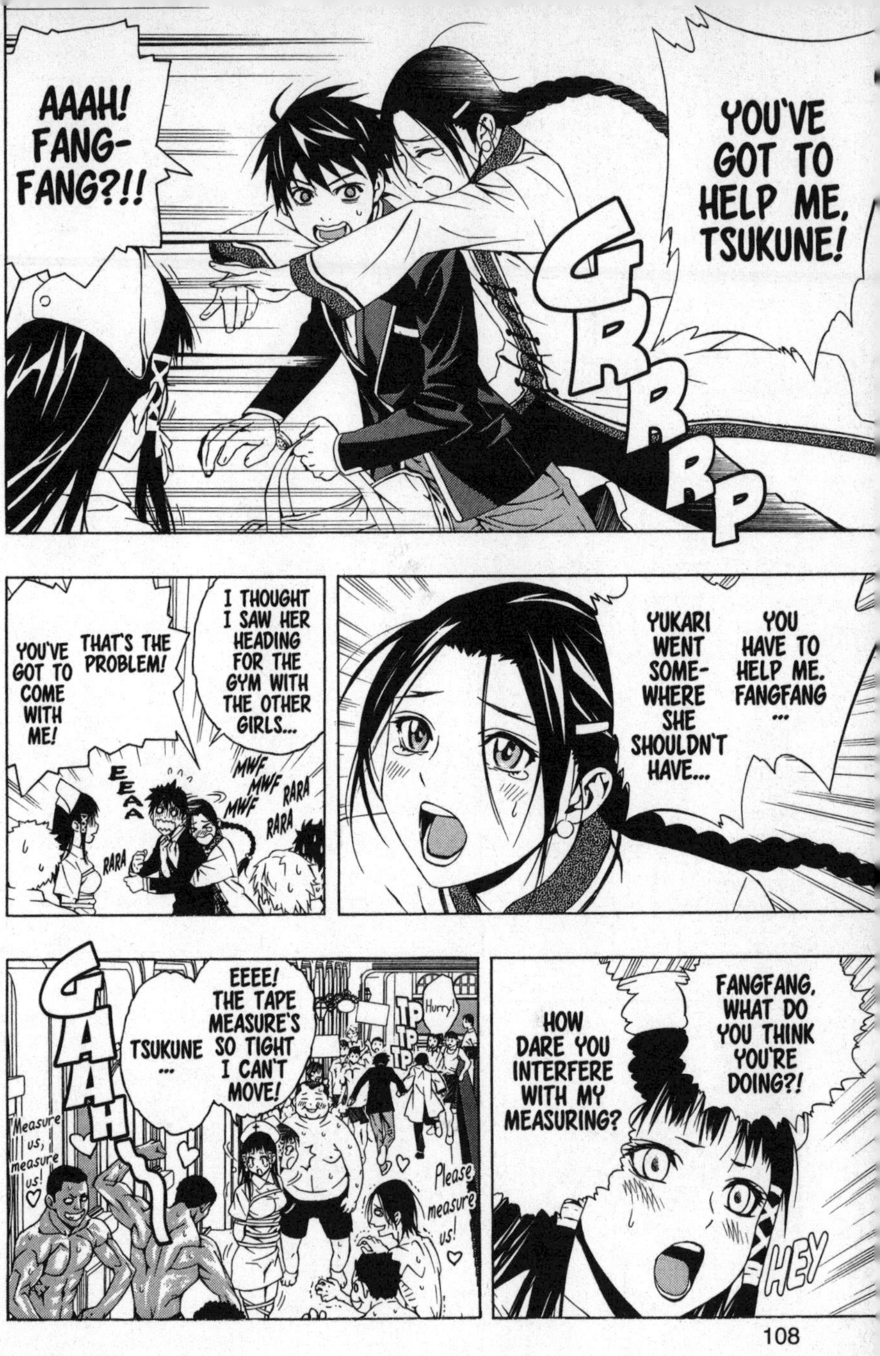
YOU'VE GOT TO HELP ME, TSUKUNE!
GRRRP
AAAH! FANG-FANG?!!
YOU HAVE TO HELP ME. FANGFANG ...
YUKARI WENT SOME-WHERE SHE SHOULDN'T HAVE...
I THOUGHT I SAW HER HEADING FOR THE GYM WITH THE OTHER GIRLS...
THAT'S THE PROBLEM!
YOU'VE GOT TO COME WITH ME!
EEAA
MWF MWF MWF
RARA RARA
RARA
FANGFANG, WHAT DO YOU THINK YOU'RE DOING?!
HOW DARE YOU INTERFERE WITH MY MEASURING?
HEY
EEEE! THE TAPE MEASURE'S SO TIGHT I CAN'T MOVE!
TSUKUNE ...
GAAAH
Hurry!
TP TP TP
Please measure us!
Measure us, measure us!

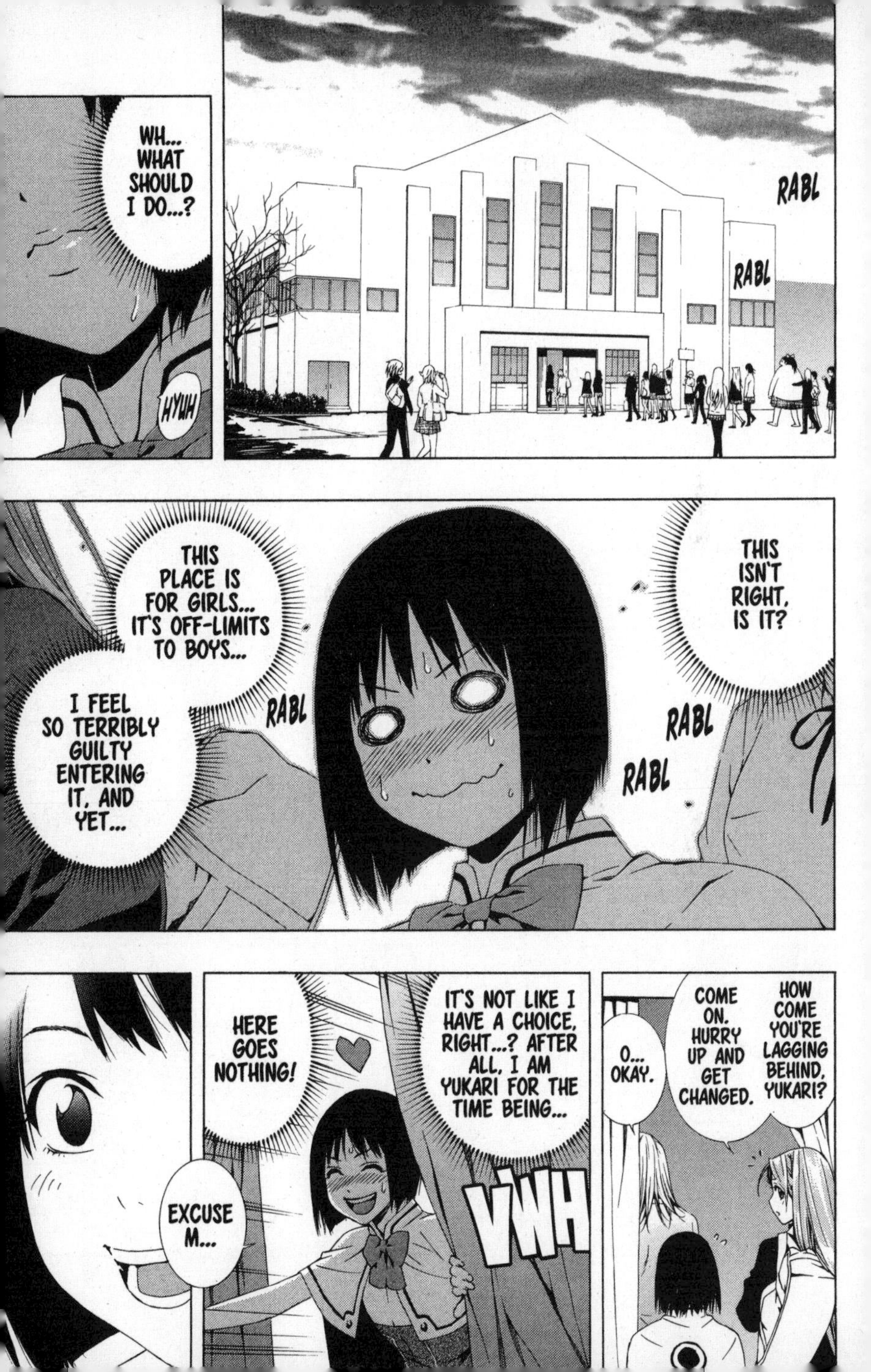
RABL
RABL
WH... WHAT SHOULD I DO...?
HYUH
THIS ISN'T RIGHT, IS IT?
RABL
RABL
RABL
THIS PLACE IS FOR GIRLS... IT'S OFF-LIMITS TO BOYS...
I FEEL SO TERRIBLY GUILTY ENTERING IT, AND YET...
HOW COME YOU'RE LAGGING BEHIND, YUKARI?
COME ON. HURRY UP AND GET CHANGED.
O... OKAY.
IT'S NOT LIKE I HAVE A CHOICE, RIGHT...? AFTER ALL, I AM YUKARI FOR THE TIME BEING...
HERE GOES NOTHING!
VNH
EXCUSE M...

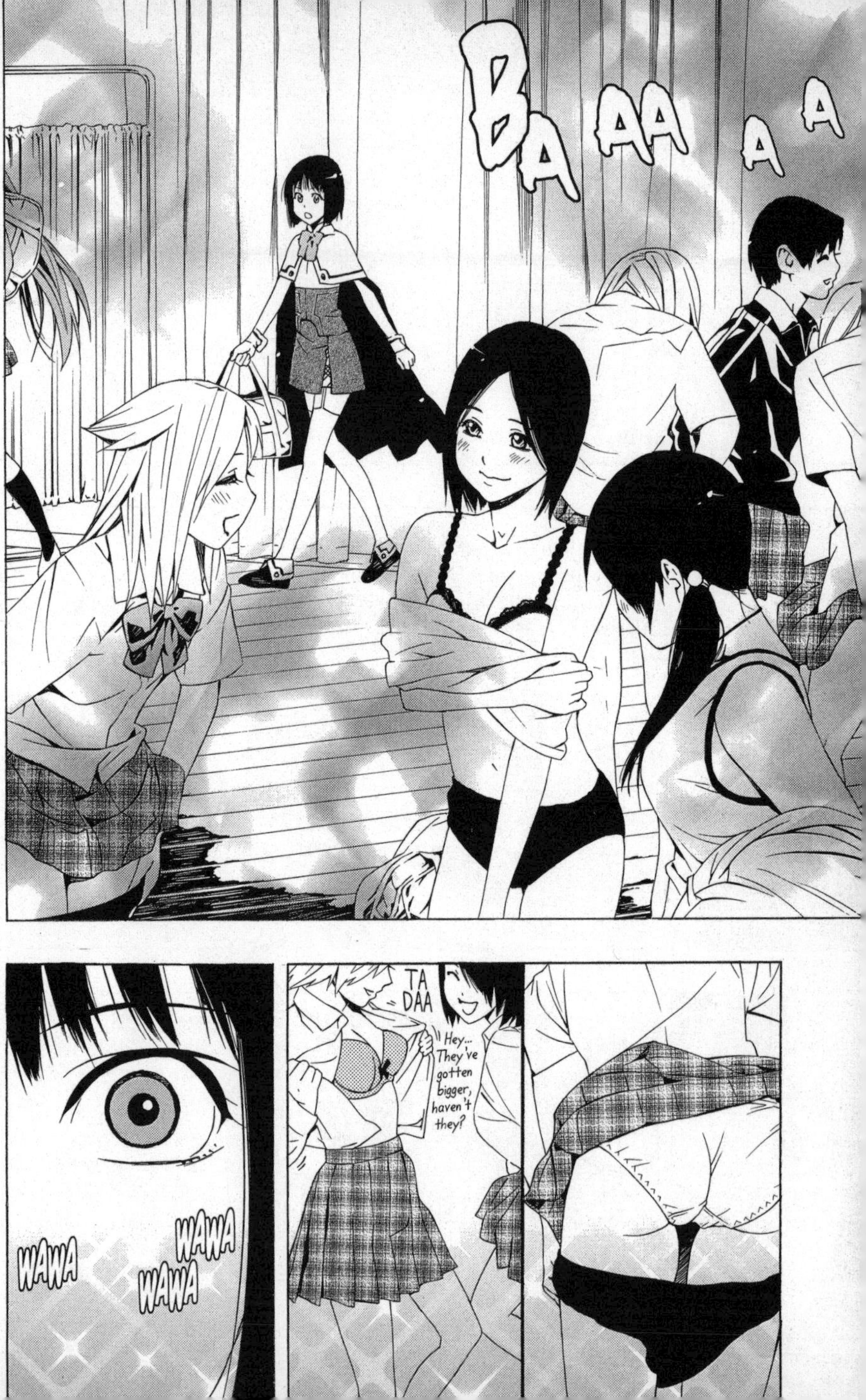
BAAAAA
TA DAA
Hey... They've gotten bigger, haven't they?
WAWA
WAWA
WAWA

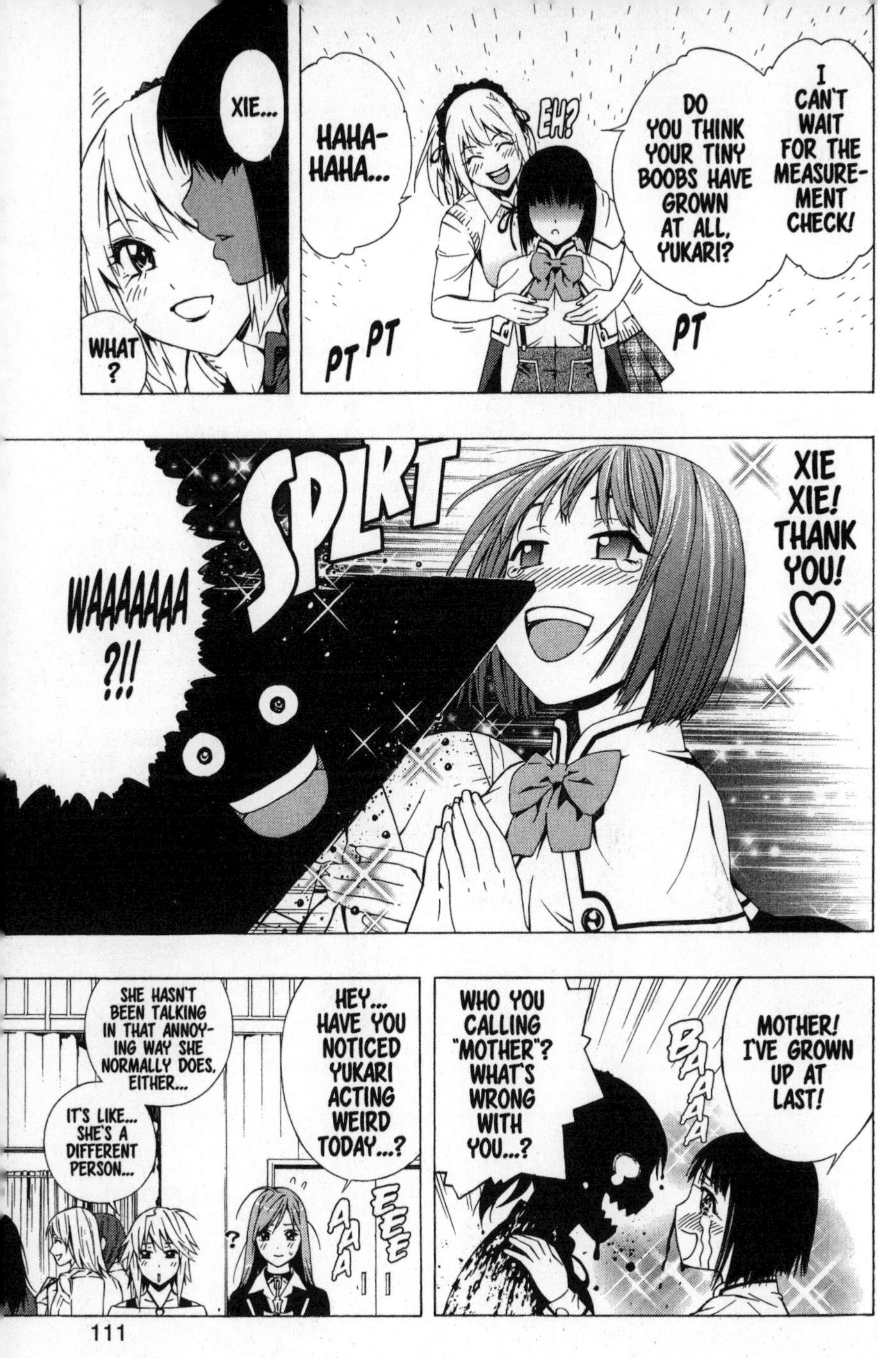
I CAN'T WAIT FOR THE MEASUREMENT CHECK!
DO YOU THINK YOUR TINY BOOBS HAVE GROWN AT ALL, YUKARI?
EH?
HAHA-HAHA...
PT
PT PT
XIE...
WHAT?
XIE XIE! THANK YOU! ♡
SPLKT
WAAAAAAA?!!
MOTHER! I'VE GROWN UP AT LAST!
BAAAA
WHO YOU CALLING "MOTHER"? WHAT'S WRONG WITH YOU...?
HEY... HAVE YOU NOTICED YUKARI ACTING WEIRD TODAY...?
EEE
AAA
SHE HASN'T BEEN TALKING IN THAT ANNOYING WAY SHE NORMALLY DOES, EITHER...
IT'S LIKE... SHE'S A DIFFERENT PERSON...

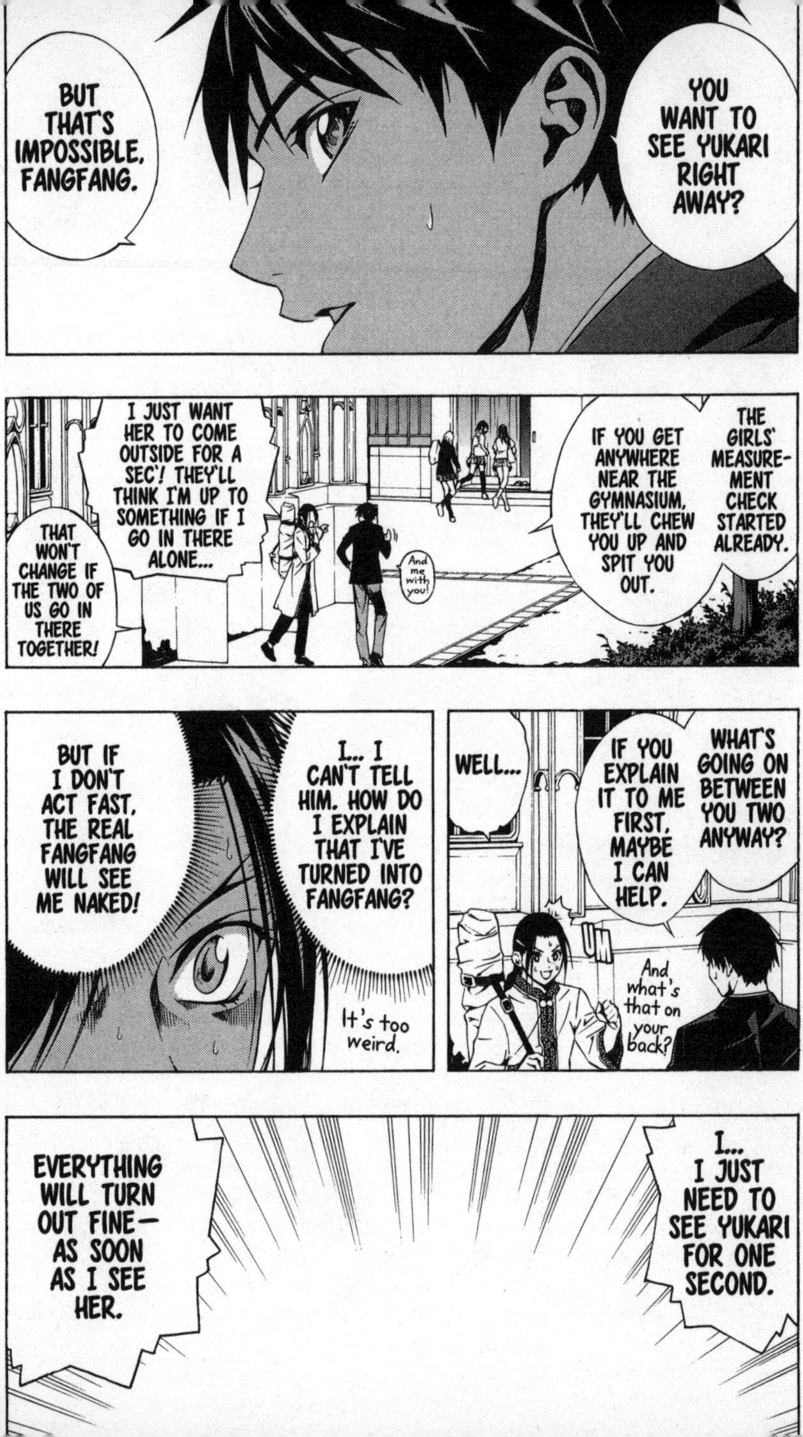
YOU WANT TO SEE YUKARI RIGHT AWAY?
BUT THAT'S IMPOSSIBLE, FANGFANG.
THE GIRLS' MEASUREMENT CHECK STARTED ALREADY.
IF YOU GET ANYWHERE NEAR THE GYMNASIUM, THEY'LL CHEW YOU UP AND SPIT YOU OUT.
And me with you!
I JUST WANT HER TO COME OUTSIDE FOR A SEC'! THEY'LL THINK I'M UP TO SOMETHING IF I GO IN THERE ALONE...
THAT WON'T CHANGE IF THE TWO OF US GO IN THERE TOGETHER!
WHAT'S GOING ON BETWEEN YOU TWO ANYWAY?
IF YOU EXPLAIN IT TO ME FIRST, MAYBE I CAN HELP.
WELL...
UM
And what's that on your back?
I... I CAN'T TELL HIM. HOW DO I EXPLAIN THAT I'VE TURNED INTO FANGFANG?
It's too weird.
BUT IF I DON'T ACT FAST, THE REAL FANGFANG WILL SEE ME NAKED!
I... I JUST NEED TO SEE YUKARI FOR ONE SECOND.
EVERYTHING WILL TURN OUT FINE— AS SOON AS I SEE HER.

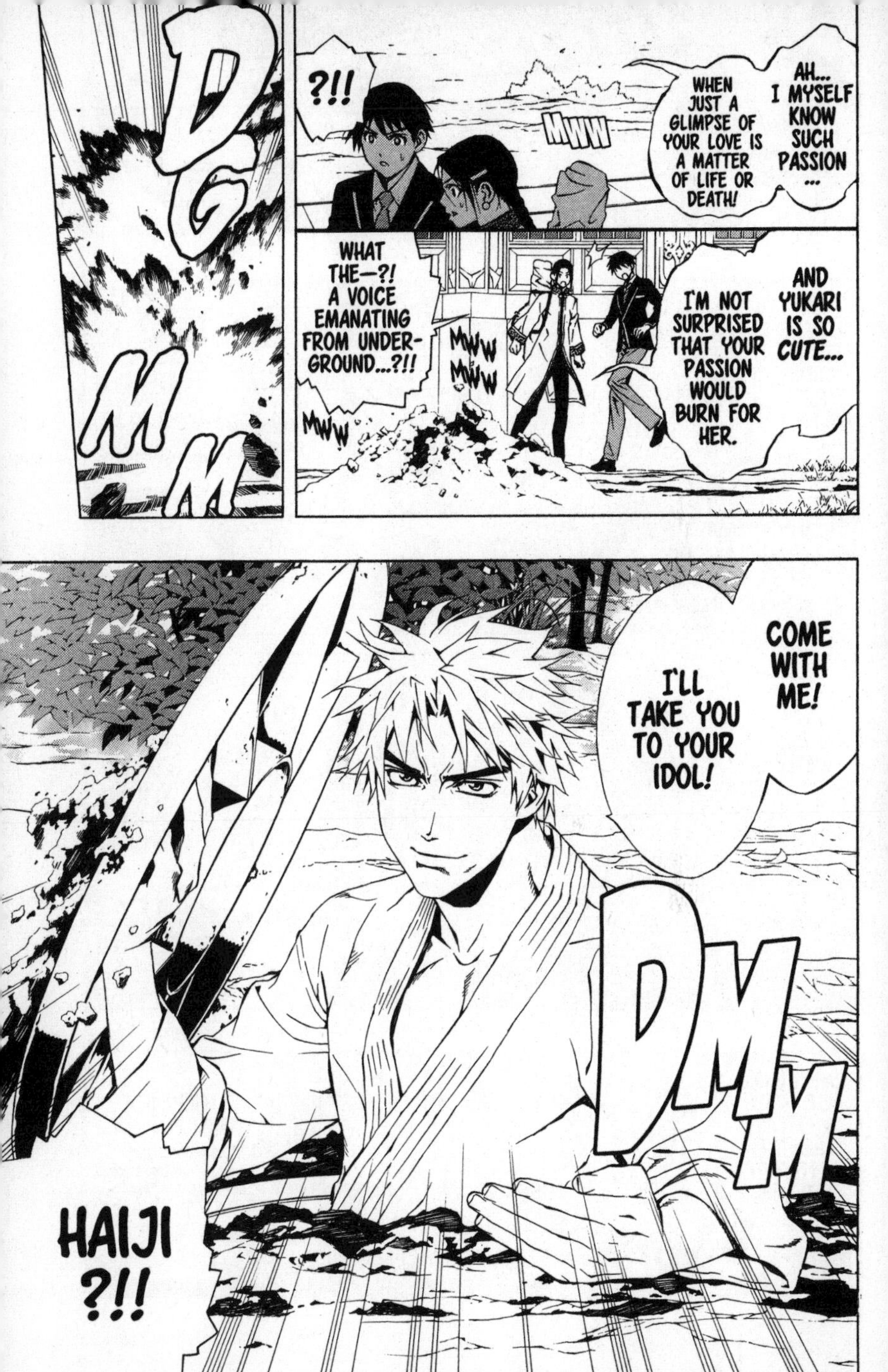
AH... I MYSELF KNOW SUCH PASSION...
WHEN JUST A GLIMPSE OF YOUR LOVE IS A MATTER OF LIFE OR DEATH!
MWW
?!!
AND YUKARI IS SO *CUTE*...
I'M NOT SURPRISED THAT YOUR PASSION WOULD BURN FOR HER.
MWW MWW
WHAT THE—?! A VOICE EMANATING FROM UNDER-GROUND...?!!
MWW
DGMM
COME WITH ME!
I'LL TAKE YOU TO YOUR IDOL!
DMMM
HAIJI ?!!

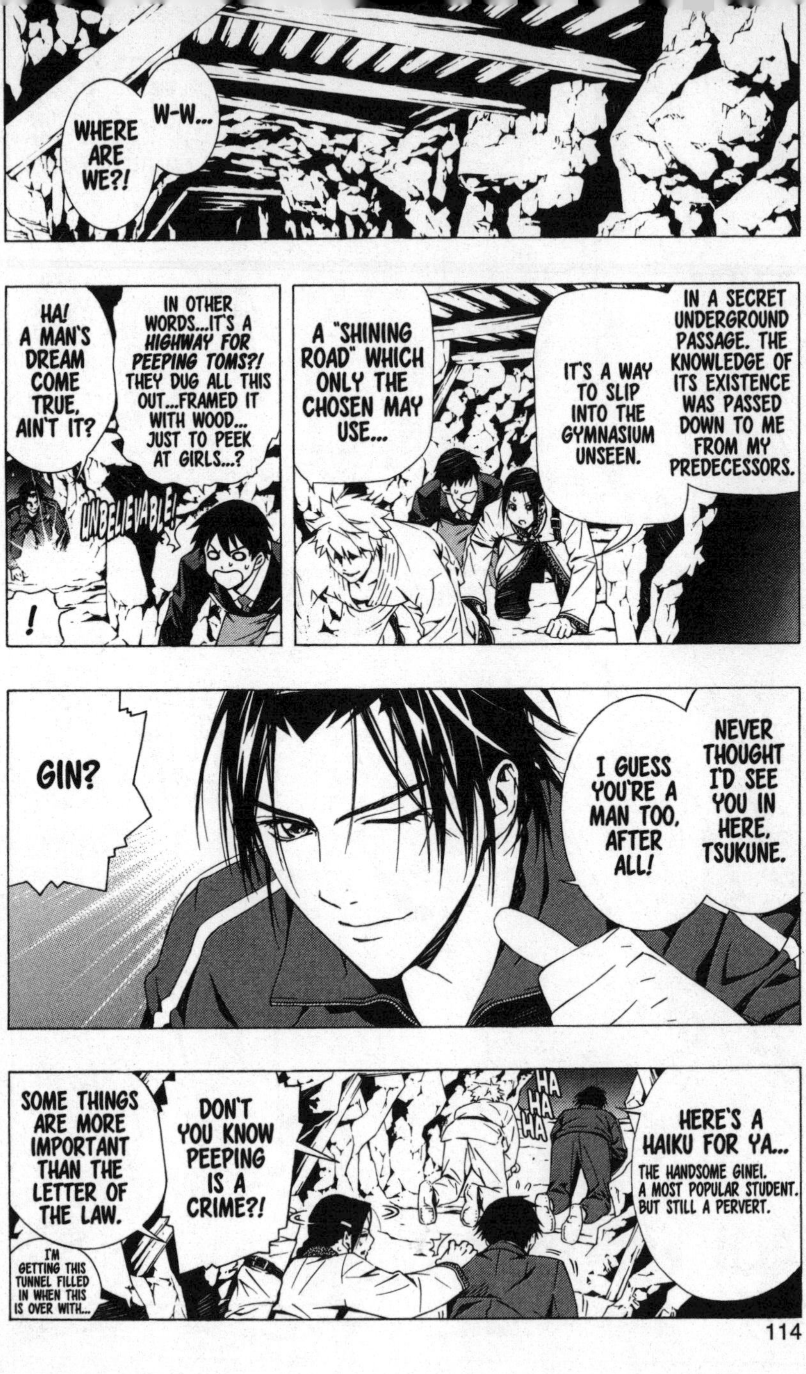
W-W...
WHERE ARE WE?!
IN A SECRET UNDERGROUND PASSAGE. THE KNOWLEDGE OF ITS EXISTENCE WAS PASSED DOWN TO ME FROM MY PREDECESSORS.
IT'S A WAY TO SLIP INTO THE GYMNASIUM UNSEEN.
A "SHINING ROAD" WHICH ONLY THE CHOSEN MAY USE...
IN OTHER WORDS...IT'S A *HIGHWAY FOR PEEPING TOMS?!* THEY DUG ALL THIS OUT...FRAMED IT WITH WOOD... JUST TO PEEK AT GIRLS...?
HA! A MAN'S DREAM COME TRUE, AIN'T IT?
UNBELIEVABLE!
!
NEVER THOUGHT I'D SEE YOU IN HERE, TSUKUNE.
I GUESS YOU'RE A MAN TOO, AFTER ALL!
GIN?
HERE'S A HAIKU FOR YA...
THE HANDSOME GINEI. A MOST POPULAR STUDENT. BUT STILL A PERVERT.
HA HA HA HA
DON'T YOU KNOW PEEPING IS A CRIME?!
SOME THINGS ARE MORE IMPORTANT THAN THE LETTER OF THE LAW.
I'M GETTING THIS TUNNEL FILLED IN WHEN THIS IS OVER WITH...

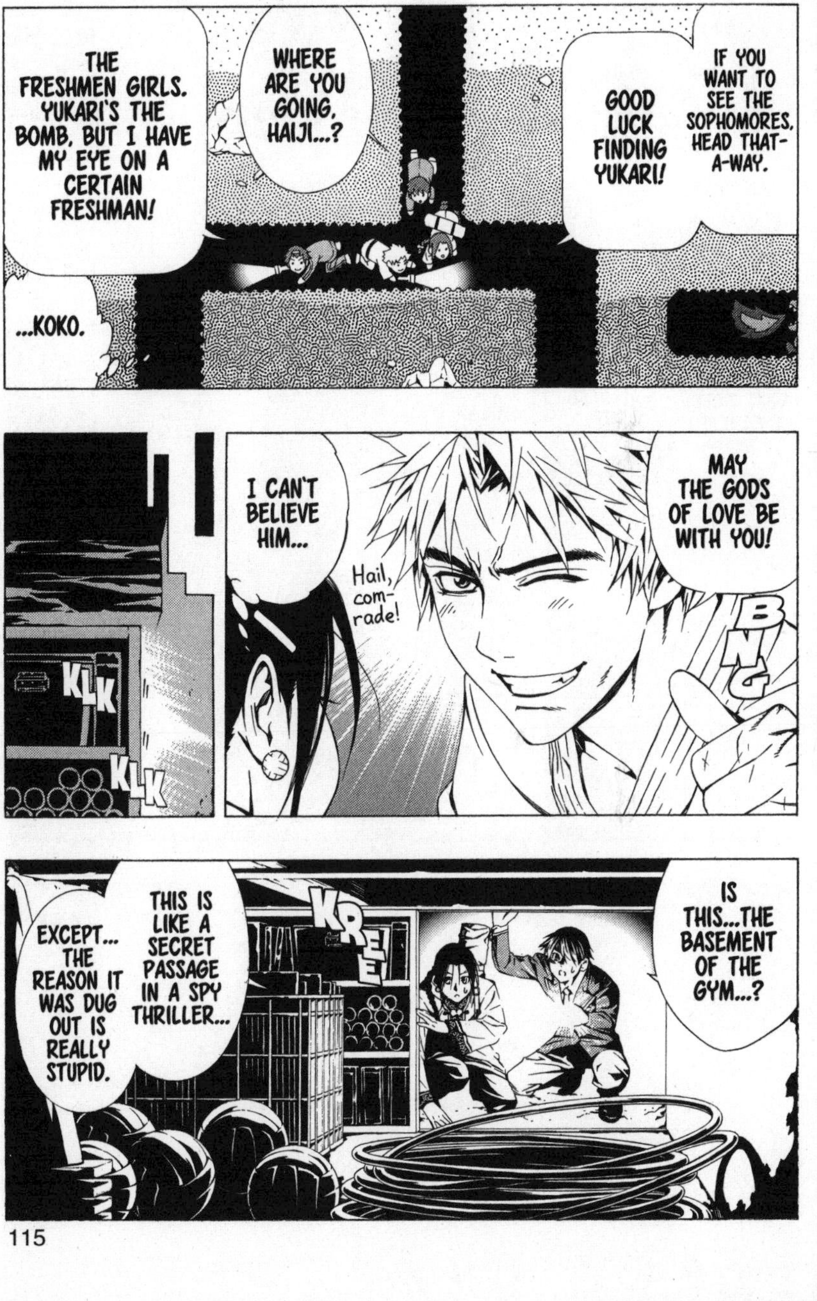
IF YOU WANT TO SEE THE SOPHOMORES, HEAD THAT-A-WAY.
GOOD LUCK FINDING YUKARI!
WHERE ARE YOU GOING, HAIJI...?
THE FRESHMEN GIRLS. YUKARI'S THE BOMB, BUT I HAVE MY EYE ON A CERTAIN FRESHMAN!
...KOKO.
MAY THE GODS OF LOVE BE WITH YOU!
BNG
Hail, com-rade!
I CAN'T BELIEVE HIM...
KLK
KLK
IS THIS...THE BASEMENT OF THE GYM...?
KREE
THIS IS LIKE A SECRET PASSAGE IN A SPY THRILLER...
EXCEPT... THE REASON IT WAS DUG OUT IS REALLY STUPID.

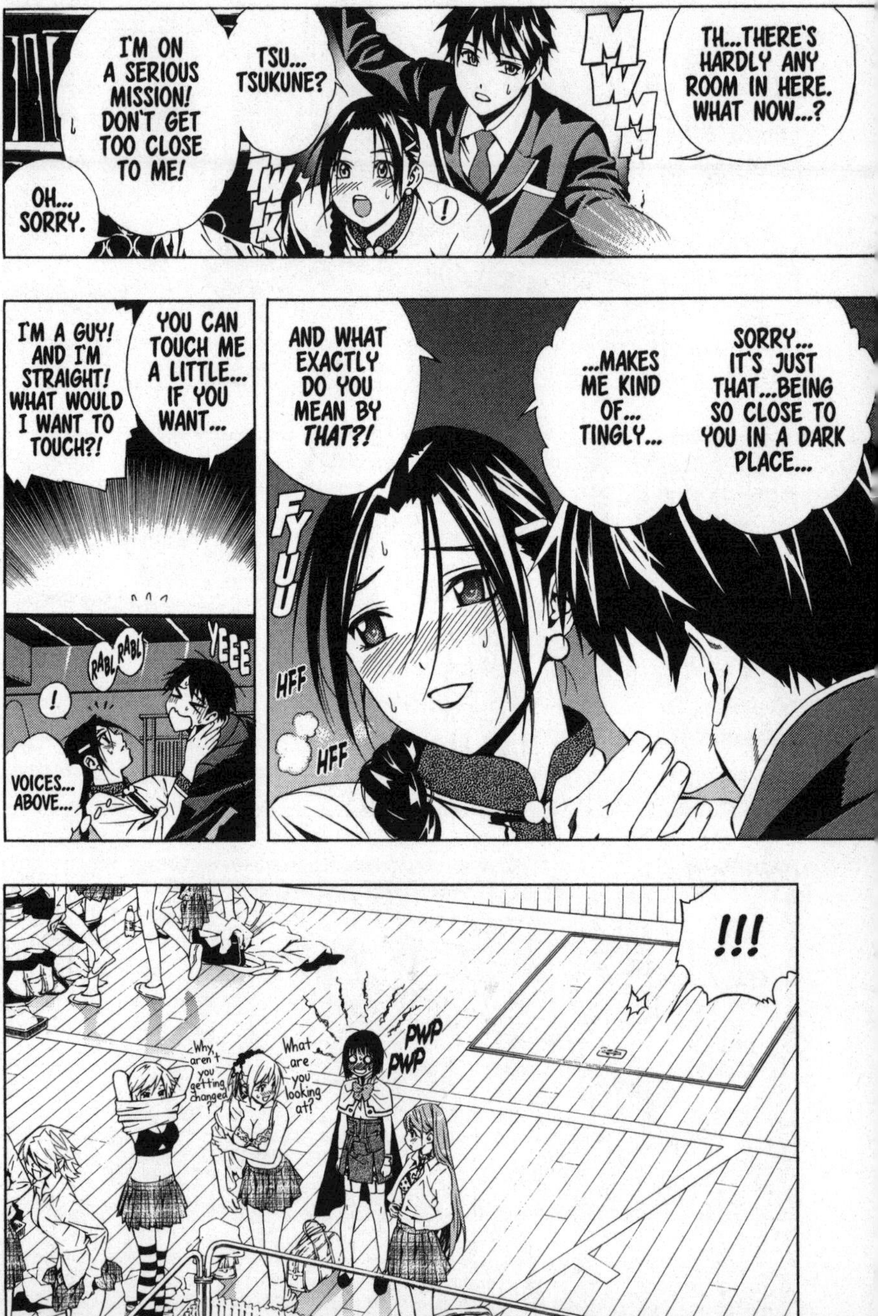
TH...THERE'S HARDLY ANY ROOM IN HERE. WHAT NOW...?
MWWMM
!
TWIK
TSU... TSUKUNE?
I'M ON A SERIOUS MISSION! DON'T GET TOO CLOSE TO ME!
OH... SORRY.
SORRY... IT'S JUST THAT...BEING SO CLOSE TO YOU IN A DARK PLACE...
...MAKES ME KIND OF... TINGLY...
AND WHAT EXACTLY DO YOU MEAN BY *THAT?!*
FYUU
HFF
HFF
YOU CAN TOUCH ME A LITTLE... IF YOU WANT...
I'M A GUY! AND I'M STRAIGHT! WHAT WOULD I WANT TO TOUCH?!
YEEE
RABL RABL
!
VOICES... ABOVE...
!!!
PWP PWP
What are you looking at?
Why aren't you getting changed?

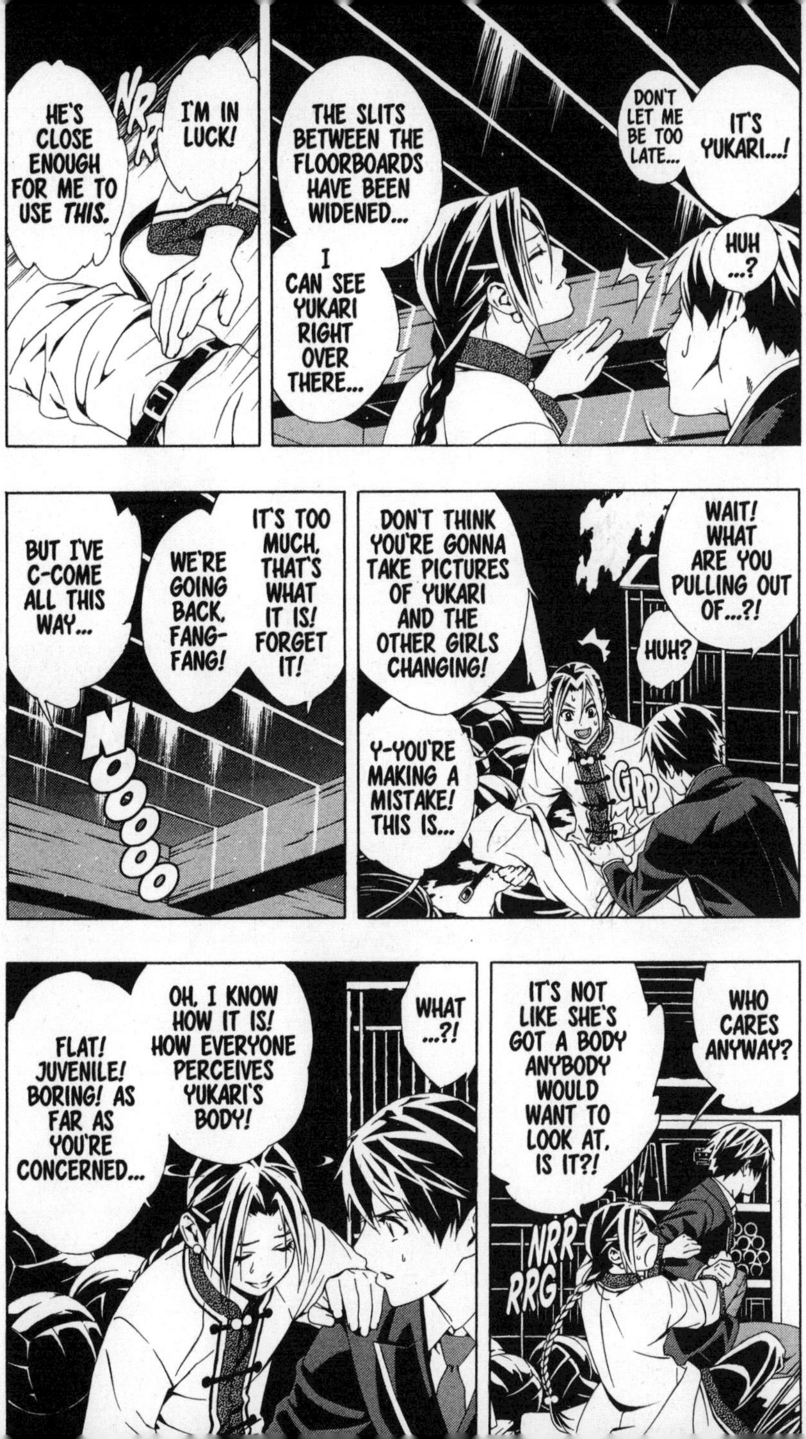
IT'S YUKARI...!
DON'T LET ME BE TOO LATE...
HUH ...?
THE SLITS BETWEEN THE FLOORBOARDS HAVE BEEN WIDENED...
I CAN SEE YUKARI RIGHT OVER THERE...
I'M IN LUCK!
NRR
HE'S CLOSE ENOUGH FOR ME TO USE THIS.
WAIT! WHAT ARE YOU PULLING OUT OF...?!
HUH?
DON'T THINK YOU'RE GONNA TAKE PICTURES OF YUKARI AND THE OTHER GIRLS CHANGING!
Y-YOU'RE MAKING A MISTAKE! THIS IS...
GRP
IT'S TOO MUCH, THAT'S WHAT IT IS! FORGET IT!
WE'RE GOING BACK, FANG-FANG!
BUT I'VE C-COME ALL THIS WAY...
NOOOOO
WHO CARES ANYWAY?
IT'S NOT LIKE SHE'S GOT A BODY ANYBODY WOULD WANT TO LOOK AT, IS IT?!
NRR RRG
WHAT ...?!
OH, I KNOW HOW IT IS! HOW EVERYONE PERCEIVES YUKARI'S BODY!
FLAT! JUVENILE! BORING! AS FAR AS YOU'RE CONCERNED...

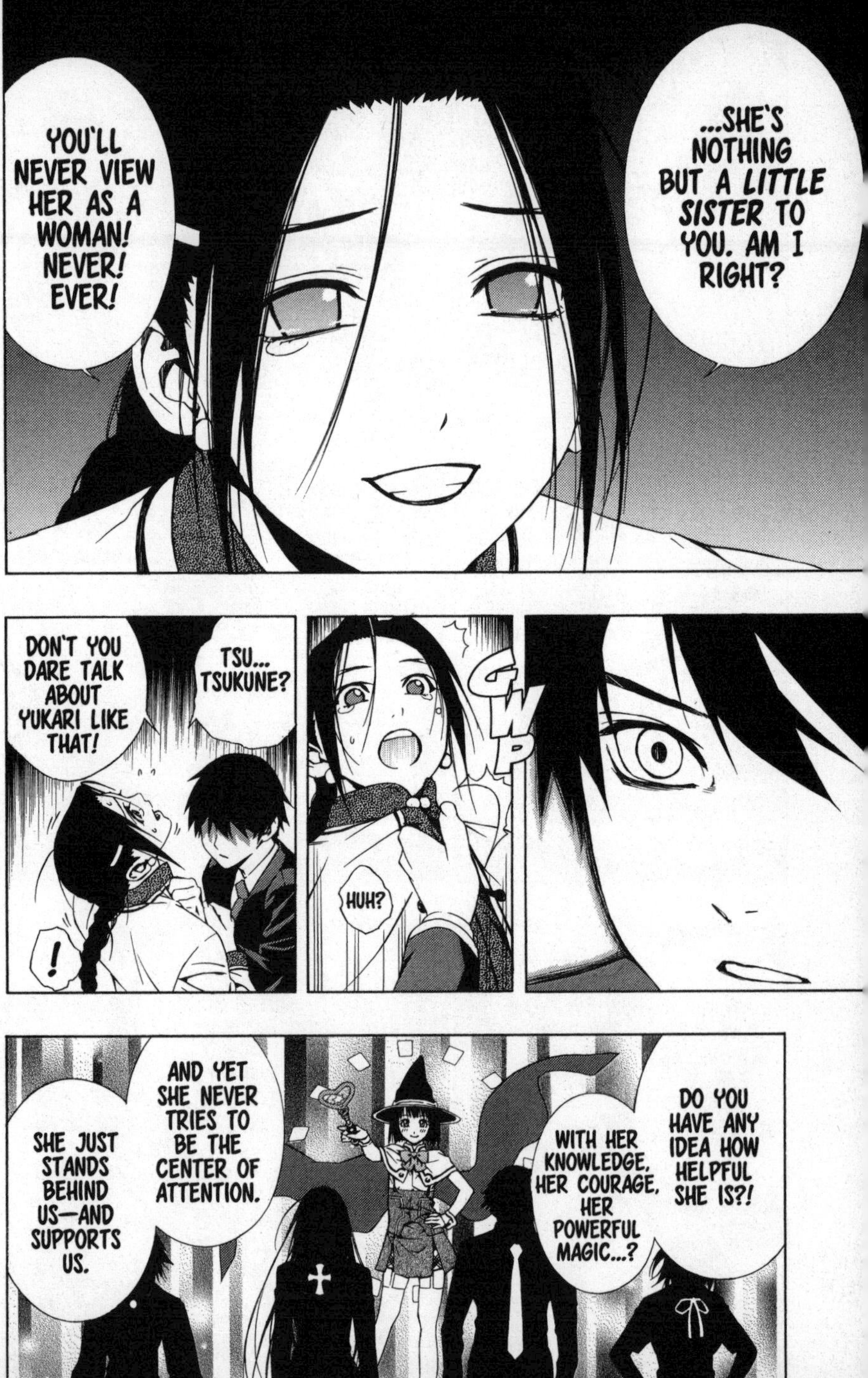
...SHE'S NOTHING BUT A *LITTLE SISTER* TO YOU. AM I RIGHT?
YOU'LL NEVER VIEW HER AS A WOMAN! NEVER! EVER!
GWP
HUH?
TSU... TSUKUNE?
DON'T YOU DARE TALK ABOUT YUKARI LIKE THAT!
!
DO YOU HAVE ANY IDEA HOW HELPFUL SHE IS?!
WITH HER KNOWLEDGE, HER COURAGE, HER POWERFUL MAGIC...?
AND YET SHE NEVER TRIES TO BE THE CENTER OF ATTENTION.
SHE JUST STANDS BEHIND US—AND SUPPORTS US.

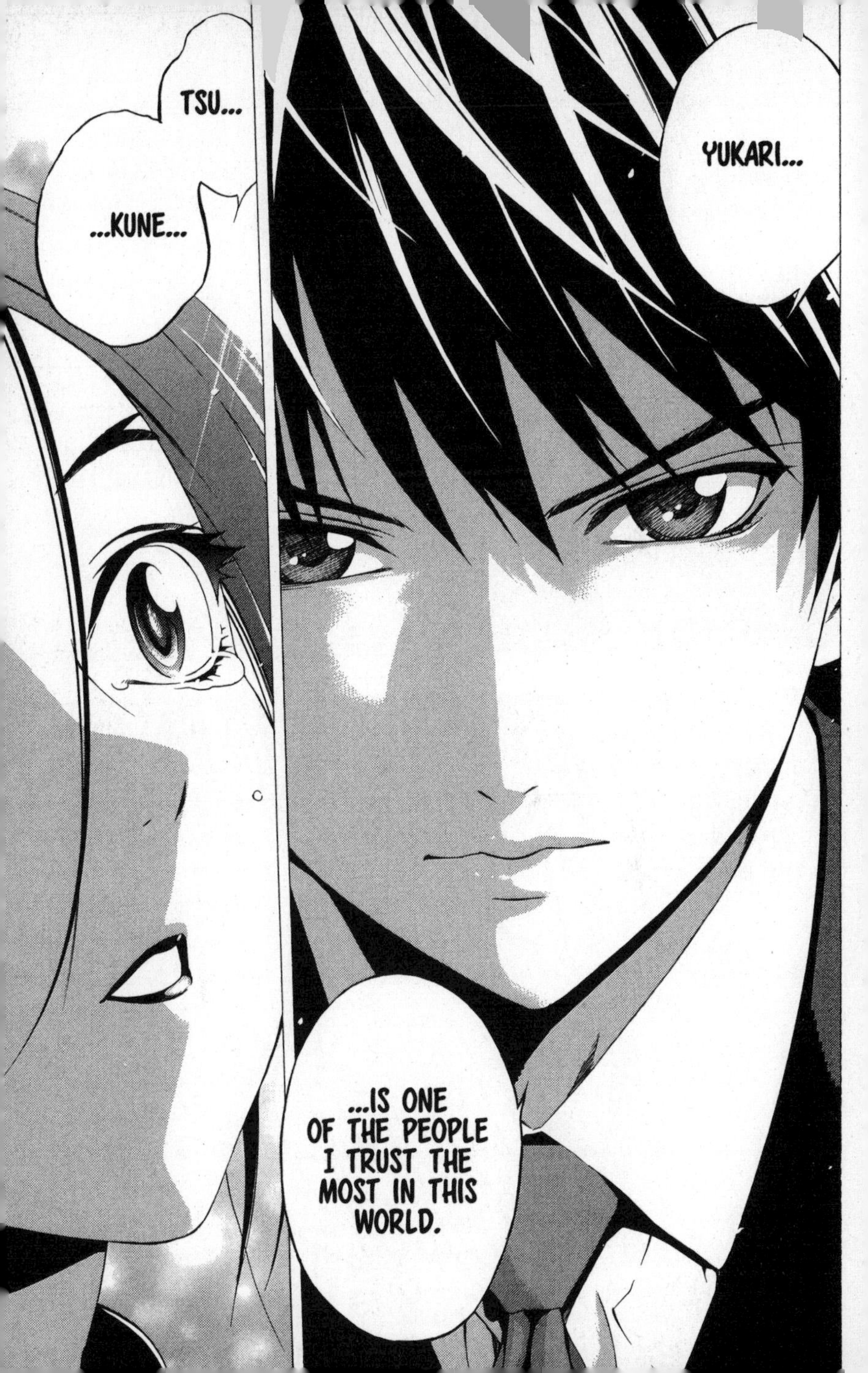
YUKARI...
...IS ONE OF THE PEOPLE I TRUST THE MOST IN THIS WORLD.
TSU...
...KUNE...

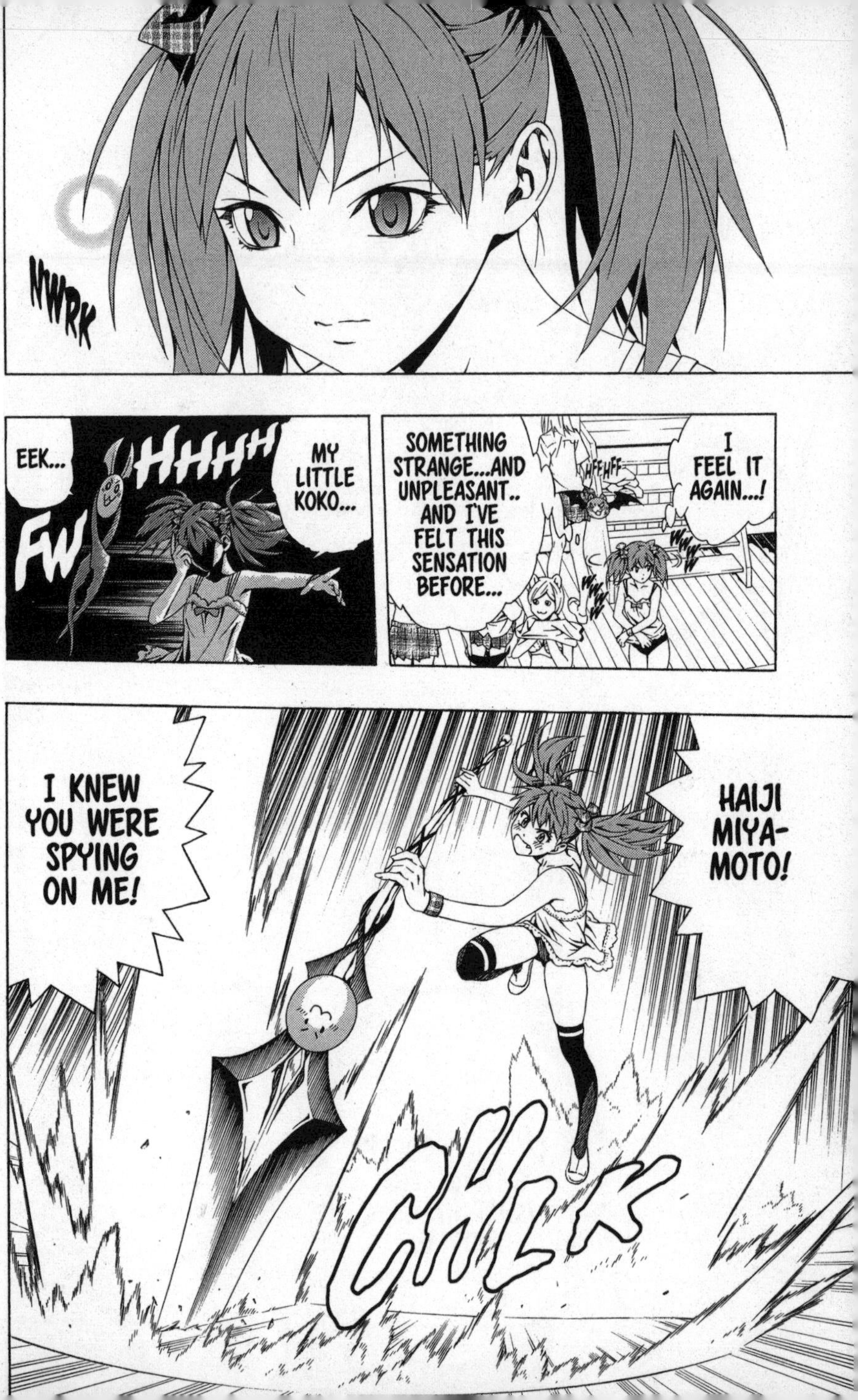
NWRK
I FEEL IT AGAIN...!
HFFHFF
SOMETHING STRANGE...AND UNPLEASANT.. AND I'VE FELT THIS SENSATION BEFORE...
MY LITTLE KOKO...
FWHHHH
EEK...
HAIJI MIYA-MOTO!
I KNEW YOU WERE SPYING ON ME!
CHLK

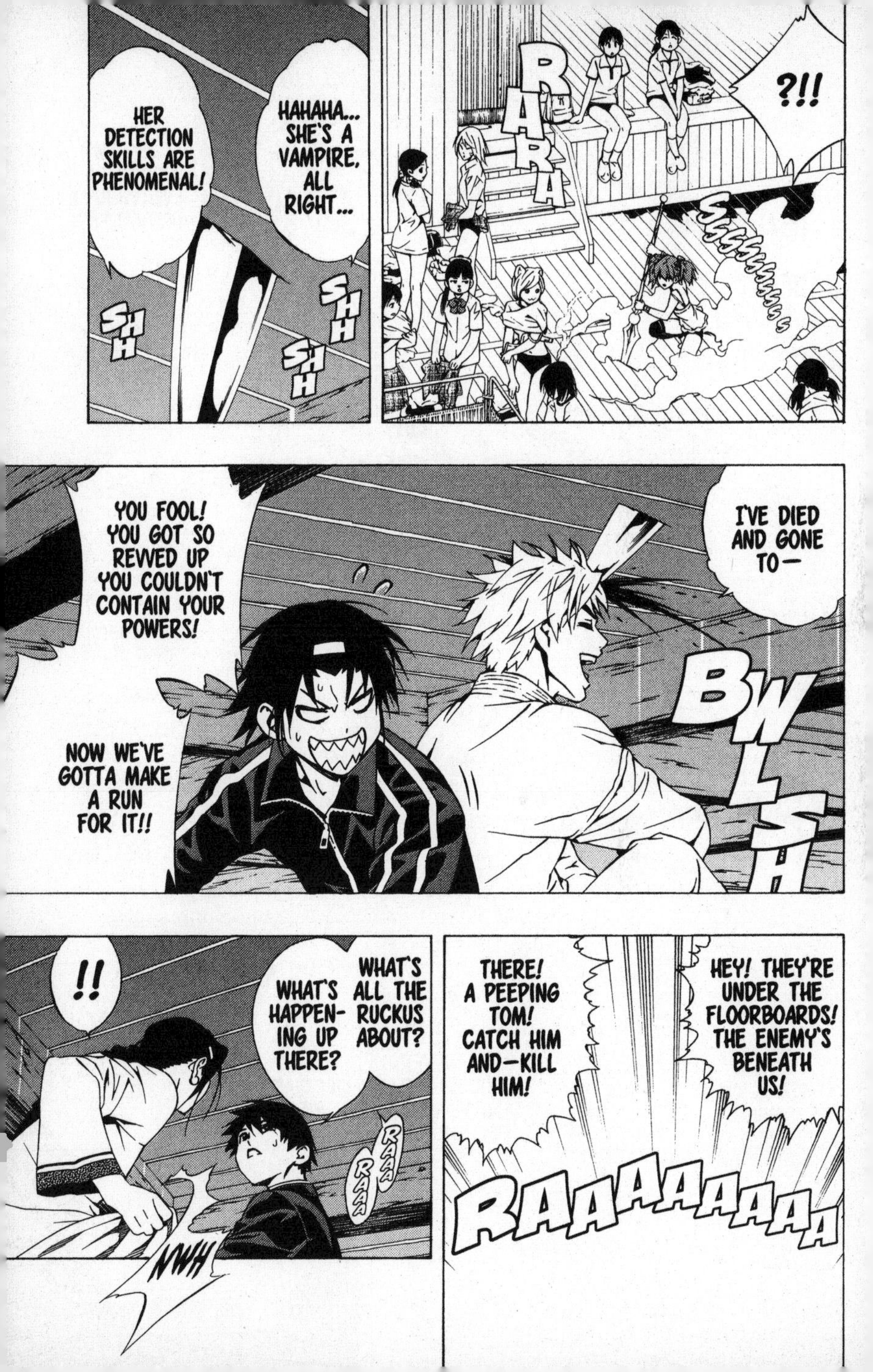
?!!
RARA
SSSSSSSSSS
HAHAHA... SHE'S A VAMPIRE, ALL RIGHT...
HER DETECTION SKILLS ARE PHENOMENAL!
SHH
SHH
SHH
I'VE DIED AND GONE TO—
BWLSH
YOU FOOL! YOU GOT SO REVVED UP YOU COULDN'T CONTAIN YOUR POWERS!
NOW WE'VE GOTTA MAKE A RUN FOR IT!!
HEY! THEY'RE UNDER THE FLOORBOARDS! THE ENEMY'S BENEATH US!
THERE! A PEEPING TOM! CATCH HIM AND—KILL HIM!
RAAAAAAAAAA
WHAT'S ALL THE RUCKUS ABOUT?
WHAT'S HAPPEN-ING UP THERE?
!!
RAAA
RAAA
NWH

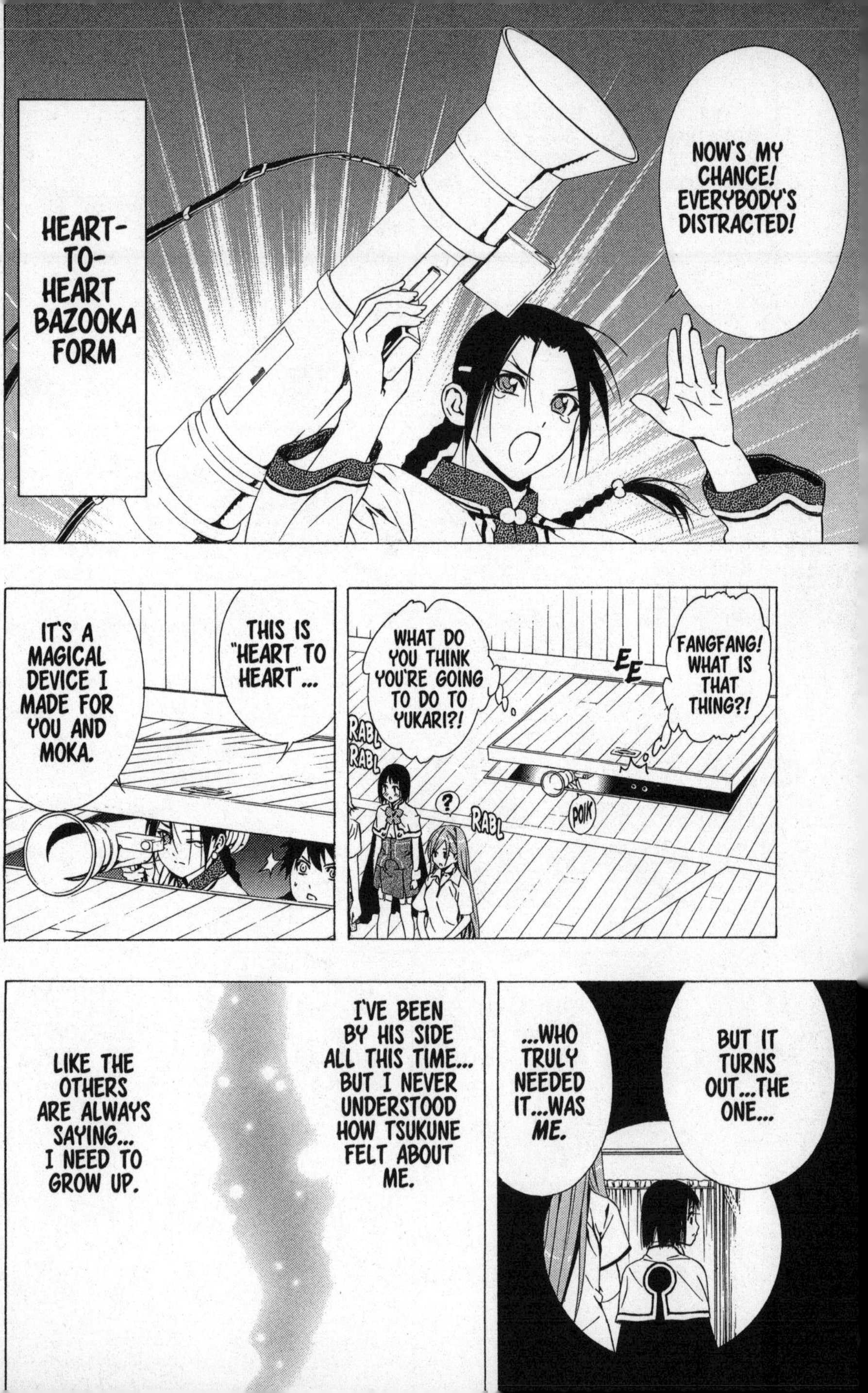
NOW'S MY CHANCE! EVERYBODY'S DISTRACTED!
HEART-TO-HEART BAZOOKA FORM
FANGFANG! WHAT IS THAT THING?!
EE
WHAT DO YOU THINK YOU'RE GOING TO DO TO YUKARI?!
RABL RABL
?
RABL
POIK
THIS IS "HEART TO HEART"...
IT'S A MAGICAL DEVICE I MADE FOR YOU AND MOKA.
BUT IT TURNS OUT...THE ONE...
...WHO TRULY NEEDED IT...WAS *ME.*
I'VE BEEN BY HIS SIDE ALL THIS TIME... BUT I NEVER UNDERSTOOD HOW TSUKUNE FELT ABOUT ME.
LIKE THE OTHERS ARE ALWAYS SAYING... I NEED TO GROW UP.

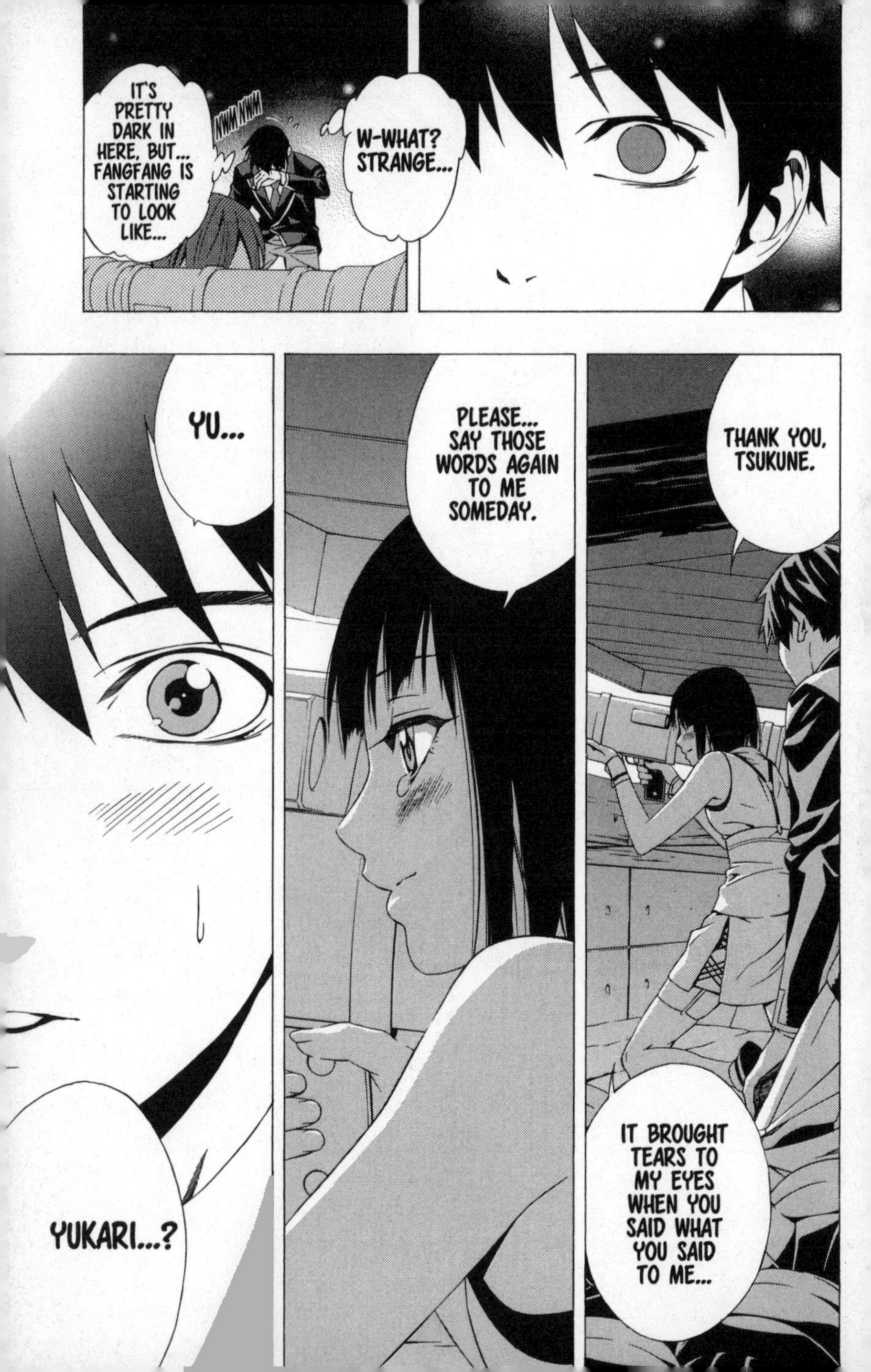
W-WHAT? STRANGE...
NWM NWM
IT'S PRETTY DARK IN HERE, BUT... FANGFANG IS STARTING TO LOOK LIKE...
THANK YOU, TSUKUNE.
IT BROUGHT TEARS TO MY EYES WHEN YOU SAID WHAT YOU SAID TO ME...
PLEASE... SAY THOSE WORDS AGAIN TO ME SOMEDAY.
YU...
YUKARI...?

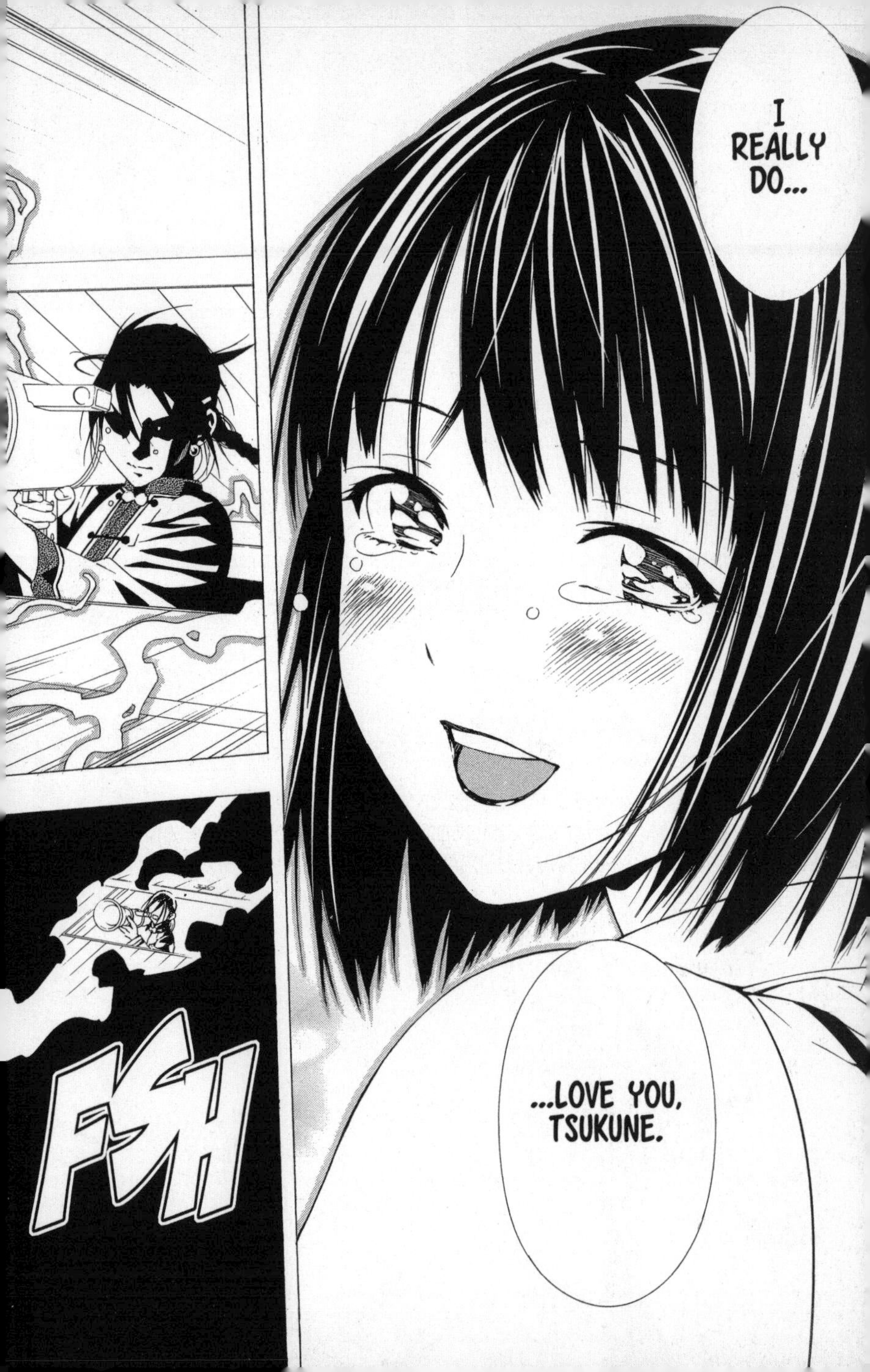
I REALLY DO...
...LOVE YOU, TSUKUNE.
FSH

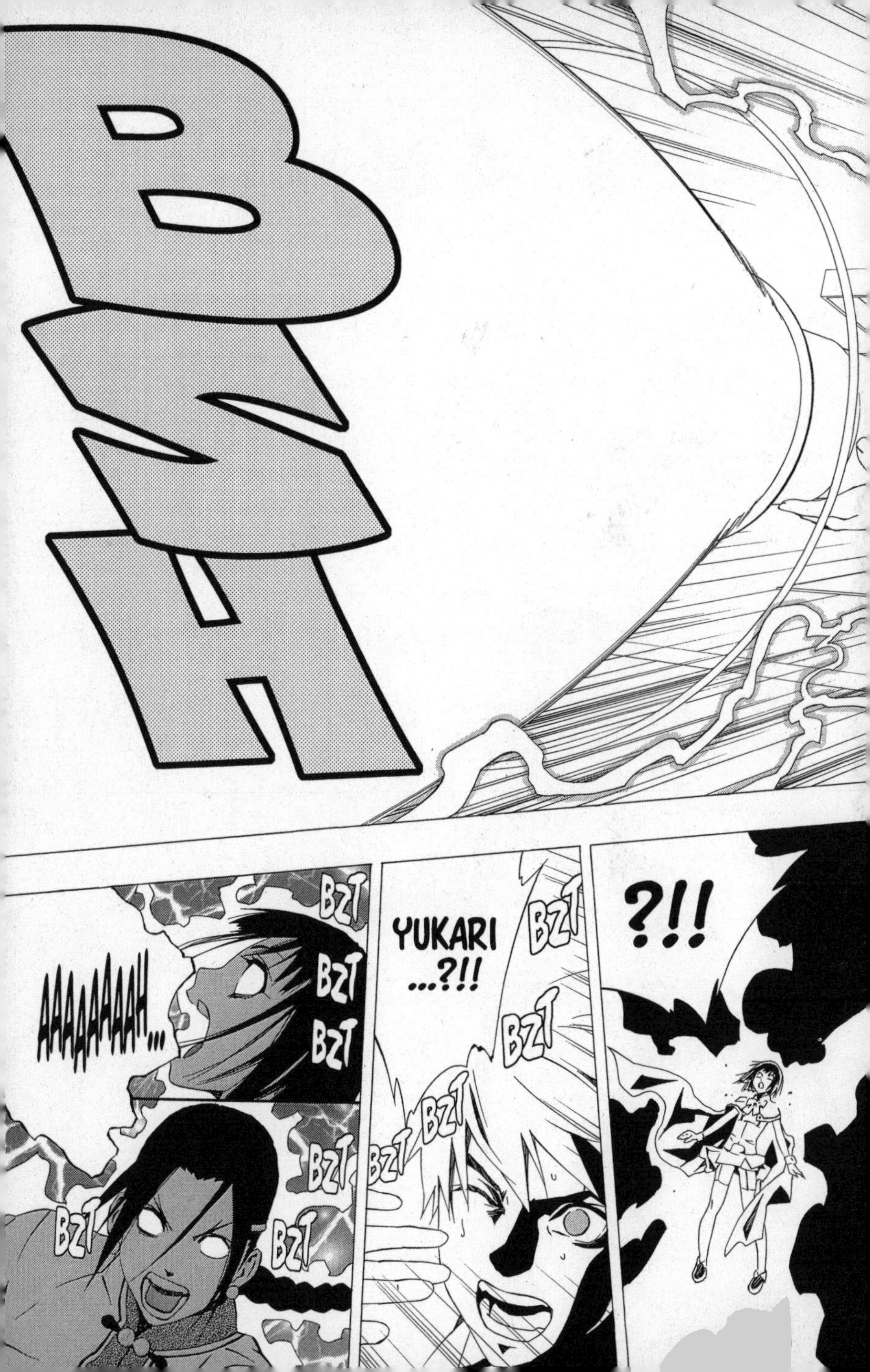
?!!
YUKARI ...?!!
BZT
BZT
BZT
BZT
BZT
BZT
BZT
AAAAAAAH...
BZT
BZT
BZT
BZT

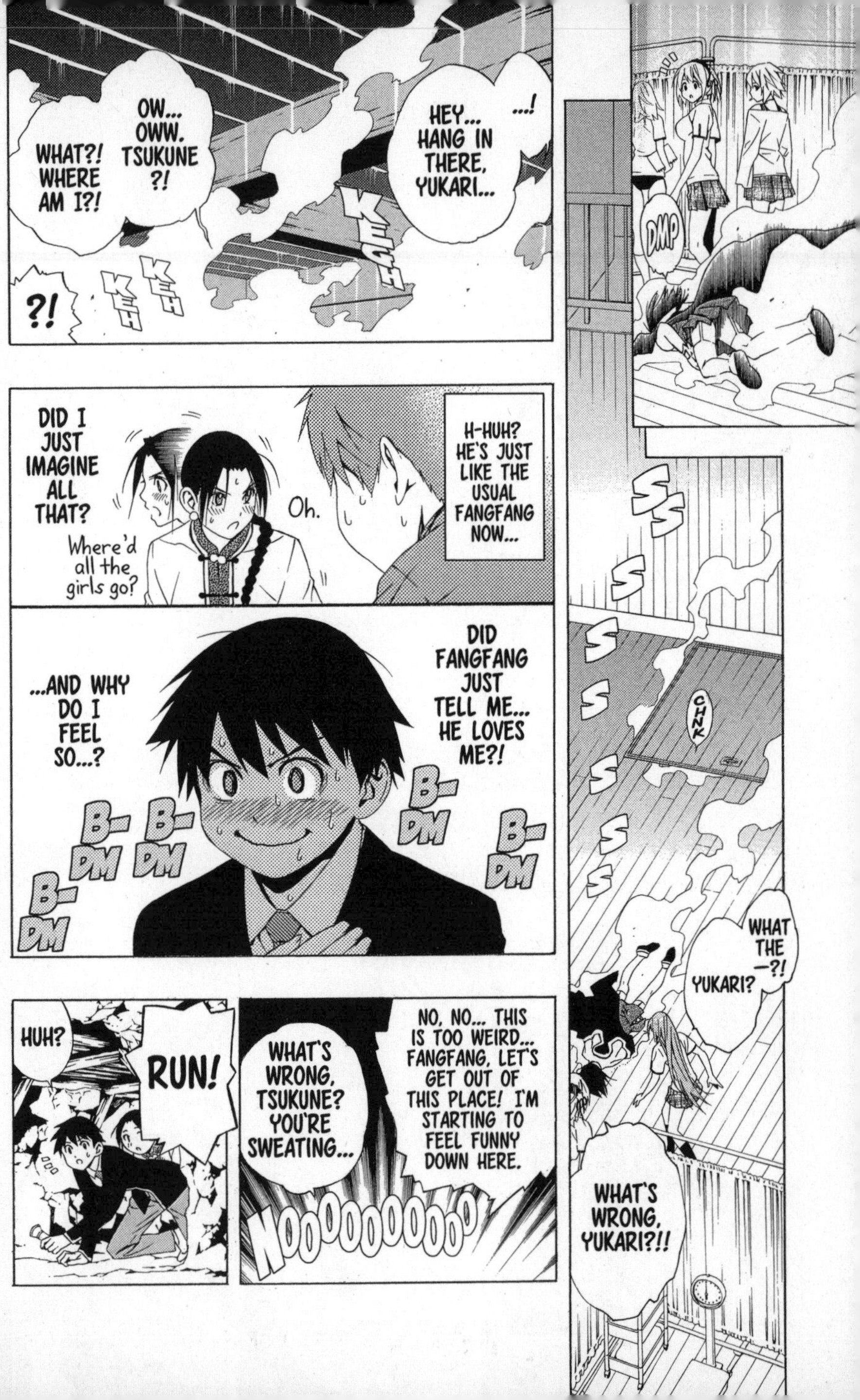
DMP
...!
HEY... HANG IN THERE, YUKARI...
KEGH
OW... OWW. TSUKUNE?!
WHAT?! WHERE AM I?!
KEH KEH
?!
SSSSSSSSS
CHNK
WHAT THE—?!
YUKARI?
WHAT'S WRONG, YUKARI?!!
H-HUH? HE'S JUST LIKE THE USUAL FANGFANG NOW...
Oh.
DID I JUST IMAGINE ALL THAT?
Where'd all the girls go?
DID FANGFANG JUST TELL ME... HE LOVES ME?!
...AND WHY DO I FEEL SO...?
B-DM B-DM B-DM B-DM B-DM
NO, NO... THIS IS TOO WEIRD... FANGFANG, LET'S GET OUT OF THIS PLACE! I'M STARTING TO FEEL FUNNY DOWN HERE.
WHAT'S WRONG, TSUKUNE? YOU'RE SWEATING...
NOOOOOOOOOO
RUN!
HUH?

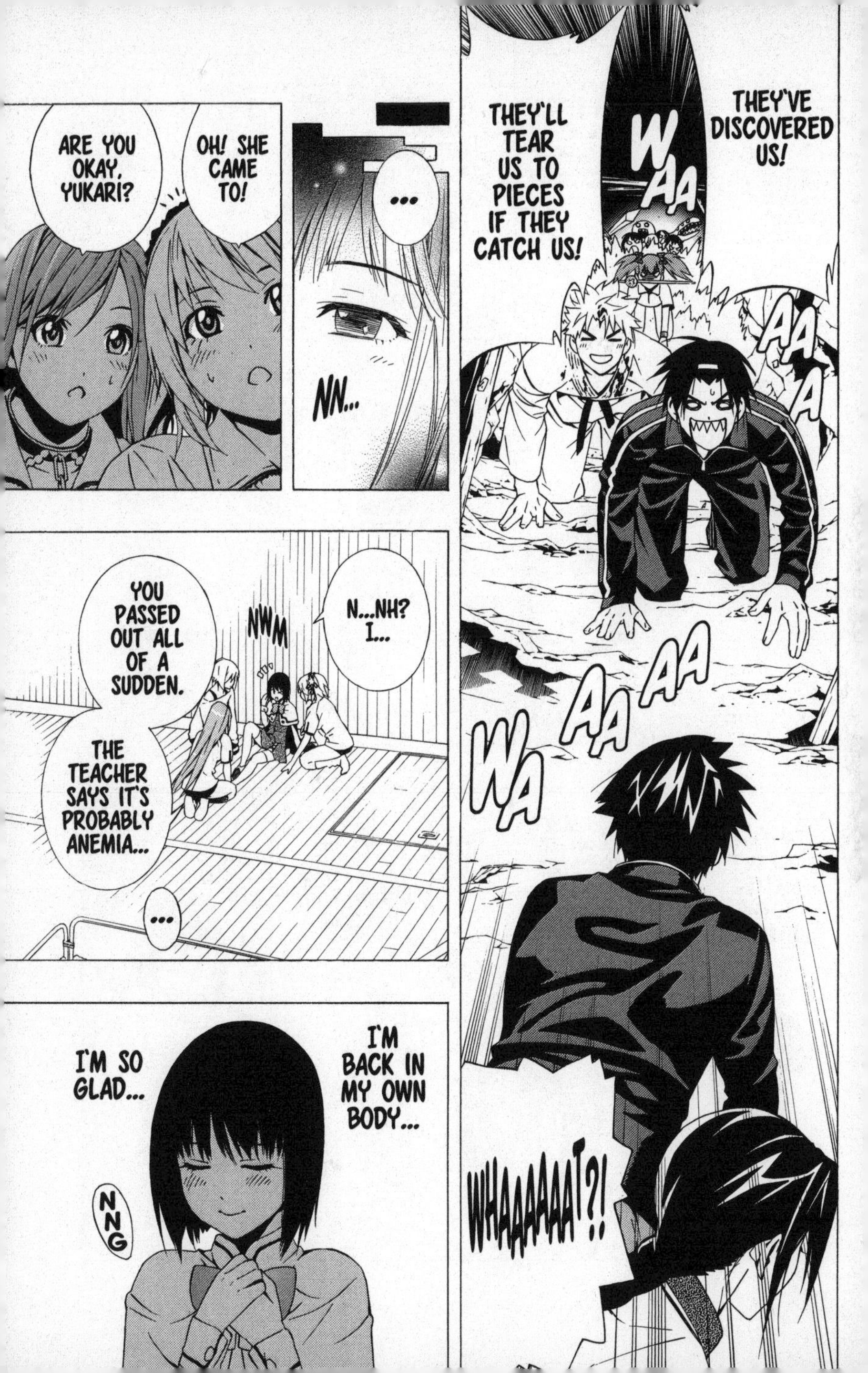
THEY'VE DISCOVERED US!
THEY'LL TEAR US TO PIECES IF THEY CATCH US!
WAA
AAAA
WAAAAAA
WHAAAAAAT?!
...
NN...
OH! SHE CAME TO!
ARE YOU OKAY, YUKARI?
N...NH? I...
NWM
YOU PASSED OUT ALL OF A SUDDEN.
THE TEACHER SAYS IT'S PROBABLY ANEMIA...
...
I'M BACK IN MY OWN BODY...
I'M SO GLAD...
NNG

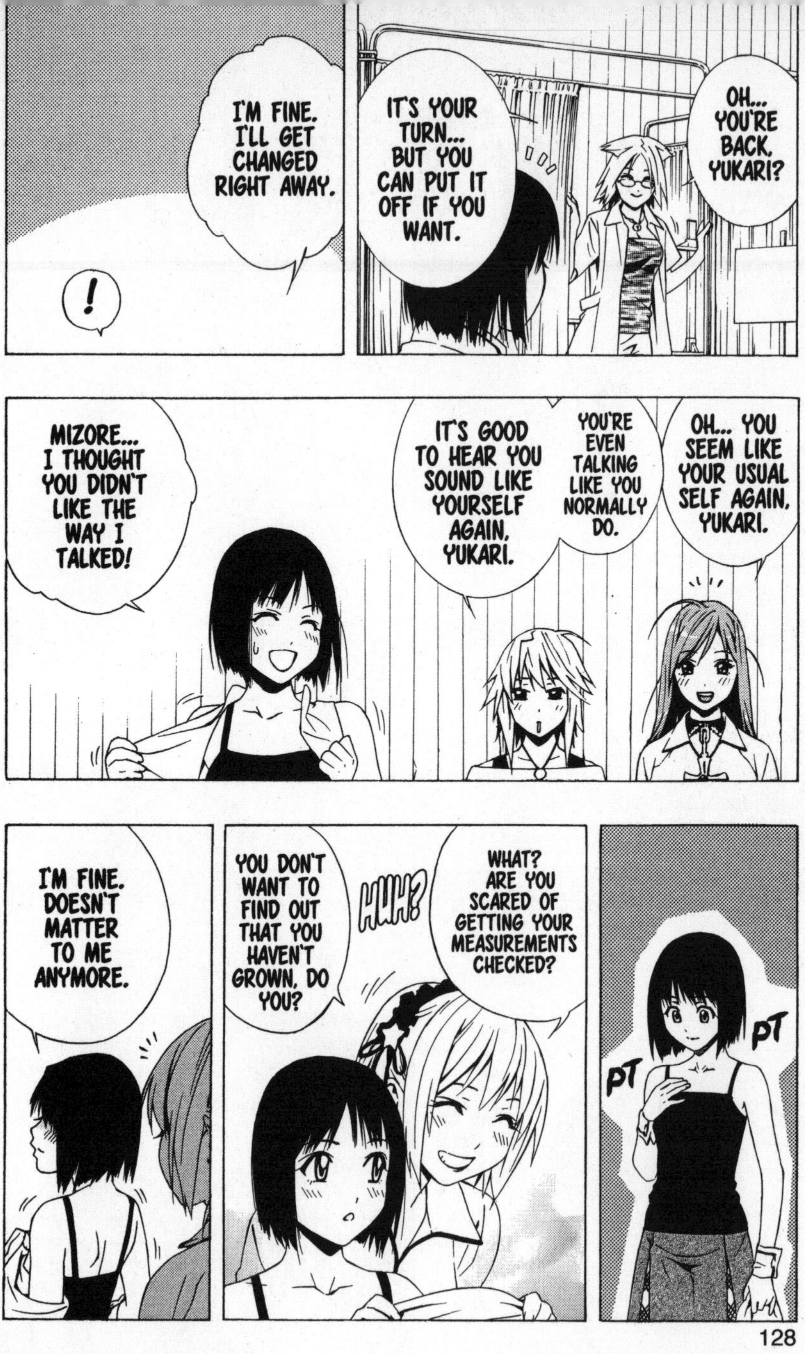
OH... YOU'RE BACK, YUKARI?
IT'S YOUR TURN... BUT YOU CAN PUT IT OFF IF YOU WANT.
I'M FINE. I'LL GET CHANGED RIGHT AWAY.
!
OH... YOU SEEM LIKE YOUR USUAL SELF AGAIN, YUKARI.
YOU'RE EVEN TALKING LIKE YOU NORMALLY DO.
IT'S GOOD TO HEAR YOU SOUND LIKE YOURSELF AGAIN, YUKARI.
MIZORE... I THOUGHT YOU DIDN'T LIKE THE WAY I TALKED!
PT
PT
WHAT? ARE YOU SCARED OF GETTING YOUR MEASUREMENTS CHECKED?
HUH?
YOU DON'T WANT TO FIND OUT THAT YOU HAVEN'T GROWN, DO YOU?
I'M FINE. DOESN'T MATTER TO ME ANYMORE.

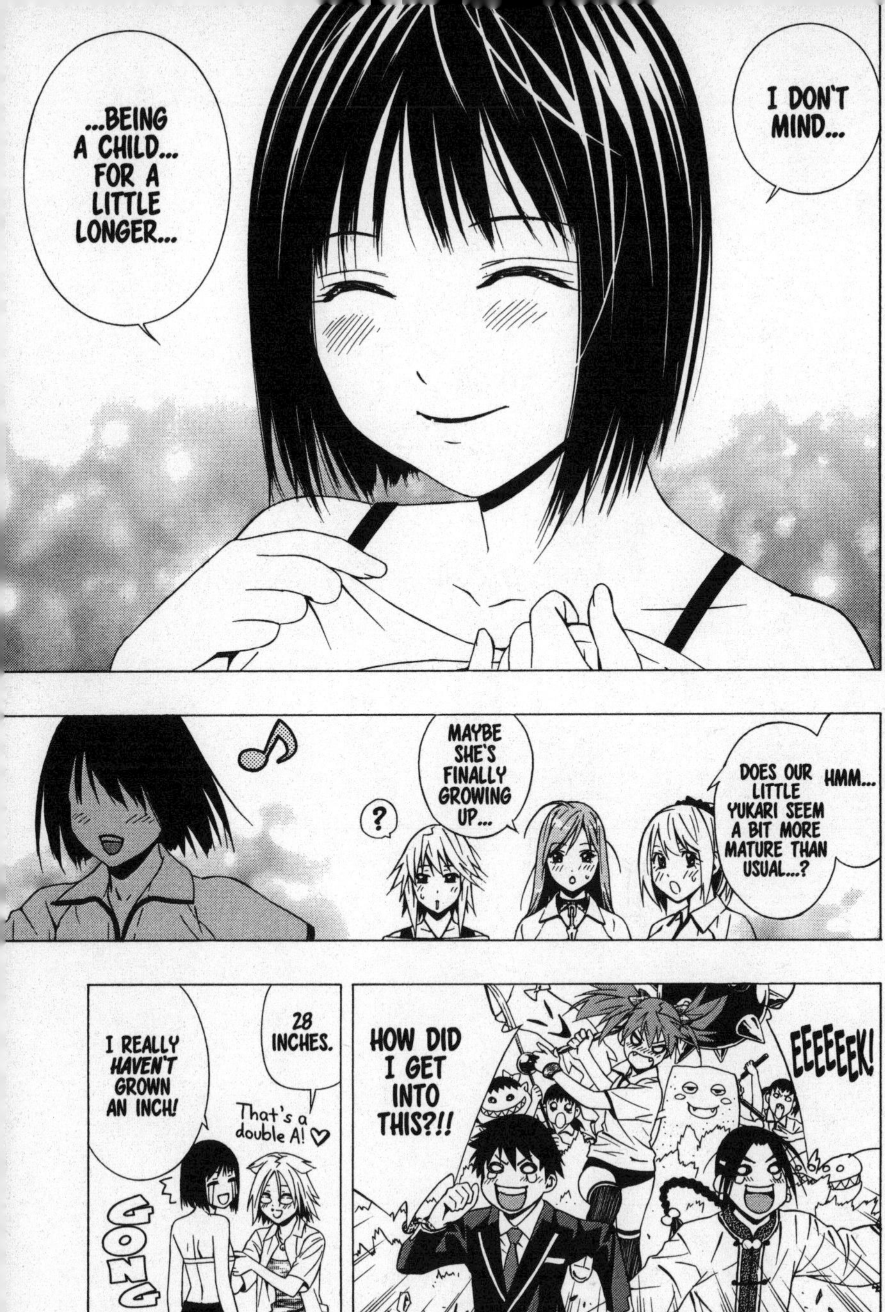
I DON'T MIND...
...BEING A CHILD... FOR A LITTLE LONGER...
HMM...
DOES OUR LITTLE YUKARI SEEM A BIT MORE MATURE THAN USUAL...?
MAYBE SHE'S FINALLY GROWING UP...
?
EEEEEEK!
HOW DID I GET INTO THIS?!!
28 INCHES.
That's a double A! ♡
I REALLY HAVEN'T GROWN AN INCH!
GONG

26: Weak Point

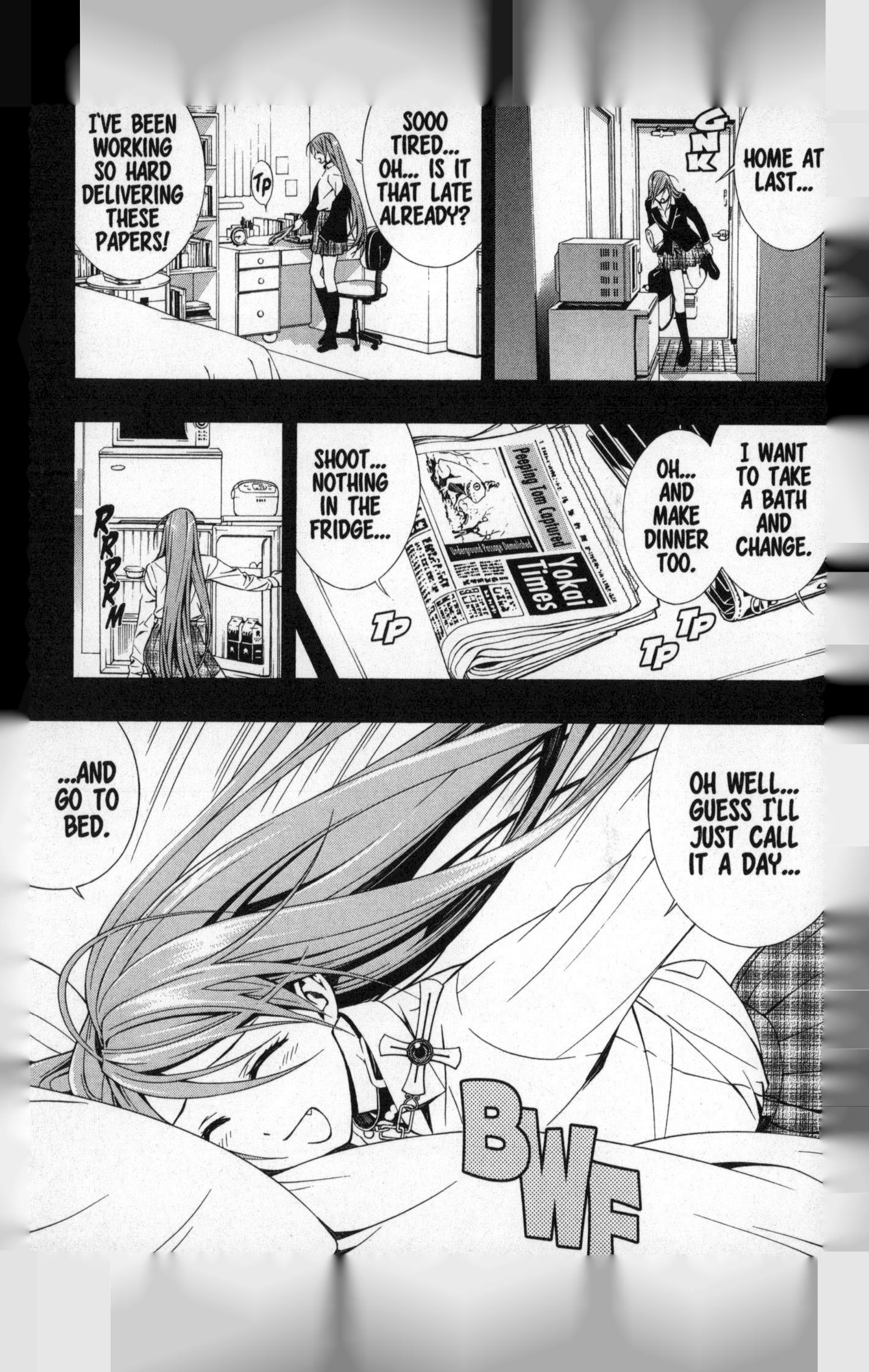
GNK
HOME AT LAST...
SOOO TIRED... OH... IS IT THAT LATE ALREADY?
Tp
I'VE BEEN WORKING SO HARD DELIVERING THESE PAPERS!
I WANT TO TAKE A BATH AND CHANGE.
OH... AND MAKE DINNER TOO.
Tp
Tp
Yokai Times
Peeping Tom Captured
Underground Passage Demolished
SHOOT... NOTHING IN THE FRIDGE...
Tp
RRRRM
OH WELL... GUESS I'LL JUST CALL IT A DAY...
...AND GO TO BED.
BWF

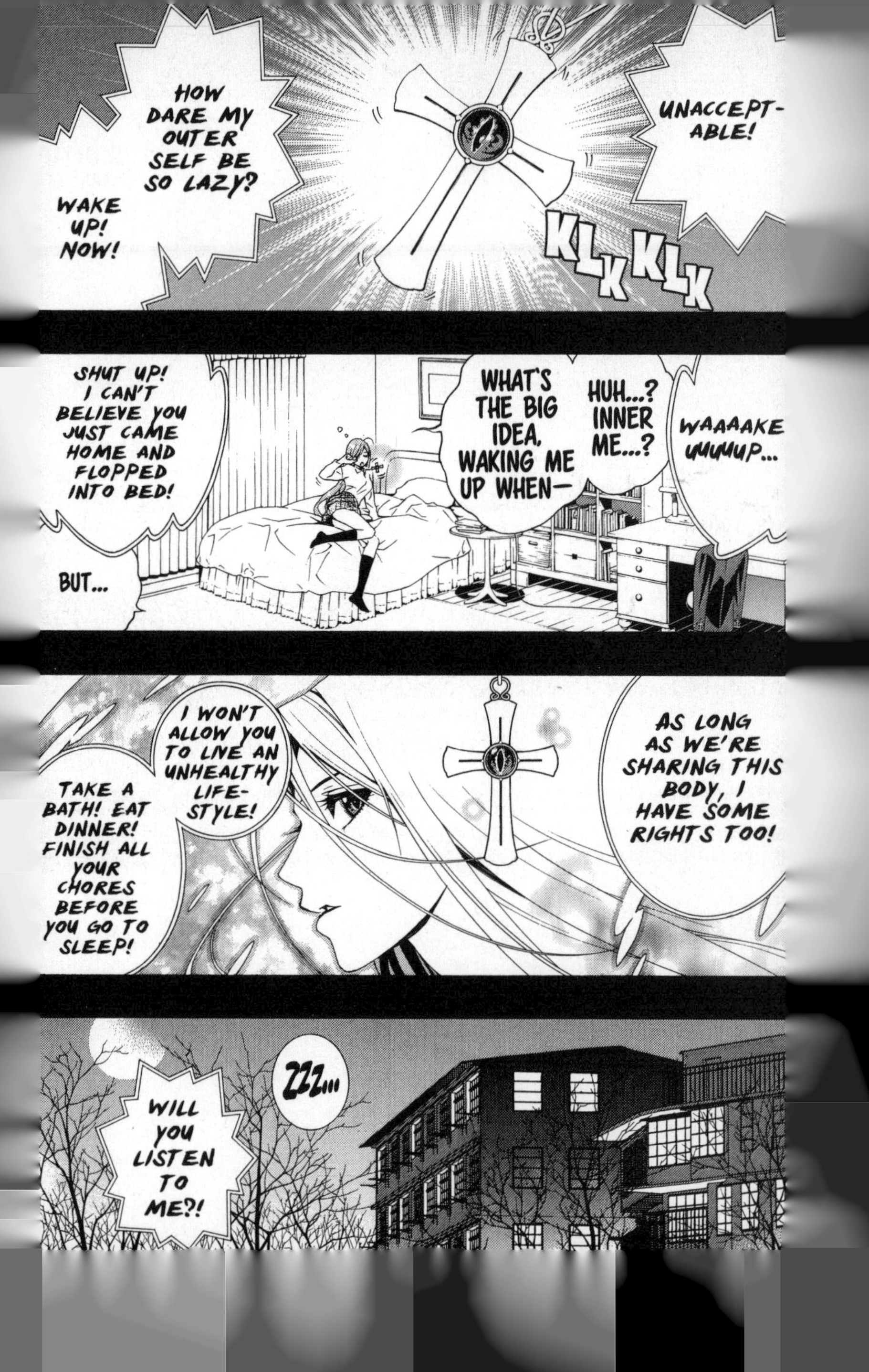
UNACCEPT-ABLE!
KLK KLK
HOW DARE MY OUTER SELF BE SO LAZY?
WAKE UP! NOW!
WAAAAKE UUUUUP...
HUH...? INNER ME...?
WHAT'S THE BIG IDEA, WAKING ME UP WHEN—
SHUT UP! I CAN'T BELIEVE YOU JUST CAME HOME AND FLOPPED INTO BED!
BUT...
AS LONG AS WE'RE SHARING THIS BODY, I HAVE SOME RIGHTS TOO!
I WON'T ALLOW YOU TO LIVE AN UNHEALTHY LIFE-STYLE!
TAKE A BATH! EAT DINNER! FINISH ALL YOUR CHORES BEFORE YOU GO TO SLEEP!
ZZZ...
WILL YOU LISTEN TO ME?!

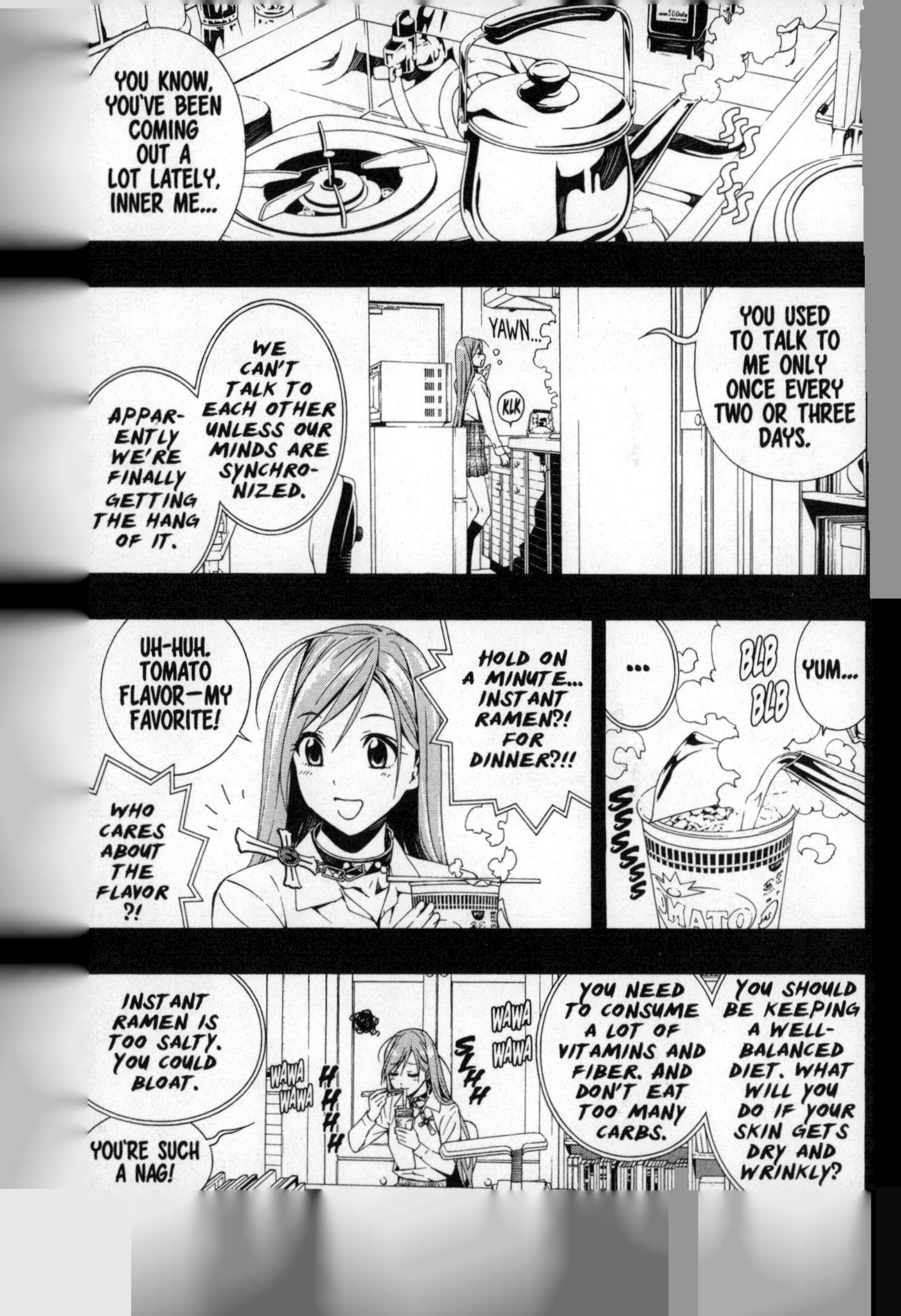
YOU KNOW, YOU'VE BEEN COMING OUT A LOT LATELY, INNER ME...
YOU USED TO TALK TO ME ONLY ONCE EVERY TWO OR THREE DAYS.
YAWN...
KLK
WE CAN'T TALK TO EACH OTHER UNLESS OUR MINDS ARE SYNCHRONIZED.
APPARENTLY WE'RE FINALLY GETTING THE HANG OF IT.
YUM...
BLB BLB
...
HOLD ON A MINUTE... INSTANT RAMEN?! FOR DINNER?!!
UH-HUH. TOMATO FLAVOR—MY FAVORITE!
WHO CARES ABOUT THE FLAVOR?!
YOU SHOULD BE KEEPING A WELL-BALANCED DIET. WHAT WILL YOU DO IF YOUR SKIN GETS DRY AND WRINKLY?
YOU NEED TO CONSUME A LOT OF VITAMINS AND FIBER. AND DON'T EAT TOO MANY CARBS.
WAWA WAWA
SLHH
HHHHH
WAWA WAWA
INSTANT RAMEN IS TOO SALTY. YOU COULD BLOAT.
YOU'RE SUCH A NAG!

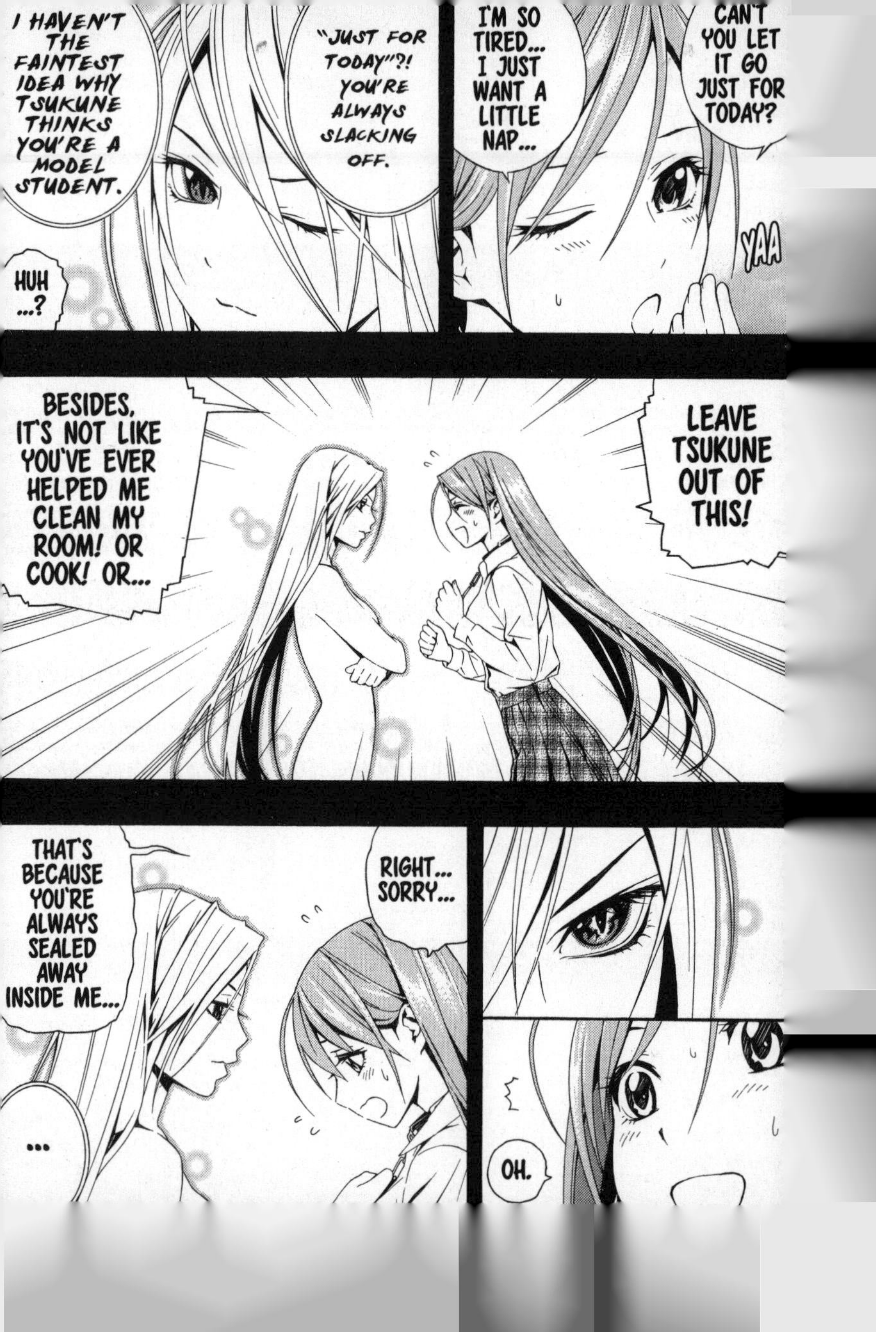
CAN'T YOU LET IT GO JUST FOR TODAY?
YAA
I'M SO TIRED... I JUST WANT A LITTLE NAP...
"JUST FOR TODAY"?! YOU'RE ALWAYS SLACKING OFF.
I HAVEN'T THE FAINTEST IDEA WHY TSUKUNE THINKS YOU'RE A MODEL STUDENT.
HUH ...?
LEAVE TSUKUNE OUT OF THIS!
BESIDES, IT'S NOT LIKE YOU'VE EVER HELPED ME CLEAN MY ROOM! OR COOK! OR...
OH.
RIGHT... SORRY...
THAT'S BECAUSE YOU'RE ALWAYS SEALED AWAY INSIDE ME...
...

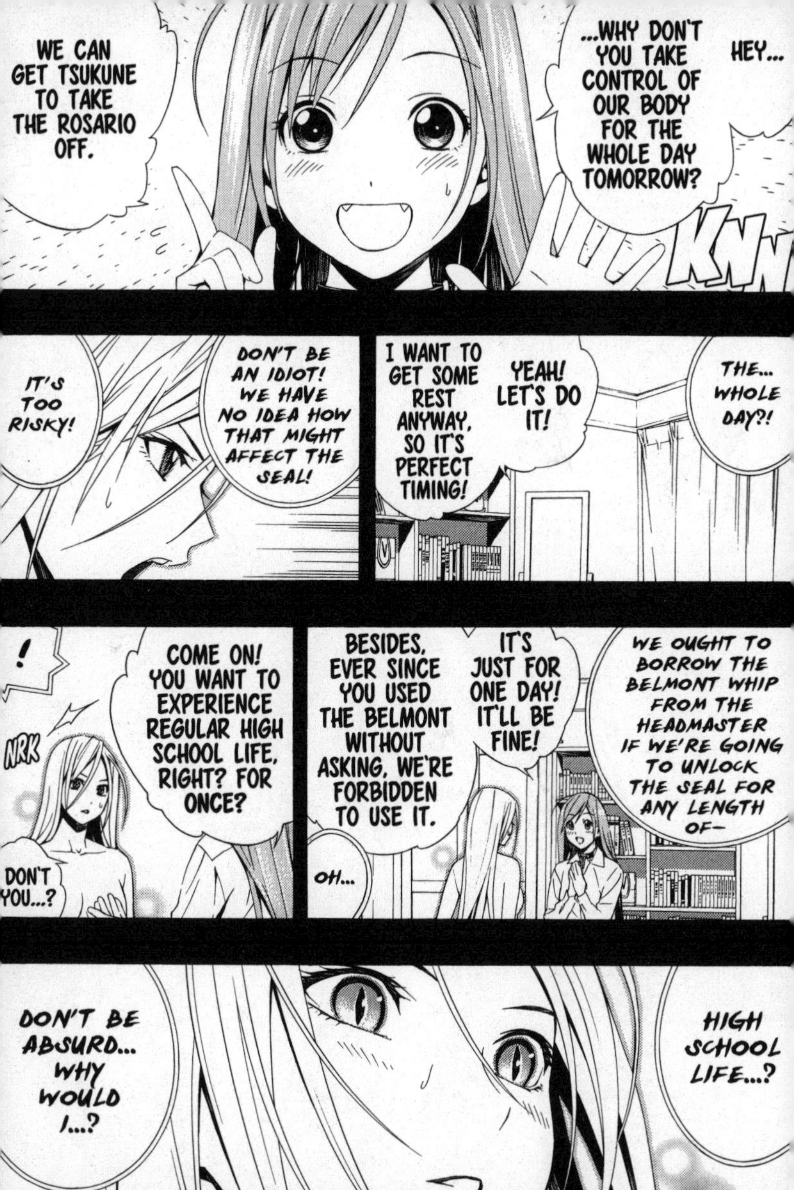
HEY...
...WHY DON'T YOU TAKE CONTROL OF OUR BODY FOR THE WHOLE DAY TOMORROW?
KNN
WE CAN GET TSUKUNE TO TAKE THE ROSARIO OFF.
THE... WHOLE DAY?!
YEAH! LET'S DO IT!
I WANT TO GET SOME REST ANYWAY, SO IT'S PERFECT TIMING!
DON'T BE AN IDIOT! WE HAVE NO IDEA HOW THAT MIGHT AFFECT THE SEAL!
IT'S TOO RISKY!
WE OUGHT TO BORROW THE BELMONT WHIP FROM THE HEADMASTER IF WE'RE GOING TO UNLOCK THE SEAL FOR ANY LENGTH OF—
IT'S JUST FOR ONE DAY! IT'LL BE FINE!
BESIDES, EVER SINCE YOU USED THE BELMONT WITHOUT ASKING, WE'RE FORBIDDEN TO USE IT.
OH...
COME ON! YOU WANT TO EXPERIENCE REGULAR HIGH SCHOOL LIFE, RIGHT? FOR ONCE?
!
NRK
DON'T YOU...?
HIGH SCHOOL LIFE...?
DON'T BE ABSURD... WHY WOULD I...?

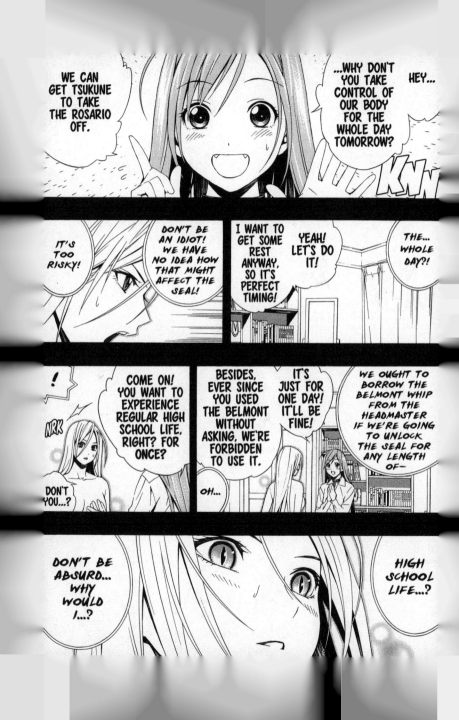

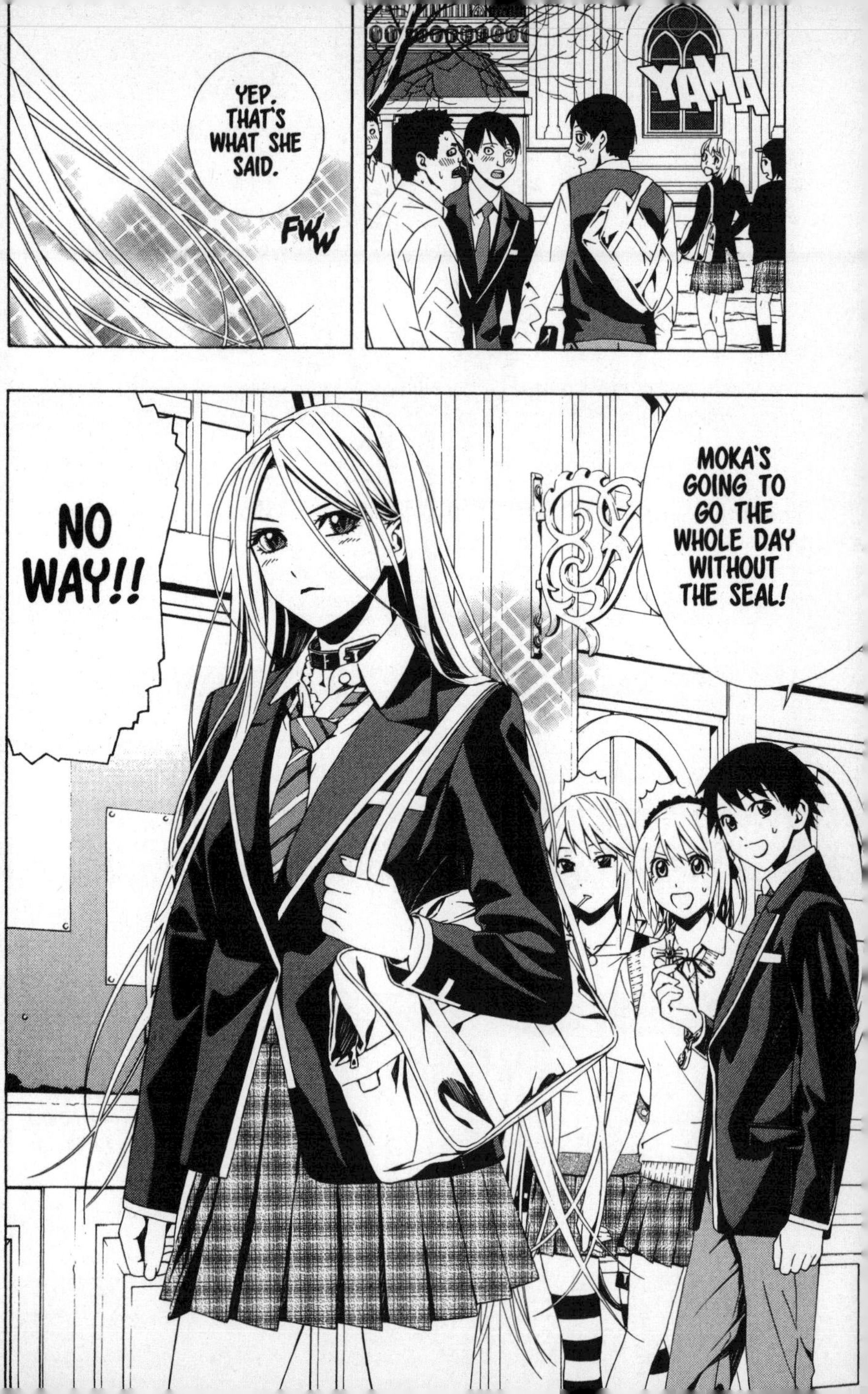
YAMA
YEP. THAT'S WHAT SHE SAID.
FWW
MOKA'S GOING TO GO THE WHOLE DAY WITHOUT THE SEAL!
NO WAY!!

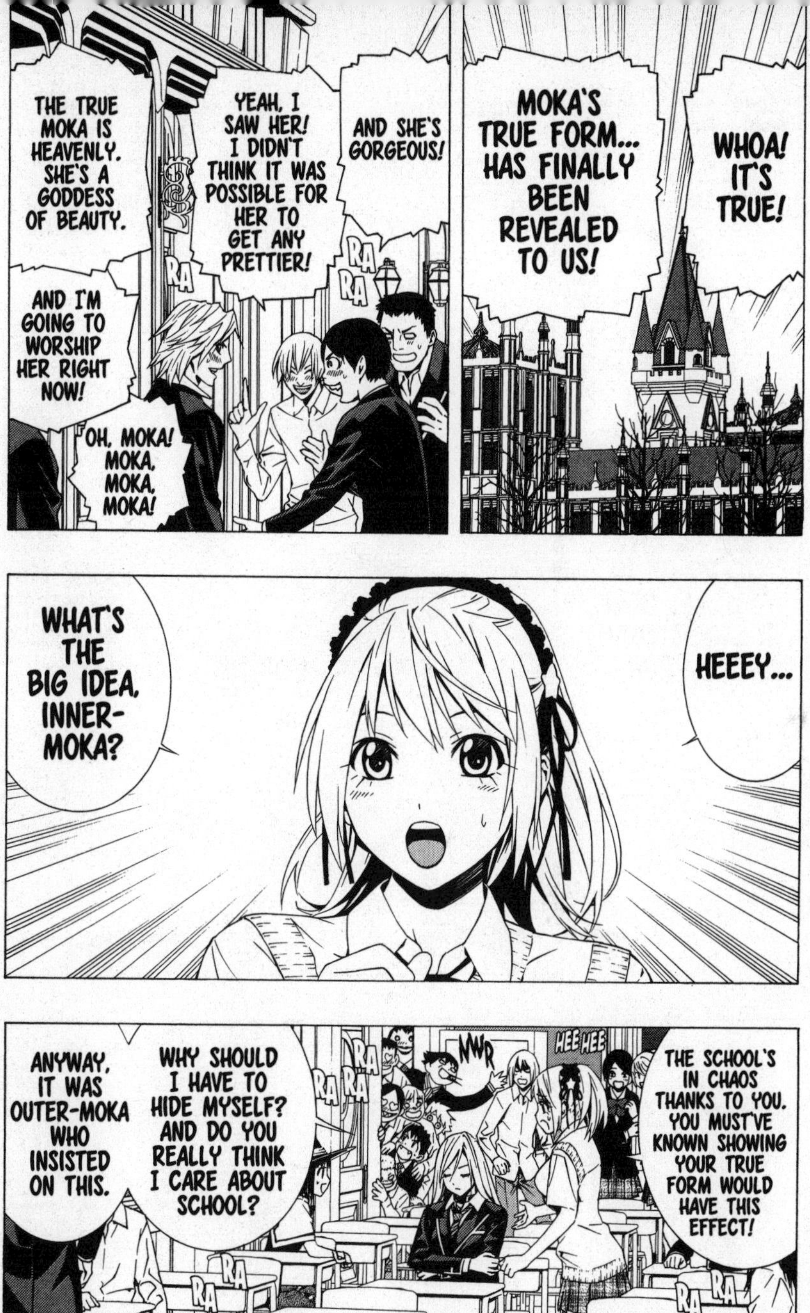

WHOA! IT'S TRUE!
MOKA'S TRUE FORM... HAS FINALLY BEEN REVEALED TO US!
AND SHE'S GORGEOUS!
YEAH, I SAW HER! I DIDN'T THINK IT WAS POSSIBLE FOR HER TO GET ANY PRETTIER!
THE TRUE MOKA IS HEAVENLY. SHE'S A GODDESS OF BEAUTY.
RA RA
RA
AND I'M GOING TO WORSHIP HER RIGHT NOW!
OH, MOKA! MOKA, MOKA, MOKA!
HEEEY...
WHAT'S THE BIG IDEA, INNER-MOKA?
THE SCHOOL'S IN CHAOS THANKS TO YOU. YOU MUST'VE KNOWN SHOWING YOUR TRUE FORM WOULD HAVE THIS EFFECT!
HEE HEE
NWR
RA RA RA
WHY SHOULD I HAVE TO HIDE MYSELF? AND DO YOU REALLY THINK I CARE ABOUT SCHOOL?
ANYWAY, IT WAS OUTER-MOKA WHO INSISTED ON THIS.
RA RA
RA RA

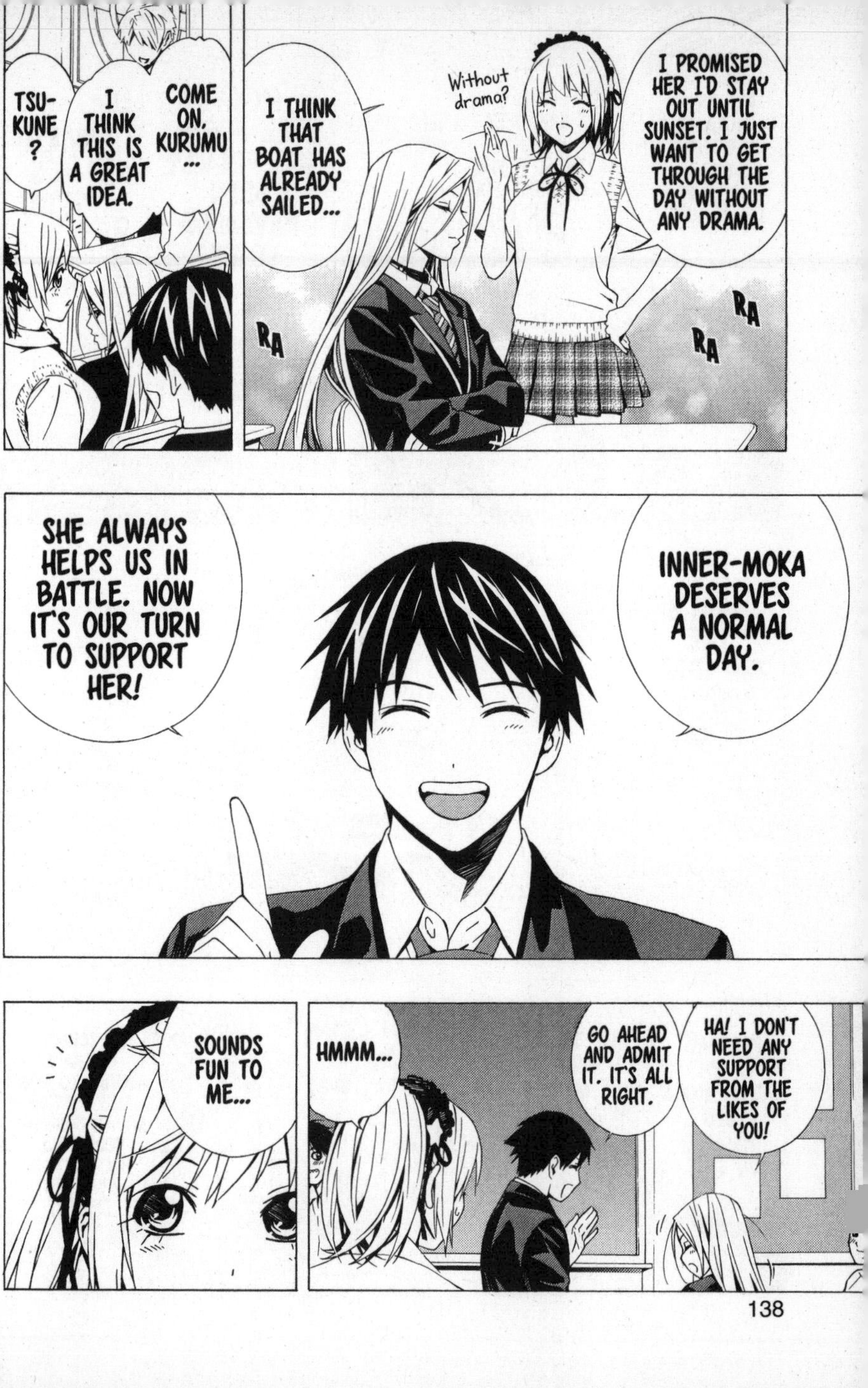
I PROMISED HER I'D STAY OUT UNTIL SUNSET. I JUST WANT TO GET THROUGH THE DAY WITHOUT ANY DRAMA.
Without drama?
RA
RA
I THINK THAT BOAT HAS ALREADY SAILED...
RA
COME ON, KURUMU...
I THINK THIS IS A GREAT IDEA.
TSU-KUNE?
INNER-MOKA DESERVES A NORMAL DAY.
SHE ALWAYS HELPS US IN BATTLE. NOW IT'S OUR TURN TO SUPPORT HER!
HA! I DON'T NEED ANY SUPPORT FROM THE LIKES OF YOU!
GO AHEAD AND ADMIT IT. IT'S ALL RIGHT.
HMMM...
SOUNDS FUN TO ME...

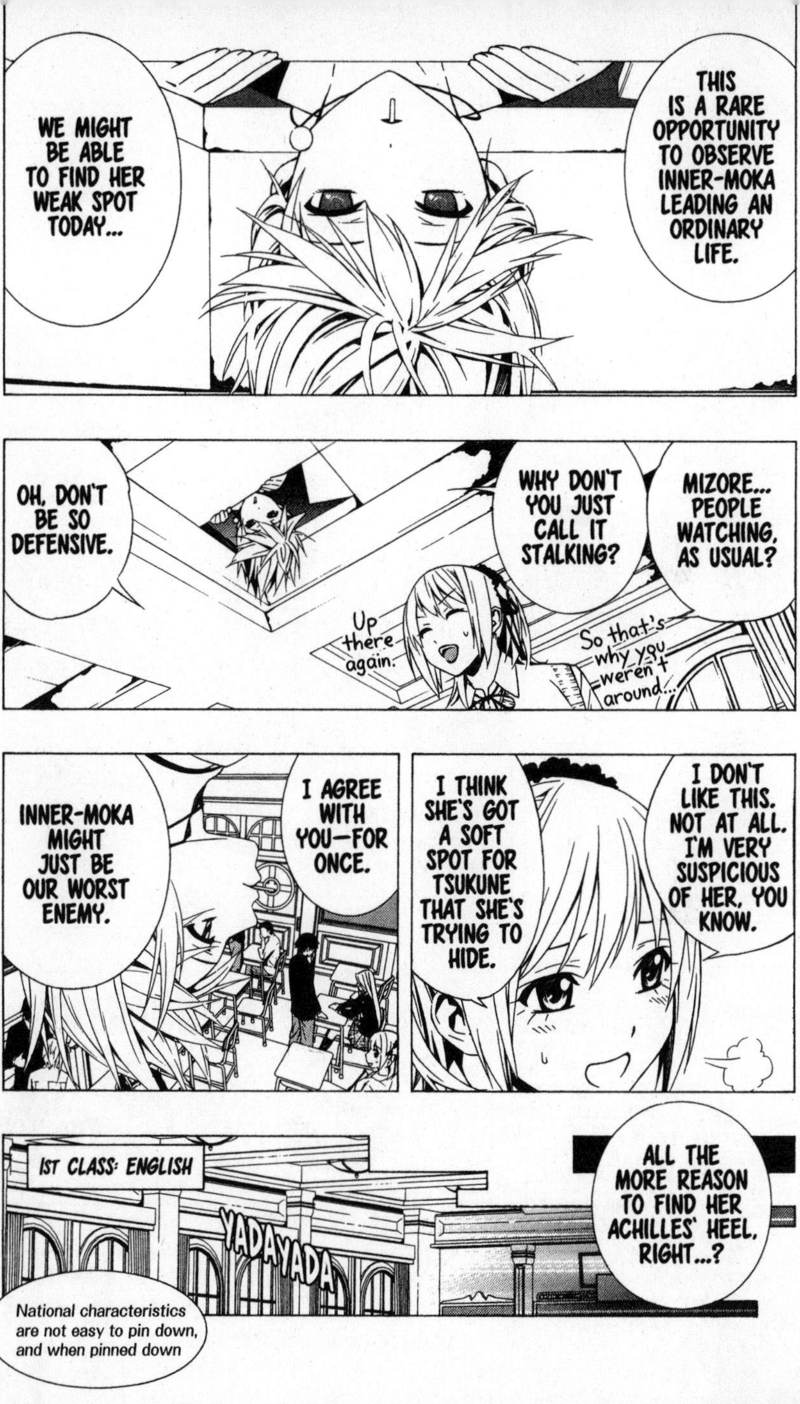
THIS IS A RARE OPPORTUNITY TO OBSERVE INNER-MOKA LEADING AN ORDINARY LIFE.
WE MIGHT BE ABLE TO FIND HER WEAK SPOT TODAY...
MIZORE... PEOPLE WATCHING, AS USUAL?
WHY DON'T YOU JUST CALL IT STALKING?
So that's why you weren't around...
Up there again.
OH, DON'T BE SO DEFENSIVE.
I DON'T LIKE THIS. NOT AT ALL. I'M VERY SUSPICIOUS OF HER, YOU KNOW.
I THINK SHE'S GOT A SOFT SPOT FOR TSUKUNE THAT SHE'S TRYING TO HIDE.
I AGREE WITH YOU—FOR ONCE.
INNER-MOKA MIGHT JUST BE OUR WORST ENEMY.
ALL THE MORE REASON TO FIND HER ACHILLES' HEEL, RIGHT...?
1ST CLASS: ENGLISH
YADAYADA
National characteristics are not easy to pin down, and when pinned down

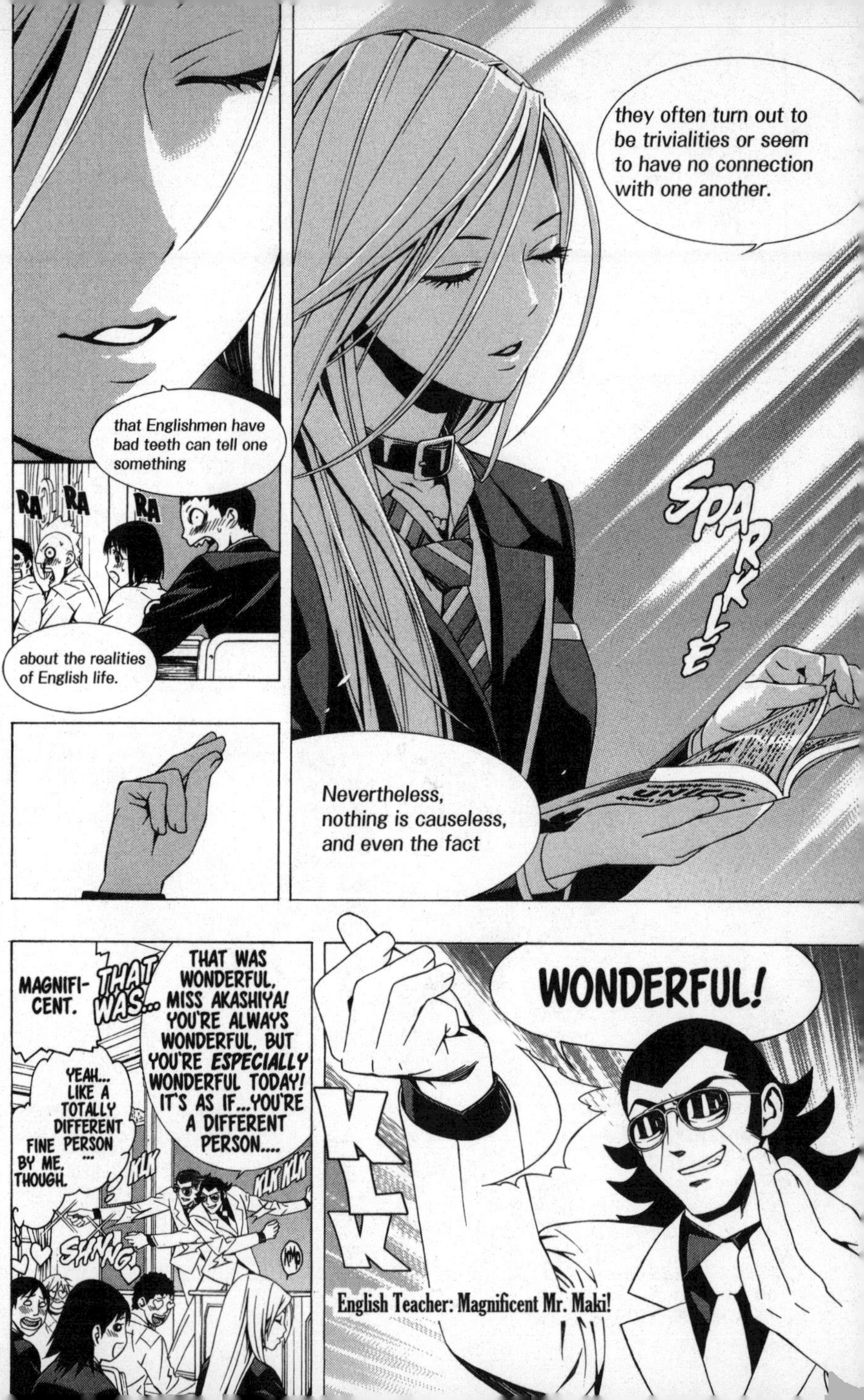
they often turn out to be trivialities or seem to have no connection with one another.
Nevertheless, nothing is causeless, and even the fact
SPARKLE
that Englishmen have bad teeth can tell one something
RA RA RA
about the realities of English life.
WONDERFUL!
KLK
English Teacher: Magnificent Mr. Maki!
THAT WAS...
THAT WAS WONDERFUL, MISS AKASHIYA! YOU'RE ALWAYS WONDERFUL, BUT YOU'RE *ESPECIALLY* WONDERFUL TODAY! IT'S AS IF...YOU'RE A DIFFERENT PERSON....
MAGNIFI-CENT.
YEAH... LIKE A TOTALLY DIFFERENT PERSON ...
FINE BY ME, THOUGH.
KLK
KLK KLK
SHING

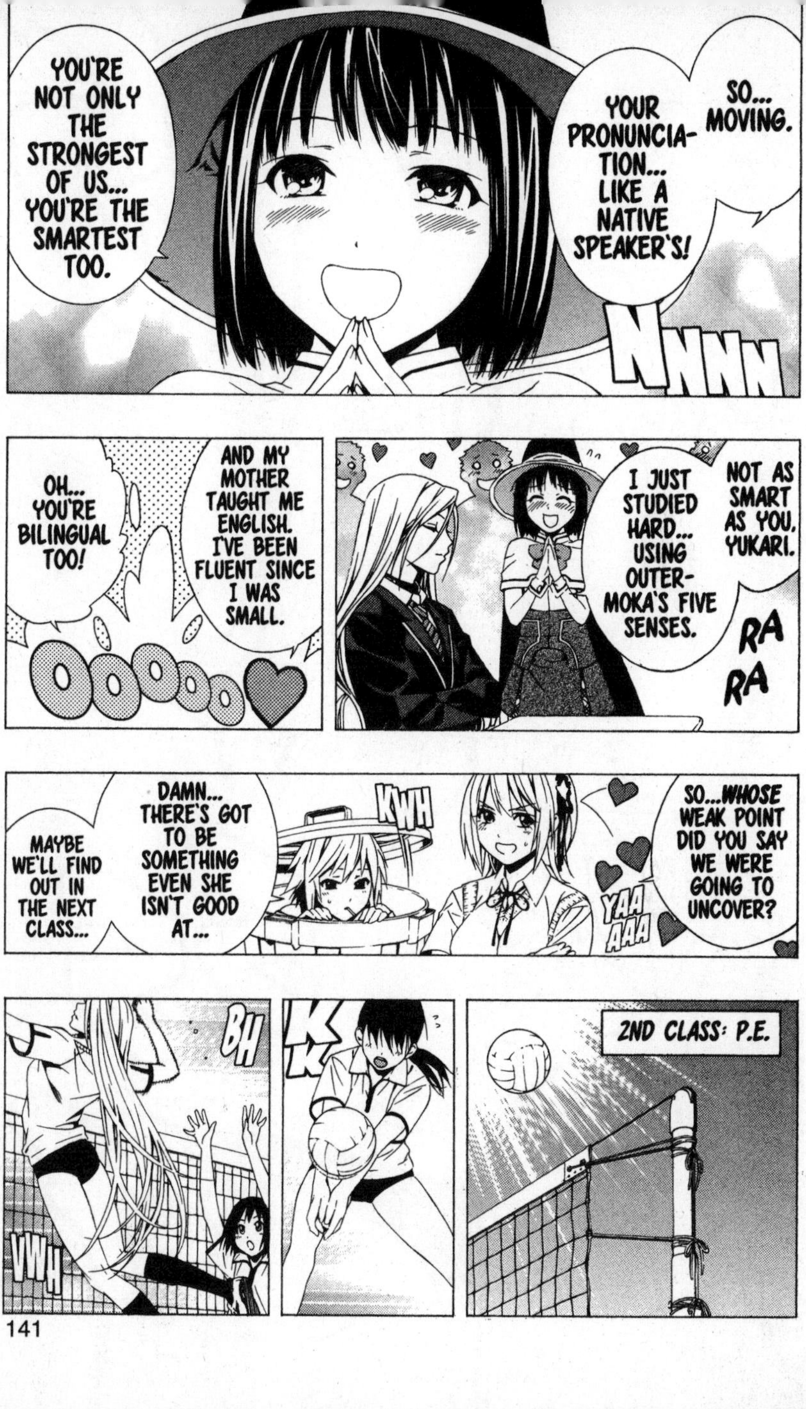
SO... MOVING.
YOUR PRONUNCIATION... LIKE A NATIVE SPEAKER'S!
YOU'RE NOT ONLY THE STRONGEST OF US... YOU'RE THE SMARTEST TOO.
NNNNN
NOT AS SMART AS YOU, YUKARI.
I JUST STUDIED HARD... USING OUTER-MOKA'S FIVE SENSES.
RA RA
AND MY MOTHER TAUGHT ME ENGLISH. I'VE BEEN FLUENT SINCE I WAS SMALL.
OH... YOU'RE BILINGUAL TOO!
OOOOOO
SO...WHOSE WEAK POINT DID YOU SAY WE WERE GOING TO UNCOVER?
YAAAAA
KWH
DAMN... THERE'S GOT TO BE SOMETHING EVEN SHE ISN'T GOOD AT...
MAYBE WE'LL FIND OUT IN THE NEXT CLASS...
2ND CLASS: P.E.
KK
BH
VWH

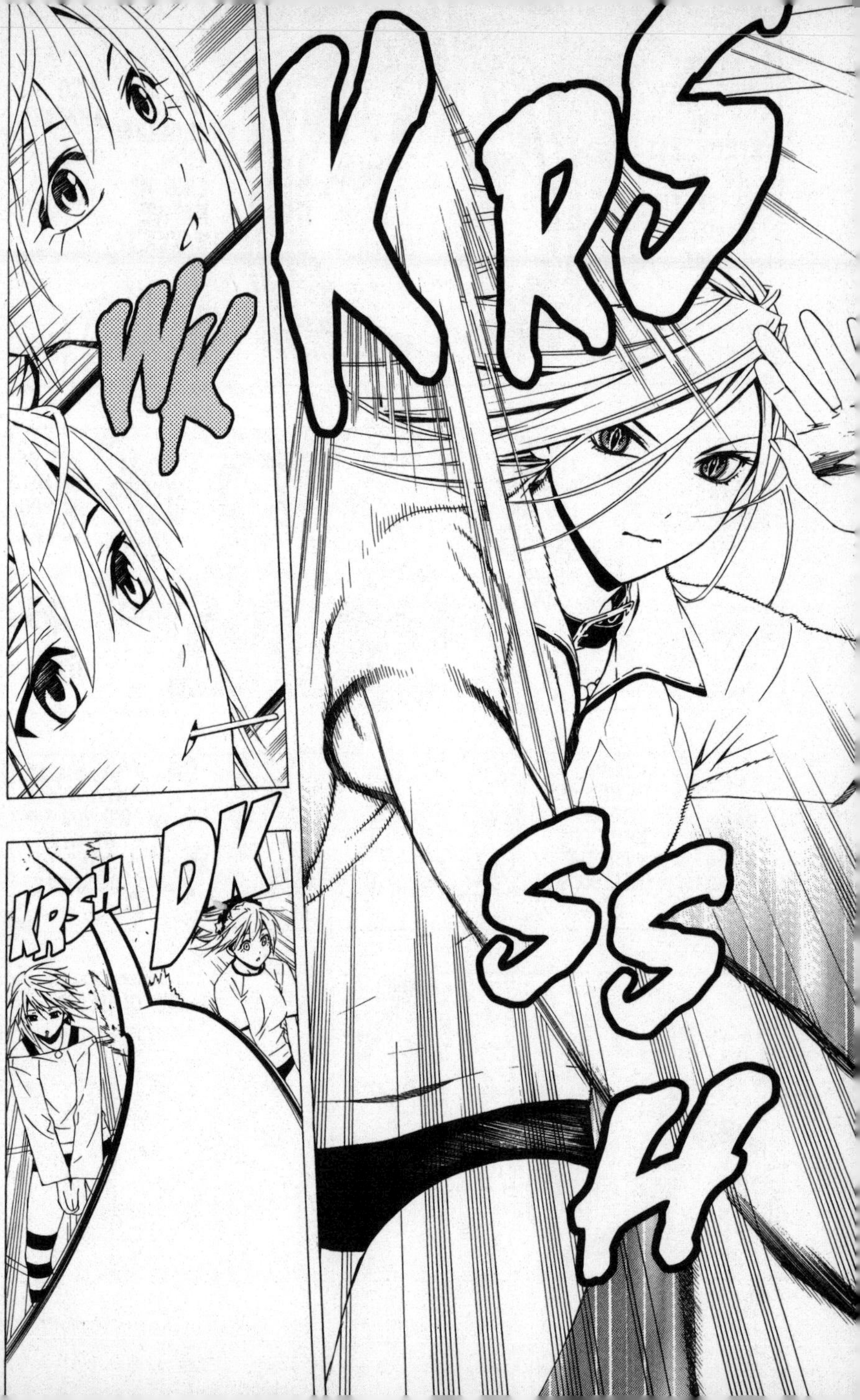
KRSSSH
WK
DK
KRSH

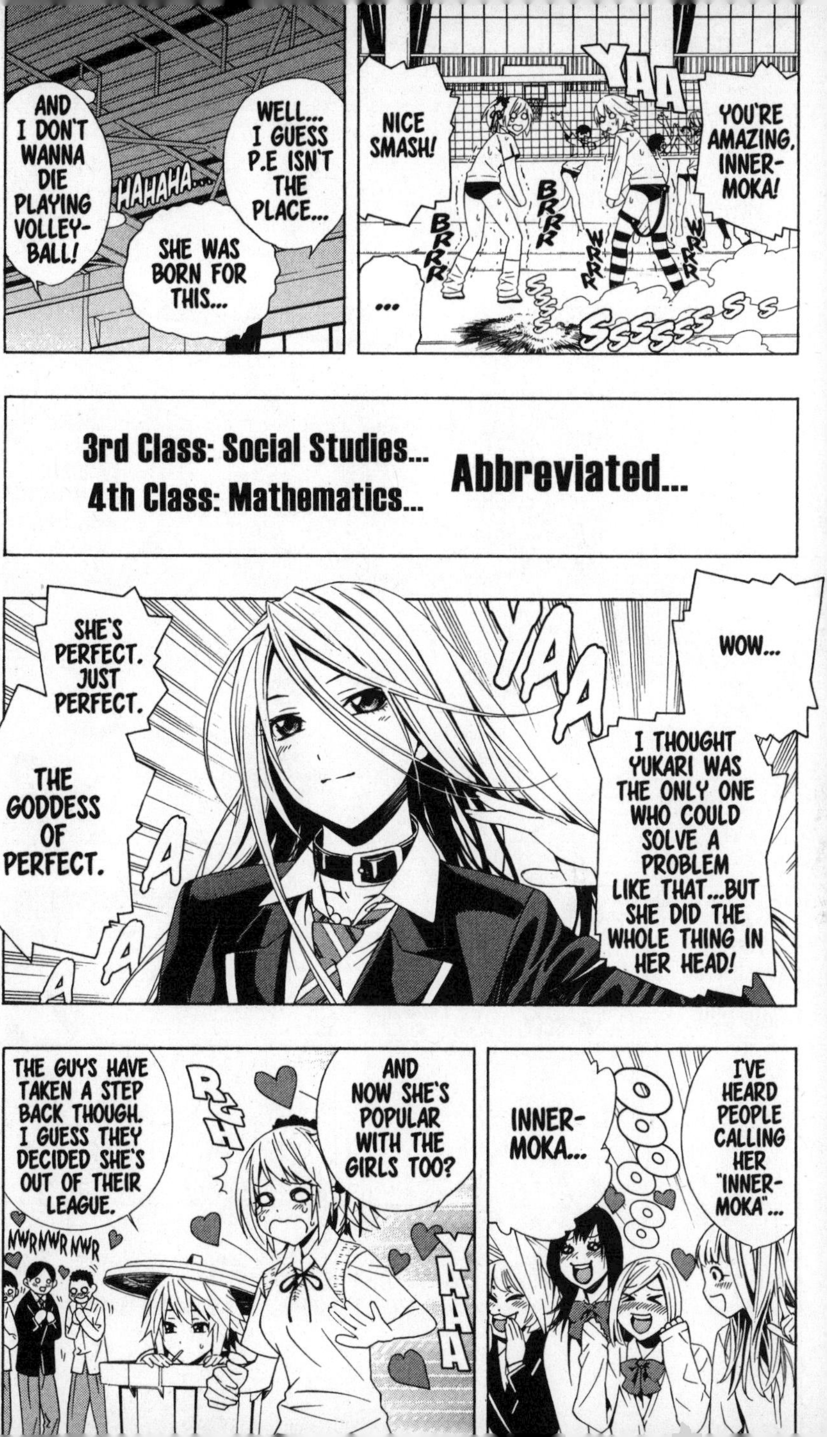
YAA
YOU'RE AMAZING, INNER-MOKA!
NICE SMASH!
BRRR
BRRR
WRRR
WRRR
...
SSSSSSSS S S
WELL... I GUESS P.E ISN'T THE PLACE...
AND I DON'T WANNA DIE PLAYING VOLLEY-BALL!
HAHAHA...
SHE WAS BORN FOR THIS...
3rd Class: Social Studies...
4th Class: Mathematics...
Abbreviated...
WOW...
YAAAAA
I THOUGHT YUKARI WAS THE ONLY ONE WHO COULD SOLVE A PROBLEM LIKE THAT...BUT SHE DID THE WHOLE THING IN HER HEAD!
SHE'S PERFECT. JUST PERFECT.
THE GODDESS OF PERFECT.
I'VE HEARD PEOPLE CALLING HER "INNER-MOKA"...
OOOOOOO
INNER-MOKA...
AND NOW SHE'S POPULAR WITH THE GIRLS TOO?
RGH
THE GUYS HAVE TAKEN A STEP BACK THOUGH. I GUESS THEY DECIDED SHE'S OUT OF THEIR LEAGUE.
NWRNWR NWR
YAAA

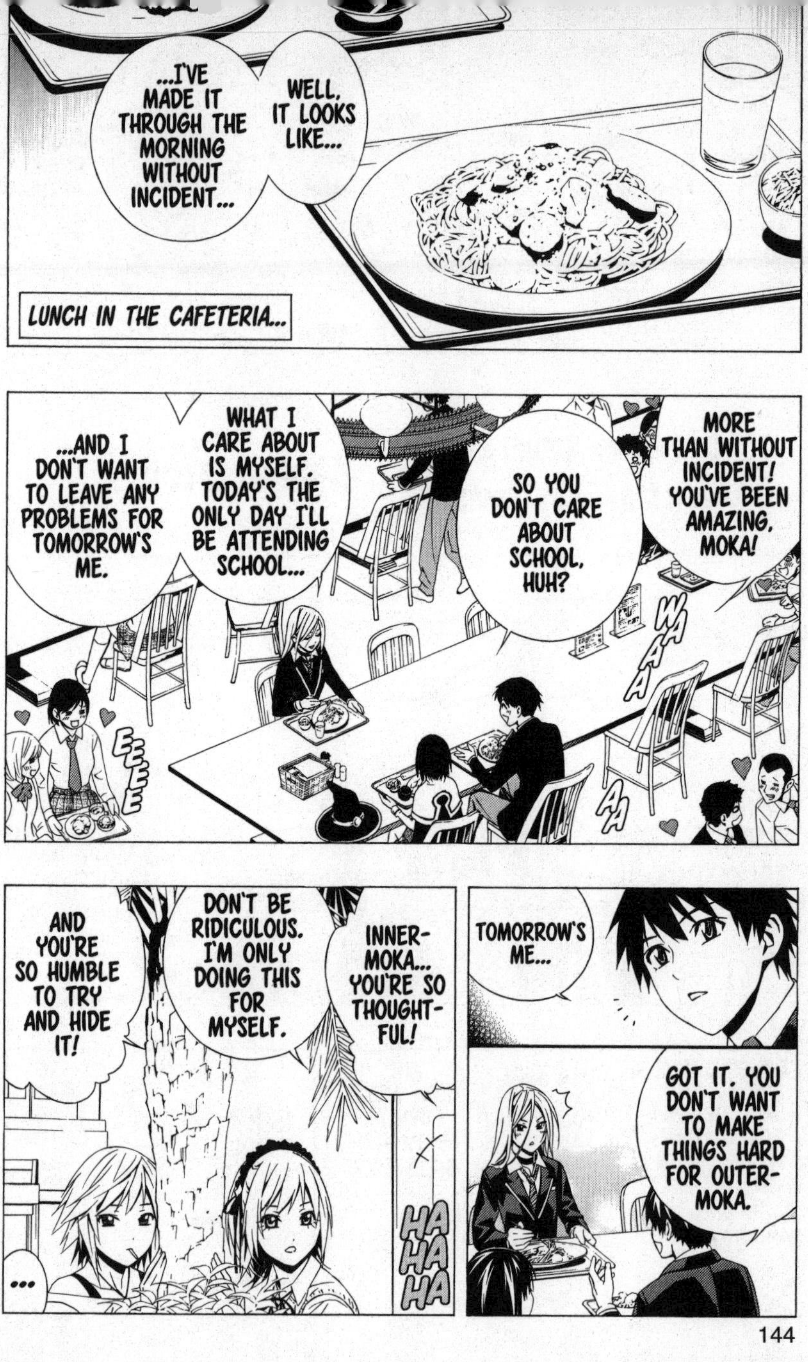
WELL, IT LOOKS LIKE...
...I'VE MADE IT THROUGH THE MORNING WITHOUT INCIDENT...
LUNCH IN THE CAFETERIA...
MORE THAN WITHOUT INCIDENT! YOU'VE BEEN AMAZING, MOKA!
WAAAA
SO YOU DON'T CARE ABOUT SCHOOL, HUH?
WHAT I CARE ABOUT IS MYSELF. TODAY'S THE ONLY DAY I'LL BE ATTENDING SCHOOL...
...AND I DON'T WANT TO LEAVE ANY PROBLEMS FOR TOMORROW'S ME.
AA
EEEE
TOMORROW'S ME...
GOT IT. YOU DON'T WANT TO MAKE THINGS HARD FOR OUTER-MOKA.
INNER-MOKA... YOU'RE SO THOUGHTFUL!
DON'T BE RIDICULOUS. I'M ONLY DOING THIS FOR MYSELF.
AND YOU'RE SO HUMBLE TO TRY AND HIDE IT!
HAHAHAHA
...

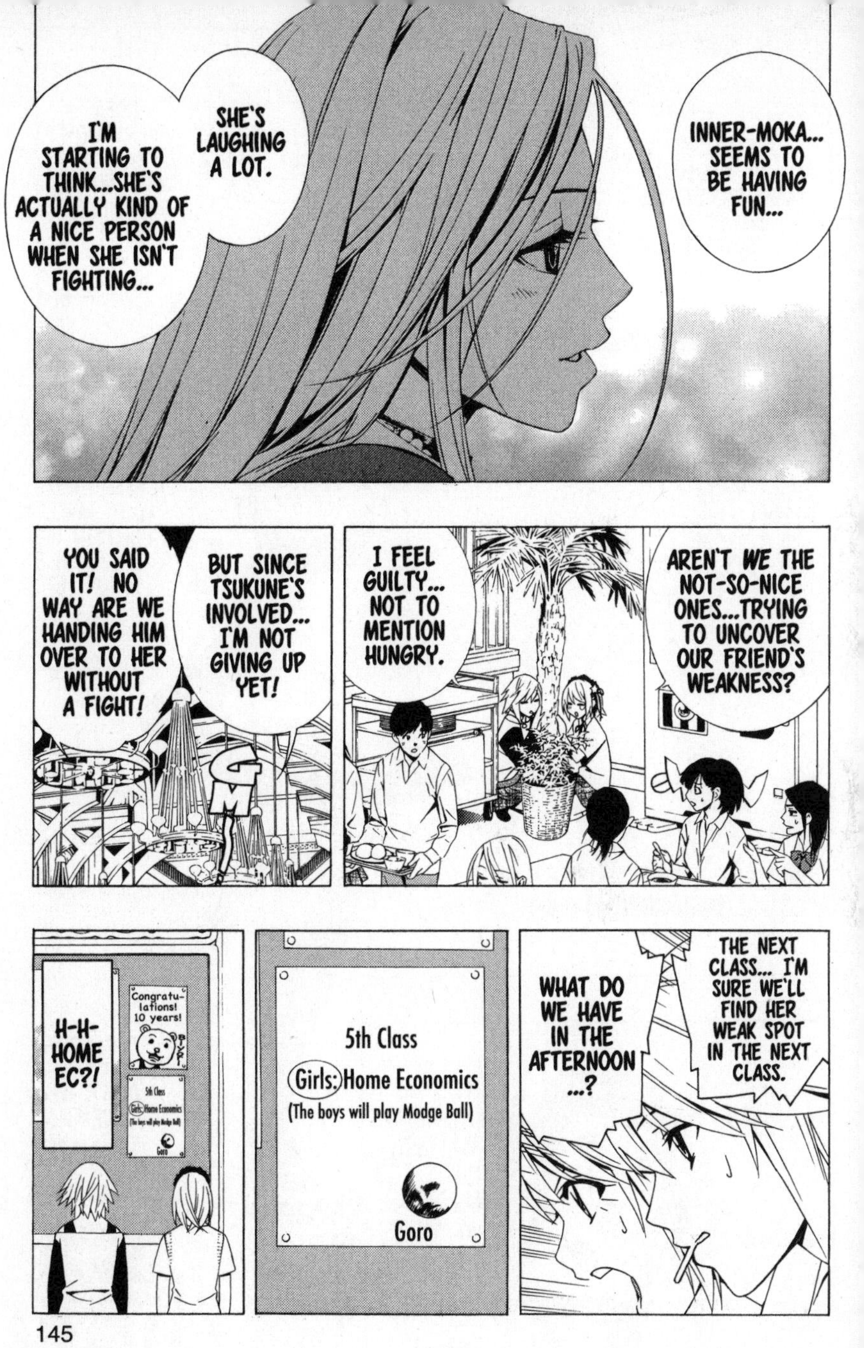
INNER-MOKA... SEEMS TO BE HAVING FUN...
SHE'S LAUGHING A LOT.
I'M STARTING TO THINK...SHE'S ACTUALLY KIND OF A NICE PERSON WHEN SHE ISN'T FIGHTING...
AREN'T WE THE NOT-SO-NICE ONES...TRYING TO UNCOVER OUR FRIEND'S WEAKNESS?
I FEEL GUILTY... NOT TO MENTION HUNGRY.
BUT SINCE TSUKUNE'S INVOLVED... I'M NOT GIVING UP YET!
YOU SAID IT! NO WAY ARE WE HANDING HIM OVER TO HER WITHOUT A FIGHT!
GM
THE NEXT CLASS... I'M SURE WE'LL FIND HER WEAK SPOT IN THE NEXT CLASS.
WHAT DO WE HAVE IN THE AFTERNOON ...?
5th Class
Girls: Home Economics
(The boys will play Modge Ball)
Goro
H-H-HOME EC?!
Congratulations! 10 years!

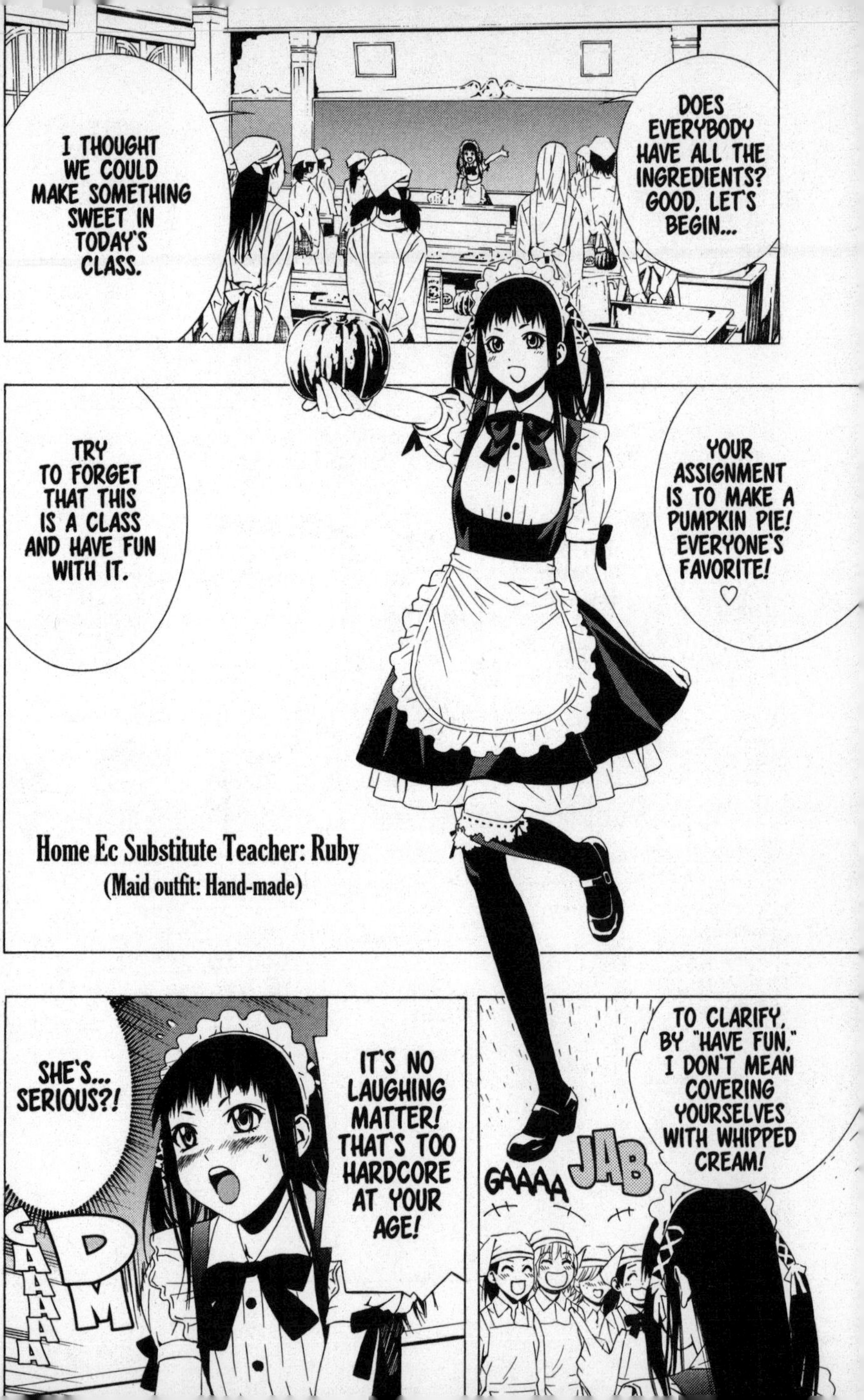
DOES EVERYBODY HAVE ALL THE INGREDIENTS? GOOD, LET'S BEGIN...
I THOUGHT WE COULD MAKE SOMETHING SWEET IN TODAY'S CLASS.
YOUR ASSIGNMENT IS TO MAKE A PUMPKIN PIE! EVERYONE'S FAVORITE! ♡
TRY TO FORGET THAT THIS IS A CLASS AND HAVE FUN WITH IT.
Home Ec Substitute Teacher: Ruby
(Maid outfit: Hand-made)
TO CLARIFY, BY "HAVE FUN," I DON'T MEAN COVERING YOURSELVES WITH WHIPPED CREAM!
JAB
GAAAA
IT'S NO LAUGHING MATTER! THAT'S TOO HARDCORE AT YOUR AGE!
SHE'S... SERIOUS?!
DM
GAAAAA

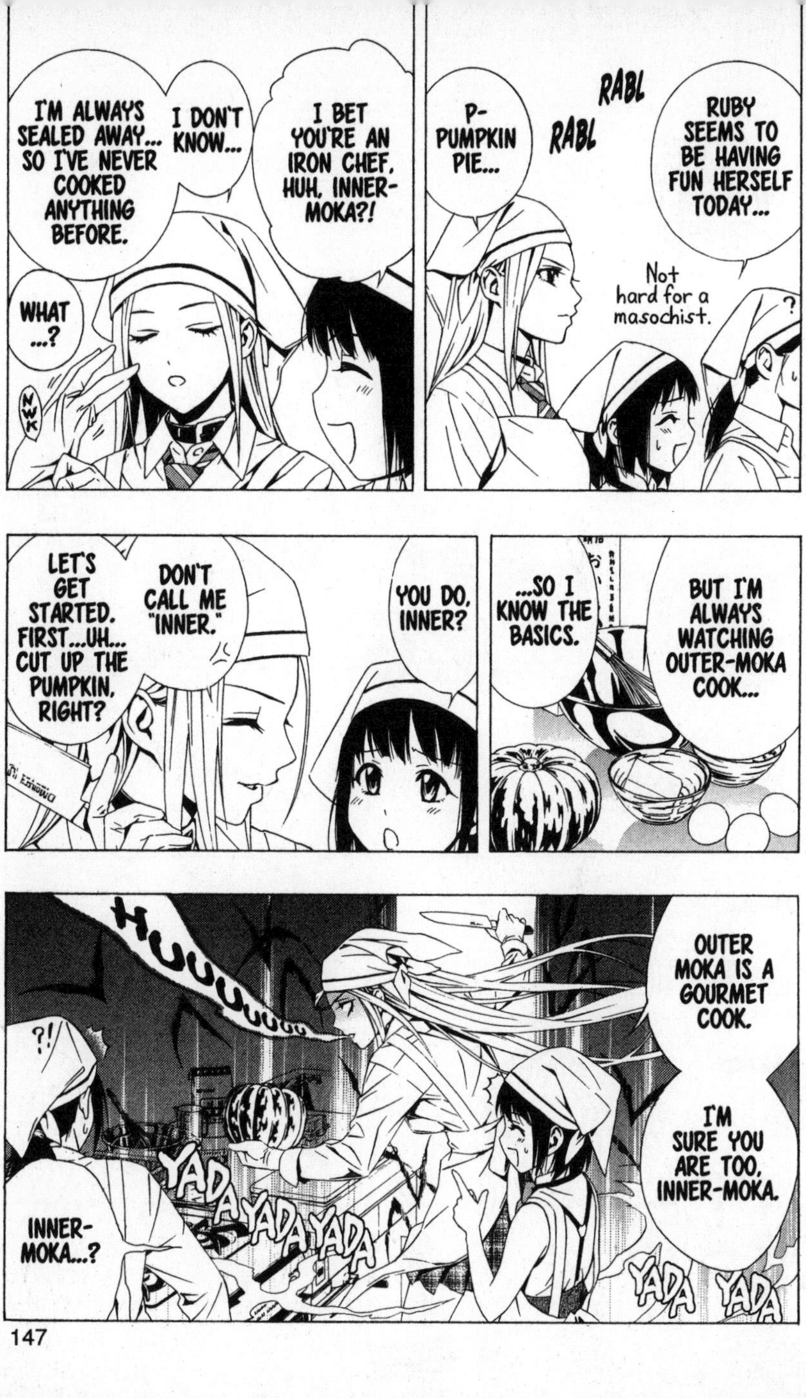
RUBY SEEMS TO BE HAVING FUN HERSELF TODAY...
RABL
RABL
P-PUMPKIN PIE...
Not hard for a masochist.
?
I BET YOU'RE AN IRON CHEF, HUH, INNER-MOKA?!
I DON'T KNOW...
I'M ALWAYS SEALED AWAY... SO I'VE NEVER COOKED ANYTHING BEFORE.
WHAT ...?
NWK
BUT I'M ALWAYS WATCHING OUTER-MOKA COOK...
...SO I KNOW THE BASICS.
YOU DO, INNER?
DON'T CALL ME "INNER."
LET'S GET STARTED. FIRST...UH... CUT UP THE PUMPKIN, RIGHT?
OUTER MOKA IS A GOURMET COOK.
I'M SURE YOU ARE TOO, INNER-MOKA.
HUUUUUUU
?!
INNER-MOKA...?
YADA YADA YADA
YADA YADA

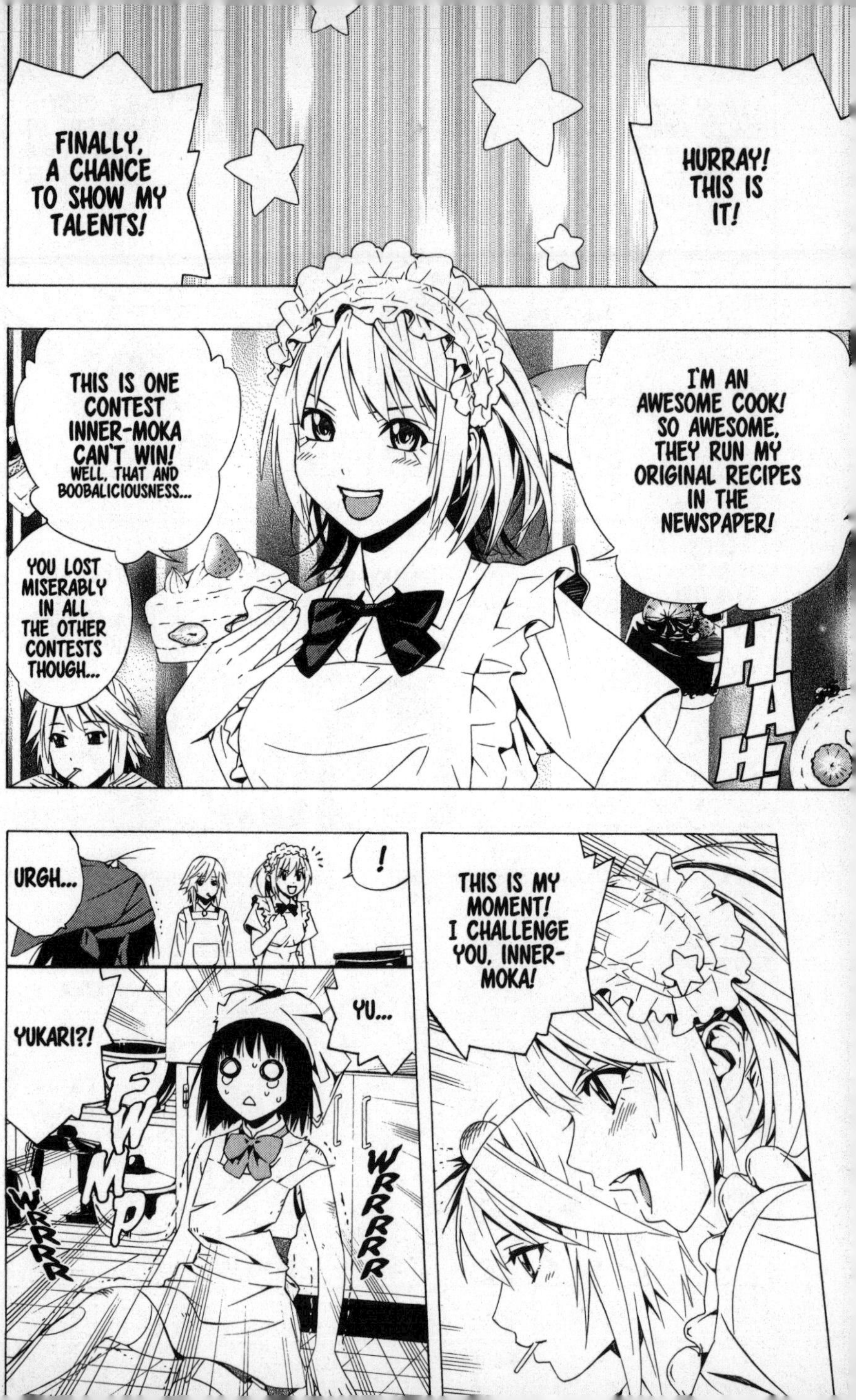
HURRAY! THIS IS IT!
FINALLY, A CHANCE TO SHOW MY TALENTS!
I'M AN AWESOME COOK! SO AWESOME, THEY RUN MY ORIGINAL RECIPES IN THE NEWSPAPER!
HAHAH!
THIS IS ONE CONTEST INNER-MOKA CAN'T WIN!
WELL, THAT AND BOOBALICIOUSNESS...
YOU LOST MISERABLY IN ALL THE OTHER CONTESTS THOUGH...
THIS IS MY MOMENT! I CHALLENGE YOU, INNER-MOKA!
!
URGH...
YU...
YUKARI?!
FWMP
WRRRRR
WRRRR

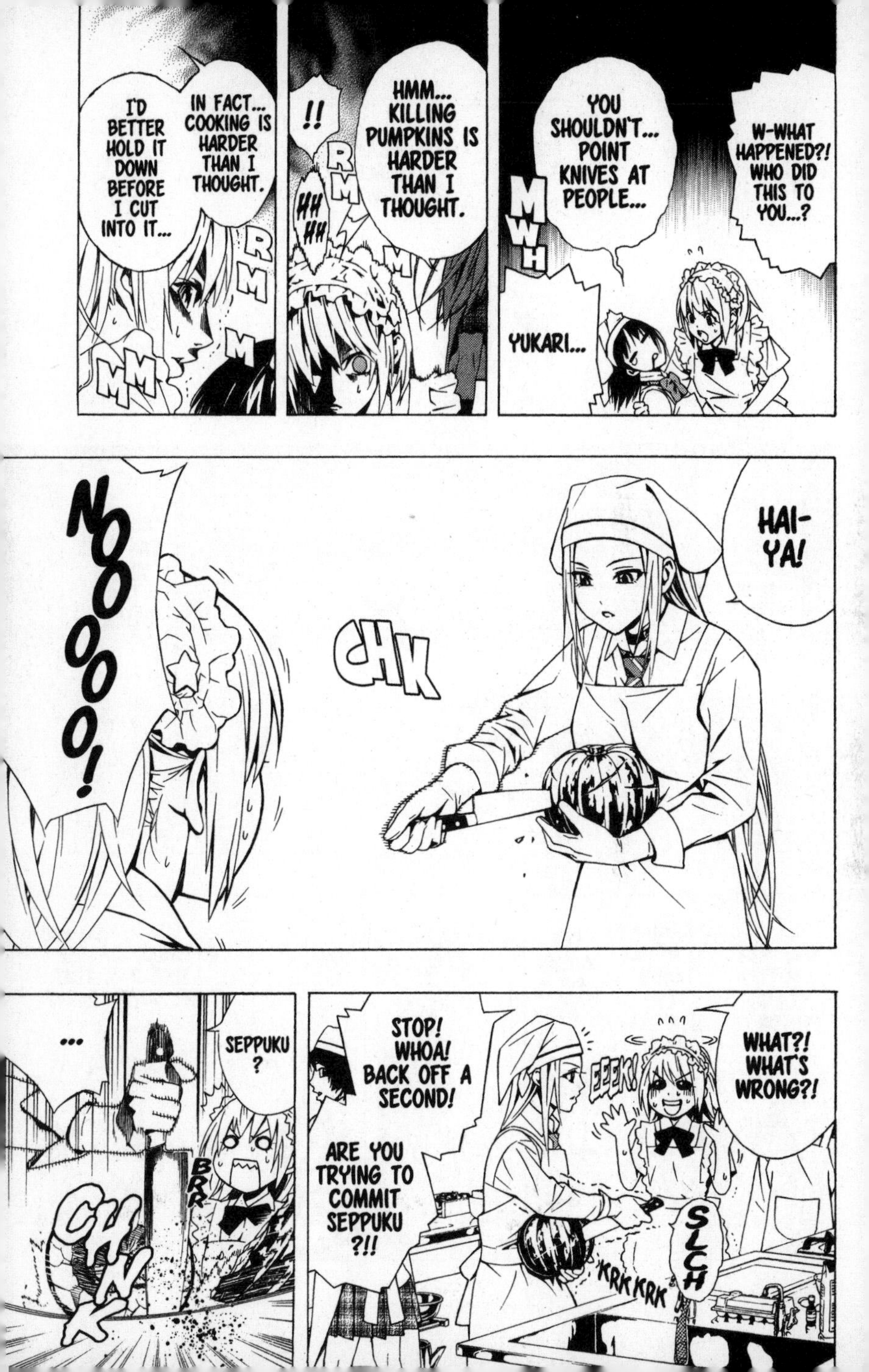
W-WHAT HAPPENED?! WHO DID THIS TO YOU...?
YOU SHOULDN'T... POINT KNIVES AT PEOPLE...
MWH
YUKARI...
HMM... KILLING PUMPKINS IS HARDER THAN I THOUGHT.
!!
RM
M
IN FACT... COOKING IS HARDER THAN I THOUGHT.
I'D BETTER HOLD IT DOWN BEFORE I CUT INTO IT...
RMM
MMM
HAI-YA!
CHK
NOOOOOO!
WHAT?! WHAT'S WRONG?!
EEEK!
STOP! WHOA! BACK OFF A SECOND!
ARE YOU TRYING TO COMMIT SEPPUKU?!!
SLCH
KRK KRK
SEPPUKU?
...
BRR
CHNK

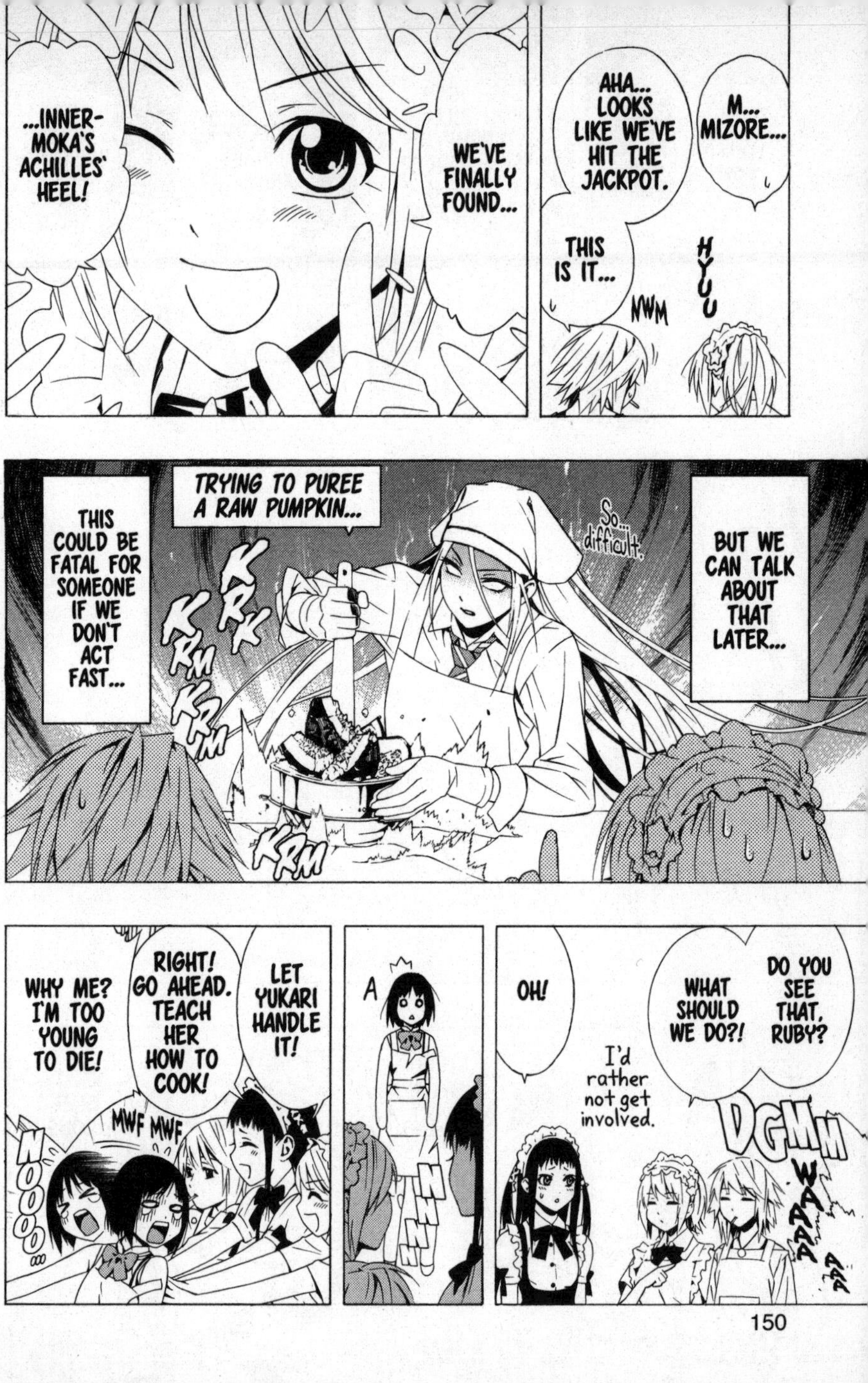
M... MIZORE...
AHA... LOOKS LIKE WE'VE HIT THE JACKPOT.
THIS IS IT...
HYUU
NWM
WE'VE FINALLY FOUND...
...INNER-MOKA'S ACHILLES' HEEL!
BUT WE CAN TALK ABOUT THAT LATER...
So... difficult.
TRYING TO PUREE A RAW PUMPKIN...
THIS COULD BE FATAL FOR SOMEONE IF WE DON'T ACT FAST...
KRK KRK
KRM KRM
KRM
DO YOU SEE THAT, RUBY?
WHAT SHOULD WE DO?!
OH!
I'd rather not get involved.
DGMM
WAAAA AAA
A
NNNNN
LET YUKARI HANDLE IT!
RIGHT! GO AHEAD. TEACH HER HOW TO COOK!
WHY ME? I'M TOO YOUNG TO DIE!
MWF MWF
NOOOOO

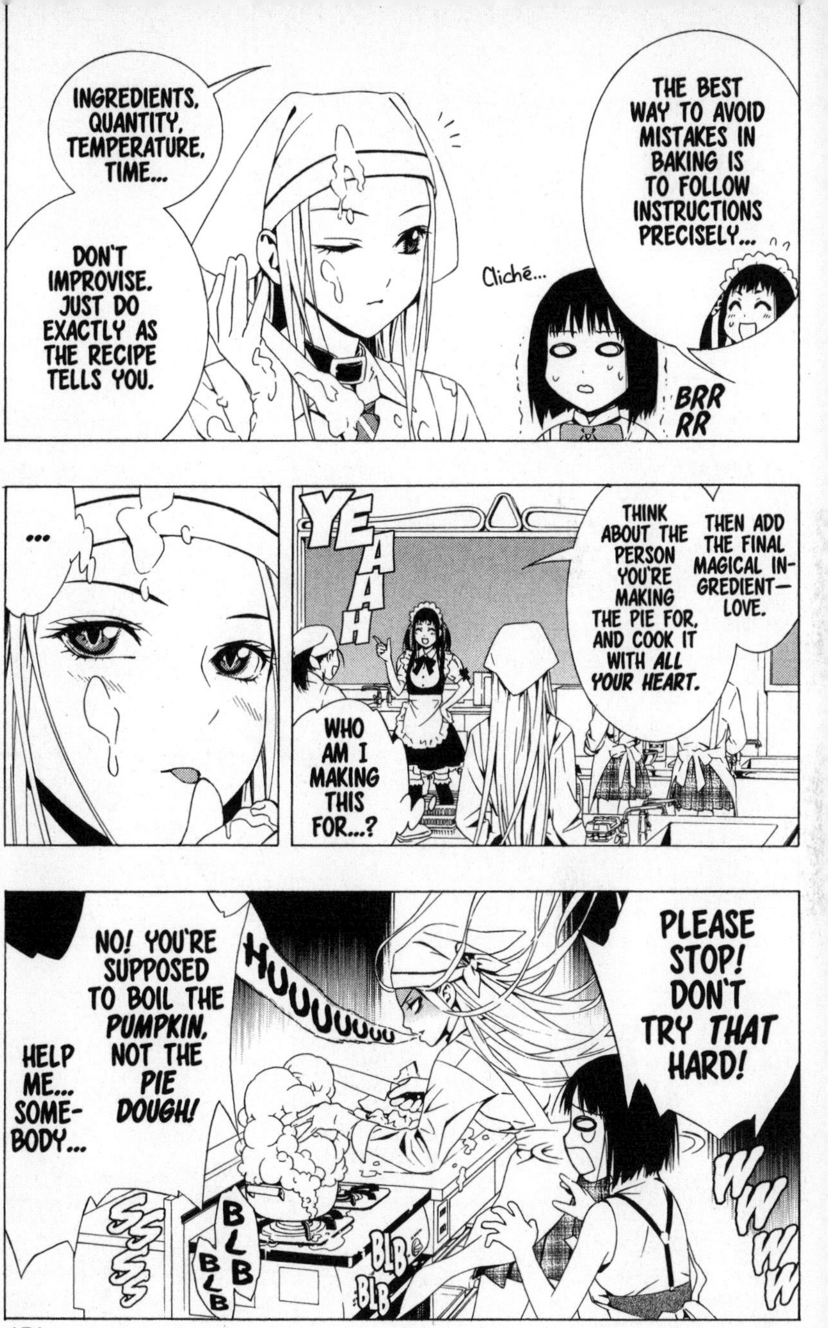
THE BEST WAY TO AVOID MISTAKES IN BAKING IS TO FOLLOW INSTRUCTIONS PRECISELY...
Cliché...
INGREDIENTS, QUANTITY, TEMPERATURE, TIME...
DON'T IMPROVISE. JUST DO EXACTLY AS THE RECIPE TELLS YOU.
BRRR RR
THINK ABOUT THE PERSON YOU'RE MAKING THE PIE FOR, AND COOK IT WITH *ALL YOUR HEART.* THEN ADD THE FINAL MAGICAL IN-GREDIENT—LOVE.
YEAAAH
WHO AM I MAKING THIS FOR...?
...
PLEASE STOP! DON'T TRY *THAT* HARD!
WWWWW
HUUUUUUU
NO! YOU'RE SUPPOSED TO BOIL THE *PUMPKIN,* NOT THE PIE *DOUGH!*
HELP ME... SOME-BODY...
SSSS
BLB BLB
BLB BLB

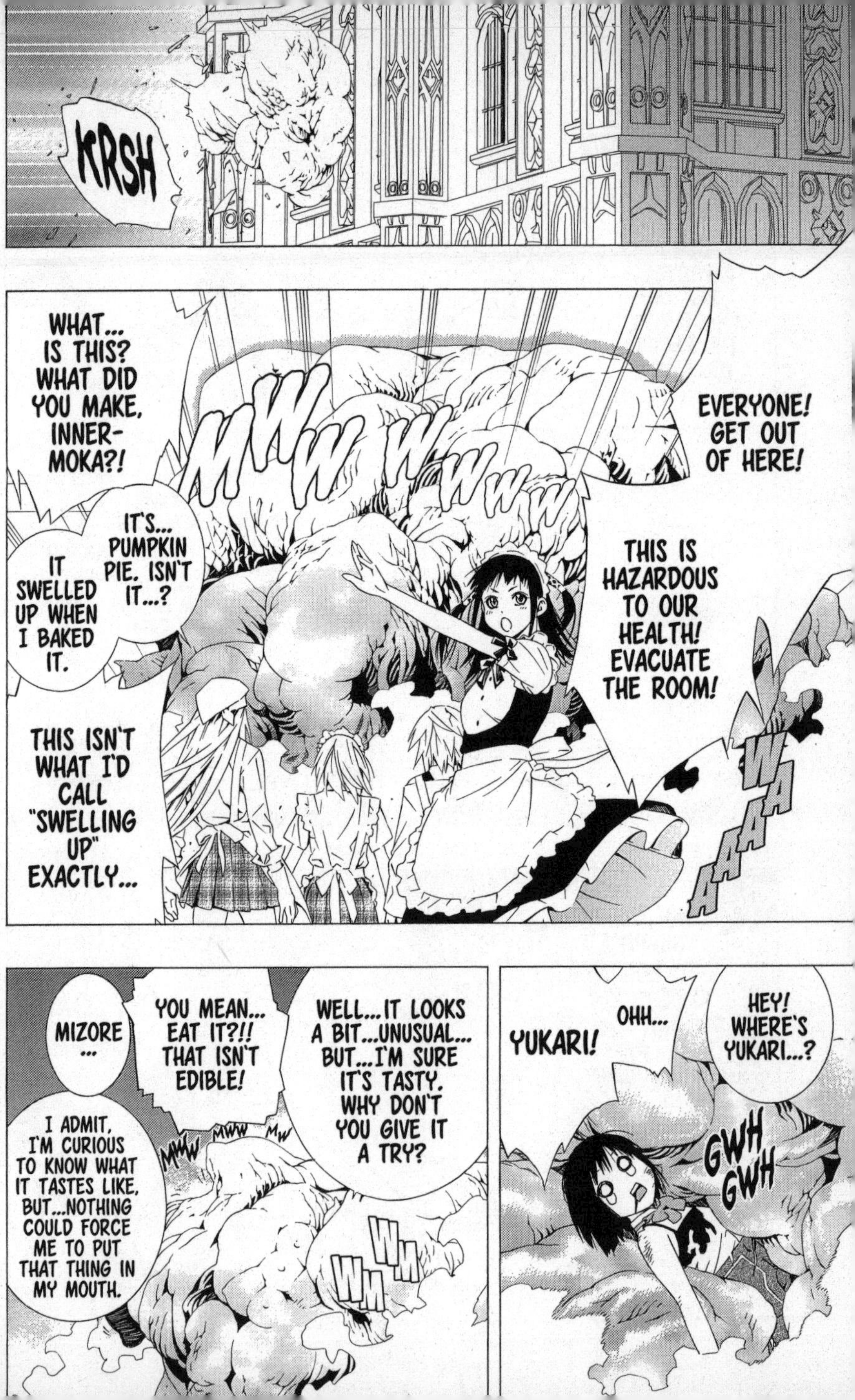
KRSH
EVERYONE! GET OUT OF HERE!
WHAT... IS THIS? WHAT DID YOU MAKE, INNER-MOKA?!
MWWWWWWW
THIS IS HAZARDOUS TO OUR HEALTH! EVACUATE THE ROOM!
IT'S... PUMPKIN PIE, ISN'T IT...?
IT SWELLED UP WHEN I BAKED IT.
WAAAAA
THIS ISN'T WHAT I'D CALL "SWELLING UP" EXACTLY...
HEY! WHERE'S YUKARI...?
OHH...
YUKARI!
GWH GWH
WELL...IT LOOKS A BIT...UNUSUAL... BUT...I'M SURE IT'S TASTY. WHY DON'T YOU GIVE IT A TRY?
YOU MEAN... EAT IT?!! THAT ISN'T EDIBLE!
MIZORE ...
I ADMIT, I'M CURIOUS TO KNOW WHAT IT TASTES LIKE, BUT...NOTHING COULD FORCE ME TO PUT THAT THING IN MY MOUTH.
MWW MWW MW
WM WM

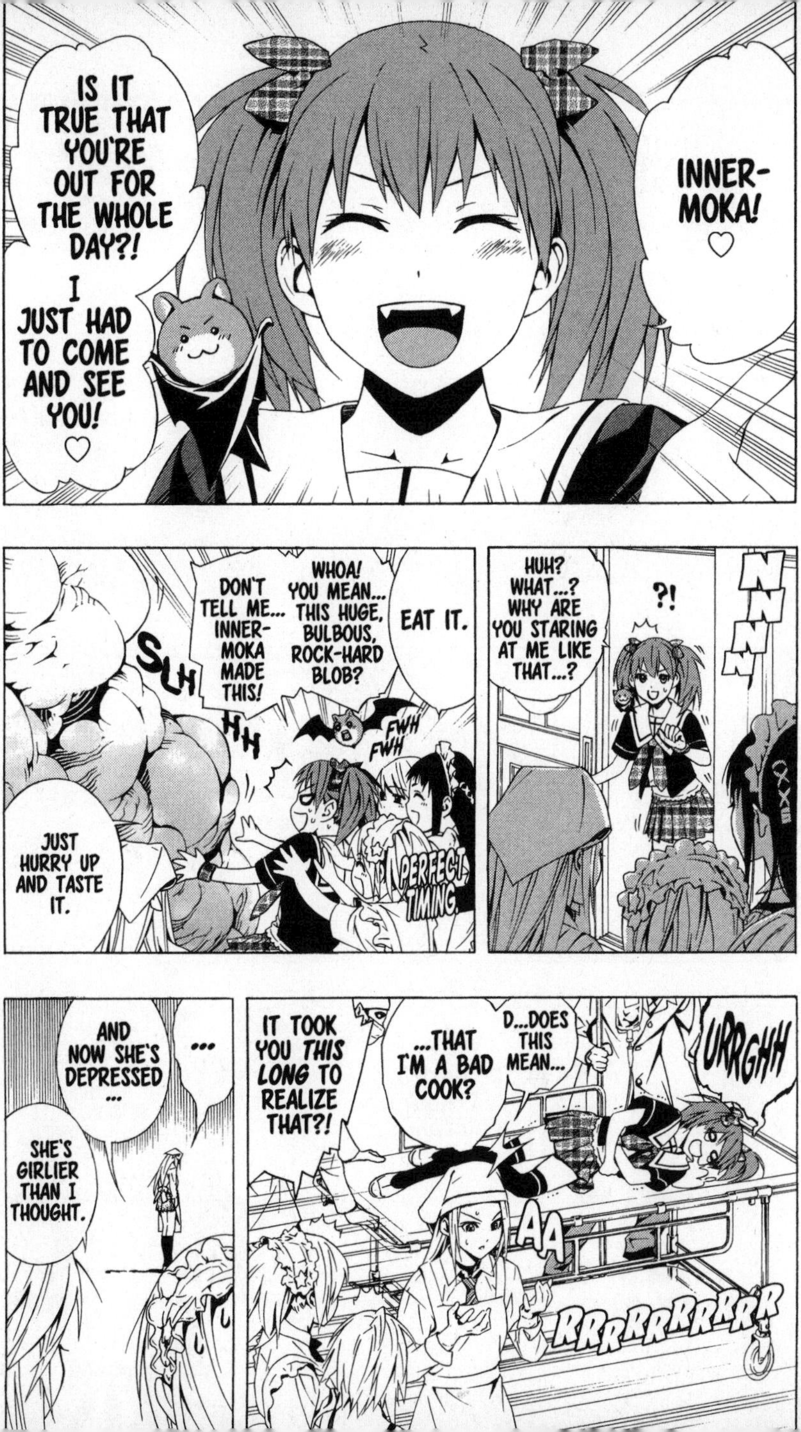
INNER-MOKA! ♡
IS IT TRUE THAT YOU'RE OUT FOR THE WHOLE DAY?!
I JUST HAD TO COME AND SEE YOU! ♡
NNNN
?!
HUH? WHAT...? WHY ARE YOU STARING AT ME LIKE THAT...?
EAT IT.
WHOA! YOU MEAN... THIS HUGE, BULBOUS, ROCK-HARD BLOB?
DON'T TELL ME... INNER-MOKA MADE THIS!
SLUHHH
FWH FWH
PERFECT TIMING.
JUST HURRY UP AND TASTE IT.
URRGHH
D...DOES THIS MEAN...
...THAT I'M A BAD COOK?
IT TOOK YOU *THIS LONG* TO REALIZE THAT?!
AA
RRRRRRRRRRR
...
AND NOW SHE'S DEPRESSED...
SHE'S GIRLIER THAN I THOUGHT.

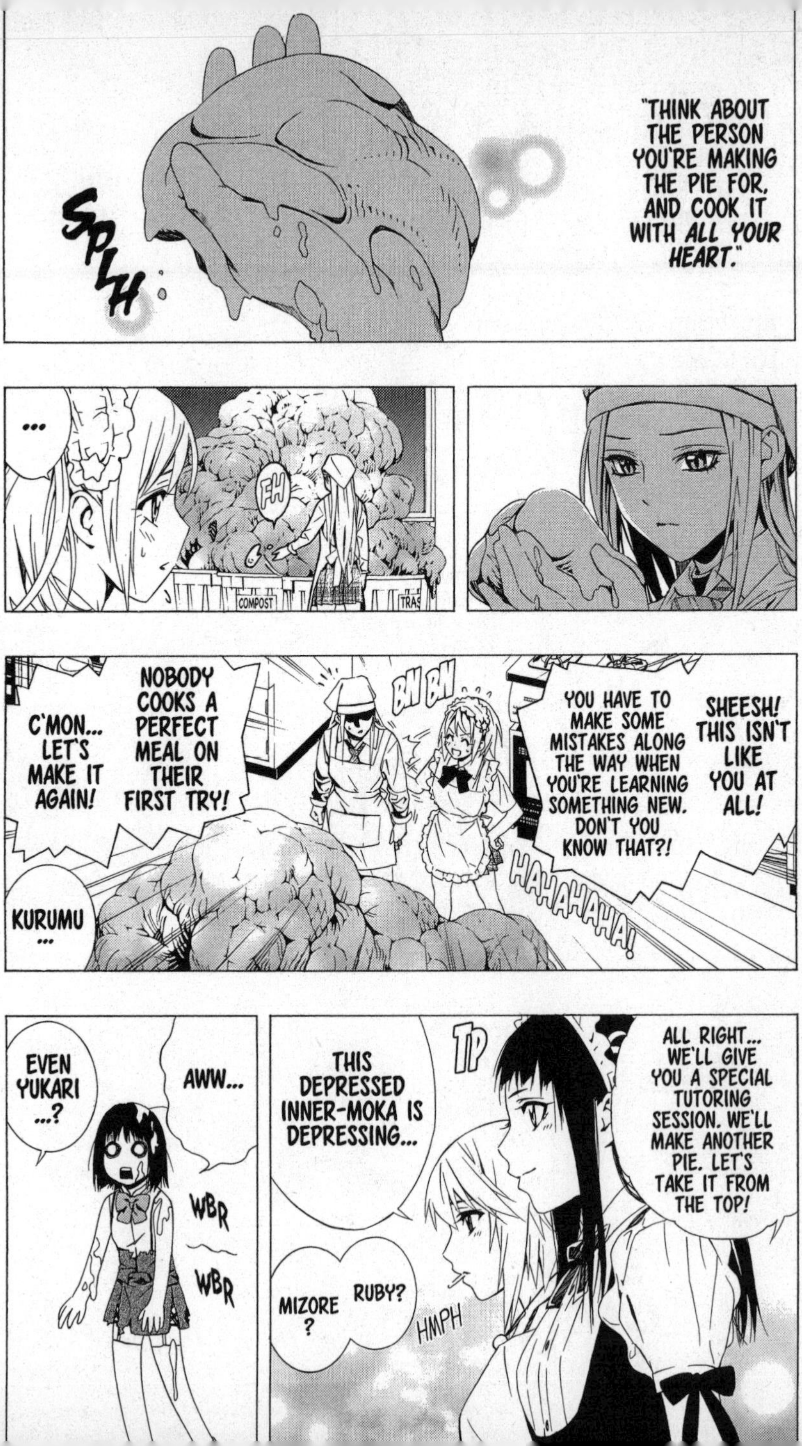
"THINK ABOUT THE PERSON YOU'RE MAKING THE PIE FOR, AND COOK IT WITH ALL YOUR HEART."
SPLH
...
FH
COMPOST
SHEESH! THIS ISN'T LIKE YOU AT ALL!
YOU HAVE TO MAKE SOME MISTAKES ALONG THE WAY WHEN YOU'RE LEARNING SOMETHING NEW. DON'T YOU KNOW THAT?!
BN BN
HAHAHAHA!
NOBODY COOKS A PERFECT MEAL ON THEIR FIRST TRY!
C'MON... LET'S MAKE IT AGAIN!
KURUMU ...
ALL RIGHT... WE'LL GIVE YOU A SPECIAL TUTORING SESSION. WE'LL MAKE ANOTHER PIE. LET'S TAKE IT FROM THE TOP!
TP
THIS DEPRESSED INNER-MOKA IS DEPRESSING...
RUBY?
MIZORE ?
HMPH
AWW...
EVEN YUKARI ...?
WBR
WBR

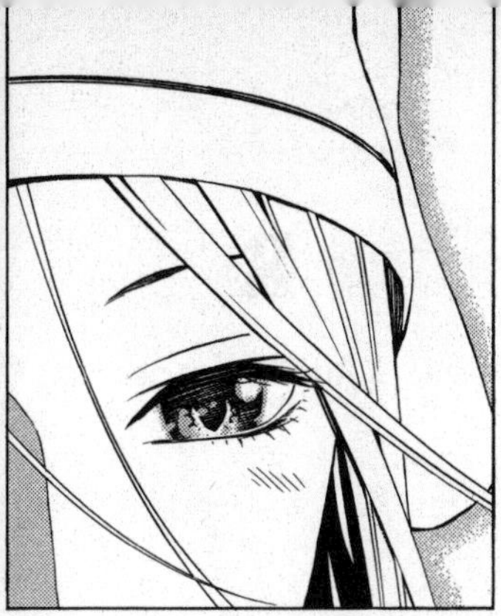
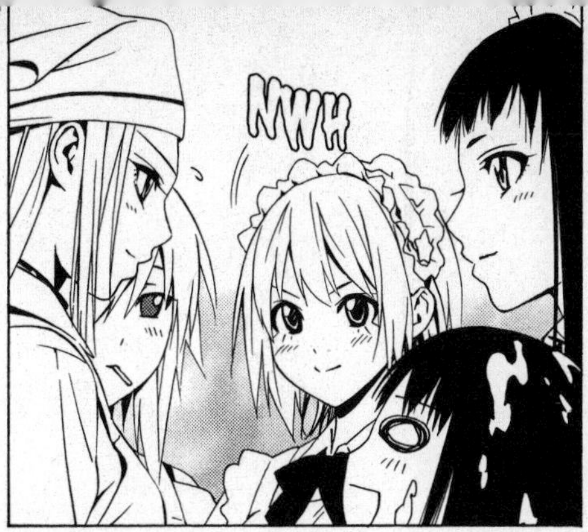
NWH
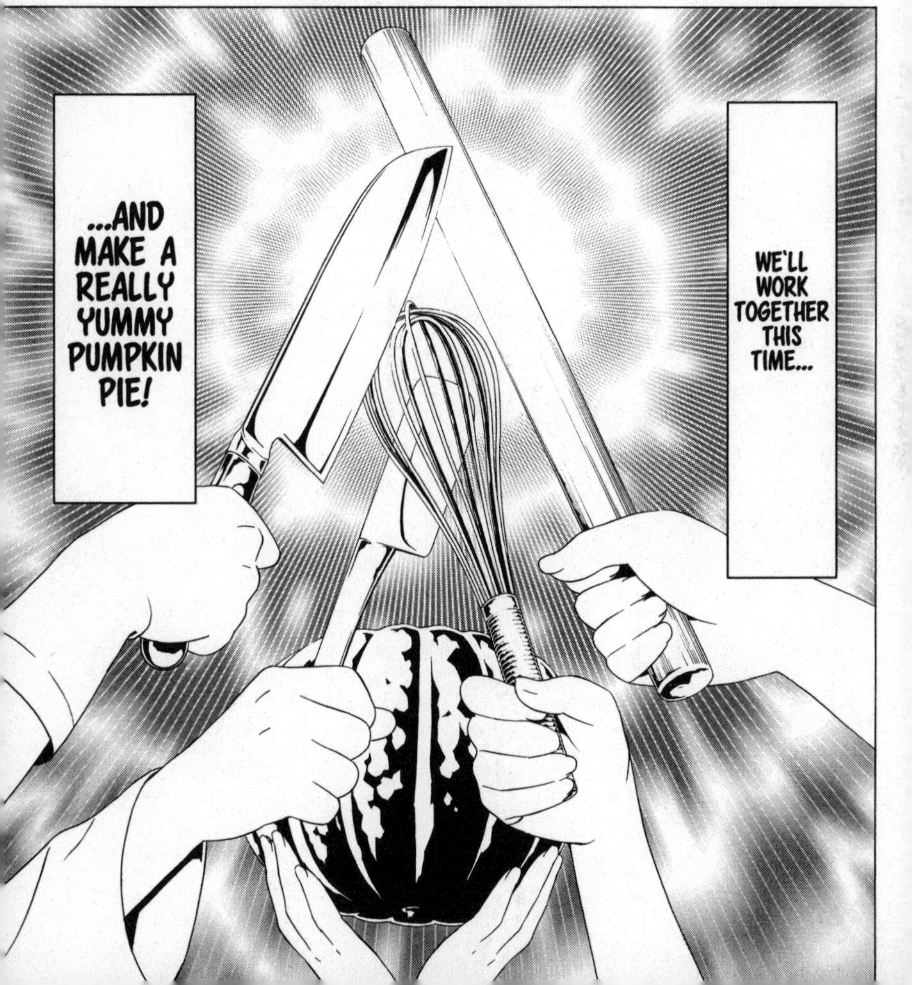
WE'LL WORK TOGETHER THIS TIME...
...AND MAKE A REALLY YUMMY PUMPKIN PIE!

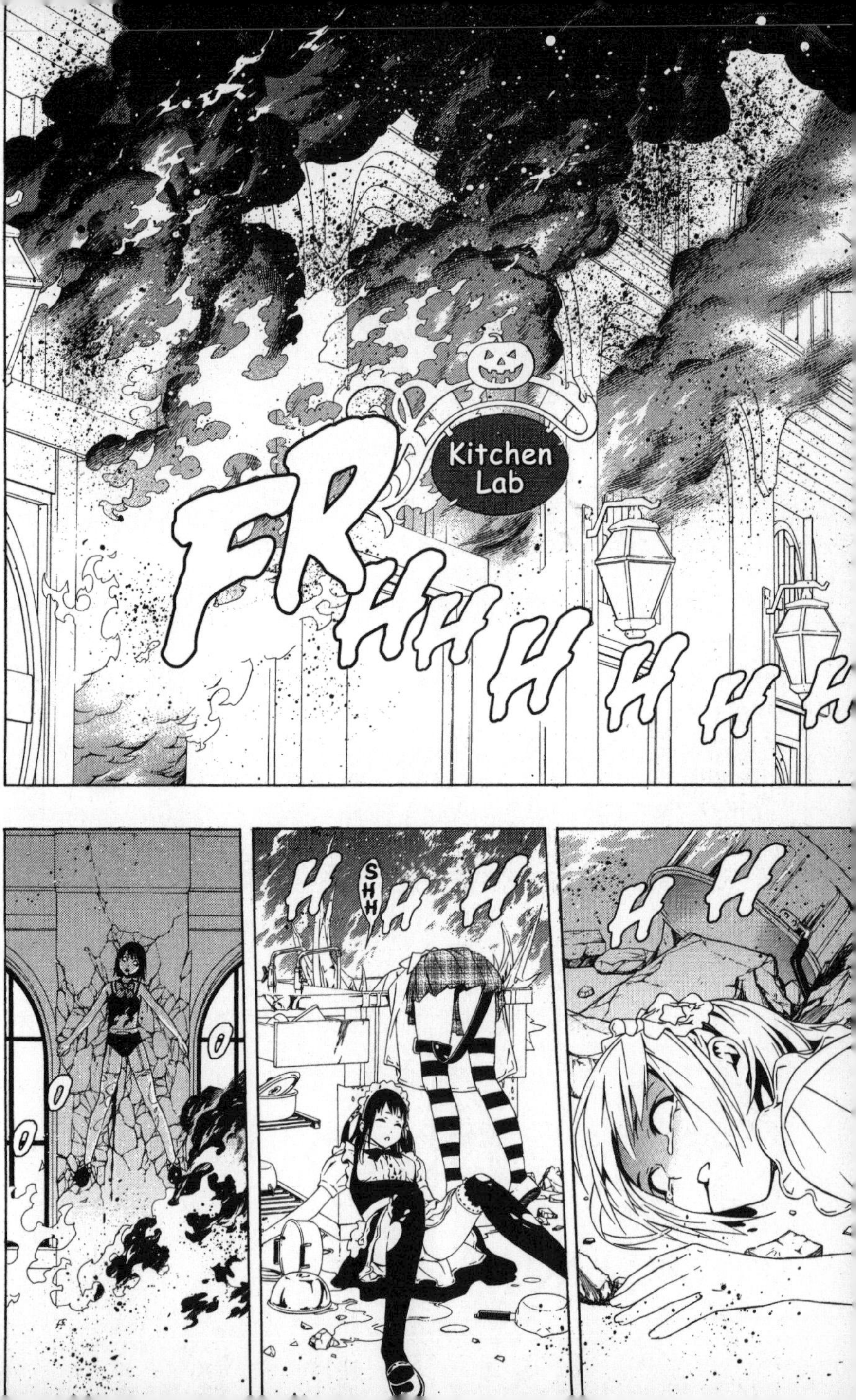
Kitchen Lab
FRHHHHHHH
H H
H SHH H H H

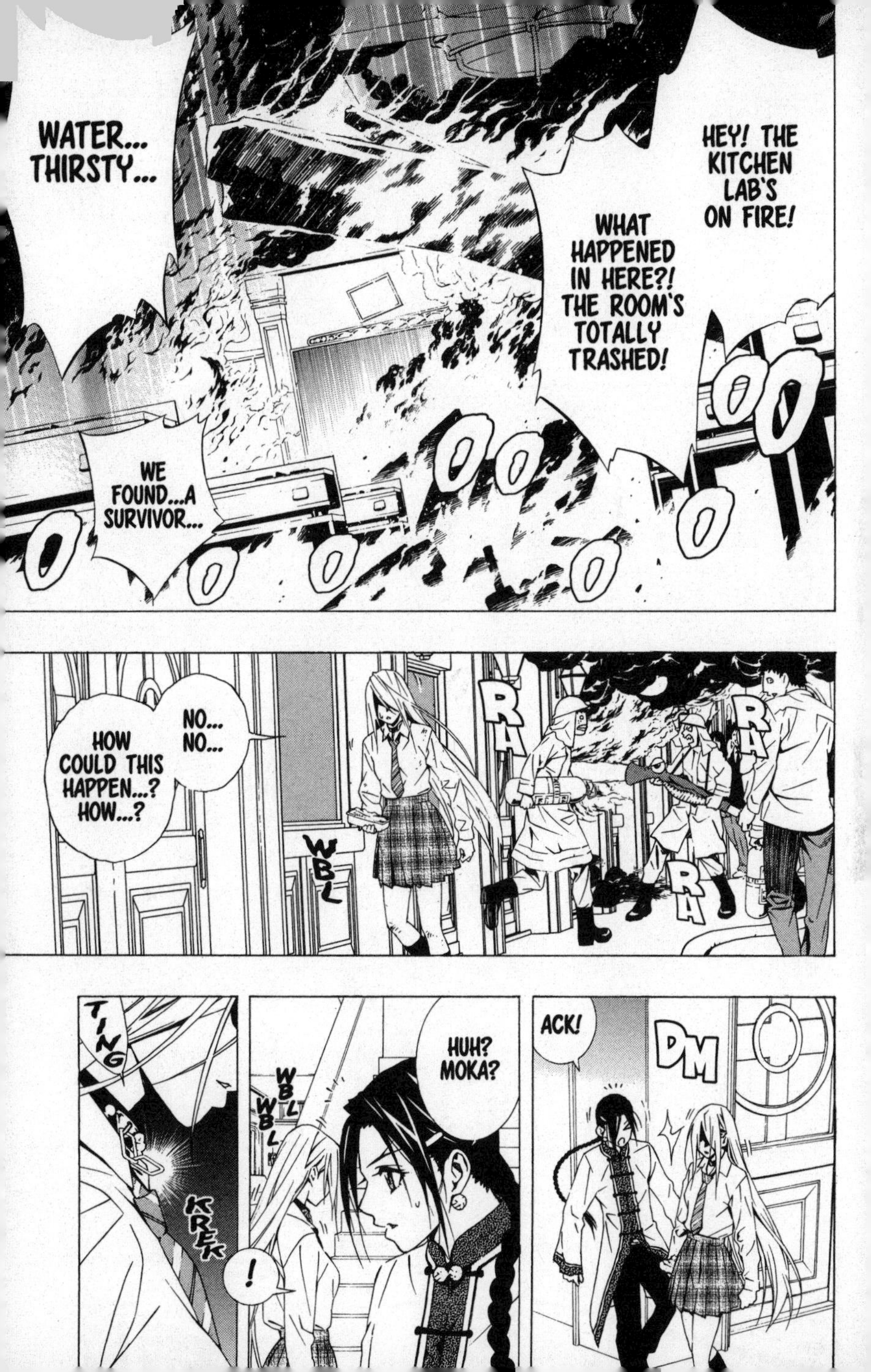
HEY! THE KITCHEN LAB'S ON FIRE!
WHAT HAPPENED IN HERE?! THE ROOM'S TOTALLY TRASHED!
WATER... THIRSTY...
WE FOUND...A SURVIVOR...
RA
RA
RA
NO... NO...
HOW COULD THIS HAPPEN...? HOW...?
WBL
ACK!
DM
HUH? MOKA?
WBL
WBL
!
TING
KREK

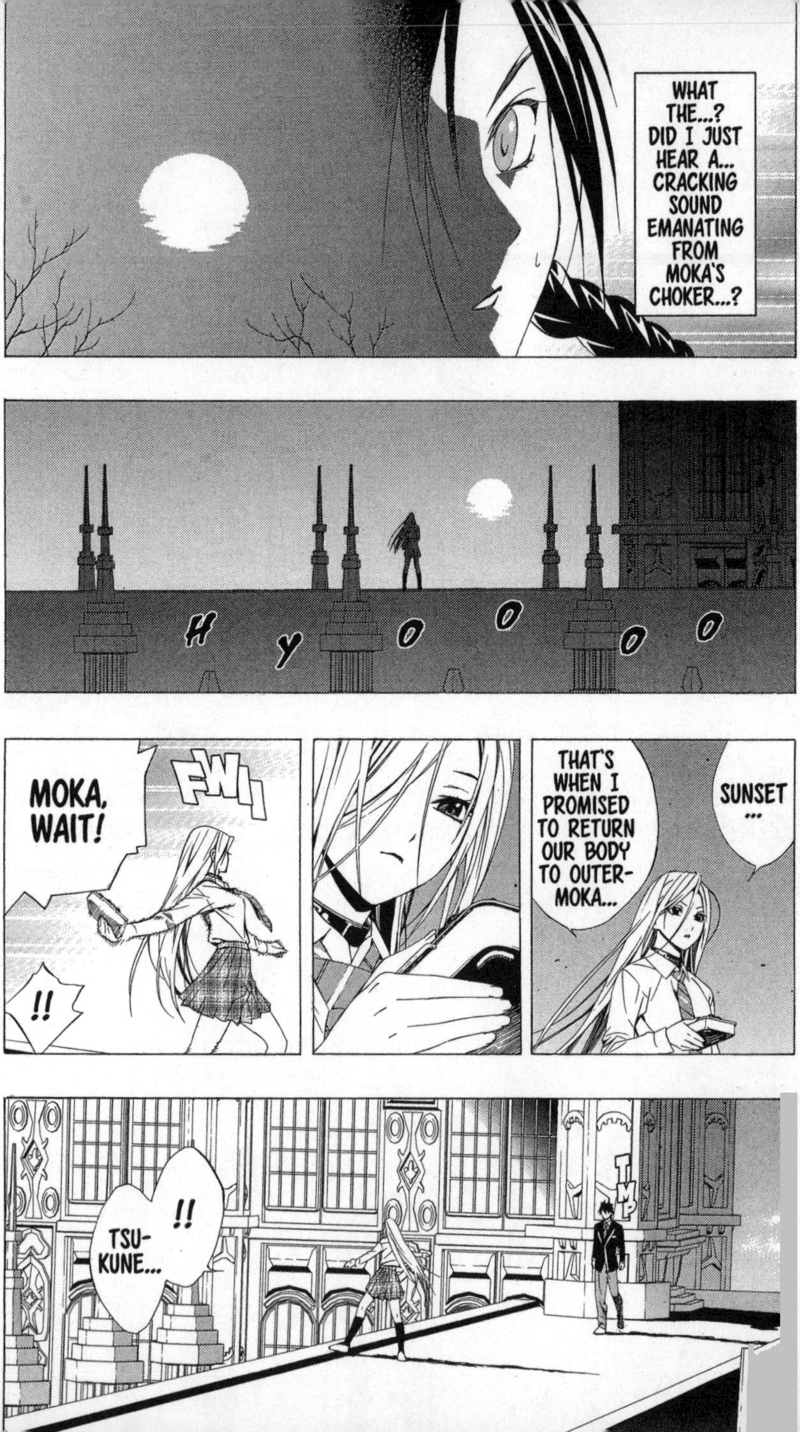
WHAT THE...? DID I JUST HEAR A... CRACKING SOUND EMANATING FROM MOKA'S CHOKER...?
HYOOOOO
SUNSET...
THAT'S WHEN I PROMISED TO RETURN OUR BODY TO OUTER-MOKA...
FWII
MOKA, WAIT!
!!
TMP
!!
TSU-KUNE...

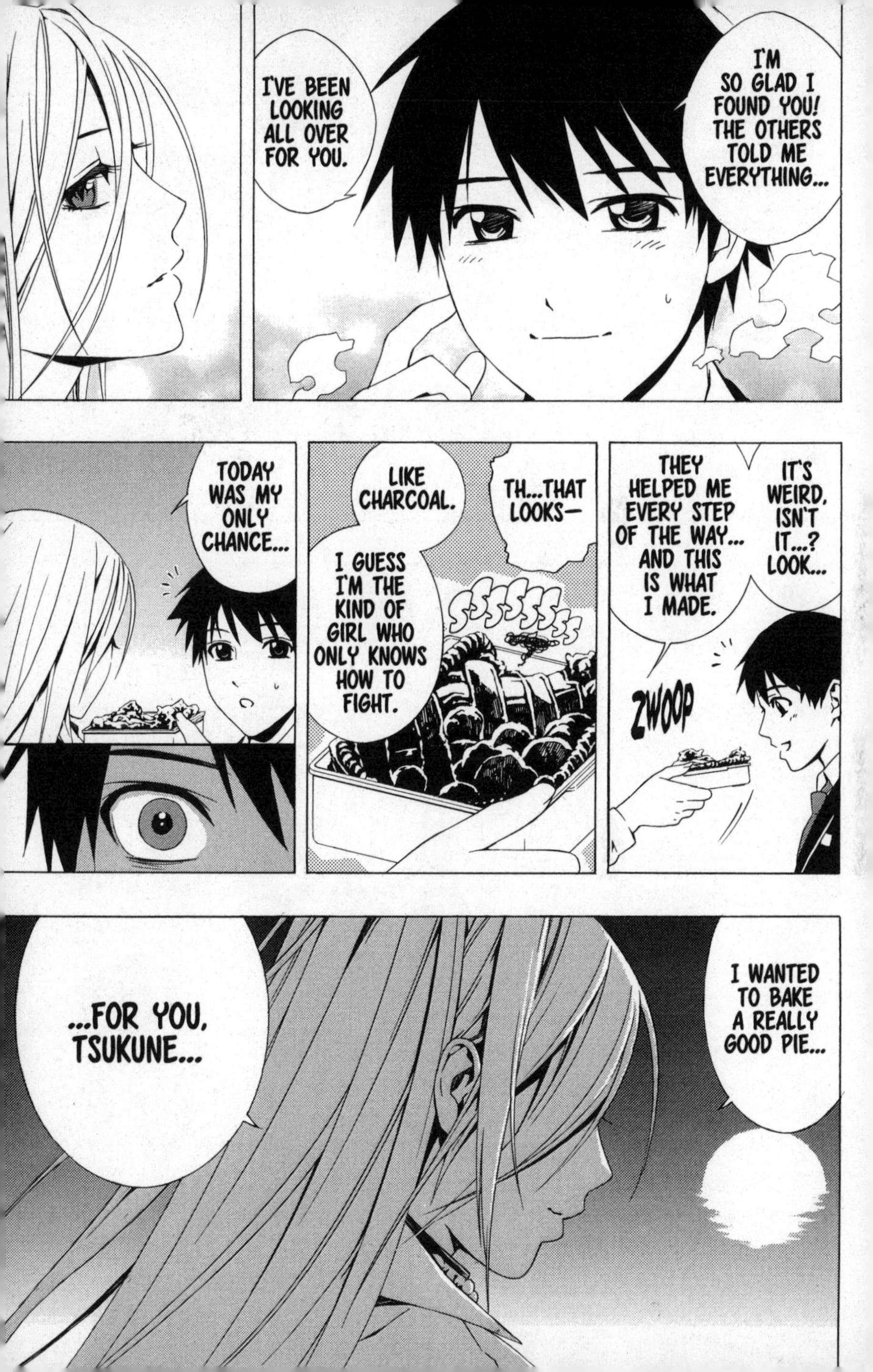
I'M SO GLAD I FOUND YOU! THE OTHERS TOLD ME EVERYTHING...
I'VE BEEN LOOKING ALL OVER FOR YOU.
IT'S WEIRD, ISN'T IT...? LOOK...
THEY HELPED ME EVERY STEP OF THE WAY... AND THIS IS WHAT I MADE.
ZWOOP
TH...THAT LOOKS—
LIKE CHARCOAL.
I GUESS I'M THE KIND OF GIRL WHO ONLY KNOWS HOW TO FIGHT.
TODAY WAS MY ONLY CHANCE...
I WANTED TO BAKE A REALLY GOOD PIE...
...FOR YOU, TSUKUNE...

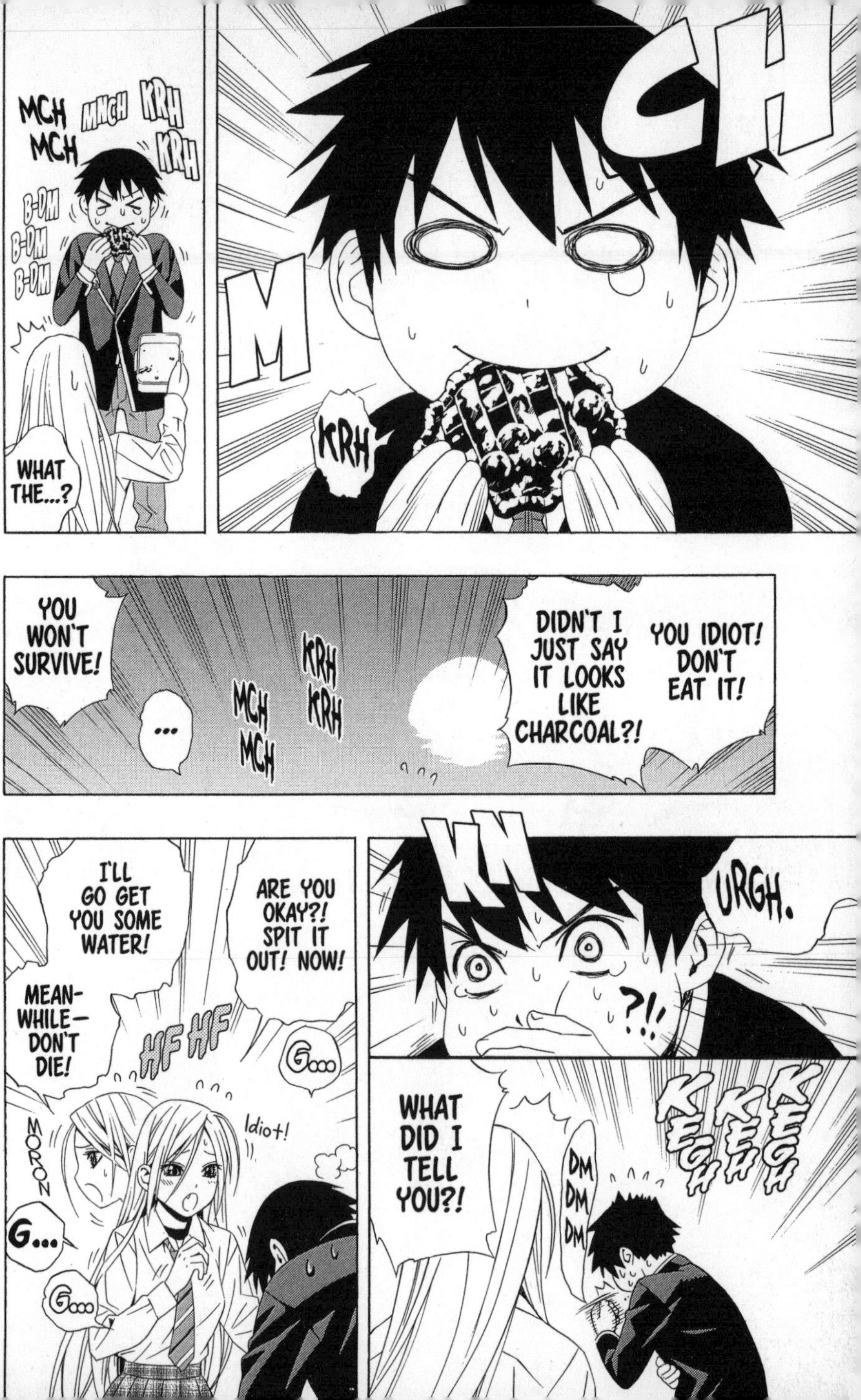
CH
M
KRH
MCH MCH
MNCH
KRH KRH
B-DM B-DM B-DM
WHAT THE...?
YOU IDIOT! DON'T EAT IT!
DIDN'T I JUST SAY IT LOOKS LIKE CHARCOAL?!
KRH KRH
MCH MCH
...
YOU WON'T SURVIVE!
WN
URGH.
?!!
KEGH KEGH KEGH
WHAT DID I TELL YOU?!
DM DM DM
ARE YOU OKAY?! SPIT IT OUT! NOW!
I'LL GO GET YOU SOME WATER!
MEAN-WHILE— DON'T DIE!
HF HF
G...
Idiot!
MORON
G...
G...

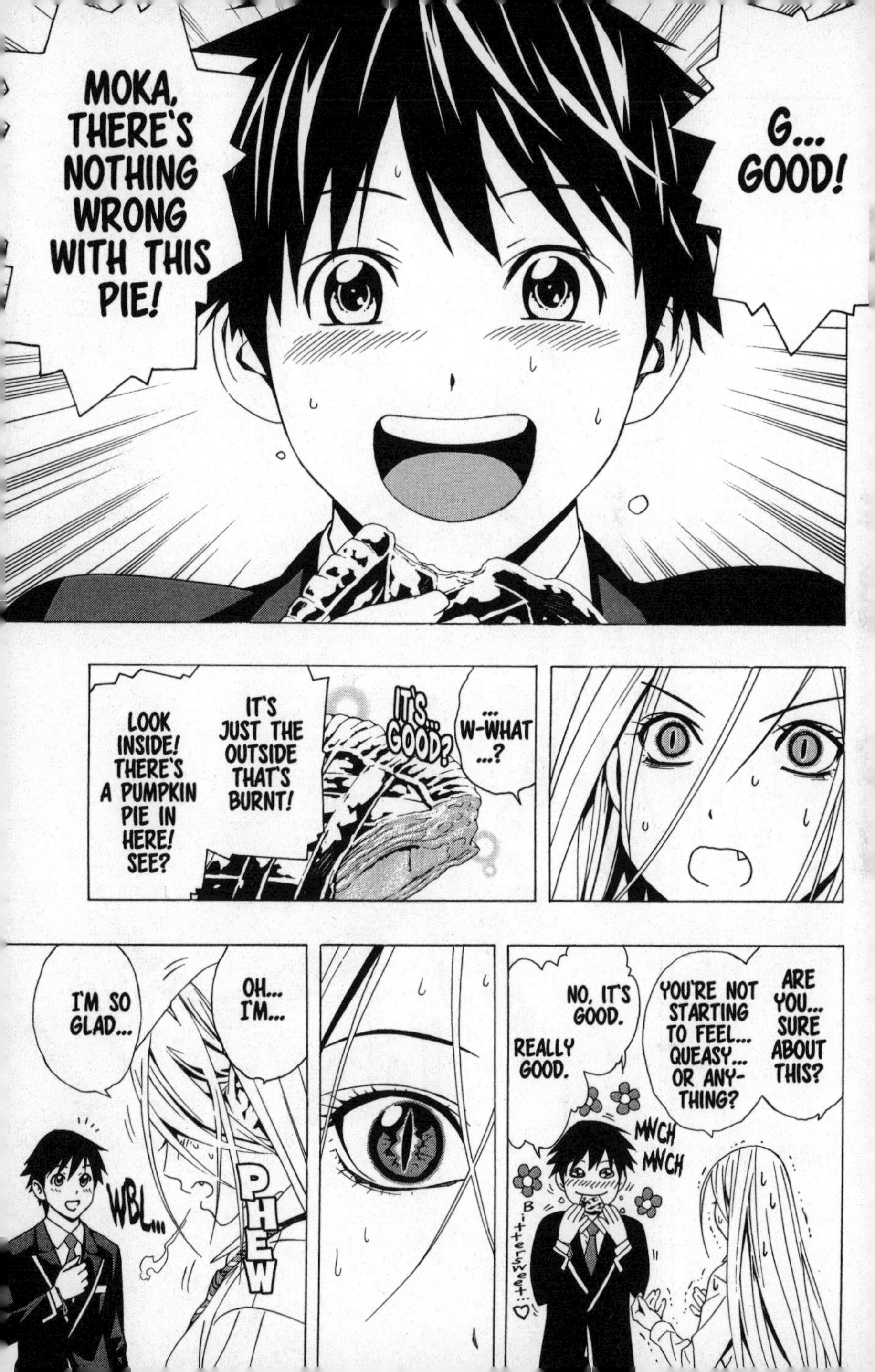
G... GOOD!
MOKA, THERE'S NOTHING WRONG WITH THIS PIE!
...W-WHAT ...?
IT'S... GOOD?
IT'S JUST THE OUTSIDE THAT'S BURNT!
LOOK INSIDE! THERE'S A PUMPKIN PIE IN HERE! SEE?
ARE YOU... SURE ABOUT THIS?
YOU'RE NOT STARTING TO FEEL... QUEASY... OR ANY-THING?
NO, IT'S GOOD.
REALLY GOOD.
MUNCH MUNCH
Bittersweet...♡
OH... I'M...
I'M SO GLAD...
PHEW
WBL...

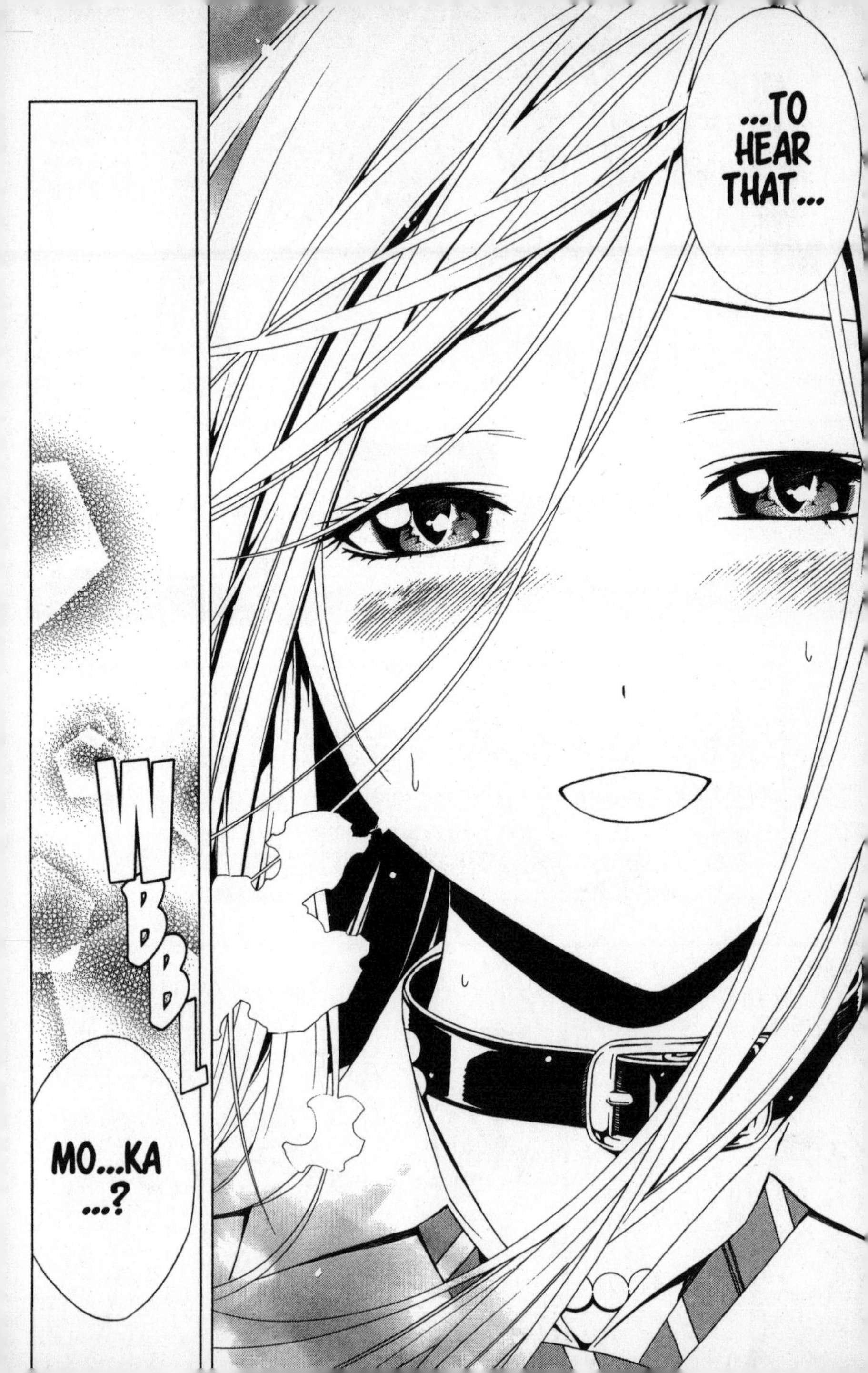
...TO HEAR THAT...
WBBL
MO...KA ...?

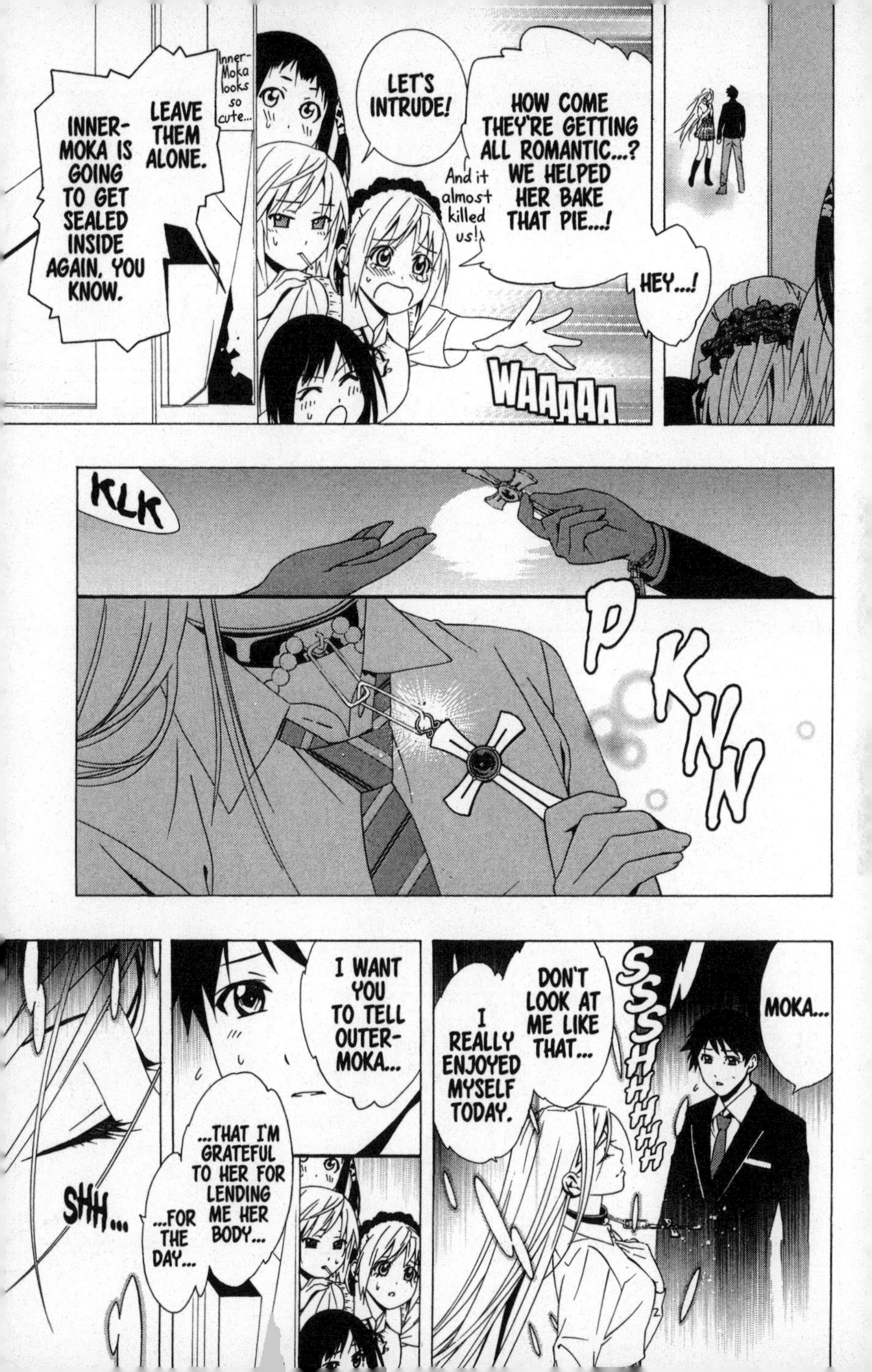
HOW COME THEY'RE GETTING ALL ROMANTIC...? WE HELPED HER BAKE THAT PIE...!
And it almost killed us!
LET'S INTRUDE!
HEY...!
WAAAAA
Inner-Moka looks so cute...
LEAVE THEM ALONE.
INNER-MOKA IS GOING TO GET SEALED INSIDE AGAIN, YOU KNOW.
KLK
PKNN
MOKA...
SSSHHHHHH
DON'T LOOK AT ME LIKE THAT...
I REALLY ENJOYED MYSELF TODAY.
I WANT YOU TO TELL OUTER-MOKA...
...THAT I'M GRATEFUL TO HER FOR LENDING ME HER BODY...
...FOR THE DAY...
SHH...

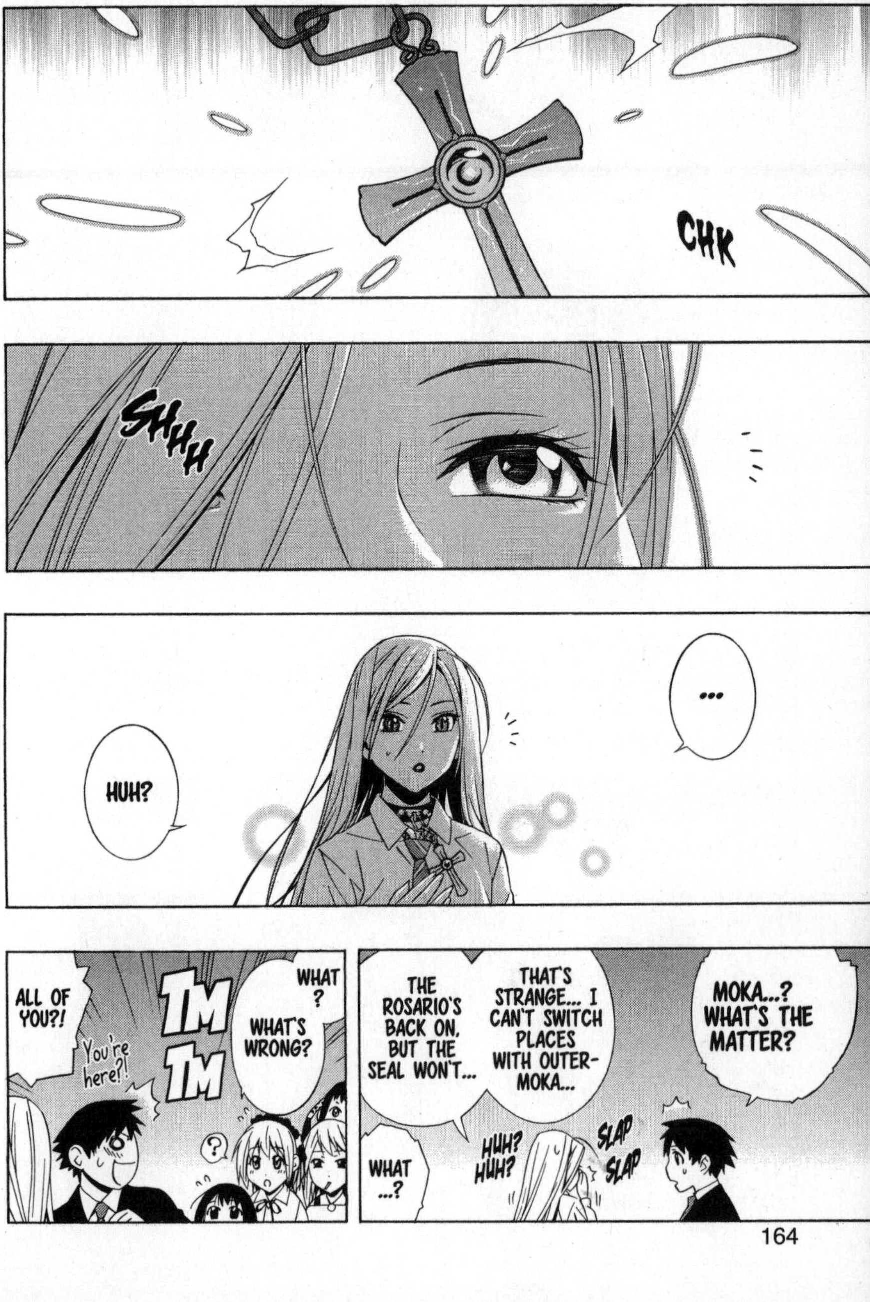
CHK
SHHH
...
HUH?
MOKA...? WHAT'S THE MATTER?
SLAP SLAP
THAT'S STRANGE... I CAN'T SWITCH PLACES WITH OUTER-MOKA...
HUH? HUH?
THE ROSARIO'S BACK ON, BUT THE SEAL WON'T...
WHAT ...?
WHAT ?
WHAT'S WRONG?
TM TM
You're here?!
ALL OF YOU?!

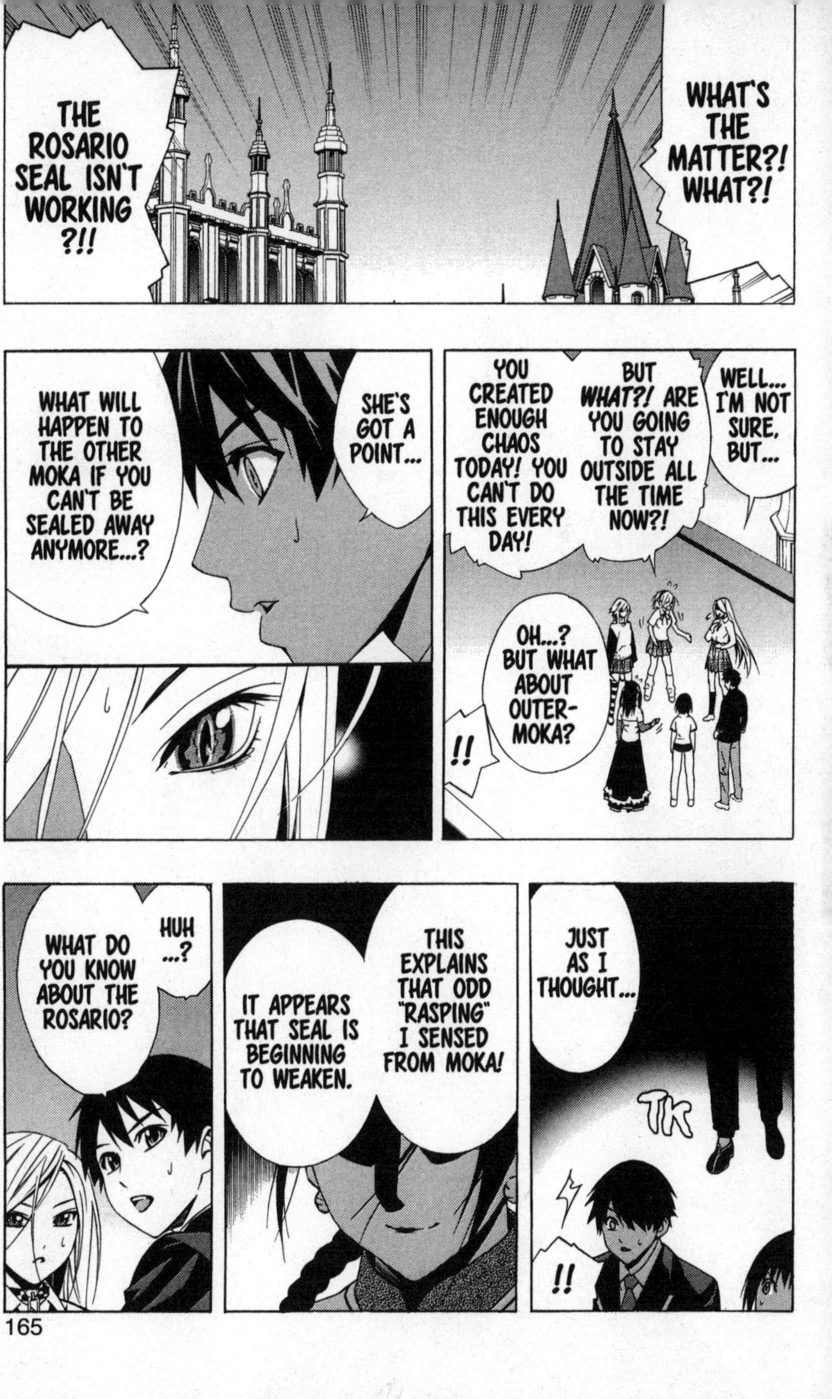
WHAT'S THE MATTER?! WHAT?!
THE ROSARIO SEAL ISN'T WORKING ?!!
WELL... I'M NOT SURE, BUT...
BUT WHAT?! ARE YOU GOING TO STAY OUTSIDE ALL THE TIME NOW?!
YOU CREATED ENOUGH CHAOS TODAY! YOU CAN'T DO THIS EVERY DAY!
OH...? BUT WHAT ABOUT OUTER-MOKA?
!!
SHE'S GOT A POINT...
WHAT WILL HAPPEN TO THE OTHER MOKA IF YOU CAN'T BE SEALED AWAY ANYMORE...?
JUST AS I THOUGHT...
TK
!!
THIS EXPLAINS THAT ODD "RASPING" I SENSED FROM MOKA!
IT APPEARS THAT SEAL IS BEGINNING TO WEAKEN.
HUH ...?
WHAT DO YOU KNOW ABOUT THE ROSARIO?

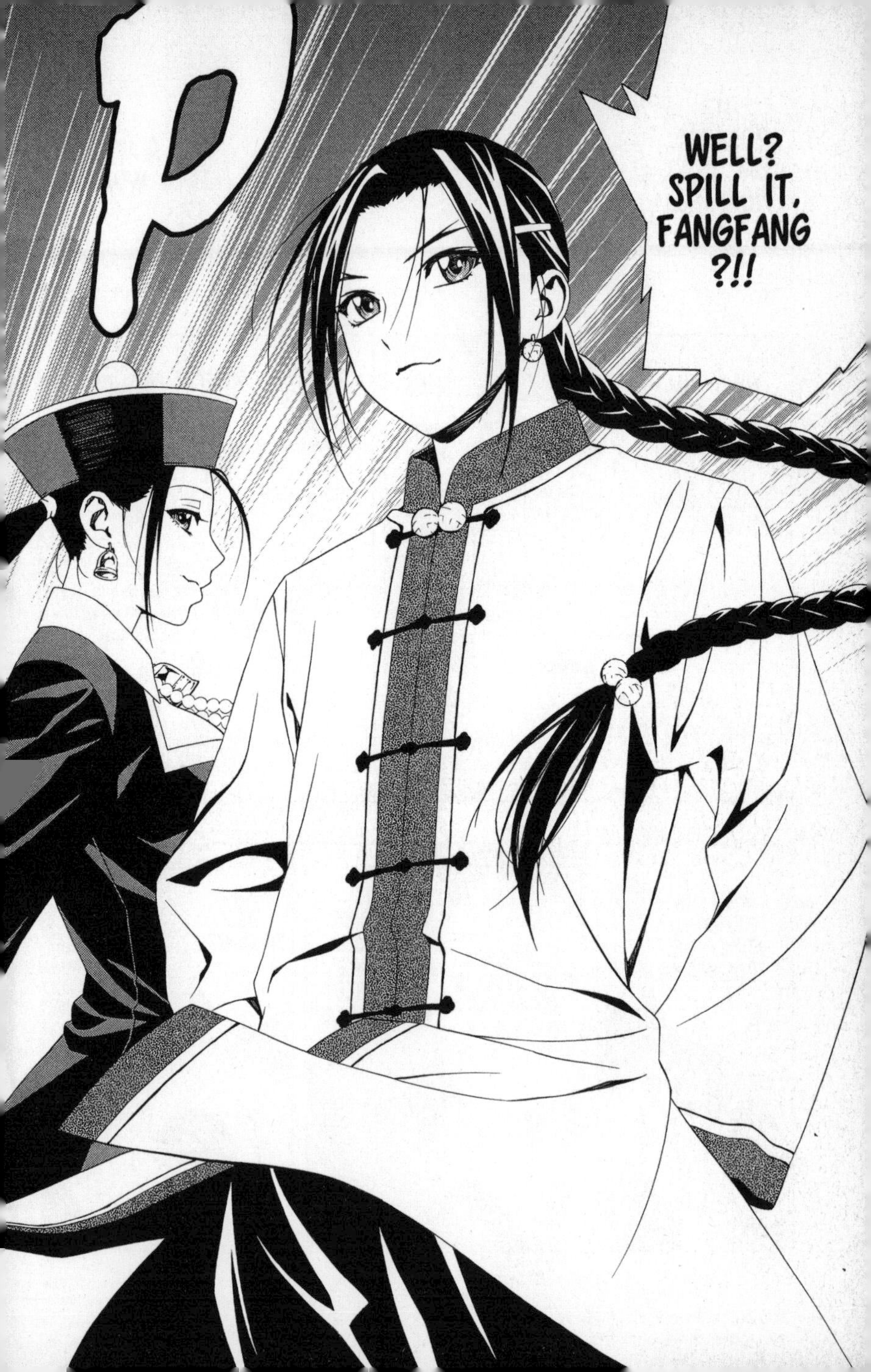
WELL? SPILL IT, FANGFANG ?!!
?

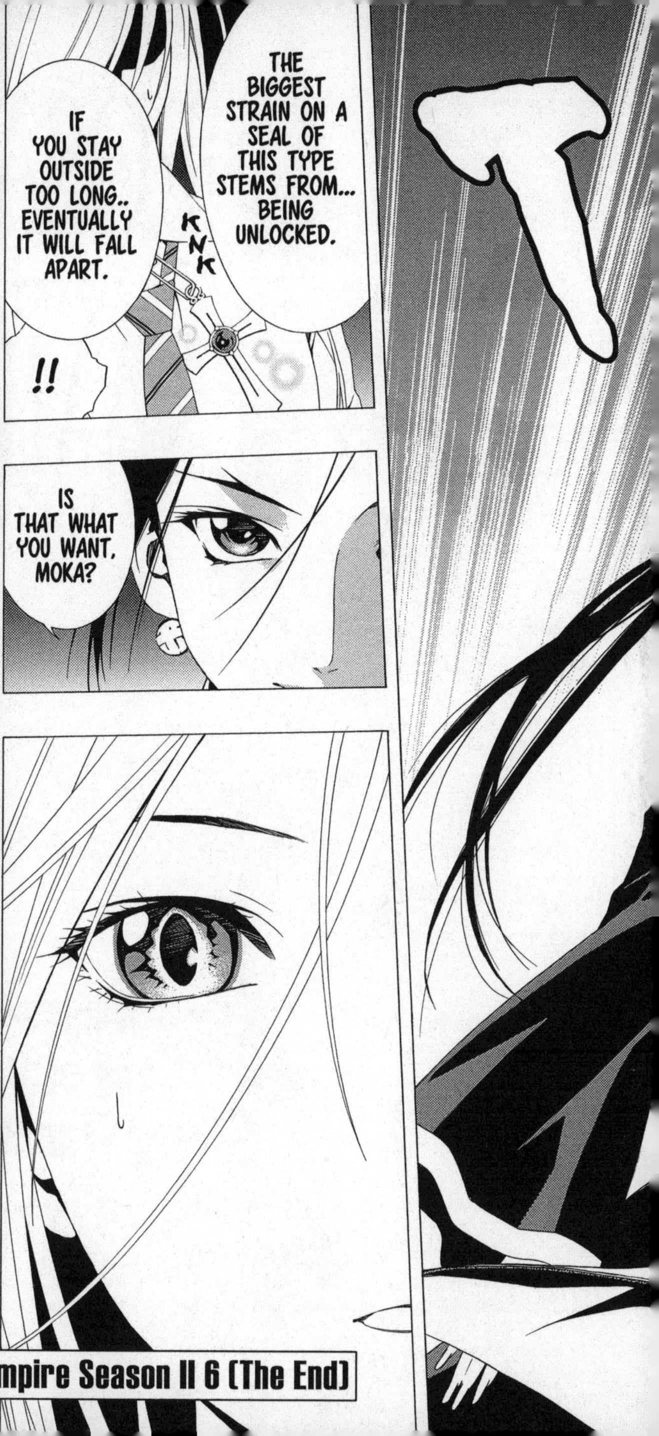
THE BIGGEST STRAIN ON A SEAL OF THIS TYPE STEMS FROM... BEING UNLOCKED.
KNK
IF YOU STAY OUTSIDE TOO LONG.. EVENTUALLY IT WILL FALL APART.
!!
IS THAT WHAT YOU WANT, MOKA?

mpire Season II 6 (The End)

From
Sports
Day

ROSARIO + VAMPIRE
Season II

**Meaningless
End-of-Volume
Theater**

VI

•Troubled Witch•

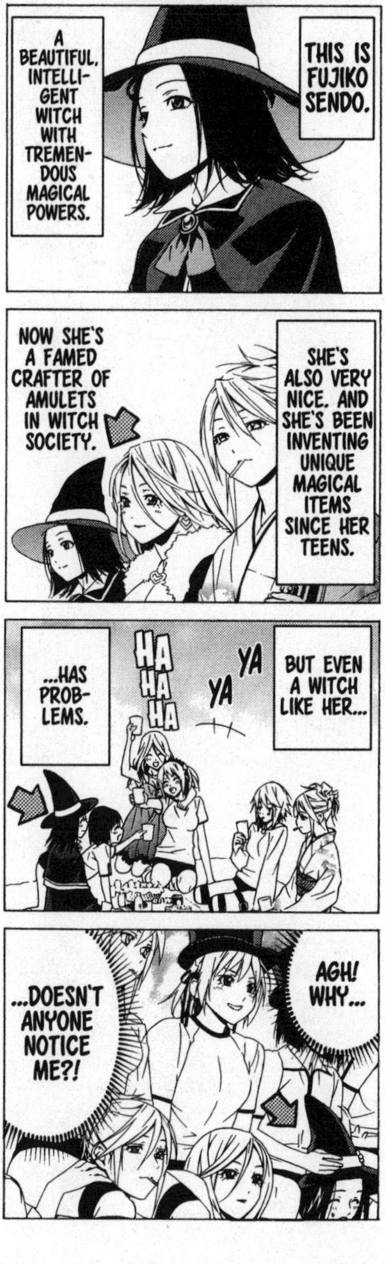
THIS IS FUJIKO SENDO.
A BEAUTIFUL, INTELLIGENT WITCH WITH TREMENDOUS MAGICAL POWERS.
SHE'S ALSO VERY NICE. AND SHE'S BEEN INVENTING UNIQUE MAGICAL ITEMS SINCE HER TEENS.
NOW SHE'S A FAMED CRAFTER OF AMULETS IN WITCH SOCIETY.
BUT EVEN A WITCH LIKE HER...
YA
YA
HA HA HA HA
...HAS PROBLEMS.
AGH! WHY...
...DOESN'T ANYONE NOTICE ME?!

•Invisible Witch•

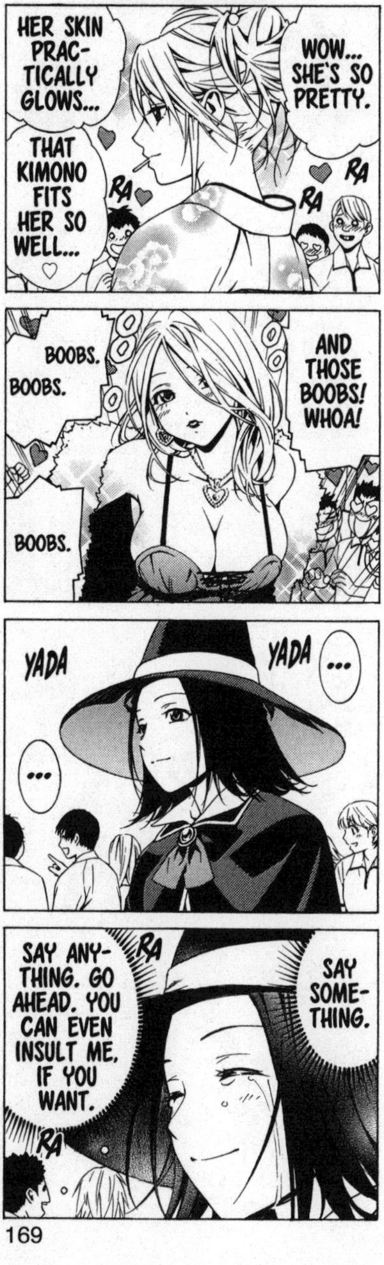
WOW... SHE'S SO PRETTY.
RA
RA
HER SKIN PRACTICALLY GLOWS...
THAT KIMONO FITS HER SO WELL... ♡
RA
AND THOSE BOOBS! WHOA!
BOOBS.
BOOBS.
BOOBS.
...
YADA
YADA
...
SAY SOMETHING.
RA
SAY ANYTHING. GO AHEAD. YOU CAN EVEN INSULT ME, IF YOU WANT.
RA

•Let's Shake on It•

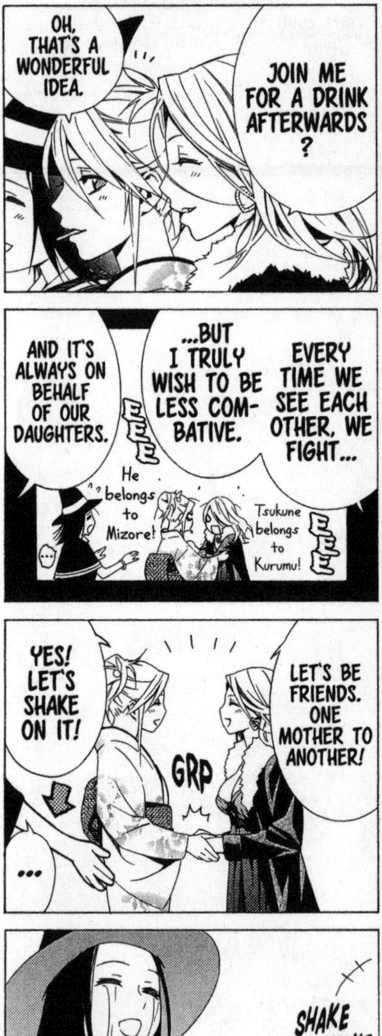
JOIN ME FOR A DRINK AFTERWARDS?
OH, THAT'S A WONDERFUL IDEA.
EVERY TIME WE SEE EACH OTHER, WE FIGHT...
...BUT I TRULY WISH TO BE LESS COM-BATIVE.
AND IT'S ALWAYS ON BEHALF OF OUR DAUGHTERS.
EEE
Tsukune belongs to Kurumu!
He belongs to Mizore!
EEE
...
LET'S BE FRIENDS. ONE MOTHER TO ANOTHER!
GRP
YES! LET'S SHAKE ON IT!
...
SHAKE SHAKE

•Plus the Brawl•

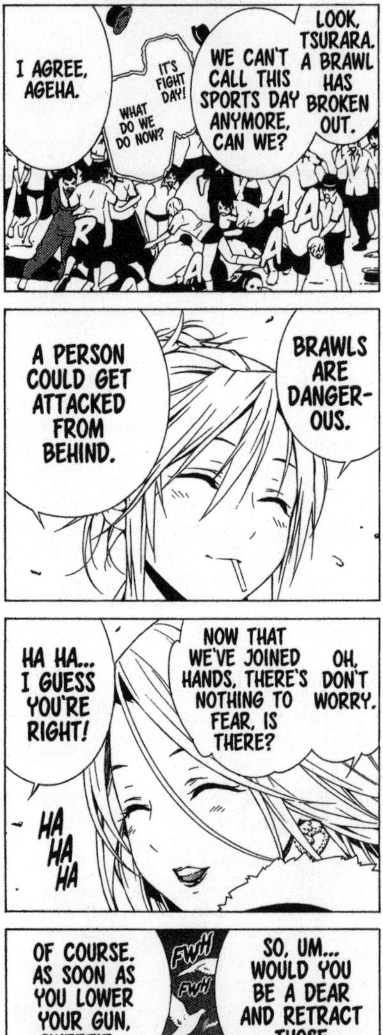
LOOK, TSURARA. A BRAWL HAS BROKEN OUT.
WE CAN'T CALL THIS SPORTS DAY ANYMORE, CAN WE?
IT'S FIGHT DAY!
WHAT DO WE DO NOW?
I AGREE, AGEHA.
BRAWLS ARE DANGER-OUS.
A PERSON COULD GET ATTACKED FROM BEHIND.
OH, DON'T WORRY.
NOW THAT WE'VE JOINED HANDS, THERE'S NOTHING TO FEAR, IS THERE?
HA HA... I GUESS YOU'RE RIGHT!
HA HA HA
SO, UM... WOULD YOU BE A DEAR AND RETRACT THOSE CLAWS?
FWH
FWH
OF COURSE. AS SOON AS YOU LOWER YOUR GUN, SWEETIE...
HAHAHAHAHAHA

Please send questions and fan letters to ➡ Rosario+Vampire Fan Mail, VIZ Media, P.O. Box 77010, San Francisco, CA 94107

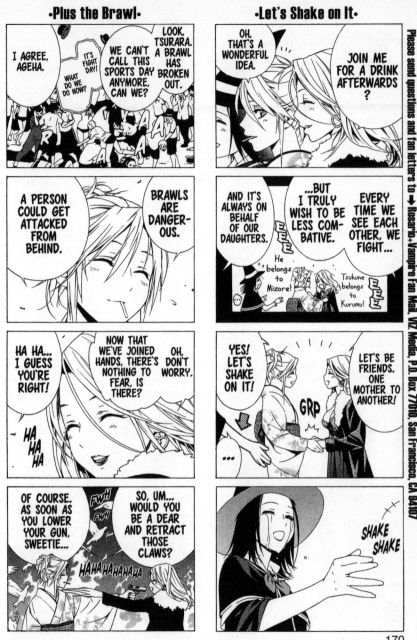

Rosario+Vampire

Akihisa Ikeda

• Staff •
Makoto Saito
Kenji Tashiro
Nobuyuki Hayashi

• Help •
Tomoharu Shimomura
Eri Ueyama

• 3DCG •
Takaharu Yoshizawa

• Editor •
Takanori Asada

• Comic •
Kenju Noro

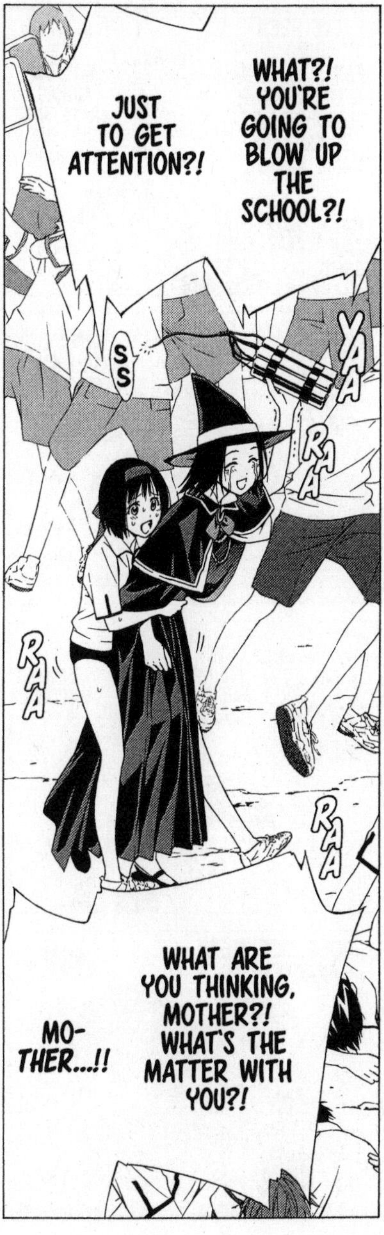
WHAT?! YOU'RE GOING TO BLOW UP THE SCHOOL?!
JUST TO GET ATTENTION?!
SS
YAAA
RAA
RAA
RAA
WHAT ARE YOU THINKING, MOTHER?! WHAT'S THE MATTER WITH YOU?!
MO-THER...!!

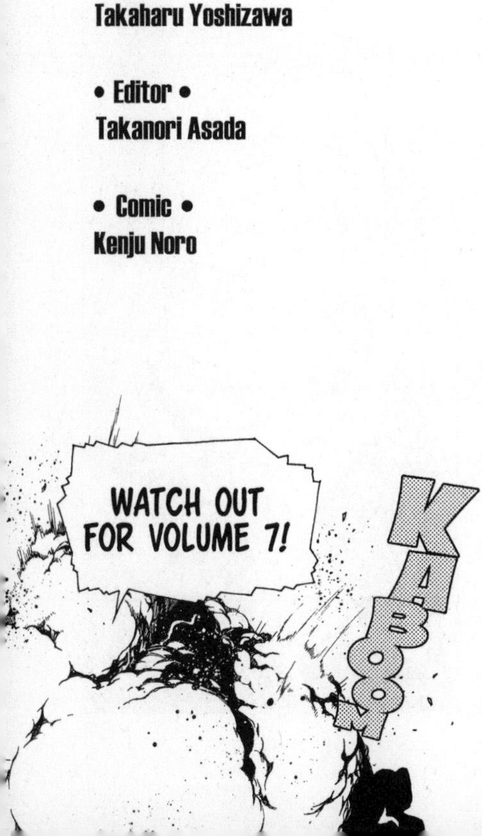
WATCH OUT FOR VOLUME 7!
KABOOM

Extra Meaningless Bonus Story

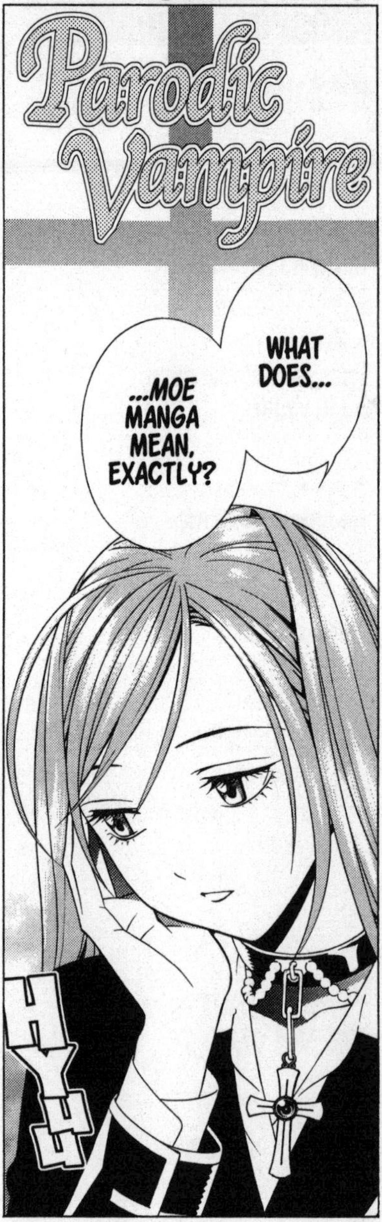
Parodic Vampire
WHAT DOES...
...MOE MANGA MEAN, EXACTLY?
HYUUU

•I Don't Get It•

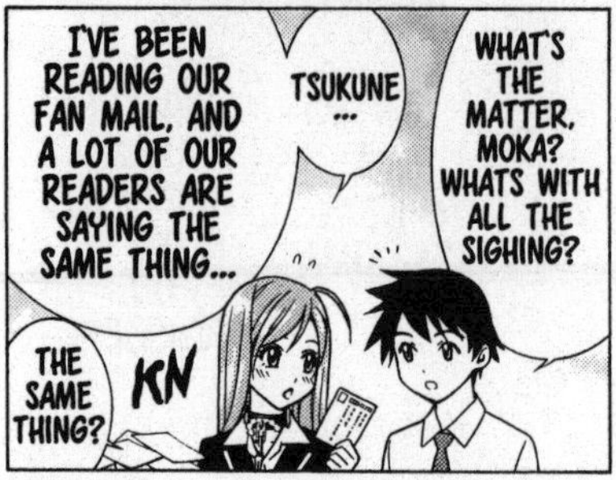
WHAT'S THE MATTER, MOKA? WHATS WITH ALL THE SIGHING?
TSUKUNE...
I'VE BEEN READING OUR FAN MAIL, AND A LOT OF OUR READERS ARE SAYING THE SAME THING...
KN
THE SAME THING?

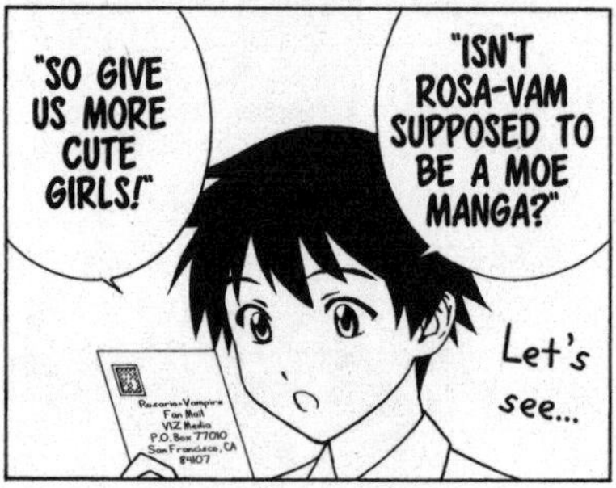
"ISN'T ROSA-VAM SUPPOSED TO BE A MOE MANGA?"
"SO GIVE US MORE CUTE GIRLS!"
Let's see...
Rosario+Vampire
Fan Mail
VIZ Media
P.O. Box 77010
San Francisco, CA
8407

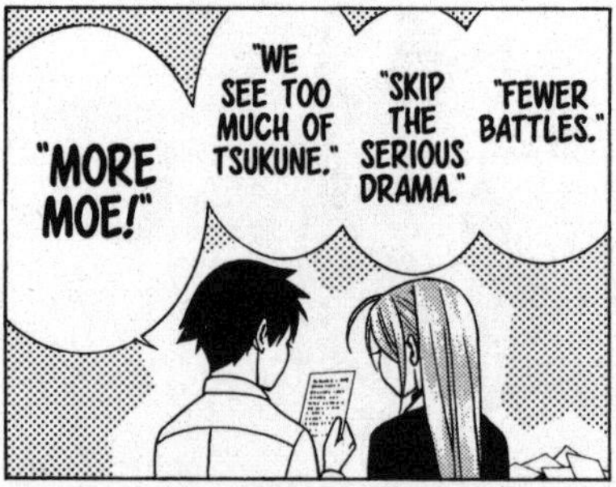
"FEWER BATTLES."
"SKIP THE SERIOUS DRAMA."
"WE SEE TOO MUCH OF TSUKUNE."
"MORE MOE!"

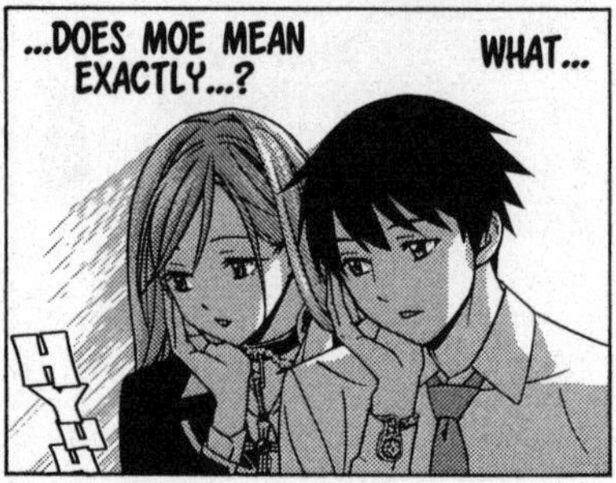
WHAT...
...DOES MOE MEAN EXACTLY...?
HYUU

•No Hard Feelings•

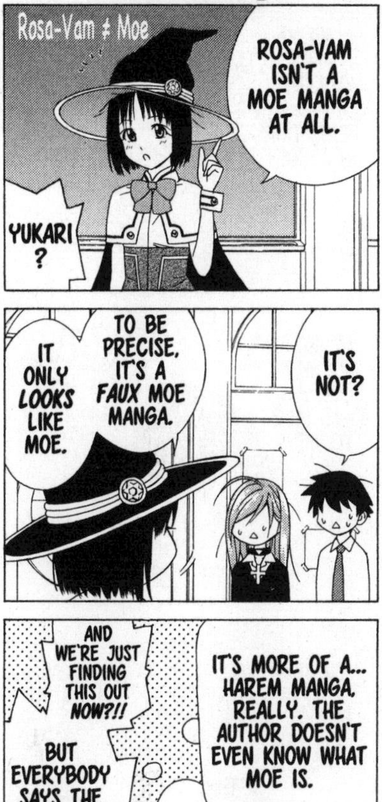
ROSA-VAM ISN'T A MOE MANGA AT ALL.
Rosa-Vam ≠ Moe
YUKARI?
IT'S NOT?
TO BE PRECISE, IT'S A *FAUX* MOE MANGA.
IT ONLY *LOOKS* LIKE MOE.
IT'S MORE OF A... HAREM MANGA, REALLY. THE AUTHOR DOESN'T EVEN KNOW WHAT MOE IS.
HA HA HA
AND WE'RE JUST FINDING THIS OUT *NOW?!!*
BUT EVERYBODY SAYS THE ROSA-VAM ANIME IS *PACKED* WITH MOE!
THE ANIME IS THE ANIME...
...AND THE ORIGINAL MANGA IS THE ORIGINAL MANGA.

•But It Just Doesn't Click•

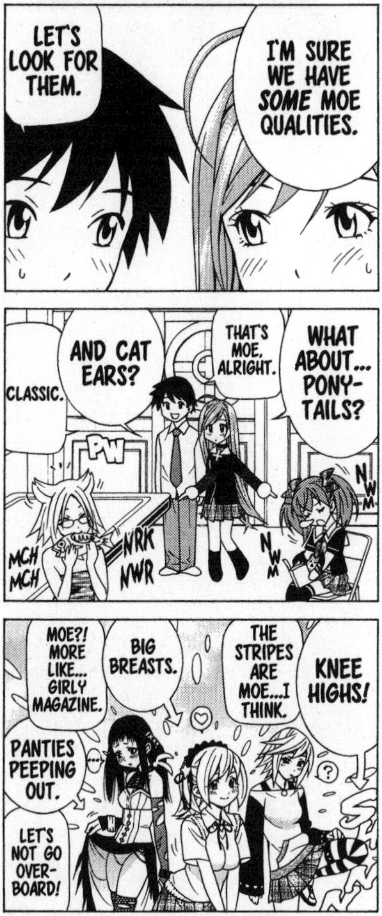
I'M SURE WE HAVE *SOME* MOE QUALITIES.
LET'S LOOK FOR THEM.
WHAT ABOUT... PONY-TAILS?
THAT'S MOE, ALRIGHT.
AND CAT EARS?
CLASSIC.
NWM
PW
NWM
NRK NWR
MCH MCH
KNEE HIGHS!
THE STRIPES ARE MOE...I THINK.
BIG BREASTS.
MOE?! MORE LIKE... GIRLY MAGAZINE.
PANTIES PEEPING OUT.
LET'S NOT GO OVER-BOARD!
ACTUALLY ...
...WE'RE CHOCKFULL OF MOE.

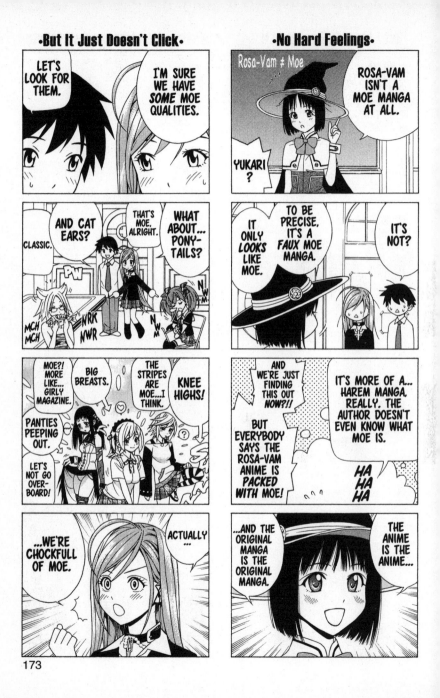

Even more Meaningless etc. etc.

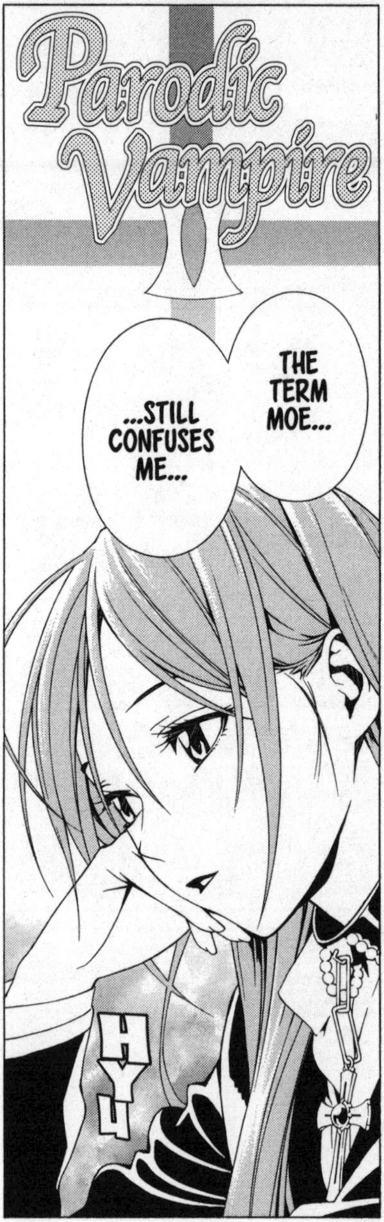
Parodic Vampire
THE TERM MOE...
...STILL CONFUSES ME...
HYU

•But I Already Explained it...•

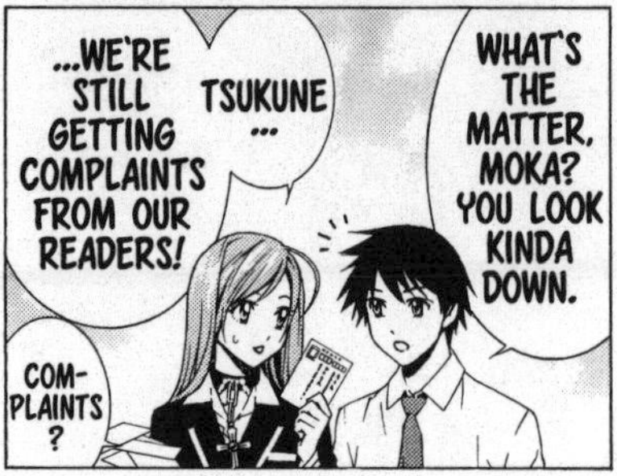
WHAT'S THE MATTER, MOKA? YOU LOOK KINDA DOWN.
TSUKUNE...
...WE'RE STILL GETTING COMPLAINTS FROM OUR READERS!
COM-PLAINTS?

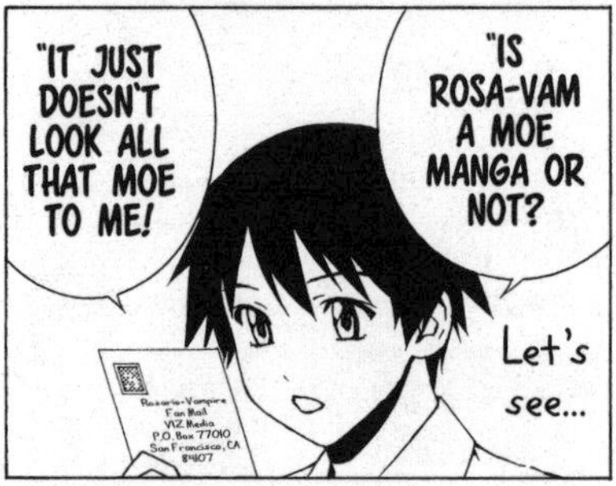
Let's see...
"IS ROSA-VAM A MOE MANGA OR NOT?
"IT JUST DOESN'T LOOK ALL THAT MOE TO ME!
Rosario-Vampire Fan Mail VIZ Media P.O. Box 77010 San Francisco, CA 94107

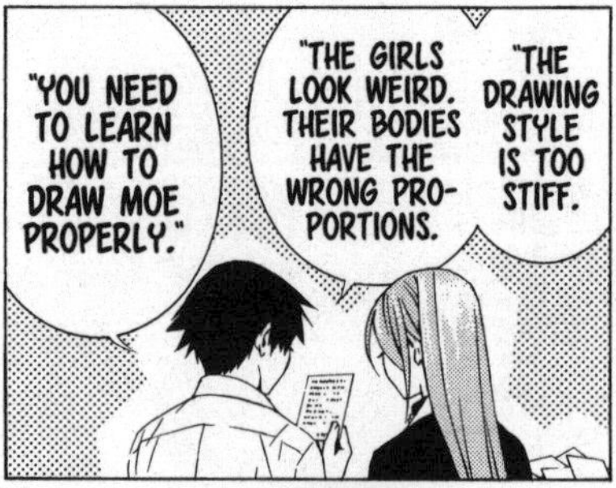
"THE DRAWING STYLE IS TOO STIFF.
"THE GIRLS LOOK WEIRD. THEIR BODIES HAVE THE WRONG PRO-PORTIONS.
"YOU NEED TO LEARN HOW TO DRAW MOE PROPERLY."

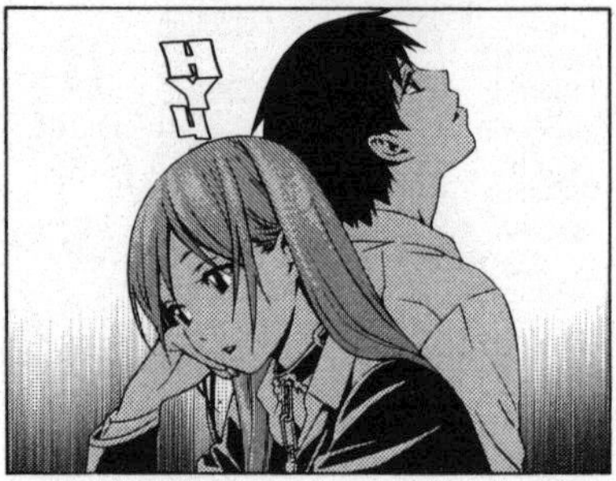
HYU

•I Did My Best•

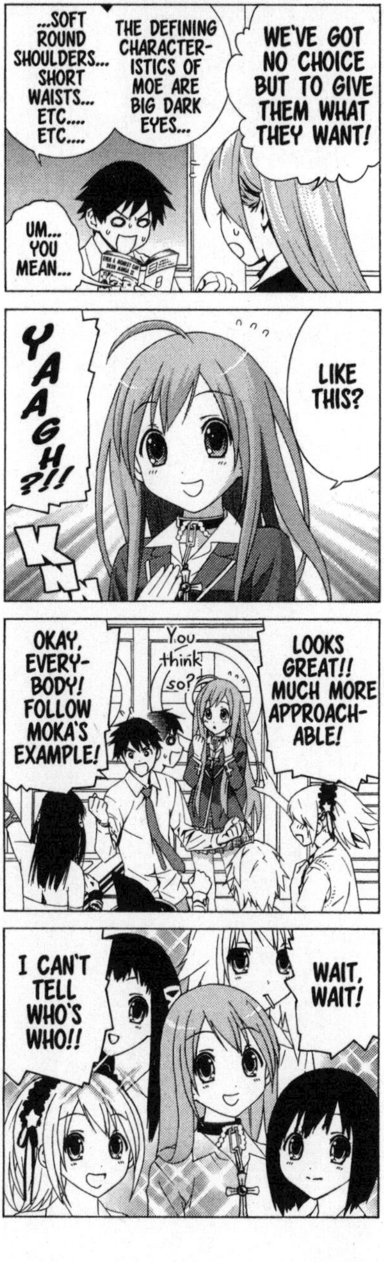
WE'VE GOT NO CHOICE BUT TO GIVE THEM WHAT THEY WANT!
THE DEFINING CHARACTER-ISTICS OF MOE ARE BIG DARK EYES...
...SOFT ROUND SHOULDERS... SHORT WAISTS... ETC.... ETC....
UM... YOU MEAN...
LIKE THIS?
YAAAGH?!!
KNN
LOOKS GREAT!! MUCH MORE APPROACH-ABLE!
You think so?
OKAY, EVERY-BODY! FOLLOW MOKA'S EXAMPLE!
WAIT, WAIT!
I CAN'T TELL WHO'S WHO!!

•A Little Too Late•

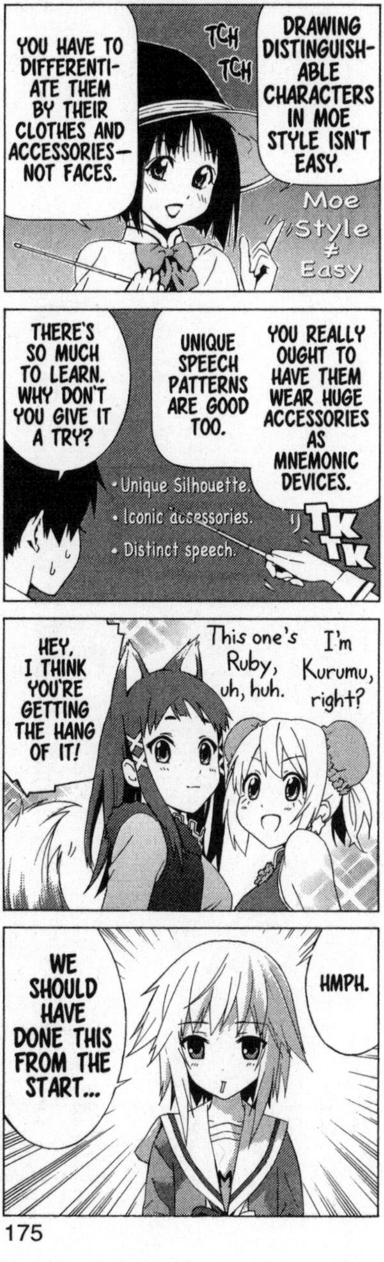
DRAWING DISTINGUISH-ABLE CHARACTERS IN MOE STYLE ISN'T EASY.
TCH TCH
YOU HAVE TO DIFFERENTI-ATE THEM BY THEIR CLOTHES AND ACCESSORIES— NOT FACES.
Moe Style ≠ Easy
YOU REALLY OUGHT TO HAVE THEM WEAR HUGE ACCESSORIES AS MNEMONIC DEVICES.
UNIQUE SPEECH PATTERNS ARE GOOD TOO.
THERE'S SO MUCH TO LEARN. WHY DON'T YOU GIVE IT A TRY?
TK TK
• Unique Silhouette.
• Iconic accessories.
• Distinct speech.
I'm Kurumu, right?
This one's Ruby, uh, huh.
HEY, I THINK YOU'RE GETTING THE HANG OF IT!
HMPH.
WE SHOULD HAVE DONE THIS FROM THE START...

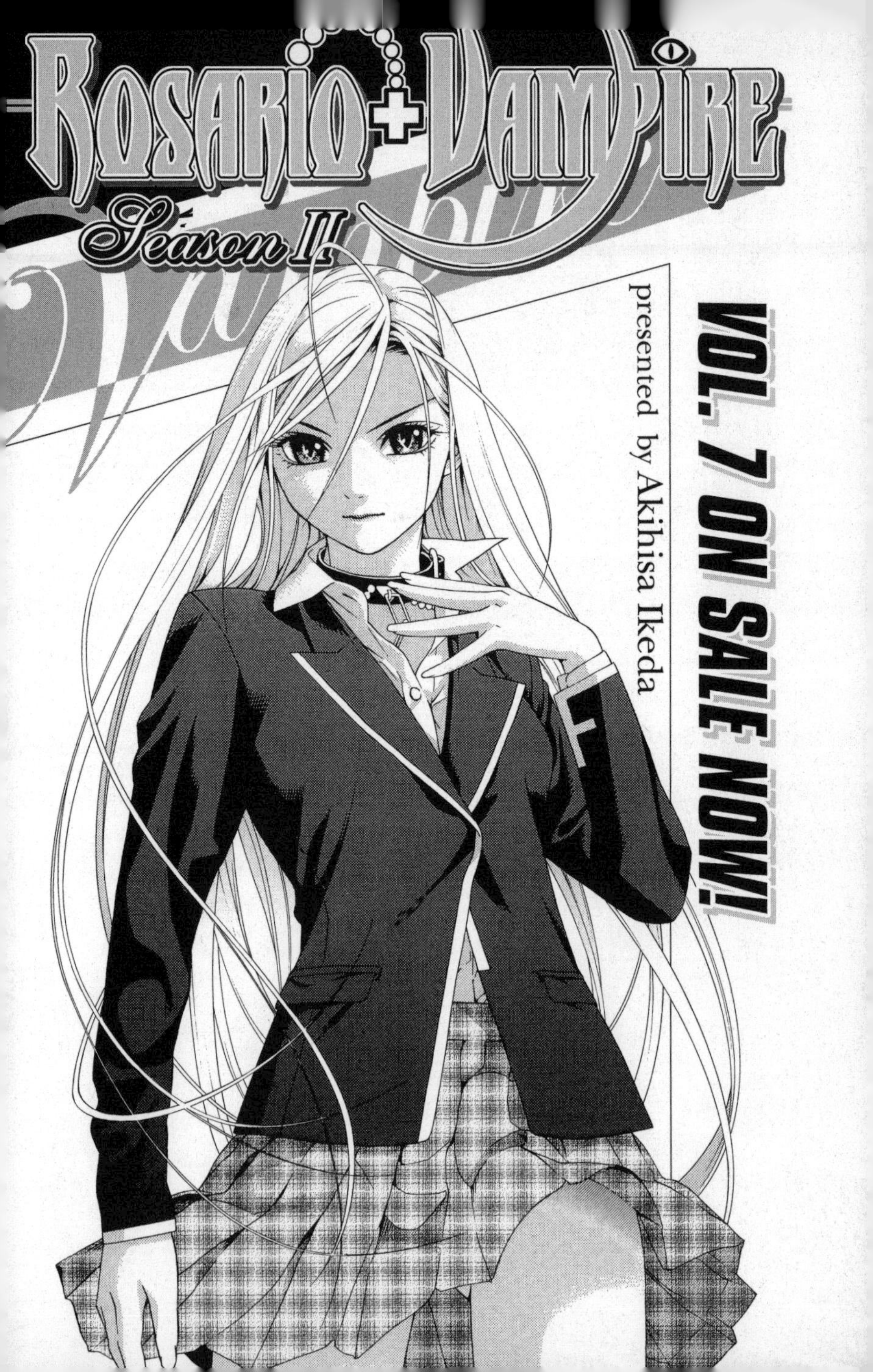
Rosario+Vampire
Season II
VOL. 7 ON SALE NOW!
presented by Akihisa Ikeda

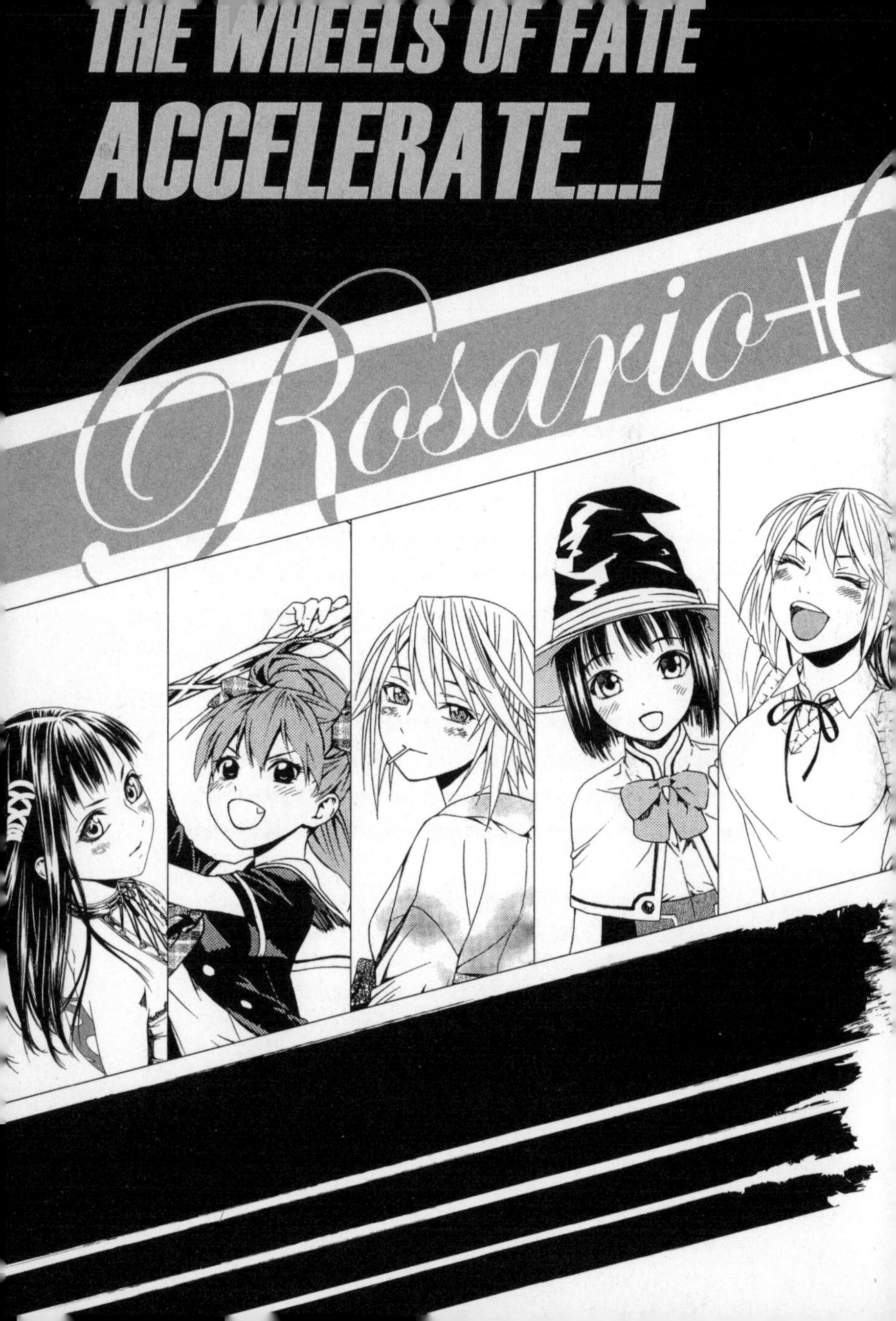
THE WHEELS OF FATE
ACCELERATE...!
Rosario+

AKIHISA IKEDA

"Those were the best days of my life..."

I'm sure everybody has a time they remember fondly. I might be experiencing that time right now, since I'm able to make a living doing my favorite thing. Even though I'm unable to get enough sleep, and I end up trapped in my house all the time... Please, somebody! Grant me more time! (LOL)

What I wanted to capture in this volume was the essence of peaceful, fulfilling days like those...days that Tsukune and the others will be able to look back on after they grow up and remember what a great time they had... I hope you enjoy reading about this happy interlude in their lives.

Akihisa Ikeda was born in 1976 in Miyazaki. He debuted as a mangaka with the four-volume magical warrior fantasy series *Kiruto* in 2002, which was serialized in *Monthly Shonen Jump*. *Rosario+Vampire* debuted in *Monthly Shonen Jump* in March of 2004 and is continuing in the magazine *Jump Square (Jump SQ)* as *Rosario+Vampire: Season II*. In Japan, *Rosario+Vampire* is also available as a drama CD. In 2008, the story was released as an anime. Season II is also available as an anime now. And in Japan, there is a Nintendo DS game based on the series.

Ikeda has been a huge fan of vampires and monsters since he was a little kid. He says one of the perks of being a manga artist is being able to go for walks during the day when everybody else is stuck in the office.

ROSARIO+VAMPIRE: Season II
6
SHONEN JUMP ADVANCED Manga Edition

STORY & ART BY AKIHISA IKEDA

Translation/Tetsuichiro Miyaki
English Adaptation/Gerard Jones
Touch-up Art & Lettering/Stephen Dutro
Cover & Interior Design/Ronnie Casson
Editor/Annette Roman

ROSARIO TO VAMPIRE SEASON II © 2007 by Akihisa Ikeda
All rights reserved. First published in Japan in 2007 by SHUEISHA Inc.,
Tokyo. English translation rights arranged by SHUEISHA Inc.

Printed in the U.S.A.

Published by VIZ Media, LLC
P.O. Box 77010
San Francisco, CA 94107

10 9 8 7 6 5 4 3 2
First printing, October 2011
Second printing, June 2014

www.viz.com

www.shonenjump.com

CRYPT SHEET FOR

ROSARIO+VAMPIRE: SEASON II, VOL. 7

VANISHING ACTS

TEST 7

WHEN YOU'RE A HOUSEGUEST AND YOUR FRIENDS START VANISHING ONE BY ONE...

a. blame your hosts

b. play hide and seek

c. move to a motel

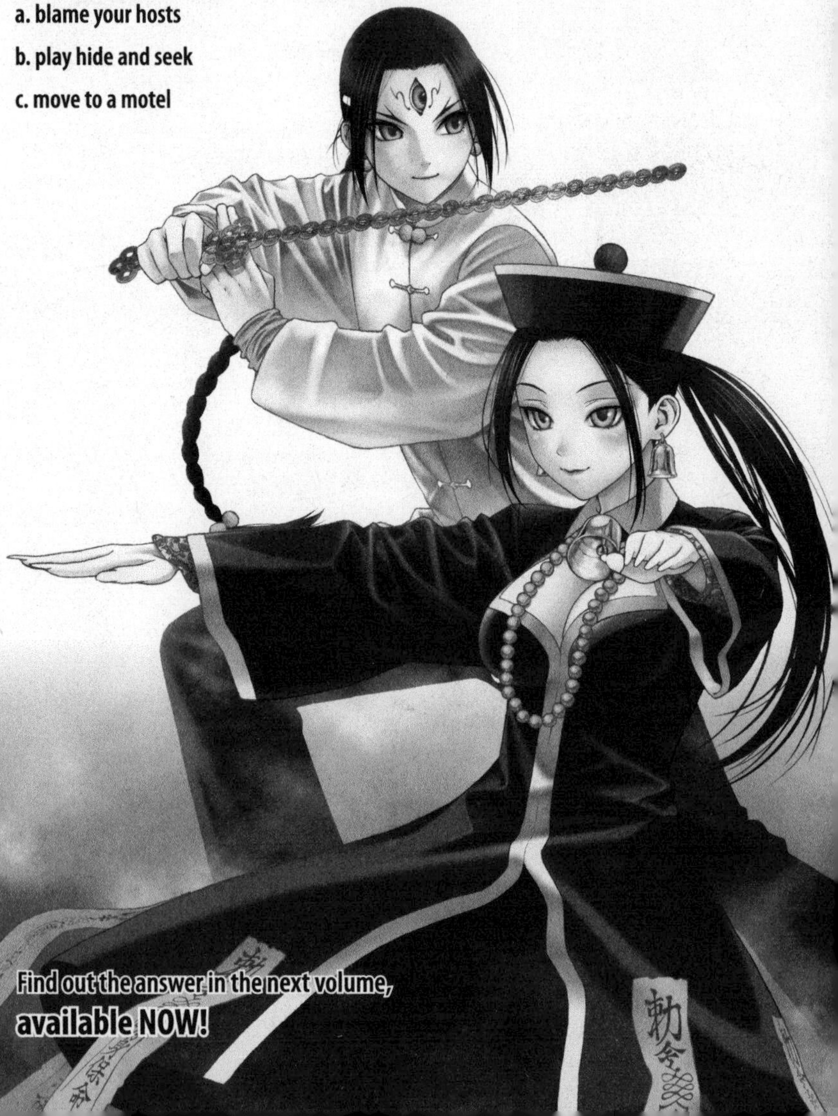

Find out the answer in the next volume, available NOW!

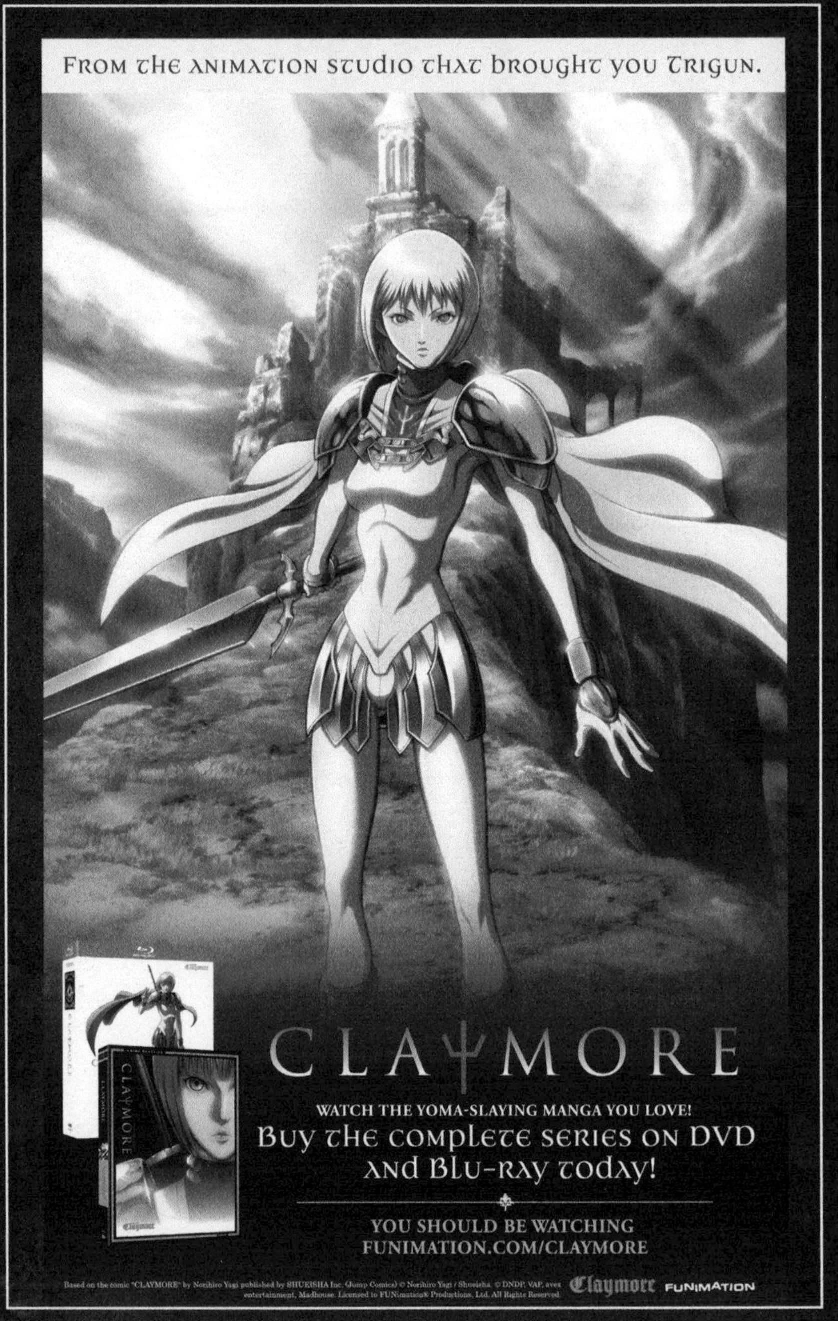
FROM THE ANIMATION STUDIO THAT BROUGHT YOU TRIGUN.
CLAYMORE
WATCH THE YOMA-SLAYING MANGA YOU LOVE!
Buy the complete series on DVD and Blu-ray today!
YOU SHOULD BE WATCHING
FUNIMATION.COM/CLAYMORE
Based on the comic "CLAYMORE" by Norihiro Yagi published by SHUEISHA Inc. (Jump Comics) © Norihiro Yagi / Shueisha. © DNDP, VAP, avex entertainment, Madhouse. Licensed to FUNimation® Productions, Ltd. All Rights Reserved.
Claymore
FUNIMATION

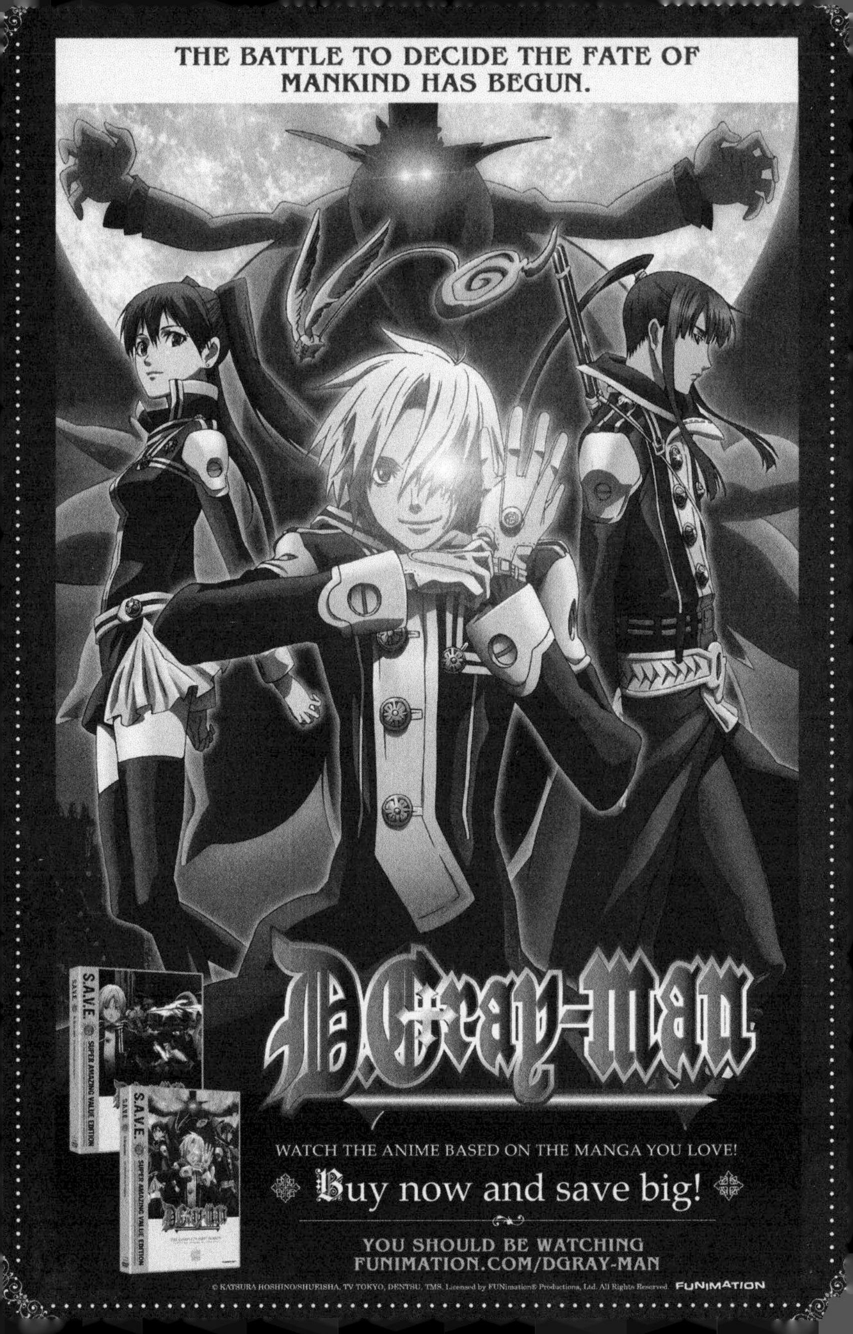
THE BATTLE TO DECIDE THE FATE OF MANKIND HAS BEGUN.
D.Gray-man
WATCH THE ANIME BASED ON THE MANGA YOU LOVE!
Buy now and save big!
YOU SHOULD BE WATCHING FUNIMATION.COM/DGRAY-MAN
© KATSURA HOSHINO/SHUEISHA, TV TOKYO, DENTSU, TMS. Licensed by FUNimation® Productions, Ltd. All Rights Reserved.
FUNIMATION

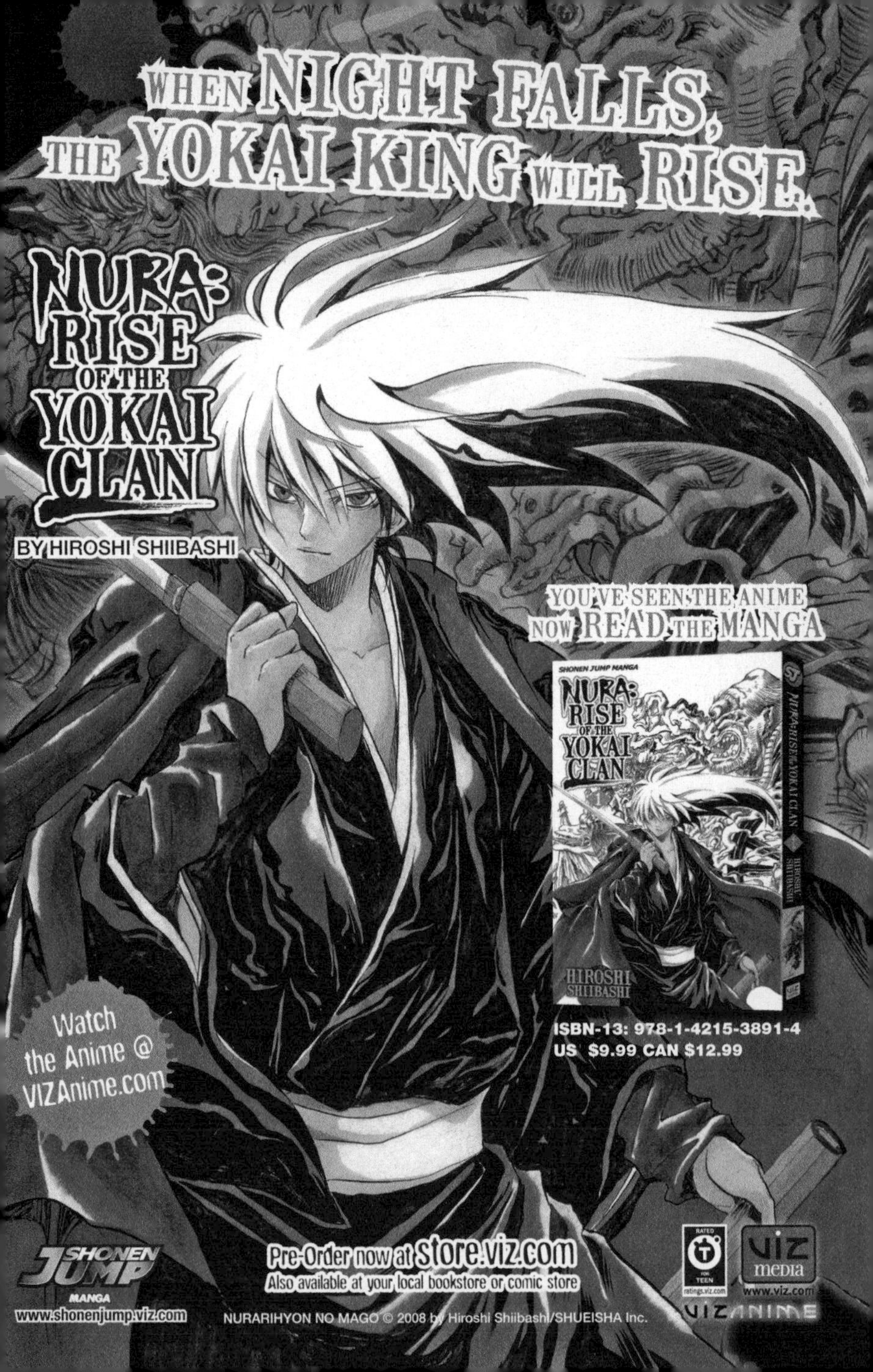
WHEN NIGHT FALLS, THE YOKAI KING WILL RISE.
NURA: RISE OF THE YOKAI CLAN
BY HIROSHI SHIIBASHI
YOU'VE SEEN THE ANIME NOW READ THE MANGA
SHONEN JUMP MANGA
NURA: RISE OF THE YOKAI CLAN
HIROSHI SHIIBASHI
ISBN-13: 978-1-4215-3891-4
US $9.99 CAN $12.99
Watch the Anime @ VIZAnime.com
SHONEN JUMP MANGA
www.shonenjump.viz.com
Pre-Order now at store.viz.com
Also available at your local bookstore or comic store
RATED T FOR TEEN ratings.viz.com
VIZ media
www.viz.com
VIZANIME
NURARIHYON NO MAGO © 2008 by Hiroshi Shiibashi/SHUEISHA Inc.

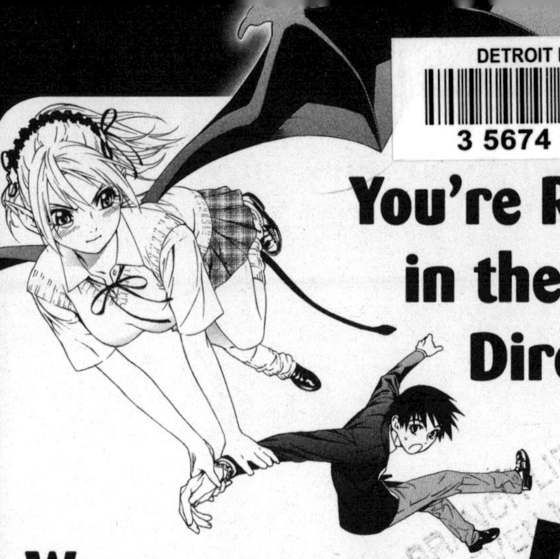

You're Reading in the Wrong Direction!!

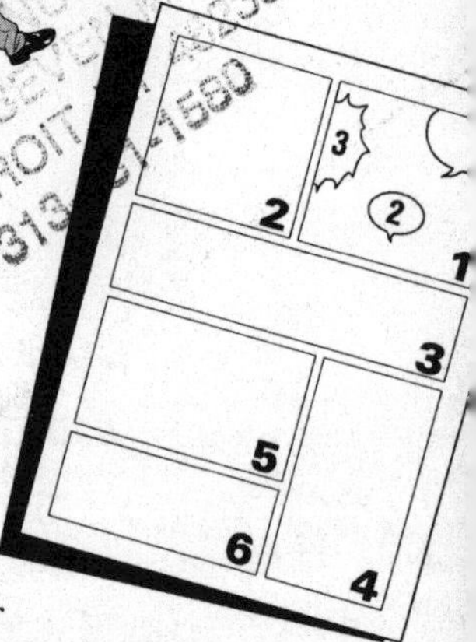
1
2
3
2
3
4
5
6

Whoops! Guess what? You're starting at the wrong end of the comic!

...It's true! In keeping with the original Japanese format, **Rosario+Vampire** is meant to be read from right to left, starting in the upper-right corner.

Unlike English, which is read from left to right, Japanese is read from right to left, meaning action, sound effects and word-balloon order are completely reversed... something which can make readers unfamiliar with Japanese feel pretty backwards themselves. For this reason, manga or Japanese comics published in the U.S. in English have sometimes been published "flopped"—that is, printed in exact reverse order, as though seen from the other side of a mirror.

By flopping pages, U.S. publishers can avoid confusing readers, but the compromise is not without its downside. For one thing, a character in a flopped manga series who once wore in the original Japanese version a T-shirt emblazoned with "M A Y" (as in "the merry month of") now wears one which reads "Y A M"! Additionally, many manga creators in Japan are themselves unhappy with the process, as some feel the mirror-imaging of their art skews their original intentions.

We are proud to bring you Akihisa Ikeda's **Rosario+Vampire** in the original unflopped format. For now, though, turn to the other side of the book and let the haunting begin...!

—Editor

◀••••••••••••••••